In the Weeds

CLAYTON J. MOSHER
AND SCOTT AKINS

In the Weeds

Demonization, Legalization, and the Evolution of U.S. Marijuana Policy

TEMPLE UNIVERSITY PRESS
Philadelphia • *Rome* • *Tokyo*

TEMPLE UNIVERSITY PRESS
Philadelphia, Pennsylvania 19122
tupress.temple.edu

Library of Congress Cataloging-in-Publication Data

Names: Mosher, Clayton James, author. | Akins, Scott, author.
Title: In the weeds : demonization, legalization, and the evolution of U.S. marijuana
 policy / Clayton J. Mosher and Scott Akins.
Description: Philadelphia : Temple University Press, [2019] | Includes bibliographical
 references and index. |
Identifiers: LCCN 2018030215 (print) | LCCN 2018030655 (ebook) |
 ISBN 9781439913321 (E-Book) | ISBN 9781439913307 (cloth : alk. paper) |
 ISBN 9781439913314 (pbk. : alk. paper)
Subjects: LCSH: Marijuana—Law and legislation—United States. | Marijuana—
 Therapeutic use—United States. | Marijuana—Government policy—United States. |
 Marijuana abuse—United States. | Drug legalization—United States.
Classification: LCC KF3891.M2 (ebook) | LCC KF3891.M2 M69 2019 (print) |
 DDC 345.73/0277—dc23
LC record available at https://lccn.loc.gov/2018030215

9 8 7 6 5 4 3 2 1

Contents

Preface

This book provides a historically grounded examination of marijuana policy reform and ultimately the move toward legalization over a period extending back more than one hundred years. In the context of the recent legalization of marijuana in nine states and Washington, D.C., and a time when a significant majority of the population of the United States is in favor of the legalization of recreational marijuana, we look back to consider how we arrived at this point. We argue that, examined under a larger historical lens, the prohibition of marijuana constitutes a historical anomaly. More specifically, considered with a larger historical lens (and also in light of scientific evidence on marijuana), if the passage of the federal Marihuana Tax Act constitutes the beginning of marijuana prohibition in the United States and the 1996 passage of medical marijuana legislation in California its end, complete prohibition of marijuana in the United States lasted fifty-nine years. We agree with Andrea Reiman (2015a), policy manager for the Drug Policy Alliance, who comments, "When the entire history of cannabis is taken into account, its use as a medicine and a source of healing dwarfs its time as a dangerous recreational drug with no medical benefit."

The book also considers the effects of marijuana, both the good and the bad; the evidence on its medicinal applications; and the (absurd) persistence of the U.S. government to retain the substance as a Schedule I drug under the Controlled Substances Act (enacted in 1970). The state of denial on the part of the federal government with its continued refusal to reschedule the drug (reaffirmed in August 2016) is sadly entirely consistent with the government's long-standing, science-optional, and essentially evidence-free approach to marijuana. It is also consistent with a variety of marijuana demonization strategies employed by the government that essentially began in the 1930s with Harry Anslinger, first director of the Federal Bureau of Narcotics. These strategies of demonization, and the organizations and agents primarily used to deploy them, are addressed in depth and deconstructed in the chapters to follow. In the final two chapters of the book we consider the rapidly changing landscape of marijuana policy, both in the United States and in a select group of other countries, a landscape that seems to shift on an almost monthly basis, and where we may be going from here.

Our approach in this book is somewhat different from that of drug policy scholars such as Mark Kleiman and Jonathan Caulkins. While we respect their work, we believe that drug policy scholars have been too focused on the negative outcomes (some real, some imagined) of marijuana policy reform and have not devoted sufficient attention to the historical record on marijuana and the incremental developments with respect to policy reforms. By no means do we ignore some of the negative outcomes associated with marijuana legalization, but these have often been overstated, while many of the positive outcomes have been ignored or neglected. We argue that, while it is still somewhat early to evaluate the successes and failures of marijuana law reform, the absence of serious negative outcomes constitutes a positive.

A Note on the Sources Used in This Book

In discussing the history, effects, and legal reforms related to marijuana, we, of course, include extensive (although by no means exhaustive) coverage of research published in medical, scientific, social scientific, and other academic journals. However, in contrast to most "academic" books, this book also relies heavily on so-called gray literature—publications and reports that are not peer reviewed and are produced by organizations such as various government agencies, nonprofit organizations, and think tanks, as well as what are sometimes referred to as special interest groups. The benefit of employing such sources is that they often provide the most up-to-date information and current data on issues of relevance because they are usually not subject to the long delays associated with the publication of peer-reviewed studies.

The specific gray literature sources we utilize include a number of reports produced by both federal agencies (e.g., the Drug Enforcement Administration [DEA], the National Institute on Drug Abuse, and the Office of National Drug Control Policy [ONDCP], as well as federally sponsored programs such as regional High Intensity Drug Trafficking Areas) and various state agencies (especially agencies in states that have legalized recreational marijuana that are responsible for cannabis regulation, such as the Washington

State Liquor and Cannabis Board). We also draw on materials from organizations such as the Drug Policy Alliance (DPA), the Marijuana Policy Project (MPP), and the National Organization for the Reform of Marijuana Laws (NORML). We are aware that some view these organizations as "advocacy groups" in the marijuana policy context, and we would tend to agree. However, we demonstrate that many of the arguments made by these organizations are compelling. For the most part, these so-called advocacy groups refer to actual scientific studies in their publications. In contrast, much of the information on marijuana published by federal government organizations is often misleading and, in some cases, simply false. It is also important to note that, while government agencies are not typically referred to as advocacy groups, some might be appropriately characterized as such. For example, under the Office of National Drug Control Policy Reauthorization Act of 1988, the director of the agency is mandated to "ensure that no federal funds appropriated to the Office of National Drug Control Policy shall be expended for any study or contract relating to the legalization (for a medical or any other use) of a substance listed in Schedule I of the Controlled Substances Act and take such actions as necessary to oppose any attempt to legalize the use of a substance (in any form) listed in Schedule I" (White House 1998). Such mandates can (and do) lead to significant biases in the publications of the ONDCP and often lead to questionable actions on the part of ONDCP officials and other federal government agencies in their response to marijuana.

We also draw extensively on print and Internet media discussions related to marijuana—in particular the publications of several reporters/journalists who have, as part of their work, focused specifically on marijuana issues and have published numerous well-written, thoroughly researched, and important articles related to topics addressed in this book.[1] Similar to the advantages associated with using information from gray media sources, print and Internet media sources provide the most current information on important marijuana-related topics. In many instances, these sources have the

---

1. We are indebted to the following reporters/journalists (some of whom we have contacted), as our research benefited tremendously from their reporting: Ricardo Baca, the founding editor of the *Denver Post*'s *Cannabist* edition (established in 2013); Russ Belville of the *Huffington Post*; Noelle Crombie of the *Oregonian*; Jake Ellison of the *Seattle Post-Intelligencer*; Thomas Fuller of the *New York Times*; Evan Halper of the *Los Angeles Times*; Josh Harkinson of *Mother Jones*; Jack Healy of the *New York Times*; Josiah Hesse of the *Guardian*; Rob Hotakainen of *McClatchy*; John Ingold of the *Denver Post/ Cannabist*; Christopher Ingraham of the *Washington Post*; Patrick McGreevy of the *Los Angeles Times*; Melissa Santos of the (Tacoma) *News Tribune*; Brooke Staggs of the *Orange County Register/Cannifornian*; Jacob Sullum of *Forbes*; Alicia Wallace and Polly Washburn of the *Denver Post/Cannabist*; Kristen Wyatt of the *Associated Press*; and Bob Young of the *Seattle Times*.

additional advantage of providing local, "on-the-ground" information that we use to emphasize the considerable variation across and within states with respect to the implementation of marijuana law reform.

In incorporating information from this wide array of sources in our narrative, we are cognizant of the perils associated with "fake news." However, based on our assessments of these sources, and as we demonstrate throughout this book, fake news (or, at least, alternative/distorted/decontextualized "facts") is a more common feature in some reports produced by federal government agencies and opponents of marijuana law reform.

Outline of the Book

Chapter 1 considers the major policy shifts and trends occurring in the United States with respect to marijuana as of late 2017. Among the issues discussed is the recently rejected proposal to reschedule marijuana under the Controlled Substances Act. Marijuana has been considered a Schedule I drug under this act since 1970. Under the provisions of the act, a Schedule I substance "has a high potential for abuse, has no medical use in the United States, and has a lack of accepted safety for use under medical supervision" (Drug Enforcement Administration 2005). Currently, marijuana is placed alongside drugs such as heroin and LSD, which are also Schedule I substances.

The refusal of the federal government to reschedule marijuana is problematic in several ways, including but not limited to the fact that is deprives researchers of access to quality marijuana (the kind typically available on the street) for the research needed to demonstrate its possible medicinal applications and its possible negative effects, depriving patients of medicine that could assist them in treating their conditions and maintaining a war stance on marijuana that the vast majority of Americans have long since tired of and largely rejected. Only three months after the DEA refused to reschedule marijuana, in November 2016 four more states (California, Maine, Massachusetts, and Nevada) legalized recreational marijuana (Alaska, Colorado, Oregon, Washington State, and Washington, D.C., legalized recreational marijuana between 2012 and 2014), meaning that one in five Americans now lives in a state where recreational marijuana is legalized. In addition, thirty states have legalized medical marijuana.

Chapter 1 also devotes considerable attention to the shifting support for the reform of marijuana laws over time. When marijuana legalization was first considered in Gallup opinion polls in 1969, only 12 percent of Americans supported it, but this figure reached 60 percent in October 2016 (Ingraham 2016e), and currently support for medical marijuana legalization is in excess of 90 percent (Washburn 2017a). Support for marijuana legalization varies considerably across demographic categories as well as political affiliation and remains in flux. But, as the sky has not fallen following the legalization of marijuana in several states, and as the substance has become increasingly normalized and accepted, it is likely that public support for legalization will continue to rise.

Chapter 1 also examines marijuana use patterns over time and discusses in detail the concern that heavy use and youth use may be especially likely to increase following legalization. While we agree that these issues are worthy of concern because the harms associated with marijuana use appear to be greatest among heavy users and young users, we consider whether available data support the claim that heavy and youth use is significantly greater under legalization. Data on the sales of marijuana and the associated tax revenue for states that have legalized the substance are also considered, as is the "mainstreaming" of marijuana, as reflected in myriad goods, services, practices, and references to marijuana's presence in American culture and entertainment.

Chapter 1 also considers the forces that have driven reform in marijuana policy over the last several decades, most notably fiscal issues (states can collect significant tax revenues from the sale of legal marijuana, revenues that are not available when marijuana is illegal); changes in normative attitudes, especially among the young; and an increased recognition of the profound and disproportionate harm the drug war in general and the war on marijuana in particular has done (and continues to do) to racial and ethnic minorities in the United States.

Chapter 2 traces the social, political, and legal history of marijuana, beginning with a review of medical and scientific literature on the substance in the 1800s and the seminal 1893–1894 Indian Hemp Drugs Commission report. This chapter also devotes significant attention to what is the most influential (and controversial) period of marijuana regulation in the history of the United States, the 1930s and 1940s, what some have referred to as the "reefer madness" era, and the role of Harry Anslinger. As director of the Federal Bureau of Narcotics, Anslinger was the primary architect of a campaign to demonize marijuana and gain approval for the Marihuana Tax Act, passed in 1937, which resulted in the first federal prohibition of marijuana. To accomplish this, Anslinger used a variety of strategies designed to create fear of marijuana, many of which persist in anti-marijuana rhetoric and campaigns to the present day. Drawing heavily on racist beliefs and fears during this period, Anslinger emphasized that marijuana was a substance used primarily by Mexicans and "Negroes" and that the substance led to the commission of crime, especially violent crime and sexual depravity.

Chapter 2 also considers the report of the La Guardia Committee, appointed by New York City mayor Fiorello La Guardia to provide a thorough examination of marijuana's risks and effects on society. The report included a consideration of all available scientific literature on the topic of marijuana, an examination of the prevalence of marijuana use in society (focusing on New York City), and a clinical study examining the physiological and psychological effects of marijuana on users. The findings refuted virtually every claim made by Anslinger and other anti-marijuana propagandists. Among the highlights of the La Guardia Committee report were that chronic marijuana users could quit using the substance without experiencing withdrawal or craving, that the use of marijuana did not lead to the use of cocaine or heroin (rejecting the so-called gateway drug theory), and that the use of marijuana did not increase an individual's propensity to commit criminal acts (Mayor's Committee on Marihuana 1944). Also during the 1930s–1940s period, interesting debates regarding marijuana's harm emerged in medical and scientific literature; Chapter 2 discusses these debates in some detail.

Following a brief discussion of marijuana-related developments in the 1950s through the 1970s, a period in which an increasing percentage of American youth (and youth in other Western countries) began to use marijuana, we proceed to a discussion of developments during the administration of President Richard Nixon, the most significant of which was the first (official) declaration of a war on drugs and the (at the time, supposedly temporary) placement of marijuana in Schedule I of the Controlled Substances Act. Chapter 2 devotes significant attention to the reports of a number of committees/commissions appointed in several countries to examine drug (particularly marijuana) problems and to recommend policy alterations. With one exception, each of these reports concluded that marijuana was not a dangerous drug and its use did not lead consumers to the use of harder drugs and, most important, emphasized that penalties for possession of the substance should be reduced if not eliminated altogether. The conclusions of these various commissions/committees, which have been almost completely ignored by contemporary drug scholars as well as marijuana prohibitionists, are vitally important to consider, as they rejected a number of common myths about the drug.

The second part of Chapter 2 addresses developments related to marijuana and other illicit drugs during the presidencies of Richard Nixon, Gerald Ford, Jimmy Carter (who supported decriminalization of marijuana), Ronald Reagan, George H. W. Bush, Bill Clinton, and George W. Bush. Reagan initiated what might be referred to as the "second" (with Nixon's being the first), and much more intense, war on drugs (including marijuana) and the administrations of George H. W. Bush, Clinton, and George W. Bush continued the war. We devote considerable attention to the views and actions of the directors of the ONDCP, as these "drug czars" were highly influential in the approach and outcomes associated with the drug war. Chapter 2 also discusses developments during the Obama administration; although Obama had indicated that his administration would deemphasize federal government intervention in states with legalized medical and recreational marijuana, by no means did the war on drugs or the war on marijuana end under his administration. We conclude with a discussion of two key developments with respect to recreational and medical marijuana at the federal level—the Cole memorandum of 2013 and the Rohrabacher-Farr amendment of 2014, which provided guidelines regarding federal intervention in states with recreational and medical marijuana laws and have proven to be important even today.

In Chapter 3 we address the effects of marijuana and its classification as a Schedule I drug. As noted previously, this designation indicates the substance has no approved medical use and a high potential for abuse (however, more harmful drugs such as methamphetamine and cocaine are included in the less restrictive Schedule II). Given the federal justification of the Schedule I status of marijuana, we discuss the scientific evidence concerning the drug's relative harms across a variety of domains. We consider its acute (including psychoactive) and chronic effects, its addictive potential, and its medicinal uses, drawing extensively on a 2017 comprehensive report by the National Academies of Sciences, Engineering, and Medicine (NASEM) that reviewed approximately ten thousand studies on the substance. The report concluded that although marijuana poses some public health risks, the available evidence indicates that it has several medicinal applications. The NASEM report also concluded that the Schedule I status of marijuana impedes research on both the benefits and relative harms of marijuana.

Given that several opponents of marijuana law reform (some of whom will admit that marijuana is relatively benign compared to other psychoactive substances) have emphasized that its use leads to consumption of "harder" drugs, in Chapter 3 we critically examine the logic of and (generally lack of) empirical support for the timeworn and stubbornly enduring gateway drug theory. We also address the emerging important scientific evidence indicating that users of more harmful drugs (most notably opiate drugs) are replacing these drugs with marijuana. Considering the evidence reviewed in Chapter 3 in its totality, it is clear that marijuana should not be placed in Schedule I of the Controlled Substances Act; in fact, many argue that it should be removed from the act entirely (Drug Policy Alliance 2013).

Chapter 4 examines and deconstructs a number of themes commonly employed by individuals and organizations opposed to marijuana law reform. Drawing on Chris Mooney's (2005) concept of "science abuse," which he defines as "any attempt to undermine, alter, or otherwise interfere with the scientific process, or scientific conclusions, for political or ideological reasons," we consider the various strategies used to frame what is known about marijuana. Dating back to roughly the reefer madness era of the 1930s and 1940s, common strategies to demonize the substance include providing information that is known to be a lie; decontextualizing (for example, not providing information on the relative risks of marijuana against those of a commonly used alternative psychoactive substance, such as alcohol); deny-ing, particularly as demonstrated with respect to the long-standing and clear empirical evidence on the medicinal benefits of marijuana; and cherry-pick-ing anecdotes to create the impression that an outcome allegedly associated with marijuana use is in some way typical rather than aberrant.

With these contextual frames in mind we consider the available scien-tific evidence on topics such as whether marijuana use leads to cognitive deficits or declines in IQ and whether providing legal access to marijuana (medicinal or recreational) will lead to increased use of the drug by young people, as well as claims that more permissive marijuana laws will lead to an increase in automobile collisions and traffic fatalities. In this chapter we em-phasize that marijuana, like any psychoactive substance, has the potential to generate adverse effects. But we also emphasize that the harms of the sub-stance are all too often presented in a context that overstates, distorts, and (often deliberately) insufficiently contextualizes these harms. It thus seems necessary to remind people that *legalization did not create marijuana*; it has existed, and humans have consumed the substance, for thousands of years.

In Chapter 5, we continue our examination of marijuana demonization, but we focus on the most prominent agents and agencies of demonization, including federal government agencies such as the ONDCP, the DEA, and the National Institute on Drug Abuse. At the state and local levels, the most notable marijuana demonizers are certain law enforcement organizations (especially federally funded High Intensity Drug Trafficking Areas) and of-ficials, as well as criminal justice system officials more generally. We include a critical overview of reports produced by these organizations, as well as the specific actions they have taken with respect to marijuana. Several of the reports distort the available scientific evidence on marijuana, cherry-pick information from sources that are consistent with their anti-marijuana phi-losophy, and deliberately or conveniently ignore evidence that is inconsistent with their prohibitionist arguments. We also briefly consider opposition to marijuana legalization as manifested in the stances of purveyors of legal drugs (pharmaceutical companies and beer and alcohol producers/distribu-tors) and professional medical associations. The chapter also includes a dis-cussion of the views (and misinformation propagated by) the most promi-nent U.S. organization opposed to marijuana legalization—Project SAM (Smart Approaches to Marijuana) and its president, Kevin Sabet. The chapter concludes with a consideration of other recent contributions to the mari-juana legalization debate offered by former drug czars John Walters and William Bennett.

Chapter 6 examines the path to marijuana legalization in several U.S. states, as well as developments with respect to the regulation of marijuana in several foreign countries. We address in depth the four states (Alaska, Colo-rado, Oregon, and Washington) and Washington, D.C., that legalized recreational marijuana prior to 2016 and also cover states that legalized the substance in 2016 (California, Massachusetts, Maine, and Nevada). The most recent state to legalize marijuana (Vermont) is also discussed.[2]

In this chapter we consider the techniques and strategies employed by groups and individuals who have supported these various legalization measures and document how constituencies opposing marijuana legalization have emphasized many of the same themes of demonization that we cover in Chapter 4. Chapter 6 also addresses some of the nuances of various legalization schemes, including differing tax rates, allowance for home cultivation of marijuana, the vertical integration of cannabis businesses, and local variation in the implementation of marijuana legalization—in particular, local bans and moratoria on marijuana sales. The chapter concludes with a discussion of marijuana policy developments in other countries, with a particular focus on Canada (where recreational marijuana will be legal as of July 2018),[3] Uruguay (where marijuana was legalized in 2014), and the Netherlands.

Chapter 7 considers the rapidly shifting marijuana policy landscape as of late 2017. Among the issues addressed are the ongoing debates surrounding marijuana's Schedule I federal status and a number of problems arising from this status, including conflicting or absent guidelines in banking and taxation. The chapter also considers a number of controversial issues, including the absence of people of color in the marijuana industry (both ironic and glaring given the profound harm that prohibitionist drug policies have done to minority communities over the past several decades) and the fear that the marijuana industry will be "corporatized," or eventually controlled by a few powerful and influential producers that through lobbying, advertising, and other strategies will strive to increase use of marijuana (and thereby increase their profits). We also address the effects of legalization on the black market in marijuana—of particular importance because many states have not legalized the substance and cannabis from legal markets can be diverted to states where it remains illegal.

Chapter 7 also examines signs that the federal government's approach to marijuana (which, under the Obama administration, was largely, although not completely, characterized by a hands-off approach in states where marijuana has been legalized medically and/or recreationally) may be shifting. We pay particular attention to President Donald Trump's attorney general, Jeff Sessions,[4] who is staunchly opposed to marijuana (both medicinal and

---

2. As this book was going to press, on November 6, 2018, voters in Michigan approved a ballot measure legalizing recreational marijuana, and voters in Missouri and Utah approved the legalization of medical marijuana. A recreational marijuana legalization measure in North Dakota failed.

3. Sales of recreational marijuana in Canada were scheduled to begin on July 1, 2018, but were delayed until October 17, 2018.

4. Sessions "resigned" as attorney general on November 7, 2018.

recreational) and who, in August 2017, sent a series of rather threatening letters to the governors of four states (Alaska, Colorado, Oregon, and Washington) that had legalized marijuana. Sessions's letters (which were largely based on highly suspect and, in some cases, false "data" from High Intensity Drug Trafficking Area reports) asserted that marijuana legalization was attended by a number of problems in these states and hinted that the federal government would take action. However, as we address in some detail, the governors of these states largely rejected these claims and responded to Sessions's somewhat veiled threats by emphasizing that legalization had not created severe problems—in fact, there are several benefits arising from it. The governors indicated that they would defend marijuana legalization in their states, especially given that voters had approved it. The chapter concludes with a discussion of further interesting developments with marijuana at the federal level, including a proposal by Senator Corey Booker to completely legalize marijuana through the Marijuana Justice Act.

In the Weeds

.

1

The Changing Landscape of Marijuana

Marijuana is one of the safest therapeutically active
substances known to man. . . . The provisions of the
[Controlled Substances] Act permit and require the
transfer of marijuana from Schedule I to Schedule II.
—JUDGE FRANCIS YOUNG, quoted in U.S. Department of Justice,
  "In the Matter of Marijuana Rescheduling Petition"

In August 2016, in a much-anticipated decision, the Drug Enforcement Administration (DEA) refused to reschedule marijuana to a Schedule II drug under the Controlled Substances Act. This decision was in response to a December 2011 petition by Governors Christine Gregoire of Washington State and Lincoln Chaffee of Rhode Island (and a second petition by New Mexico nurse practitioner Bryan Krumm) officially requesting that marijuana be rescheduled. In defending her position on rescheduling, Governor Gregoire explained, "We have patients who really either feel like they're criminals or may be engaged in some criminal activity, and really are legitimate patients who want medical marijuana" (quoted in Cooper 2011). Chafee, a former Republican-turned-Independent, whose joining the petition signaled that it was a bipartisan effort, added, "It is time to show compassion and time to show common sense" (quoted in Cooper 2011).

This decision marked at least the fourth time the DEA had refused to reschedule marijuana since its *temporary* placement in Schedule I of the Controlled Substances Act in 1970, (the first petition was initiated by the National Organization for the Reform of Marijuana Laws [NORML] in 1972). It came some forty-four years after the Shafer Commission, appointed by the Nixon administration to make recommendations on the rescheduling of marijuana, concluded that rescheduling was not sufficient but that the drug should be completely decriminalized (National Commission on Marihuana and Drug Abuse 1972). It also came some twenty-eight years after Judge Francis Young's recommendation quoted in the epigraph, which was overruled by DEA administrator John Lawn in 1989 (Miron 2015). The DEA's decision effectively means that marijuana (alongside other Schedule I substances such as heroin and LSD) has been deemed to be a substance that "has a high potential for abuse, no medical use in the United States, and has a lack of accepted safety for use under medical supervision" (Drug Enforcement Administration 2005). At the same time, other highly addictive substances such as cocaine, fentanyl, oxycodone, and methamphetamine remain in Schedule II of the Controlled Substances Act and are thereby subject to fewer restrictions.

In his letter to the petitioners explaining the decision not to reschedule marijuana, Chuck Rosenberg (2016), acting administrator of the DEA, conceded that marijuana was less dangerous than some substances in Schedules II through V but noted that "the criteria for inclusion in Schedule I is not relative danger." Asserting that there was not sufficient scientific evidence to support rescheduling, Rosenberg commented that "research is the bedrock of science" and that "if the scientific understanding about marijuana changes—and it could change—then the decision could change." The DEA continues to assert that well-controlled clinical trials would provide the best support for marijuana's possible medicinal benefits but refuses to acknowledge the role the agency itself (as well as the National Institute on Drug Abuse [NIDA]) plays in preventing such studies from occurring. Marijuana's status as a Schedule I drug results in researchers having to obtain multiple approvals from (1) the NIDA to obtain the marijuana that many researchers have reported to be of low quality); (2) the Food and Drug Administration (FDA) to submit an "investigational new drug application"; and (3) the DEA to "obtain investigator registration and site licensure to conduct studies using marijuana" (Throckmorton 2016). And although it was published after Rosenberg issued the DEA's decision, a 2017 review of more than ten thousand scientific abstracts (the overwhelming majority of which were published prior to the DEA decision) on cannabis published by the National Academies of Sciences, Engineering, and Medicine (NASEM) concluded that cannabis was effective in treating chronic pain in adults, in reducing spasms in multiple sclerosis patients, and in preventing and treating nausea and vomiting in adults undergoing chemotherapy. Marijuana's medicinal benefits have been reported in medical literature and scientific studies as far back as five thousand years.

The DEA's August 2016 decision not to reschedule marijuana was met with considerable derision; several major U.S. newspapers wrote editorials condemning it, some of which were scathing. The *New York Times* (2016b), while partially commending the DEA's indication in the decision that it would remove some restrictions preventing research into marijuana's potential medical uses, led with the headline "Stop Treating Marijuana like Heroin" and noted that "having marijuana on that list [Schedule I] is deeply misguided." The editorial added that the DEA's claim that there was not enough scientific evidence to support the rescheduling of marijuana was a "disingenuous argument; the government itself has made it impossible to do the kinds of trials and studies that could produce the evidence that would justify changing the drug's classification." The *Los Angeles Times*, which in prior years had opposed marijuana-related legal reforms in California, said the decision was based on a "bizarre circular logic, a different kind of reefer madness. . . . The DEA opted to keep its policies mired in the 1970s, which will only exacerbate the growing divide between the states and feds" (quoted in Downs 2016a). The *Seattle Times* (2016) referred to the decision as "astonishingly tone deaf" and added that the policy was "absurd . . . and should be changed. . . . Bureaucratic obfuscation on medical marijuana is a rear-guard action on a fight already lost in the public's view. Congress must act. End the reefer madness."

Some three months after the DEA's decision, in the November 2016 elections, four states legalized recreational marijuana, and an additional four states legalized medicinal marijuana (a ballot measure to legalize recreational marijuana in Arizona was the only one of nine marijuana-related measures on state ballots that failed in that year). As a result of the passage of these ballot measures, as of December 2016, one in five Americans lives in a state in which recreational use of marijuana is legal (McMaken 2016). Recreational marijuana is now legal up and down the entire West Coast of the United States and Alaska and will be legal in Canada in 2018. As Christopher Ingraham (2016f) notes, in the 2016 elections "advocates of reforming marijuana laws made progress in regions of the country they'd previously had little success in." In 2016, Florida became the first state in the South to approve the legalization of medical marijuana, although a 2014 measure in the state had failed; Arkansas similarly passed medical marijuana legislation, and, perhaps most surprisingly, in North Dakota, which Gallup ranks as the second most conservative state in the country (Newport 2017), two-thirds of voters approved medical marijuana legalization (Ingraham 2016f). Recreational marijuana is also now legal in Massachusetts, Maine, and California, the most populous state in the country, as well as in Nevada. Even more recently, in January 2018, Vermont became the first state to legalize recreational marijuana through the legislature (Zezima 2018). Thus, as of mid-2018, recreational marijuana is legal in nine U.S. states (in addition to California, Maine, Massachusetts, and Nevada, recreational legalization measures had previously passed in Alaska, Colorado, Oregon, and Washington State) and Washington, D.C.

While the DEA decision not to reschedule marijuana and the legalization of recreational marijuana by ballot measures in eight states and D.C. since 2012 may seem to be unrelated on the surface, we argue that they are in fact strongly connected. The intransigence of the federal and state governments and government agencies and their collective refusal to acknowledge that in comparison to currently legal drugs such as alcohol, tobacco, and several prescription drugs, marijuana is a relatively benign substance (which also has several benefits), have forced political/social movements to change marijuana laws through ballot (or so-called bottom up) measures. Because many elected officials rely on the (frequently distorted) "information" on cannabis provided by federal government agencies (such as the DEA, NIDA, and the Office of National Drug Control Policy [ONDCP]) and are labeled as being "soft on crime" if they support marijuana law reform, political/social movements committed to marijuana law reform have been forced to rely on ballot measures to effect change in the laws.

Support for Marijuana Law Reform as Revealed in Public Opinion Polls

Increasing support for marijuana law reform has also been revealed in public opinion polls conducted in recent years. When Gallup opinion polls first asked questions about support for marijuana legalization in 1969, only 12 percent of Americans were in support, and as recently as 2005, support for legalization was only at 36 percent (Swift 2016; see also Ingraham 2016e). However, a Gallup poll released in October 2016 found that 60 percent of Americans were in favor of marijuana legalization—the results of this poll mirrored those of a Pew Research poll conducted around the same time, which found 57 percent of adults in support of marijuana legalization (Geiger 2016). While Gallup and Pew polls are more susceptible to sampling error (because of their relatively small sample sizes) and additional methodological problems, even the General Social Survey (GSS), considered by many to be the gold standard of public opinion polls in the United States, has revealed significant increases in support for marijuana legalization in recent years. In 2016, 57 percent of respondents to the GSS indicated they approved the legalization of marijuana (GSS Data Explorer, n.d.), representing an increase of 9 percent since 2012. The most recent poll addressing the issue of marijuana legalization, conducted by Quinnipiac and released in August 2017, revealed that 94 percent of Americans supported medical marijuana legalization and, similar to the results of the Gallup, Pew, and GSS polls, placed support for marijuana legalization at 61 percent (Washburn 2017a).

However, support for marijuana legalization is by no means universal and reflects larger political divisions in the United States; there is considerable variation across demographic categories (especially age but also gender and race/ethnicity) and according to political affiliation. The 2016 Pew poll found that 60 percent of men and 55 percent of women supported legalization. With respect to age, 71 percent of millennials (ages eighteen to thirty-five), 57 percent of Generation X (ages thirty-six to fifty-one), 56 percent of baby boomers (ages fifty-two to seventy), and only 33 percent of those from the "silent generation" (ages seventy-one to eighty-eight) supported legalization in the 2016 Pew poll (Geiger 2016). The support for legalization among Generation X and baby boomers is likely at least partially related to personal experiences using marijuana—an earlier national survey conducted in 2012 found that among those who had tried marijuana, 70 percent supported legalization, but only 35 percent of those who had not used the substance supported legalization (Galston and Dionne 2013). Concerning millennials' support of marijuana legalization, Lapidos (2014) comments, "As with same sex marriage, young people don't seem to understand what all the fuss is about." As William Galston and E. J. Dionne note with respect to the importance of these demographic differences, "Unless the younger generation substantially alters its views as it ages, generational change alone is likely to keep support [for legal marijuana] well above the levels of the relatively recent past, even if enthusiasm for legalization wanes" (2013, 1).

Differences in support for marijuana legalization across political affiliation are also significant. Similar to the results from the 2016 Pew poll, the 2016 Gallup poll found that 70 percent of those identifying as Independents, 67 percent of Democrats, but only 42 percent of Republicans supported legalization (Swift 2016). However, and importantly, an earlier 2015 Pew poll found that 63 percent of Republican millennials (who are also more supportive than older Republicans of issues such as same-sex marriage) supported marijuana legalization (Devaney 2015). And a 2017 CBS News poll revealed that, even among Republicans, 63 percent were opposed to the federal government enforcing marijuana laws in states where the substance is legal (Scott 2017).

While the results of public opinion polls and the reality of recreational marijuana legalization in nine states and in Washington, D.C., are of course reflective of changing attitudes toward the substance in the United States, legalization measures have not passed by overwhelming margins. Although D.C.'s 2014 (recreational marijuana legalization) Initiative 71 passed with 70.6 percent of voters in favor, in the eight states that have legalized recreational marijuana via ballot measures since 2012, support averaged 54.2 percent of voters in favor, with Maine's Measure 1 passing by a margin of only four thousand votes. This indicates that there is still by no means consensus on the issue of marijuana legalization (again reflecting, to a certain extent, larger political divisions within the United States).

And even in states that have passed recreational marijuana legalization measures, there has been considerable variation in support across counties and cities. In Washington State, for instance, although 55.7 percent of voters approved Initiative 502, the majority of voters in nineteen of the state's thirty-nine counties did not support legalization (Washington Secretary of State 2012), with most of the opposition in the state's rural counties (once again, reflecting larger political divisions within the United States). In addition, as of July 2016, 30 percent of Washington State residents lived in jurisdictions that had implemented temporary or permanent bans on retail marijuana sales (Dilley et al. 2017). Similarly, in Colorado, while 54.8 percent of voters statewide approved Amendment 6 in 2012, voters in thirty-one of the state's sixty-four counties did not approve the amendment (*Denver Post* 2012); and as of August 2016, eighty-five cities in Colorado had enacted bans on retail marijuana outlets (Boudreau 2016). In Oregon, 56.1 percent of voters approved the legalization of recreational marijuana in 2014, with support being highest in the Portland metropolitan area and western counties (Oregon Secretary of State 2014). However, voters in fourteen of the state's thirty-six counties did not approve Measure 91, and as of June 2016, sixteen counties prohibited retail sales of cannabis (Oregon Liquor Control Commission 2017).

Trends in Marijuana Use

The increasing levels of support for marijuana legalization have been mirrored in trends in use of the substance by adults. Although estimates vary (and in some cases, widely), most surveys (whether large-scale surveys such as the National Household Survey on Drug Use and Health [NSDUH] or others, such as a 2017 survey conducted by Yahoo News and Marist University) indicate that marijuana use among adults in the United States is increasing.

The 2017 Yahoo/Marist poll revealed that more than half of adults in the United States had tried marijuana at least once in their lives and estimated that 22 percent (fifty-five million) currently use the substance (in contrast to most surveys on drug use, the Yahoo/Marist poll defined current use as having consumed marijuana at least one or twice in the previous year), while nearly thirty-five million were regular users (consuming marijuana at least once or twice per month) (Marist Poll 2017). The Yahoo/Marist poll estimates of the number of past-year marijuana users are considerably higher than the most recent figures from the NSDUH (Substance Abuse and Mental Health Services Administration [SAMHSA] 2017), which estimated that thirty-three million adults were current users of marijuana (defined in the NSDUH as use in the past month). As Ingraham (2017c) notes, the varying estimates are likely due to methodological differences in the way the surveys were conducted—the Yahoo/Marist poll is a phone survey, while the NSDUH relies on in-home, face-to-face interviews of subjects, who may be less willing to admit using marijuana. Data from the 2016 NSDUH indicated that the percentage of individuals over the age of eighteen reporting past-month marijuana use increased from 10.4 percent in 2002 to 14.1 percent in 2016 (SAMHSA 2017). While this increase is not inordinately large, it has generated concerns regarding the impact of legalization on cannabis consumption. However, earlier NSDUH surveys revealed that adult current marijuana use, as well as daily or near-daily use, began increasing in 2009, prior to the legalization of recreational marijuana. It is also not possible to determine from these survey data how much of the reported increase in marijuana use among adults is attributable to social desirability effects. That is, as marijuana use has become increasingly normalized and acceptable in the United States over the past decade, survey respondents may simply be more willing to admit use of the substance.

The same 2016 NSDUH survey also found that close to 19 percent of people who used marijuana in 2016 used it on at least three hundred days during the year; only 12 percent reported using the substance daily or nearly daily in 2002 (SAMHSA 2017). Data from a report by the Washington State Institute for Public Policy, analyzing trends in marijuana use under legalization, similarly signaled an increase in frequent and heavy use by adults (defined as use on twenty or more days over the previous month)—individuals twenty-one years of age and older in counties in Washington State with higher retail cannabis sales were more likely to report using cannabis in the past month and also to report heavy use (Darnell and Bitney 2017).

Drug policy scholars and commentators have expressed legitimate concerns about these increases in frequent and heavy use of marijuana among adults in the United States. Considered by many to be among the top drug policy scholars in the United States, Jonathan Caulkins of Carnegie Mellon University has been the most prominent in expressing concerns about the upward trend in so-called heavy and frequent marijuana use. Using data from the 2013 NSDUH (and based on somewhat questionable assumptions and estimates), Caulkins suggested that marijuana legalization under which the substance would be sold at low prices could increase the amount of time "spent stoned" (although the specific psychological effects associated with being "stoned" were not defined) by fifteen billion person-hours per year (Kleiman 2014).[1] Caulkins (2016) further asserted that this increase would be concentrated among frequent heavy users rather than casual recreational users of the substance and commented, "Choosing legalization means choosing greater drug dependence." This increase in heavy use has also been emphasized by another preeminent drug policy scholar, Mark Kleiman of New

---

1. Caulkins's analysis of the NSDUH survey indicated that there were an equivalent of 228 million days of marijuana use in the previous thirty days reported by respondents. However, he estimated that the underreporting of cannabis use increases the number of marijuana-use days by 33 percent, although it is not entirely clear how this assumption can be justified. He then multiplied this figure by the number of times an individual consumed marijuana on any given day (once again, making largely unsubstantiated assumptions). Finally, the number of sessions was multiplied by the number of hours of intoxication, which can range from one to four, to arrive at the figure of fifteen billion (Wile 2015).

York University. In a 2013 symposium on marijuana legalization organized by the National Institute of Justice, Kleiman repeated Caulkins's claim: "The primary impact of legalizing cannabis is that there will probably be six hundred and fifty thousand fewer arrests every year and forty thousand fewer people behind bars. And there will be an additional . . . fifteen billion stoned hours" (quoted in Keefe 2013). Similarly, in an op-ed published in the *Los Angeles Times* opposing a 2010 recreational marijuana legalization ballot measure in California, Kleiman asserted, "The only way to sell a lot of pot is to create a lot of potheads—not casual, moderate, recreational users but chronic, multiple-joints-per-day zonkers" (quoted in Keefe 2013).

While we share the concerns of Caulkins, Kleiman, and others regarding the problems associated with an increased number of heavy marijuana users, for the most part,[2] they have not acknowledged the emerging research indicating that marijuana may actually serve as a substitute for other drugs such as alcohol, opiates (both prescription opiates and heroin), and even stimulant drugs. And although it is beyond the scope of this book to deconstruct Caulkins's and others' arguments regarding heavy use, it is by no means clear that such use is attributable to the legalization of recreational or medical marijuana. That is, marijuana use, including heavy marijuana use, existed well before legalization of the substance. We also agree with the comments of Alison Holcomb, primary architect of Washington State's recreational marijuana legalization measure (Initiative 502) who commented, "Would it bother me if problematic use went way up? Yes. Would it make me think we should go back to treating it as a crime? No" (quoted in Keefe 2013).

A final important issue to consider regarding trends in use of marijuana is that of youth use. As we discuss in considerable detail in Chapter 4, one of the major concerns of those opposed to marijuana legalization is that under legalization, youth use of marijuana would increase. Both national data and data from states that have legalized recreational marijuana do not support this claim. In the same NSDUH survey referred to previously, only 6.5 percent of twelve- to seventeen-year-olds reported past-month use of marijuana, the lowest level in more than two decades (SAMHSA 2017). Roughly similar trends in youth use have been revealed in the 2016 University of Michigan's school-based Monitoring the Future Survey. Although past-year marijuana use in 2016 was at 36 percent among twelfth-graders and had held steady since 2011, past-year use among eighth-graders (at 9.4 percent in 2016) has been declining since 2010. Past-year use of marijuana among tenth-graders (24 percent) has also been declining since 2013. Similar declines in daily or

---

2. Mark Kleiman has acknowledged that "if marijuana turns out to be a substitute for alcohol, if allowing people to smoke pot decreases heavy drinking, that's a huge win. If that were true, I'd be a strong legalizer" (quoted in Haglage 2013).

near-daily use (twenty or more occasions in the past month) were reported for eighth- and tenth-graders, although there was no change in this metric for twelfth-graders (Monitoring the Future 2016). These trends in youth use prompted Nora Volkow, director of the National Institute on Drug Abuse, to comment, "We had predicted based on changes in legalization, culture in the U.S. as well as decreasing perceptions among teenagers that marijuana was harmful [and] that [accessibility and use] would go up. But it hasn't gone up" (quoted in Ingraham 2017a).

Sales of Cannabis Products and Employment in the (Legal) Marijuana Industry

The changing landscape of marijuana in the United States is also reflected in legal sales of the drug (both medical and recreational), which reached $6.7 billion in North America in 2016 and were projected to be $10.2 billion by 2021 (Marks 2017). In Washington State, marijuana sales increased from $31 million between July 8, 2014, and December 31, 2014, to $696 million in 2016, and the state collected $256 million in excise taxes from sales of the substance in 2016 alone (Washington State Liquor and Cannabis Board 2017b). In Colorado, sales of marijuana in March 2017 reached $131.7 million, and monthly sales of $100 million or more had become the "new norm" in the state (Wallace 2017c). In Oregon retail sales of marijuana were estimated at approximately $287 million in 2016 (Oregon Department of Revenue 2018), and between January 4, 2016, and August 31, 2017, the state collected more than $108 million in state and local taxes (Crombie 2017c).

The cannabis industry is also contributing to employment by creating significant numbers of jobs. In the first six months of legal recreational marijuana sales in Colorado (January 2014 to July 2014) it was estimated that more than eleven thousand people were employed in various aspects of the industry (Healy and Johnson 2014), and by early 2016, some twenty-one thousand Colorado residents held occupational licenses to work in marijuana-related businesses (Powell 2016). Nationally, it was estimated that 100,000 to 150,000 workers were employed in marijuana-related businesses in 2016, and projections suggested that by 2020 the legal cannabis market would create more than 250,000 jobs (more than the expected number of jobs in manufacturing, utilities, or government) (Borchardt 2017). While some have questioned whether the jobs created in the marijuana industry have simply been transferred from the black market to the legal cannabis industry (Subritzky, Pettigrew, and Lenton, 2016), it is important that unlike those who were involved in black-market marijuana "businesses," individuals in these newly created jobs are paying taxes.

The Mainstreaming and Normalization of Marijuana

The changing landscape of marijuana is also evidenced in the mainstreaming of the substance, the increasing number of products and forms of the substance that can be purchased, and the growing array of methods of consumption. Along with the more traditional marijuana flower, which is smoked in cigarettes, pipes, and bongs, the substance can now be ingested via vaporizers and "e-pens." And in addition to brownies, we now have several types of marijuana-infused edible products that have become increasingly popular among consumers—these include "beef" jerky, nuts, ice cream, root (and alcoholic) beer and other beverages, gummy bears, lemon drops, marshmallows, and several others. Marijuana-infused topicals, ingestible oils, tinctures, and suppositories are also available to consumers.[3]

Marijuana has also become increasingly prominent in U.S. culture, social life, entertainment, and professional sports. Consider the following:

- In Colorado, there are organized bus tours of marijuana dispensaries and cultivation facilities, and the Avalon Group, publishers of the popular Rick Steves travel guides, include a section on marijuana tourism for cities in Colorado (Baca 2016c). The state also features "bud and breakfast" establishments (Hesse 2016a). In Washington State, a company known as Kush Tours offers "cannabis friendly lodging" and tours of Seattle's cannabis businesses (Kush Tours, n.d.; see also E. Bush, 2015b).
- In both Oregon and Washington State, drive-through marijuana stores have opened (Rose 2016). In some locations, marijuana can be purchased online (Fuller 2017a), and we are even seeing delivery of marijuana by drones (Harbarger 2015). In California, a company sometimes referred to as the "Uber of marijuana," delivers the substance and is active in more than eighty cities in the state (Corbyn 2015).
- In Colorado, there are marijuana cooking classes and dinner parties, sushi and joint-rolling classes, and the "munchie crawl" (the marijuana equivalent of a pub crawl; Wenzel 2015). There are also cannabis-and-wine-pairing dinners in the Sonoma wine region of Northern California (Fuller 2017b). Dozens of cannabis cookbooks have been published, with titles such as *Cannabis Cocktails, Mocktails, and Tonics: The Art of Spirited Drinks and Buzz-Worthy Libations*; *The Ganja Kitchen Revolution: The Bible of Cannabis Cuisine*;

---

3. There is even a product known as the Peter Piper Pecker Puffer. Although it has now been discontinued, this hybrid "weed pipe and sex toy," manufactured by the online sex toy company Pipedreams, was marketed as "smoke it then poke it!" (Bess 2015).

Baked: Over 50 Tasty Marijuana Treats; and *The Vegan Stoner Cookbook: 100 Easy Vegan Recipes to Munch* (Bringetto 2016).

- Online dating services such as My420mate.com, which claims to be the "#1 online and mobile dating app for 420 friendly singles," allows such singles "who are acceptable of the green lifestyle to meet, connect, and grow a relationship."[4] A competing dating website and app is High There, created by Todd Mitchem, who indicated he established the website after one of his dates ended when his companion discovered that he smoked marijuana (Bell 2015). High There's website indicates it is a "social network that promotes uniting cannabis users and enthusiasts with each other in a friendly and judgment-free environment" (High There, n.d.).
- In Centennial, Colorado (a suburb of Denver), there is a Stoner Jesus Bible study group; one member of this group commented, "Jesus didn't hang out with the Pharisees, if somebody passed him a pipe, he wouldn't say no" (quoted in Wiedeman 2015).
- In 2016, marijuana plants were displayed and judged at the Oregon State Fair (Crombie 2016a).
- Portland, Oregon, has hosted "Toke Talks," modeled after the popular "Ted Talks" at local theaters. These events are advertised as "taking the discussion about cannabis to a higher level" (*Mercury* 2017).
- The cannabis company American Green Inc. purchased the town of Nipton (on the California/Nevada border—population twenty) to turn it into a marijuana tourist destination (*Time* 2017).
- In May 2014, the Colorado symphony held a "classically cannabis" fund-raiser (Healy 2014b).
- Former National Football League running back (and admitted cannabis user) Ricky Williams has opened a "cannabis gym" in San Francisco (Daley 2016).
- In the bong pong game (analogous to the popular college game beer pong), players throw ping-pong balls along a line of bongs instead of cups of beer, and whenever a ball lands in a bong, players are supposed to take a hit of marijuana (N. Shapiro 2012).
- There are reports that parents in Colorado are dressing their children as marijuana plants for Halloween (Baca 2015b).
- Companies such as Canna Companion (a hemp-based pet supplement company); Seattle's "Canna-Pet, which also markets cannabis products for pets; and Austin + Kat, Therabis, and Treatibles have been established to serve pet owners who believe that their

---

4. See the site's home page, at http://www.my420mate.com.

pets can receive some of the same medicinal benefits as humans from cannabis products (Mosendz 2016).

- Law enforcement agencies in several locations in the United States, particularly in states where marijuana is legal, are "detraining" or removing drug sniffing dogs that search for marijuana (Bailey 2015).
- In cannabis culture, the term "4-20" is a code that refers to the consumption of cannabis, especially smoking marijuana around 4:20 in the afternoon and celebrating cannabis on April 20. Although most U.S. highways do not cover four hundred miles, to deal with thieves who want to own 420 milepost markers, Idaho changed its milepost 420 sign to 419.9. It has also been reported that Colorado has consistently had to replace the 420 signs on its highways (Kruesi 2015).

The mainstreaming of marijuana has also extended to language—in 2014, "vape" was chosen as the *Oxford English Dictionary*'s "word of the year," "greenout" is the new blackout, marijuana entrepreneurs are referred to as "ganjapreneurs," people who serve customers in legal marijuana stores are "budtenders," a marijuana connoisseur is a "cannaseur," and bias against marijuana users is referred to as "cannabigotry" (Bennett 2014). Related to the mainstreaming of marijuana in language, cannabis businesses have come up with numerous creative names for their medical and recreational businesses and products. Among the more interesting business names are Alice's Secret Garden, Bloom Room, Calm and Collective, Ganja Gourmet, Grass Roots, Grateful Meds, Green Light District, Hard Pot Café, Kush Mart, New Vansterdam, Rip City Remedies, Planet Hollyweed, Puffin Stuff, the Coughy Shop, the Releaf Center, the Secret Stash, Starbuds, and Weedidit Association (*Herb* 2015).

Cannabis brand names include Agent Orange, Alaskan Thunderfuck, Brown Buddha, Bubbleicious, Charlotte's Web, Chernobyl, Chunky Cheese, Cookies 'n Cream, Frosty Lemonade, Galactic Jack, Girl Scout Cookies, Gorilla Glue, Grape Ape, Green Crack, Psychocrack, Space Queen, Skywalker, Smurf, Spirit in the Sky, and Trainwreck (Crombie 2016b; Main St. Marijuana 2018).

And as marijuana laws have changed in several jurisdictions across the country, "higher?" educational institutions (both alternative and traditional) have chosen to get a piece of the action. For example, Oaksterdam University, founded by medical marijuana activist Richard Lee in 2007, was the first "cannabis college" in the United States—it offers classes on legal issues and politics surrounding marijuana, horticulture, and "cannabusiness" among other topics; at one time, Oaksterdam University had more than fifteen thousand students and more than one hundred instructors (Thomas 2013a).

The Cannabis Training University (n.d.), an online university founded in 2009 in San Francisco and now headquartered in Denver, has a mission to "teach students about the medical marijuana industry and prepare them for a cannabis career." Some traditional universities have also introduced marijuana-related courses, with several focusing on cannabis laws: The University of Denver has a class titled "Representing the Marijuana Client"; it also began offering a course in cannabis journalism in 2015, in which "students will visit and interview dispensaries, industry professionals and private citizens to produce a portfolio of narrative journalism" (quoted in Baca 2015a). Even Harvard University's Law School offers the seminar "Tax Planning for Marijuana Dealers" (Migoya 2015) (we are assuming the curriculum in this course relates only to *legal* marijuana dealers).

And of course, not surprisingly, this mainstreaming of marijuana has also extended to print media, television, and the Internet, as well as entertainment and professional sports. Although primarily focused on research on marijuana, in June 2015, *National Geographic*'s cover showed a photograph of a marijuana plant and included a thirty-plus-page article titled "Weed: The New Science of Marijuana"; *Time* published an entire special issue titled "Marijuana Goes Main Street" in 2015. And similar to the way that television shows such as *Will and Grace*, *Ellen*, and *Modern Family* that feature gay characters have contributed to changing Americans' attitudes toward homosexuality (Bond and Compton 2015) and influenced growing support for same-sex marriage, it is likely that portrayals of marijuana and marijuana users in popular media are influencing Americans' attitudes toward the substance. The following examples show the mainstreaming of marijuana in the media, professional sports, and entertainment:

- On the popular ABC comedy series *Modern Family*, the couple living next door to the Dunphy family (the main characters in the show) owns a marijuana dispensary (Jurgensen 2015).
- On the Fox procedural crime drama *Bones*, one of the characters consumes marijuana to treat the side effects of cancer (Jurgensen 2015).
- Comedian Doug Benson has a weekly series on YouTube (the show has close to three hundred thousand subscribers) called *Getting Doug with High*; guests have included Sarah Silverman and Cheech and Chong (Rottenberg 2015).
- *Weeds*, which ran for eight seasons on the Showtime network, features a woman who, after her husband dies, begins selling cannabis to make money. The show, a "female spin on Breaking Bad," which focused on a high school chemistry teacher who began producing and selling methamphetamine, featured "heavy marketing aimed at the pot friendly demographic" (Virtue 2017).

- The 2014 Super Bowl, in which the Denver Broncos played the Se-attle Seahawks, was referred to by some as the "bud bowl," "bong bowl," "doobie bowl," "clash of the tokers," and "'The Evergreen State' vs. 'The Mile High City'" (Glaser 2014) because the home states of both teams had legalized recreational marijuana.
- During the 2016 Super Bowl, with the Denver Broncos playing the Carolina Panthers (held at Levi Stadium in the San Francisco Bay Area city of Santa Clara), medical cannabis stores in the area mar-keted new marijuana brands such as Bronco Mile High and Cam Crush (the latter named after Panthers quarterback Cam Newton) (Vekshin 2016). This was taken a step further in the 2017 Super Bowl, which included an advertisement for T-Mobile featuring Martha Stewart and Snoop Dog (well known for his marijuana use), with several not-so-subtle references to marijuana (Suri 2017).

Another obvious and related sign of mainstreaming is use of marijuana (and public acknowledgment of use) by celebrities and its appearance in various aspects of popular culture. Prominent filmmakers Robert Altman and Oliver Stone have both admitted to being lifelong marijuana consumers, and Jennifer Aniston, Sarah Silverman, Brad Pitt, Jane Fonda, Seth Rogan, Matthew McConaughey, and Woody Harrelson (although he announced in 2017 that he was quitting marijuana [Tracy 2017]) have publicly endorsed marijuana (Fox, Armentano, and Tvert 2009). Perhaps the most prominent celebrity advocate for marijuana and confirmed consumer is HBO's Bill Ma-her, who actually smoked a "giant joint" on his television show on February 12, 2016 (YouTube 2016). Morgan Freeman told the *Daily Beast* that only marijuana could alleviate the pain he experienced from fibromyalgia (Downs 2015).

In addition to publicly endorsing marijuana, several celebrities and sports figures have become directly involved in the marijuana industry, such as Snoop Dogg, who has a new line of cannabis products called Leafs by Snoop (Tablang 2016); country music icon Willie Nelson, whose company, Willie's Reserve, opened in Colorado in 2016 (Baca 2016d); actor Seth Rogan (Keyes 2015); Whoopi Goldberg, who has a line of cannabis topicals and edibles (Nathman 2016); and Melissa Etheridge, who produces a marijuana-infused wine (Wyatt 2016). Former Seattle Seahawk Marcus Trufant is a co-owner of a marijuana retail outlet in Lacey, Washington (E. Bush 2015c), and the Queen Anne Cannabis Club in Seattle named one of its marijuana strains Beast Mode after former Seattle Seahawks running back Marshawn Lynch. According to the owner of Queen Anne, the Beast Mode strain of cannabis "hits you like its namesake. . . . Marshawn has gears when he's run-ning and it's kind of like that. It has a little bit of a slow start and then kicks in" (quoted in Young 2014).

Marijuana Law Reform in the United States: Forces Driving Change

Given the relatively long history of prohibitionist drug policies in the United States, and given that these policies (including those related to marijuana) are among the most stringent of any in Western industrialized nation, pundits likely would not have predicted that the United States would be the first country to embrace the legalization of recreational marijuana (albeit, up to this point, in only nine states and Washington, D.C.). But a unique confluence of factors has contributed to this reform. Certainly part of the equation was fiscal: There has been a realization that hundreds of millions of dollars were being spent on the drug war, with much of the raw material for this war involving marijuana offenses, and a realization that, given relatively high levels of consumption of the substance in the United States, governments could derive substantial tax revenues from legalizing marijuana. For example, a study by the Tax Foundation estimated that the federal government and states where marijuana was not legal were forfeiting $28 billion in annual tax revenue by not legalizing the drug (Ingraham 2016m). And while opponents of marijuana law reform have argued that collection of tax revenues should not be a justification for legalization, it is important to remain aware that without legalization of marijuana, people still consume it and the state receives nothing.

Marijuana law reform has also been fueled by larger changes in (especially young people's) views about certain social issues—particularly relevant here are changes in attitudes toward homosexuality and same-sex marriage; as Bruce Barcott suggests, "Gay marriage and marijuana are neighbors" (2015, 293). In 1996, only 27 percent of Americans supported same-sex marriage (Leonhardt and Parlapiano 2015), and in 2001, only 35 percent were in support, but a Pew poll conducted in June 2017 revealed that 62 percent of Americans favored allowing gays and lesbians to marry (Pew Research Center 2017). Reflective of these changes in attitudes, as of 2017, thirty-seven states had legalized same-sex marriage (Governing the States and Localities 2018).

Importantly, the legalization of medical marijuana (beginning in 1996 in California) and the fact that there have not been significant problems in states that allow medical marijuana have to some extent paved the way for the legalization of recreational marijuana—one commentator has referred to medical marijuana legalization as "gateway legislation" (Balko 2014b). As of August 2017, there were an estimated 2,354,403 state-legal medical marijuana patients in the United States (Statista 2017).

While all of these factors, as well as the efforts of marijuana and other drug policy reform organizations such as the Drug Policy Alliance (DPA), the National Organization for the Reform of Marijuana Laws (NORML), and the Marijuana Policy Project (MPP) have been major driving forces in marijuana legalization, it is our contention that concerns over the racial and social injustices associated with the war on marijuana (and the war on drugs more generally) have been a central force in producing change.

Engines of Reform: Social and Racial Justice Issues

Two of the primary factors influencing marijuana law reform, which have been emphasized to a greater or lesser degree in marijuana legalization efforts in several states and Washington, D.C., are the huge numbers of arrests for marijuana offenses and the exorbitant costs associated with the enforcement of marijuana laws—a 2013 report by the American Civil Liberties Union (ACLU) estimated that states spent more than $3.6 billion enforcing marijuana possession laws in the year 2010 alone. A second and related issue is the tremendous racial and ethnic disparities in arrests for marijuana and other illegal drugs in the United States. Galston and Dionne (2013) note that public opinion polls indicate that support for marijuana legalization is driven more by concerns over the negative outcomes related to its prohibition than by strong support for marijuana per se.

In a 2013 article published by the James Baker III Institute for Public Policy, Kevin Sabet (2013a) of Smart Approaches to Marijuana (SAM) asserted that "private, personal use of marijuana is rarely pursued by law enforcement."[5] In addition to Sabet, drug policy expert Jonathan Caulkins and former drug czars John Walters and William Bennett (the latter in a book published in 2015 and coauthored with federal prosecutor Robert White titled *Going to Pot: Why the Rush to Legalize Marijuana Is Harming America*) apparently believe that the hundreds of thousands of marijuana arrests each year are not relevant to consider in the debate over marijuana legalization.

The number of marijuana arrests seems to tell a different story than what Sabet and other marijuana prohibitionists would have us believe—in fact, in any given year, police make more arrests for marijuana possession than for all violent crimes combined. Between 1998 and 2013, police in the United States made more than ten million arrests for marijuana possession (Levine 2013), and while marijuana arrests constituted 22.4 percent of all drug arrests in 1981, they made up 44 percent in 2010. Although the number of marijuana arrests declined from 872,720 in 2007 to 643,121 in 2015 (at least partially due to the legalization of recreational marijuana in Alaska, Colo-

---

5. Although, interestingly, some two paragraphs later, Sabet (2013a) notes that "about 700,000 arrests are made yearly for marijuana possession." It would seem to us that 700,000 arrests is not a trivial number and does not provide evidence that personal use of marijuana is not being pursued by law enforcement.

rado, Oregon, Washington State, and Washington, D.C., between 2012 and 2014),[6] Jacob Sullum (2016) refers to the number of arrests as an "outrage" and comments, "Still, 643,121 marijuana arrests are 643,121 too many."

Data on marijuana arrests in particular cities and states are also relevant to consider here. For example, police in New York City, who made fewer than eight hundred marijuana arrests in 1991, made more than fifty-nine thousand such arrests in 2010, and over the 1998 to 2013 period, arrested more than eight hundred thousand people for marijuana possession (Levine 2013). A 2014 report on disparities in marijuana law enforcement in New York City found that the predominantly black Washington Heights area had a rate of 882 marijuana possession arrests per 100,000 residents, which was 110 times higher than the rate in Forest Hills; Harlem's rate of 1,128 per 100,000 marijuana possession arrests was similarly 110 times higher than the rate on the Upper East Side of the city (Drug Policy Alliance 2014c).

While campaigning for mayor of New York City in 2013, Bill de Blasio stated, "Low-level marijuana possession arrests have disastrous consequences for individuals and their families. These arrests limit one's ability to qualify for student financial aid and undermine one's ability to find stable housing and good jobs. What's more, recent studies demonstrate clear racial bias in arrests for low-level possession. . . . This policy is unjust and wrong" (quoted in Drug Policy Alliance 2014c).

But a more recent report on marijuana arrests, commissioned by the DPA, found that, despite Mayor de Blasio's promise to end marijuana possession arrests in New York City, during the first three years of his administration, the City of New York Police Department (NYPD) made more than sixty thousand arrests for possession of marijuana, and 86 percent of the arrests involved blacks or Latinos (Drug Policy Alliance and Marijuana Arrest Research Project 2017). The report further notes that during the twelve years under Mayor Michael Bloomberg, there was an average of more than forty thousand marijuana possession arrests per year, making New York City the "marijuana arrest capital of the world." The report also documented that marijuana possession arrests in New York City were concentrated in certain locations—in 2016, the city's housing police made 21 percent of the total of 18,121 arrests for marijuana possession, with 92 percent of arrestees being black and Latino. The outcomes of marijuana possession cases in

---

6. While marijuana legalization in these states is not the only cause of the overall decline, it is notable that in Alaska, the number of marijuana-related arrests declined from 716 in 2014 to 290 in 2015; in Colorado, the number of marijuana possession arrests fell from 9,011 in 2010 to 1,464 in 2014 (a decrease of 84 percent); in Oregon, marijuana arrests decreased from 4,723 in 2014 to 1,129 in 2015 (Sullum 2016). In Washington State "low level marijuana court filings" fell from 6,879 in 2011 to 120 in 2013 (American Civil Liberties Union of Washington 2014). In Washington, D.C., marijuana possession arrests declined from more than 2,000 in 2011 to fewer than 10 in 2015 (Sullum 2016).

courts also varied by race/ethnicity, with 15.8 percent of cases involving whites resulting in conviction and sentencing, 32.3 percent involving blacks, and 30 percent involving Hispanics.

NYPD's continuing focus on marijuana possession and the related racial/ethnic disparities in these arrests cannot be completely blamed on Mayor de Blasio, of course. Similar to the views of some other law enforcement officials, NYPD chief Bill Bratton (who eventually retired from the department in September 2016) is an ardent marijuana prohibitionist. At a 2015 press conference, Bratton blamed occasional marijuana use and marijuana trafficking for an increase in murders in the city: "In this city, people are killing each other over marijuana more than anything we had to deal with in the 80s and 90s with heroin and cocaine" (quoted in Karlin 2015). In making this statement (even if it were true), Bratton makes an all-too-common error characteristic of other marijuana prohibitionists—he is conflating the effects of prohibition with the effects of marijuana itself.

As mentioned previously, an additional defining characteristic of marijuana law enforcement in the United States is the gross racial/ethnic disparities in marijuana arrests. The 2013 ACLU report noted that, while blacks and whites use cannabis at similar rates, overall in the United States, blacks are 3.7 times more likely to be arrested for marijuana offenses—in 2010, the arrest rates for marijuana possession were 716 per 100,000 for blacks and 192 per 100,000 for whites. In some counties, the arrest rate for blacks for marijuana possession was up to thirty times higher than the rate for whites (American Civil Liberties Union 2013). There are also significant racial disparities in marijuana arrests and outcomes in other large American cities and states. For example, in Chicago, fifteen times as many African Americans are arrested for marijuana possession as whites, and forty times as many are convicted (D'Angelo 2015). In Virginia, over the three-year period spanning 2011–2013, marijuana possession arrests increased from 19,697 to 21,684, with African Americans accounting for 82 percent of the increase (Gettman 2015). Looking at a longer historical period, in 2003, the marijuana arrest rate for black Virginians was 344 per 100,000 and 144 per 100,000 for whites—by 2013, the rate for black Virginians had increased to 636 per 100,000 151 per 100,000 for whites. Expressed in a different way, in 2003, blacks constituted 20 percent of Virginia's population and 39 percent of marijuana possession arrests, and while still composing 20 percent of the state's population in 2013, they accounted for nearly half of all marijuana possession arrests. In light of these gross racial disparities in the enforcement of marijuana laws in numerous cities and states, the 2013 ACLU report concluded, "Such racial disparities in marijuana possession arrests exist in all regions of the country, in counties large and small, urban and rural, wealthy and poor. . . . Just as with the larger drug war, the war on marijuana has, quite simply, served as a vehicle for police to target Blacks."

While the overall number of marijuana arrests has declined, particularly in jurisdictions where the substance has been legalized for recreational purposes, racial disparities in marijuana law enforcement persist. After legalization in Washington, D.C., marijuana arrests have decreased significantly. However, it is still a crime to smoke marijuana in public (a misdemeanor offense that can result in a $500 fine and ninety days in jail), and in 2015 African Americans made up 109 (85 percent) of the 128 arrests in D.C. for smoking marijuana in public (A. Davis 2016). In Colorado, black adults were arrested at a rate slightly less than double the rate for whites in 2012, but two years after legalization, they were arrested at triple the rate for whites (Colorado Department of Public Safety 2016; see also Lewis 2016). These racial/ethnic disparities also manifest in the juvenile justice system. According to a report by the Colorado Department of Public Safety (2016), while juvenile arrests of whites for marijuana offenses declined by 8 percent between 2012 and 2014, arrests of blacks increased by 58 percent, and arrests of Latinos increased by 29 percent.

Just as they dismiss marijuana arrests as being of little relevance in the debate on marijuana law reforms, marijuana prohibitionists seem unaware of (or conveniently neglect) the gross racial/ethnic disparities in the enforcement of marijuana laws. Although we have certainly not read all of his publications, to the best of our knowledge, Jonathan Caulkins has not commented on this issue. Speaking at a symposium on the impacts of marijuana legalization at Colorado Christian University in October 2016, Kevin Sabet of SAM asserted that marijuana legalization was not about social/racial justice issues and, referring to the data on juvenile arrests in Colorado mentioned previously, implied that legalization had actually exacerbated racial disparities (Pasquariello 2017). And while William Bennett and Robert White should perhaps be commended for acknowledging racial disparities in the enforcement of marijuana laws, their proposed solution to the problem is rather bizarre. Referencing a 2014 *New York Times* editorial that highlighted racial disparities in marijuana arrests as one justification for legalization, Bennett and White suggest that more, not fewer, marijuana arrests are the solution to the racial disparity problem: "The [*New York Times*] editorial tried to bolster its case by citing racial disparities in these arrests. . . . If a good many non-minorities are breaking the law, any law, target them more, and we advocate that absolutely, but do not let up on enforcement simply because one group is getting away with what another group is not" (2015, 169).

While not conceding that the number of arrests for marijuana is much cause for concern or acknowledging that racial disparities in these arrests are problematic, Kevin Sabet, John Walters, William Bennett, and Jonathan Caulkins have emphasized that such arrests are not a problem because very few, if any, of those arrested for violations of marijuana laws end up being incarcerated. While these critics are correct in noting that most of those incarcerated for marijuana offenses were involved in cultivation and/or trafficking of the substance, while others have had additional offenses and/or prior criminal histories (see also Pfaff 2017), it is important to deconstruct these arguments.

In the foreword to an ONDCP report titled "Who's Really in Prison for Marijuana?" then drug czar John Walters commented, "While we cannot categorically state that no simple marijuana user has ever received a jail or prison sentence, the evidence is overwhelming that these cases are rare" (2003, 7). Speaking at a press conference in 2008, Walters further asserted, "Finding somebody in jail or prison for marijuana for first-time, non-violent possession of marijuana is like finding a unicorn—it doesn't exist" (quoted in Fox, Armentano, and Tvert 2009, 79). Jonathan Caulkins has similarly asserted that one of the biggest myths surrounding marijuana is that the United States has prisons full of marijuana users—"that's basically wrong" (quoted in Dorris 2016). And while we are somewhat hesitant to include it here, given her influence in American culture (especially on the political right), it is worth mentioning the views of Ann Coulter, conservative syndicated columnist, *New York Times* bestselling author, and frequent Fox News contributor, on the issue of incarceration of marijuana offenders. Speaking at a Politicon event in July 2017, Coulter commented that marijuana legalization was "destroying the country" and that the substance "makes people retarded." She also noted, "No, I know, you're all potheads, and you're going to have trouble following what I'm about to say, but almost 90% of people in prison are in prison as a result of a plea bargain. No one gets arrested and tried for possession of marijuana" (quoted in J. Williams 2017).

On its website, SAM (n.d.a) similarly claims that "in total, one tenth of one percent (0.1 percent) of all state prisoners were marijuana-possession offenders with no prior sentences" (a footnote appears to indicate that this is in reference to data from 2004). Further, although not providing a specific reference (or, in this case, any dates to which the cited statistics refer), SAM (n.d.a) notes that, according to Jonathan Caulkins, "only about a half a percent of the total prison population was there for marijuana possession." While including these two different estimates of the percentage of state prisoners incarcerated for marijuana possession is problematic itself, if we use data on the number of individuals in state prisons in 2010 (1,402,624) (Guerino, Harrison, and Sabol 2011), the one-tenth of one percent estimate would translate to 1,420 inmates, while the half a percent figure would translate to 7,103 inmates. We assert that this is not a trivial number of individuals in prison for marijuana offenses. In addition, although we were unable to obtain precise numbers, given that in any given year, more than ninety thousand people are housed in local jails as a result of drug possession charges (Human Rights Watch 2016), the majority of whom are likely charged with marijuana possession, it is certainly the case that thousands more are incarcerated for marijuana possession. And as Ingraham (2016f) notes, many of these individuals may languish in jail for several days or months because they cannot post bail.

Even if it were true that large numbers of people do not go to prison for marijuana possession (which, as we demonstrate, is not the case), Sabet, Caulkins, and others seem to be unaware of (or perhaps conveniently neglect?) the fact that a simple arrest for marijuana possession results in numerous "collateral costs." In many states, most people arrested for marijuana offenses, including simple possession, are held in jail for at least a day and obtain arrest and/or criminal records that show up on background checks when individuals are applying to rent apartments or obtain and keep their current jobs. As Tom James (2016) suggests, arrests are "often treated by society as de facto markers of guilt" and constitute a "scarlet letter."

Additional data also indicate that large numbers of people *do* end up in jail or prison for marijuana offenses, including for possession of the drug. According to a 2015 report issued by the Department of Justice, 11,533 people in the United States were in prison on marijuana-related charges (but only 5,800 for heroin and 3,237 for OxyContin and ecstasy) (Sottile 2016). In addition, 75 individuals convicted of simple possession of marijuana were serving time in federal prisons in 2014 (United States Sentencing Commission 2014)—higher than the number for powder and crack cocaine, heroin, and methamphetamine and representing 40 percent of the total number of individuals incarcerated in federal prisons for drug possession.

In discussing the incarceration of marijuana offenders, it is also important to consider that, according the 2015 Clemency Report, since 1996 (data for the years prior to 1996 were not available) federal judges had sentenced fifty-four people to life in prison without parole for marijuana offenses (these numbers do not include those sentenced to life in prison who are in state prisons). An investigative reporter for *Mother Jones* estimated that there were sixty-nine people serving life sentences for marijuana-related offenses as of 2015 (Schatz 2015). And as a *New York Times* (2016a) editorial noted, individuals can actually receive life in prison without parole for what is essentially marijuana possession.

As we address in more detail in Chapter 6, these injustices that have resulted from the war on marijuana have been central factors in legal reforms dealing with the substance. And while we are by no means suggesting that marijuana legalization has not been attended by problems, we believe that the alarmist positions taken by marijuana prohibitionists such as Kevin Sabet and academics such as Jonathan Caulkins are contrary to what the data tell us so far—in addition, they often attribute certain negative outcomes to marijuana legalization when they are simply part of larger trends in the United States. Also, in states where recreational marijuana has been legalized, governments and state regulatory agencies have responded to problems through alterations to legislation and regulations.

In the next chapter we examine the social, political, and legal history of marijuana. The chapter devotes considerable attention to the reefer madness era of the 1930s and 1940s, what is arguably the most important period of marijuana regulation in the history of the United States. We proceed to a discussion of developments from the 1950s through the 1970s, a time during which marijuana went from a heavily demonized substance to relatively mainstream but also a time when the first official "war on drugs" was initiated during the administration of President Richard Nixon. We also review the findings of several commissions/committees appointed to inform policy makers on marijuana's effects on users and society and to make policy recommendations regarding the substance. These reports were commissioned in the United States, Britain, the Netherlands, Canada, and Australia, and with one exception, they concluded that marijuana was a relatively benign substance and did not lead to the use of hard drugs; most important, these reports recommended that penalties for possession of the substance should be reduced or eliminated entirely. The last part of the chapter considers developments related to marijuana and other drugs from the administrations of President Gerald Ford through Barack Obama, with significant attention being paid to the views and actions of drug czars appointed under these administrations.

2

The Larger Picture

The Social, Political, and Legal History of Marijuana

> Cannabis policy reform is not a daring step forwards so much
> as a righting of historical wrongs, a reversion to what the
> drug's status should always have been, had it been treated
> impartially.
> —BORIS STARLING, "The Tide Effect"

In this chapter, we trace the social, political, and legal history of marijuana. We begin with a discussion of the substance in popular literature and scientific/medical journals in the 1800s as well as the findings of the Indian Hemp Drugs Commission (published in 1894). These early writings on cannabis are worth exploring in some detail, as they provide several insights that have contemporary relevance. For example, in emphasizing the applicability of the Indian Hemp Drugs Commission report to current debates over marijuana legalization, Dave Bewley-Taylor, Tom Blickman, and Martin Jelsma comment, "Had the wisdom of the Indian Hemp Drugs Commission's recommendations prevailed, we might now have a system not dissimilar to the new legislation on cannabis regulation adopted recently in Uruguay or the regulation models being implemented in Colorado and Washington" (2014, 11).

After briefly discussing two little-known reports addressing marijuana use by soldiers in the Panama Canal region (*Military Surgeon* 1933), we proceed to a discussion of arguably the most important period in the history of marijuana regulation in the United States—the 1930s and 1940s, what some have referred to as the "reefer madness era." During this period, the head of the Federal Bureau of Narcotics, Harry Anslinger, engaged in a concerted campaign to demonize and ban marijuana. Anslinger was an instrumental figure in the passage of the 1937 Marihuana Tax Act and demonized marijuana largely through assertions that it was consumed primarily by members of minority groups (Mexicans and "Negroes") and led to the commission of criminal acts.[1] Many of the themes articulated by Anslinger and in the popular media in the 1930s continue to frame current debates over the marijuana into the twenty-first century, but many were challenged and refuted in the 1944 La Guardia Committee report and in scientific studies published in leading medical journals in the late 1930s and 1940s.

As use of marijuana (and other drugs) by youth in several Western countries increased significantly in the 1960s, and as thousands of these youth were subject to criminal justice system sanctions, legislators in several countries (many of whom were not comfortable seeing large numbers of middle-class youth being subjected to severe penalties for drug use) established committees or commissions to study the problems surrounding marijuana and other drugs and to provide recommendations regarding possible changes to drug policies. After discussing marijuana and other drug policies established during the Nixon era, we review the findings and recommendations of the 1962 President's Advisory Commission on Narcotic and Drug Abuse; the 1967 U.S. Task Force on Narcotics and Drug Abuse; the 1968 Wootton Committee (Great Britain); the Hulsman (1968–1971) and Baan (1968) Commissions (Netherlands); the 1972 Le Dain Commission (Canada); the 1972 U.S. Shafer Commission; the U.S. Eastland Committee report (United States Congressional Record 1974); and the Baume Committee (Commonwealth of Australia 1977). With the exception of the 1974 Eastland report, to a greater or lesser extent each of these reports refuted claims that marijuana was a dangerous drug and recommended softening the laws addressing its possession and use. The findings and recommendations of these various reports are vital to consider, as they underscore one of the central themes of this book— in the larger historical context, marijuana prohibition is a historical anomaly. As Johann Hari suggests, "It's not the new wave of legalization [of marijuana] that is radical—prohibition was radical" (2015, 273). The substance's prohibition is simply not justifiable if we consider the best scientific evidence on the drug.

After reviewing these reports, we proceed to a discussion of key developments in general U.S. drug policies and marijuana policies at the federal level under the Gerald Ford, Jimmy Carter, Ronald Reagan, George H. W. Bush, Bill Clinton, and George W. Bush presidencies. While President Carter recommended the decriminalization of marijuana at the federal level (this obviously did not occur), the Reagan and George H. W. Bush eras signaled a renewal and intensification of the Nixon-initiated war on drugs. Despite a rhetorical commitment to drug treatment and other possibly progressive

---

1. In the early 1900s through the 1970s, but particularly in the 1930s, the word "marihuana" was "popularized in the United States by advocates of prohibition who sought to exploit prejudice against despised minority groups, especially Mexican immigrants" (Lee 2012, 6).

drug policies, drug arrests increased significantly during the Clinton administration and there was no abatement in the drug war. Following Clinton, George W. Bush increased budgets to fund the drug war to unprecedented levels, supported antidrug advertisement campaigns that attempted to tie drug use to terrorism (particularly resonant after the September 11, 2001, terrorist attacks), and expanded drug testing programs in schools. We also discuss the views of directors of the Office of National Drug Control Policy ("drug czars"), a position that was first officially established during the administration of George H. W. Bush. The views and actions of these drug czars had a significant impact on drug (including marijuana) policies from 1990 to 2008.

We then consider key developments in U.S. drug policy during the Obama administration. While Obama stated that (in contrast to Bill Clinton) "I inhaled frequently, that was the point" (quoted in Kaczynski 2014) and in reference to the legalization of recreational marijuana in Colorado and Washington State in 2012 that "we've got bigger fish to fry [than marijuana consumers]" (Weiner 2012), the actions of agencies and individuals within his administration with respect to marijuana are not consistent with the argument that the war on marijuana had ended. The chapter concludes with a discussion of two key developments in regulations related to marijuana at the federal level during the Obama administration—the Cole memorandum and the Rohrabacher-Farr amendment, which set out priorities for federal intervention in states with legal recreational and medicinal marijuana.

The Early History of Cannabis

The cannabis plant has a long and fascinating social, economic, and legal history. It has been cultivated for its fiber, leaves, flowering tops, and resin for thousands of years. Its use has been documented as far back as twelve thousand years ago, making it one of the earliest cultivated plants (Drug Policy Alliance 2016a). The fiber from cannabis plants has been used for centuries in linen, canvas, and rope; the seeds used in bird food and for oil; and the leaves, flowering tops, and resin for religious, medicinal, and psychoactive purposes.

Cannabis is also probably the world's oldest medicine, with the earliest written record of its use for medicinal effects appearing in a pharmacy book written by the Chinese emperor Shen Nung in 2737 BC (Ray and Ksir 2004). Other early writings on the substance can be found in the *Atharvaveda,* a holy text written in India in approximately 1400 BC, which noted that the god Shiva took pity on humans and brought marijuana down from the Himalayas to relieve stress and provide pleasure and good health (Earleywine 2002). Arabian texts from AD 950 indicate that cannabis was being used to deal with depression and headaches (Commonwealth of Australia 1977), and by AD 1000, the use of cannabis had spread to North America and the Muslim world. Of course, not all writings on cannabis were positive about the substance; for example, an Arabic text titled *On Poisons* written during this period warned that hashish "renders one blind and mute, eventually leading to continuous wretching [*sic*] and death" (cited in Earleywine 2002, 11). In 1484, Pope Innocent VIII condemned the use of cannabis as "a tool of the Satanic Mass" (Gahlinger 2001), and when Napoleon invaded Egypt in the early nineteenth century, he prohibited his troops from engaging in the use of hashish. However, by the early 1830s hashish and other cannabis products were being widely used in France and other parts of Continental Europe for both medical and recreational purposes.

The Pilgrims brought cannabis with them to New England in 1632, and in 1639, to meet the need for hemp in England, colonists in Virginia were required by law to cultivate and harvest a certain number of cannabis plants each year (Gahlinger 2001); those who did not comply with the law could be subject to imprisonment (Ventura 2016). Hemp farming and processing of the plant played a significant role in American history—it is well known that President George Washington grew hemp for seed and fiber, as did Thomas Jefferson (Lee 2012). There is also some evidence to suggest that Washington consumed hemp preparations for medicinal purposes (primarily to deal with toothaches) (Belville 2014).[2] The production of cannabis as a source of fiber and cloth gradually increased in the colonies, so that by the time America declared its independence in 1776, approximately 90 percent of all clothing in the United States was made from cannabis (Gahlinger 2001), and by the mid-1880s, hemp was the third-largest crop in the United States (Lee 2012). In fact, the 1850 U.S. census counted 8,327 hemp plantations in the country, the majority of which were located in Kentucky (Ventura 2016).

Cannabis became a commonly used painkiller (along with laudanum) in the 1840s, and Queen Victoria's physician, Dr. J. R. Reynolds, prescribed it to her for menstrual cramps. Discussions of cannabis began to appear in the scientific and medical literature in the 1800s, and by the end of the century, more than one hundred articles on the substance had been published, with many of the commentators offering important insights regarding its benefits and effects. In 1890, Dr. Reynolds published a paper in the British medical journal the *Lancet* on the therapeutic uses of cannabis, noting that he had been prescribing the drug for thirty years and considered it "one of the most valuable medicines we possess" (quoted in Commonwealth of Australia 1977, 128).

---

2. Other early U.S. presidents who are believed to have consumed cannabis for medicinal and/or recreational purposes include James Madison, James Monroe, Andrew Jackson, Zachary Taylor, and Franklin Pierce (Belville 2014).

With respect to the psychoactive and behavioral effects of cannabis, several of the early publications emphasized the distorted sense of time and distance that users experience (an effect that is still emphasized today). For instance, *Harper's New Monthly Magazine* noted in 1858, "The chief peculiarity of the hasheesh vision is its immense exaggeration of time and space. Moments appear to be thousands of years." James Johnston (1855) similarly commented, "The errors of perception, in regard to time and place [while under the influence of cannabis] . . . are remarkable. Minutes seem hours, and hours are prolonged into years, till at last the idea of time seems obliterated, and the past and present are confounded together." And, prefacing Howard Becker's (1963) contention that individuals must "learn" to experience the pleasurable psychoactive effects of marijuana, Johnston commented, "It requires, indeed, a long and gradual training to its use before its boasted effects can be fully experienced."

Perhaps best known for his writing on cannabis during the 1800s is Dr. William O'Shaughnessy, who graduated from the University of Edinburgh in 1829 and then moved to Calcutta to work as a physician for the British East India Company (the journal *O'Shaughnessy's Journal of Cannabis in Clinical Practice*, founded by Tod Mikuriya and Fred Gardner in 2003, is named after him). His interest piqued by the widespread use of cannabis for therapeutic, religious, and recreational purposes in India (Lee 2012), O'Shaughnessy performed his initial tests of the drug on mice, dogs, rabbits, and cats and then gave tinctures of cannabis-infused substances he had created himself to some of his patients (Aldrich 2006; Casarett 2015). In a widely referenced paper first published in 1839, O'Shaughnessy presented case studies on the effectiveness of cannabis in treating patients suffering from rheumatism, hydrophobia, cholera, and tetanus (Aldrich 2006). Interestingly, and prefacing one of the currently more well-established benefits of cannabis, O'Shaughnessy discussed the case of an infant experiencing (likely epileptic) convulsions, who responded positively to cannabis therapy, going from near death to "the enjoyment of robust health" within a few days (1843, 368).

In addition to his focus on the medical utility of cannabis, O'Shaughnessy (1843) devoted attention to the behavioral and psychological effects of the substance. He notes that "hemp is used in various forms, by the dissipated and the depraved, as the ready agent of pleasing intoxication. In the popular medicine [of these nations] we find it extensively employed for a multitude of afflictions" (343). Referring to the consumption of cannabis-infused beverages (*bang* or *sidhee*) in India during this period, he noted that intoxication occurred within one hour of ingestion and that "the inebriation is of the most cheerful kind, causing the person to sing and dance, to eat food with great relish, and to see aphrodisiac enjoyments" (344). Similar to some of the commentators quoted previously, O'Shaughnessy also recognized the variable effects of cannabis on users: "In persons of a quarrelsome disposition it occasions, as might be expected, an exaggeration of their natural tendency," and "the kind of mental excitement it produces depends on the temperament of the consumer" (344, 347). Importantly, O'Shaughnessy also compared the effects of cannabis to the effects of other psychoactive substances: "As to the evil sequelae so unanimously dwelt on by all writers, these did not appear to me to be so numerous, so immediate, or so formidable, as which may be clearly traced to over-indulgence in other powerful stimulants or narcotics—viz. alcohol, opium, or tobacco" (363).

The Indian Hemp Drugs Commission

> That this report, which remains today by far the most complete collection of information on marijuana in existence, should have been so completely forgotten in an era when controversy over the effects of the drug and, the wisdom of its criminalization, has increased to such fervor is almost inexplicable.
> —WILLIAM MACKWORTH YOUNG AND JOHN KAPLAN, *Marijuana*

The Indian Hemp Drugs Commission was appointed by the British government in 1892 in response to a question raised in the House of Commons by temperance crusaders who expressed concerns regarding the consumption of hemp in India, asserting that the "lunatic asylums of India are filled with ganja smokers" (quoted in Bewley-Taylor, Blickman, and Jelsma 2014, 10–11). Over the course of its investigations, the commission ultimately heard testimony from almost two thousand witnesses (including more than three hundred medical practitioners) and conducted eighty meetings in more than thirty cities. The commission also examined the records of every admission (a total of 222) to mental hospitals in India in which there was an alleged connection between the consumption of hemp drugs and insanity, as well as eighty-one violent crimes committed in the country that were purported to be caused by cannabis. In its report, the commission concluded, "On the whole, the weight of the evidence is to the effect that moderation in the use of hemp drugs is not injurious. . . . The temptation to excess is not so great as with alcohol" (1894, 1:186). With regard to the mental/psychological effects of the drug, the commission noted that "the moderate use of hemp drugs produces no injurious effects on the mind. . . . [It does not] produce moral injury," and "there is little connection between the use of hemp drugs and crime" (1:264).

The Indian Hemp Drugs Commission also made recommendations with respect to policies to regulate the substance, which, it emphasized, should be directed at suppressing excessive use and restraining moderate use (1894, 1:287). These policies included taxation of hemp products, a licensing system for cultivation, limitations on the number of locations where it could be sold, and restrictions on the amount of hemp drugs that could be possessed by individuals. All of these suggestions have been incorporated to some extent in the legalization models adopted in several U.S. states, as well as in Uruguay and Canada.

Interestingly (and presciently) the commission also indirectly emphasized that hemp may serve as a "substitute" drug: "Total prohibition of the cultivation of the hemp plant for narcotics, and of the manufacture or the sale, or use of drugs derived from it, is neither necessary nor expedient in consideration of their ascertained effects, of the prevalence of the habit of using them, of the social and religious feeling on the subject, and on the possibility of its *driving the consumers to have recourse to other stimulants or narcotics which may be more deleterious* (quoted in Bewley-Taylor, Blickman, and Jelsma 2014, 9; emphasis added).

Although the findings of the Indian Hemp Drugs Commission were referenced in several countries' government-commissioned reports on marijuana published in the 1960s and 1970s, Bewley-Taylor, Blickman, and Jelsma observe, "Its absence from international discussions is pertinent today since almost nothing of significance in the conclusions of the landmark report on the cannabis problem in India has been proven wrong in over a century since its publication" (2014, 11).

Consistent with the conclusions of the commission, during the same period, an article published in the *Journal of Mental Science* argued, "It would seem that the moderate use of hemp drugs may be beneficial under certain conditions; at any rate such moderate use cannot be harmful. . . . There is not, in my opinion, any specific property in hemp drugs which incites to violence or crime" (J. Walsh 1894, 23). An accompanying editorial in the same journal concluded that "apparently, it [hemp] is much less liable than alcohol to induce men to commit violent actions" (*Journal of Mental Science* 1894, 107).

Marijuana in the United States: Late 1800s and Early 1900s

During the mid- to late 1800s and early 1900s, before the passage of local and state ordinances banning the drug, cannabis was fully legal in the United States, with pharmaceutical companies such as Lilly and Squibb manufacturing various cannabis-infused tinctures and hashish candies (similar to edible cannabis products available today) (Weiss 2015). In fact, Mark Twain, who was friends with Fitz Hugh Ludlow, author of the 1857 book *The Hasheesh Eater*, reported that his drug of choice was hashish candy (Murrieta 2015). And although data on the extent of recreational use of marijuana during this period are not available, in San Francisco, a newspaper article published in 1865 noted, "It appears that a 'hasheesh' mania has broken out among our Bohemians" (quoted in Komp 2011).

The 1906 Food and Drug Act was the first federal legislation in the United States to mention cannabis (Lee 2012). Prompted by concerns surrounding the dangers associated with patent medicines (Musto 1999), this law prohibited interstate and foreign commerce in adulterated and misbranded food and drug products and required manufacturers to list the ingredients, including the quantity of alcohol and other drugs (including cannabis) contained in their products (Janssen 1981). However, the Food and Drug Act did not attempt to regulate the purchase of drugs or the quantity of a drug that could be contained in a particular product (Lester, Andreozzi, and Appiah 2004).

The first comprehensive U.S. federal drug legislation—the Harrison Narcotics Act of 1914—did not include cannabis on its list of prohibited substances. However, some legislators argued for its inclusion because of alleged uses of the drug in certain sectors of the population. Echoing the racist theme that has characterized American drug legislation for the past one hundred years, Harry Finger, a member of the California Board of Pharmacy and friend of Hamilton Wright (primary author of the act), wrote to Wright in 1911, "Within the last year we in California have been getting a large influx of Hindoos and they in turn started quite a demand for cannabis indica, they are a very undesirable lot" (quoted in D'Angelo 2015, 22). Wright pushed to have cannabis included in both international drug agreements and in U.S. legislation, asserting that if dangerous drugs such as heroin and cocaine were prohibited, drug addicts would shift to another substance such as marijuana (Bewley-Taylor, Blickman, and Jelsma 2014). Congress ultimately decided not to include cannabis in the Harrison Narcotics Act, partially because of opposition from the pharmaceutical industry (Bewley-Taylor, Blickman, and Jelsma 2014) and also because of witnesses who testified that "as a habit-forming drug its [cannabis's] use is almost nil" (quoted in Fox, Armentano, and Tvert 2009, 41).

As marijuana use in the United States gradually spread in the 1910s and 1920s when Caribbean sailors introduced it in port towns such as New Orleans, and as Mexican immigrants brought the substance into labor towns in the American West, a number of states banned the drug—California in 1915, Texas in 1919, and Louisiana in 1924 (Barcott 2015). In justifying antimarijuana legislation in his state, and once again underscoring the racist underpinnings of drug legislation, a Texas senator stated, "All Mexicans are crazy, and this stuff [marijuana] is what makes them crazy" (quoted in D'Angelo 2015, 23). Between 1914 and 1937, at least thirty states passed antimarijuana laws.

The Panama Studies

While the findings of the La Guardia Committee report on marijuana are fairly well known, a less well-known but important study on marijuana and its effects was commissioned in 1931 to investigate the effects of smoking marijuana on military personnel in the Panama Canal region. Marijuana was being grown by farmers in the region and the surplus sold to soldiers, so marijuana smoking had apparently become "prevalent" among soldiers in the early 1920s, with "cases of delinquency" being attributed to its consumption (*Military Surgeon* 1933). After marijuana use was prohibited in the region in 1923, a committee appointed by the Panama governor to investigate use of the drug concluded in 1925 that "there is no evidence that mariahuana [*sic*] as grown here is a 'habit-forming drug' in the sense in which that term is applied to alcohol, opium, cocaine, etc., or that it has any appreciably deleterious influence on the individuals using it" (*Military Surgeon* 1933).

However, as reported in the *Military Surgeon* in 1933, many officers in the Panama Canal region continued to believe that marijuana was addictive and that its use "undermine[d] the morale of a military organization," so in 1931, a second committee was formed to investigate the problem. In an interesting "research design," the committee's method was to hospitalize thirty-four soldiers who were known to be marijuana users, allow them to use the substance, observe them for six days, then withdraw the marijuana, and have them evaluated by a psychiatrist. Presaging the popular notion that people consuming marijuana get the "munchies," the committee's report noted that "all [the marijuana-using soldiers] stated they were hungry after smoking and the quantity of food consumed at subsequent meals confirmed this." Similarly to the 1925 Panama Canal report, the 1933 report concluded that marijuana was not a habit-forming drug similar to opium and cocaine and that "the evidence suggests that organization commanders in estimating the efficiency and soldierly qualities of delinquents in their command have unduly emphasized the effects of mariahuana [*sic*], disregarding the fact that a large proportion of the delinquents are morons or psychopaths, which conditions themselves would serve to account for delinquency." While the conclusions of these two Panama Canal studies that marijuana was not a dangerous drug should not be overstated, given the limited scope of the investigations, it is notable that they are consistent with the findings of several other reports on marijuana discussed in this chapter.

Harry Anslinger, the Federal Bureau of Narcotics, and the Emergence of Reefer Madness

Harry Anslinger was appointed commissioner of the Federal Bureau of Narcotics (FBN) in 1930 and served in the position until 1962—some consider him to be the nation's first drug czar. Anslinger had previously been employed as a railroad detective, entered the U.S. diplomatic service, and in 1926 was appointed U.S. consul in Nassau in the British Bahamas, which at the time was a key location from which alcohol was smuggled into the United States during the Prohibition era (Mosher 2011a). He served as the chief U.S. delegate to international drug conventions from 1930 to 1970 and played a key role in drafting various international drug control agreements over this period, including the 1961 Single Convention on Narcotic Drugs, which further strengthened controls on the production and consumption of illegal drugs and established the International Narcotics Board (Mosher 2011a).

Anslinger is perhaps best known for his pivotal role in creating a moral panic over marijuana in the 1930s, which eventually led to the passage of the Marihuana Tax Act. In 1932, Anslinger apparently did not view marijuana as a serious problem in the United States and even suggested that the media were overplaying the extent of use of the drug:

> A great deal of public interest has been aroused by newspaper articles appearing from time to time on the evils of the abuse of marihuana. . . . The publicity tends to magnify the extent of the evil and lends color to an influence that there is an alarming spread of the improper use of the drug, whereas actual use may not have been inordinately large. (Quoted in Abel 1980, 241)

Despite these comments, Anslinger would express a markedly different attitude toward cannabis only a few years later. In the midst of the Depression, Congress began to examine the budgetary requirements of federal agencies, and the Bureau of Narcotics budget was reduced by $200,000 (Abel 1980). One obvious solution to this bureaucratic crisis was to create a new drug scare to justify the bureau's existence, and marijuana was suddenly transformed into the new "assassin of youth" (*Scientific American* 1936, 150). Anslinger and the FBN began to provide community-service groups and the popular media with information concerning the alleged atrocities and serious crimes committed by people under the influence of marijuana.

A key tactic of Anslinger's anti-marijuana campaign was to associate use of the drug with the two most despised and feared minority groups in the United States—Mexican immigrants and African Americans—who, he argued, were more likely to use marijuana than white people. Although racist views were certainly held by a large proportion of the U.S. population during this period, Anslinger arguably took this to a new level, while stoking additional fears through reference to miscegeny in his claim that "most marihuana smokers are Negroes, Hispanics, jazz musicians, and entertainers. Their satanic music is driven by marihuana, and marihuana smoking by white women makes them want to seek sexual relations with Negroes, entertainers, and others. It is a drug that causes insanity, criminality, and death—the most violence-causing drug in the history of mankind" (quoted in Bewley-Taylor, Blickman, and Jelsma 2014, 17–18). Anslinger also asserted that marijuana use by blacks made them forget the appropriate racial barriers and "unleashed their lust for white women" (quoted in Hari 2015, 17). Other articles appearing in newspapers and magazines during the 1930s emphasized that Mexicans were perhaps the most prominent users and traffickers of the drug. One commentator from Sacramento, California, noted, "Marihuana, perhaps now the most insidious of narcotics, is a direct by-product of Mexican immigration. . . . Mexican peddlers have been caught distributing sample marihuana cigarettes to schoolchildren" (cited in Musto 1999, 220).

Andrew Mellon and William Randolph Hearst were also key figures in the 1930s anti-marijuana campaign. Anslinger married Martha Denniston, who was the niece of Andrew Mellon, owner of the Mellon Bank of Pittsburgh, and who was President Hoover's secretary of the Treasury (the federal agency that oversaw the FBN). Mellon appointed Anslinger to run the FBN and was also the chief financial backer of DuPont, a company that had significant interests in the forest industry, and given its potential use as paper, hemp was obviously a threat to DuPont and Mellon's operations (Ventura 2016).

William Randolph Hearst was head of the Hearst newspaper chain, which owned some of the most popular newspapers in the United States, including the *San Francisco Examiner* and the *New York Journal*. Hearst also had significant financial interests in the paper industry and became an ally of Anslinger, publishing numerous articles in his newspapers from Anslinger's "gore file" (a collection of hideous crimes committed by individuals allegedly under the influence of marijuana, which were collected by FBN field agents). In numerous articles appearing in Hearst-owned newspapers, marijuana use was associated with "foreigners, who smoked (and distributed) marihuana," which exacerbated "anti-Mexican sentiment during the Great Depression, when many Anglos felt they were competing with brown-skinned migrants for scarce jobs" (Lee 2012, 51).

In addition to the claim that cannabis was a drug used primarily by members of minority groups, several additional themes in articles on the drug appearing in popular magazines and other sources (Anslinger supplied information to many of them) in the 1930s contributed to the demonization of the substance (Mosher 1999). These themes included that the marijuana habit was spreading to young people; that its use led to a variety of adverse psychological effects; and, most prominently, that its use resulted in the commission of acts of crime, sexual immorality, and violence. For example, an article issued by the International Narcotics Association in 1936 noted that "while the marihuana habit leads to physical wreckage and mental decay, its effects upon character and morality are even more devastating. The victim frequently undergoes such degeneracy that he will lie and steal without scruple. . . . Marihuana sometimes gives man the lust to kill unreasonably and without motive" (quoted in Mayor's Committee on Marihuana

1944). Similarly, an article appearing in the popular magazine *Survey Graphic* referred to "Victor Lacata [who] while under the influence of marijuana, murdered his mother, father, sister, and two brothers with an axe" (1938, 221). Yet another article reported, "The role of marijuana as a crime instigator is suggested by the report of the public prosecutor in New Orleans who in 1930 found that of 450 prisoners he dealt with, 125 were marijuana addicts. Slightly less than half the murderers, about 20% of the larceny men, and about 18% of the robbery prisoners smoked what they called 'Merry Wonder'" (*American Mercury* 1935, 487).

With respect to sexual immorality among marijuana users, the *Survey Graphic* article referred to "Lewis Harris, 26, arrested for the rape of a nine-year old girl while under the influence of marihuana" (1938, 221). Some articles cited bizarre incidents committed by users in order to emphasize that marijuana could potentially lower sexual inhibitions, as in the following description in *American Mercury*: "A Negro was brought to a New York hospital because he had run after and threatened two women while under the influence of reefers, he said he had seen in his reefer dream 'a bunch of naked wimmin [*sic*] some of 'em in bed, black an' white together, like dey was expectin men'" (1935, 489).

In addition to supplying "information" on marijuana to popular magazines and newspapers regarding the evils of marijuana, the FBN played a key role in the 1936 film *Tell Your Children* (better known today as *Reefer Madness*), which depicted the drug as a demon weed whose consumption altered the personalities of young people, driving them to insanity, suicide, and murder sprees (Mosher 2011a).

With these decidedly negative images of marijuana as the backdrop, the Marihuana Tax Act was introduced in Congress in 1937. In his testimony before Congress justifying the need for the legislation, Anslinger repeated many of the alarmist statements regarding the drug, including, "I believe in some cases one [marijuana] cigarette might develop a homicidal mania, probably to kill his brother" (quoted in Galliher and Walker 1977, 371).

In hearings regarding the Marihuana Tax Act, Dr. William Woodward, legislative counsel of the American Medical Association (AMA), questioned the need for the legislation: "No one has been produced from the Bureau of Prisons to show the number of prisoners who have been found addicted to the marihuana habit. . . . No one has been summoned from the Children's Bureau to show the nature and extent of the habit among children" (quoted in Fox, Armentano, and Tvert 2009, 53). Later, Woodward wrote to the Senate Finance Committee, lamenting the fact that the provisions of the Marihuana Tax Act effectively prohibited the use of cannabis for medicinal purposes: "Since the medicinal use of cannabis has not caused and is not going to cause addiction, the prevention of the use of the drug for medicinal purposes can accomplish no good end whatsoever. How far it may serve to deprive the public of the benefits of a drug that on further research may prove to be of substantial value, it is impossible to foresee" (quoted in Eddy 2010, 2).

The Marihuana Tax Act was modeled on the National Firearms Control Act, which used taxation to control the spread of machine guns across the United States (Ferraialo 2007; Dills, Goffard, and Miron, 2016). Steve D'Angelo refers to the act as "one of the most stunning abdications of legislative responsibility ever seen in the United States" (2015, 32). Under the legislation, a tax of $100 per ounce tax was levied on the transfer of marijuana to members of the general public; an annual tax of $50 per ounce was imposed on manufacturers, compounders, and importers of the substance, as well as $15 for dealers, $25 for producers, and $1 for researchers and medical professionals (Martin and Rashidian 2014).

Martin Lee notes that, during the last three months of 1937 after passage of the act, the FBN seized approximately five hundred pounds of bulk marijuana and 2,852 marijuana cigarettes, "a rather paltry law enforcement harvest given all the hoopla about deadly weed" (2012, 55). And on October 2, 1937, the day after the act became law, a fifty-eight-year-old Colorado resident, Samuel Caldwell, was the first person to be charged for a marijuana offense. Caldwell was allegedly found to be selling marijuana to another man and was sentenced to four years of hard labor at the federal penitentiary in Leavenworth, Kansas, and a $1,000 fine (Lee 2012).

Emerging Debates over the Evils of Marijuana

Beginning in the late 1930s and into the early 1940s, the claims of Anslinger and others regarding the evils of cannabis faced challenges, especially as more scientific research regarding the drug was conducted. Walter Bromberg, a psychiatrist at New York City's mental health facility, studied 2,216 criminals who had been convicted of felonies in New York and did not find a single case of marijuana addiction. In a 1939 article published in the *Journal of the American Medical Association* (*JAMA*), Bromberg concluded that alcohol consumption was more strongly related to the commission of crime than was marijuana and that marijuana did not have the addictive qualities of opium and other drugs.

Not long after the publication of Bromberg's article, New York City mayor Fiorello La Guardia (who was opposed to the Marihuana Tax Act) became concerned about rumors suggesting widespread use of marijuana in New York City, particularly about allegations that marijuana dealers were peddling the drug in schools (Mayor's Committee on Marihuana 1944). Instead of ordering a law enforcement crackdown to address the alleged problems (Barcott 2015), La Guardia created a committee to make a "thorough sociological and scientific investigation" into the issue (Mayor's Committee on Marihuana 1944).

The La Guardia Committee's research was funded by the Commonwealth Fund, the Friedsman Foundation, and the New York Foundation,
each of which donated $7,500 to the project, and the report included a review
of the existing scientific literature on marijuana, a sociological study dealing
with the extent of marijuana smoking and the methods individuals used to
obtain it, and a clinical study to examine the physiological and psychological
effects of the substance on users (Mayor's Committee on Marihuana 1944).

The insights regarding marijuana presented in the report were in stark
contrast to the anti-marijuana propaganda offered by Anslinger and others
in the 1930s and are consistent with the findings of the Indian Hemp Drugs
Commission, as well as more recent studies on the drug. Commenting on
the possibility of addiction to marijuana, the report notes, "A person may be
a confirmed [marijuana] smoker for a prolonged period, and give up the
drug voluntarily without experiencing any craving for it or exhibiting withdrawal symptoms. . . . Others remain infrequent users of the cigarette" (May-
or's Committee on Marihuana 1944). The report emphasized the significance
of these observations, because they were "contrary to the experience of other
narcotics. This may be considered presumptive evidence that there is not
true addiction in the medical sense associated with marihuana." The report
also rejected the "gateway drug" hypothesis (the claim that marijuana use
inevitably leads to the use of other, harder drugs): "We have been unable to
confirm the opinion expressed by some investigators that smoking [mari-
juana] is the first step in the use of other drugs such as cocaine, morphine,
or heroin."

With respect to the role of marijuana in the instigation of crime, federal,
state, and local police officers interviewed by La Guardia Committee researchers "unhesitatingly stated that there is no proof that major crimes are
associated with the practice of smoking marihuana" (Mayor's Committee on
Marihuana 1944). Regarding the alleged use of marijuana in New York City
schools, after surveillance of schools, interviews with school officials, and
analysis of records from children's courts, it was concluded that "although
marihuana smoking may be indulged in by small numbers of students in
certain schools in New York City, it is apparently not a widespread or large-
scale practice" and that "marihuana is not an important factor in the development of delinquency."

The clinical component of the La Guardia report involved a study of
seventy-two subjects who were administered a variety of psychological tests
and whose behaviors were observed after consuming marijuana. Recognizing the variable effects of marijuana, the report commented, "The same dose
of marihuana does not produce identical effects in different subjects or in
one subject at different times" (Mayor's Committee on Marihuana 1944). An
additional focus of the clinical studies was the relationship between marijuana consumption and "eroticism"—the report noted that "some evidence

of eroticism was reported in about 10% of the instances in which marihuana was administered to the group" and related, somewhat amusingly, that "in some instances there was evidence of a marked lowering of inhibitions such as a loud discharge of flatus, urinating on the floor instead of in the vessels supplied, and in one instance frank exhibitionism" (although this involved a subject who had been arrested three times previously for indecent exposure).

One of the more interesting components of the La Guardia Committee's research involved an "experimental design" in which subjects who smoked between one and eight marijuana cigarettes in an hour listened to the Jack Benny "Jell-O" program, with the number and duration of their "laughs" being compared to those of the general radio audience. This study concluded that "it was obvious that under marihuana the subject laughs more readily and for longer time intervals. This is probably due both to the fact that things seem funnier to him and because when under the influence of the drug he is less inhibited." The committee also addressed the possible medicinal benefits of marijuana: "The lessening of inhibitions and repressions, the euphoric state, the feeling of adequacy, the freer expression of thoughts and ideas, the increase in appetite for food, brought about by marihuana suggests therapeutic possibilities" (Mayor's Committee on Marihuana 1944).

Although the La Guardia Committee studied and debunked almost every claim Anslinger had made about marijuana, it received little attention in the popular media (for example, Lee [2012] reports that even the *New York Times* buried a summary of the report on its last page). However, it did spark considerable debate within professional journals. For example, in a study published in the *American Journal of Psychiatry*, based on research conducted under the auspices of the La Guardia Committee, Samuel Allentuck and Karl Bowman studied seventy-seven subjects and concluded that "while exerting no permanent deleterious effects, marijuana gives rise to pleasurable sensations, calmness, and relaxation and increases the appetite" (1942, 249). The authors went on to suggest that marijuana use itself did not result in antisocial behavior and stressed that the drug was not a gateway to opiate addiction. The initial responses to the Allentuck and Bowman article were largely positive; a *JAMA* editorial praised the study and suggested, "A more exhaustive study of the possibility of these drugs as a means of relieving withdrawal symptoms in narcotic addicts would seem to be justified" (1942, 1129).

Not surprisingly, Anslinger was less than pleased with the Allentuck and Bowman study and with the more general conclusions of the La Guardia Committee. In a letter to the editor of *JAMA*, Anslinger voiced his concern over the Allentuck and Bowman study, without addressing the evidence that had been presented by the researchers:

From that point of view we feel that it is very unfortunate that Drs. Allentuck and Bowman should have stated so unqualifiedly that use

of marihuana does not lead to physical, mental, or moral deteriora-
tion. More undiscriminating readers are perhaps likely to interpret
the statement as the final word of the medical profession. Also there
may well be some unsavory persons engaged in the illicit marihuana
trade who will make use of the statement in pushing their dangerous
traffic. (1943, 212–213)

It is of course certainly questionable whether "undiscriminating readers"
would have access to, or interest in, *JAMA* in the first place and even more
doubtful that marijuana traffickers would. But further opposition to the Allentuck and Bowman study was presented by J. Bouquet, an "expert on the
Narcotics Commission of the League of Nations," who, among other things,
was extremely critical of the methodology of the study. Bouquet noted that
the subjects in the Allentuck and Bowman study were prisoners and, if they
had been allowed to, would have consumed considerably more marijuana,
with greater negative effects. The users would become "wretched ragamuffins
who are a danger and a burden to society" (Bouquet 1944, 1010–1011). Karl
Bowman responded to Bouquet's critique in a letter to the editor of *JAMA*:

Medical and popular literature is filled with old wives tails about the
effects of various narcotic drugs. It is somewhat surprising to find
objection to the publication of carefully worked out studies on the
ground that it is improper and dangerous rather than to raise the
issue of science—was the study carried out in a proper scientific
manner? (1944, 376)

A further response to the La Guardia Committee report and the Allentuck and Bowman study, which marijuana researcher Jerome Himmelstein
(1983) suggests was written by Anslinger himself, appeared in *JAMA* (no
author was identified in the piece). It noted that "for many years, medical
scientists have considered cannabis a dangerous drug" and criticized the
"narrow and thoroughly unscientific foundation" of the La Guardia report,
which led to "sweeping and inadequate conclusions which minimize the
harmfulness of marihuana" (1945, 1129). In addition, the article included a
claim that "already the book [La Guardia Committee report] has done harm.
One investigator described some tearful parents who brought their 16-year
old son to a physician after he had been detected in the act of smoking marihuana. The boy said he had read an account of the LaGuardia Committee
report and that was his justification for using marihuana" (1129).

Whether or not this 1945 *JAMA* article was authored by Anslinger, several commentators on marijuana legislation and debates in this period have
suggested that the AMA was pressured by Anslinger to adopt a critical stance
on the La Guardia Committee report and to further contribute to marijuana

demonization (Barcott 2015; Lee 2012). After the passage of the Marihuana Tax Act, in a strategy similar to what would be adopted some sixty years later by President Clinton's drug czar General Barry McCaffrey in response to the legalization of medical marijuana in California in 1996, Anslinger began prosecuting physicians for what he deemed to be "illegal purposes." By 1939, more than three thousand members of the AMA had been subject to such prosecutions (Ventura 2016). Anslinger indicated to the AMA that he would cease these prosecutions if the organization would denounce the La Guardia Committee report. Although as late as 1942 the AMA continued to accept the possibility that cannabis may have medical uses, in the years immediately following the release of the La Guardia Committee report, "the AMA did an extraordinary about face and joined Anslinger's crusade against marijuana. . . . Since then, the AMA steadfastly maintained a position on cannabis that hewed closely to the drug war orthodoxy" (Lee 2012, 62).

Continuing his attack on the report, in a 1945 piece appearing in *JAMA*, Anslinger referred to an article written by an Indian physician (R. N. Chopra) that had been published in the *Indian Medical Research Memoirs* in 1939. This "intensive study of 1,800 hemp drug addicts" found that in "quite a number of cases simple indulgence in a single ganja or charas (marijuana smoke) was responsible for a heinous crime," and, according to Anslinger, the Chopra study "destroys most of the conclusions of the New York Mayor's Committee" (1945, 1187).

Despite the criticisms of the La Guardia Committee report by Anslinger, the AMA, and others, the report did contribute to the erosion of the apparent prevailing consensus in the United States during this period that cannabis was a dangerous substance whose consumption automatically led to a host of negative outcomes, in particular, involvement in crime and violence. This change is perhaps best reflected in an article that appeared in *Time* magazine, which argued:

> Despite its lurid reputation, marihuana seems no more harmful than alcohol. Although habitual criminals often use it, psychiatrists and police experts have never been able to prove that it induces criminal tendencies in otherwise law-abiding people. It is less habit-forming than tobacco, alcohol, or opium. The most confirmed vipers have no particular craving for the drug. They just enjoy its effects. Like alcohol, it can raise hell with ordinary living, release bad as well as good personality traits. But in spite of the legend, no case of physical, mental, or moral degeneracy has ever been traced exclusively to marijuana. (*Time* 1945, 54)

With increasing skepticism regarding marijuana's dangers, it became necessary for those who wanted to demonize the drug and maintain its prohibition to posit new effects. One of the most prominent and enduring themes emphasized during this period was the notion that marijuana was a stepping-stone or gateway drug whose consumption led to the use of other drugs. Thus, a *New Yorker* article noted that "most dope addicts begin on marihuana, which though rarely habit-forming, is very apt to lure users of it on to the deadlier drugs" (1951, 18). Similarly, an article in *Newsweek* declared, "Marihuana may not be more habit-forming than alcohol, but it makes the switch to heroin easy" (1954, 17).

Interestingly, despite his larger campaign against marijuana, Anslinger initially rejected the idea that marijuana was a gateway drug. In hearings on the substance in the 1930s, Anslinger was asked whether "the marihuana addict graduates into a heroin, opium, or cocaine user." Anslinger responded, "No, sir, I have not heard of a case of that kind. The marihuana addict does not go in that direction" (quoted in Brecher 1972, 416). But in 1951, Anslinger changed his views on the subject when testifying before a congressional committee, asserting, without any scientific evidence to support the claim, that "over 50% of heroin users started on marihuana smoking . . . and they graduated to heroin, they took the needle when the thrill of marihuana was gone" (quoted in Sullum 2015).

In addition to promoting the notion that marijuana was a gateway drug, in 1948, Anslinger claimed that cannabis was part of a communist plot to weaken America's strength: "Marihuana leads to pacifism and communist brainwashing" (quoted in Lee 2012, 62). And in another strategy that is strikingly similar to tactics used today, Anslinger announced that anyone who conducted research on marijuana without the approval of the FBN would be arrested and tried on federal drug charges (Barcott 2015).

As drug use, particularly among young people, allegedly increased in the 1940s, Anslinger also engaged in an attack on judges, claiming the nation's drug problems were at least partially related to the fact that judges were imposing sentences on drug offenders that were too lenient (Mosher 2011a).

The 1950s

In the 1950s, the next wave of (increasingly harsh) drug laws emerged in the United States, when President Dwight Eisenhower in 1954 called for a "new war on narcotics addiction at the local, national, and international level" (quoted in Lee 2012, 64). The federal government also used its status as a superpower and its influence in the United Nations to push for stricter controls of cannabis and other drugs at the international level (Bewley-Taylor, Blickman, and Jelsma 2014). Although the primary concerns surrounding drugs during this period were related to heroin, marijuana was lumped in with other "narcotic" drugs in crafting new drug legislation. This occurred even though some who testified, such as Dr. Harris Isabell, the director of research at the federal government's Lexington Narcotics Farm, told members of the committee deliberating on the legislation that morphine and heroin were significant problems in the United States, but marijuana was not (Barcott 2015). Federal Bureau of Investigation director J. Edgar Hoover (apparently a close friend of Anslinger's) weighed in on the topic of marijuana, stating that users of the drug become "fiends with savage 'cave man' tendencies. [Their] desires are aroused, and some of the most horrible crimes result" (quoted in Lee 2012, 73).

At least partially because of Anslinger's concerns that judicial discretion in sentencing was contributing to drug problems, the 1951 Boggs Act and the 1956 Narcotic Control Act established mandatory minimum sentences for drug-related offenses, with a first-time offense for marijuana or other drug possession resulting in a minimum sentence of two years' and a maximum of ten years' imprisonment and a fine of up to $20,000 (Dills, Goffard, and Miron 2016). A second offense for possession or a first-time offense for trafficking in marijuana or other drugs resulted in five years in prison with no option for parole; a third-time possession or second trafficking offense resulted in ten to forty years in prison with no option for parole (Martin and Rashidian 2014). In some states, penalties for drug law violations were even more severe—for example, in Georgia, offenders could be subject to the death penalty for selling drugs (including cannabis) to minors (Lee 2012). Under Alabama's mandatory sentencing drug laws, judges were required to sentence those found guilty of marijuana possession to a five-year minimum sentence; for a second offense, convictions for possession resulted in a minimum sentence of ten years and a maximum of forty years, and suspended sentences and probation for such offenders were prohibited.

These harsh drug laws, which also applied to marijuana offenses, were enacted during a period in which much of the scientific literature on marijuana stressed that the drug was relatively benign.[3] For instance, in the

---

3. An additional issue reemerged in the 1950s that was also influenced by Anslinger's stringent anti-marijuana views: the substance's medical uses. In 1952, the World Health Organization's (WHO) Expert Committee on Drugs Liable to Produce Addiction concluded that "so far as we can see, there is no justification for the medical use of cannabis preparations" (quoted in Bewley-Taylor, Blickman, and Jelsma 2014, 22). Bewley-Taylor, Blickman, and Jelsma note that the WHO decision was largely orchestrated by Pablo Osvaldo Wolff, who directed the Addiction Producing Drugs Section of the organization and whose 1949 booklet, *Marijuana in Latin America: The Threat It Constitutes*, included a preface written by Anslinger. In this publication, Wolff engaged in a scathing critique of the La Guardia Committee report, commenting that marijuana "changes thousands of persons into nothing more than human scum" and that the substance was "an exterminating demon that is now attacking our country" (quoted in Bewley-Taylor, Blickman, and Jelsma 2014, 24). Similar to other marijuana prohibitionists, both before and after him, Wolff also distorted and misstated the findings of other studies on the drug. For instance, he claimed that "an American commission which studied marijuana addiction in the

Pharmacological Basis of Therapeutics, commonly referred to as the "Blue Bible" and the most authoritative book in pharmacology, Alfred Gilman and Louis Goodman noted that "there are no lasting ill effects from the acute use of marijuana," that no deaths had been associated with its consumption, and that there were no "pathological conditions or disorders of cerebral function attributable to the drug" (1956, 170, 172). They further commented that psychological dependence on marijuana "is not as prominent or compelling as in the case of morphine, alcohol, or perhaps even tobacco habituation" (1956, 176).

Although arrest data do not provide a completely valid measure of the extent of use of marijuana, in 1958, two years after the passage of the Narcotic Control Act, there were only 2,287 reported state and local arrests for marijuana across the entire United States (Martin and Rashidian 2014), suggesting that use of the substance was not widespread. However, cannabis use began to spread to middle-class youth in the 1960s, and by 1967, there were 55,468 state and local arrests for marijuana offenses, one-third of which involved offenders who were under twenty-one years of age (Martin and Rashidian 2014). Perhaps as a consequence, signs that the federal government might change its position on marijuana and soften the stringent drug legislation began to emerge.

The 1960s and 1970s: Signs of Rationality on Marijuana

In 1962, the President's Advisory Commission on Narcotic and Drug Abuse, appointed by President John F. Kennedy (who is believed to have consumed marijuana to deal with back pain [Belville 2014]), concluded that the dangers associated with marijuana consumption had been "exaggerated" and that the harsh penalties for drug law violations should be reconsidered (*Proceedings* 1962). The commission noted that there was inadequate evidence to support claims that marijuana consumption led to involvement in sexual offenses or other antisocial acts and that "tolerance and dependence do not develop [with marijuana] and withdrawal does not produce an abstinence syndrome" (266). With respect to sentencing for drug offenders, the commission was critical of the Bureau of Narcotics' contention that severe penalties were a deterrent to involvement in illicit drug use: "It is difficult to believe that a narcotic addict who is physically and psychologically dependent on a drug will forgo satisfaction of this craving for fear of a long prison sentence" (quoted in Bertram et al. 1996, 88). More specifically, with respect

---

Panama garrisons found among the addicts individuals who were under charges of violence and insubordination" (quoted in Bewley-Taylor, Blickman, and Jelsma 2014, 24). As noted previously, the Panama studies had in fact concluded that violence and insubordination were not caused by soldiers' consumption of marijuana but instead were related to alcohol use.

to the sentencing of "petty" marijuana offenses, the commission recommended that mandatory minimum sentences should be removed and that the law should allow for suspended sentences, probation, and parole for such offenders.

A less well-known U.S. government report published in 1967 by the Task Force on Narcotics and Drug Abuse addressed, among other issues, the theory that marijuana was a gateway drug. In rejecting the theory, the task force report offered one of the most cogent arguments on the issue:

> There is evidence that a majority of heroin users who come to the attention of public authorities have, in fact, had some prior experience with marijuana. But that does not mean that one leads to the other in the sense that marijuana has an intrinsic quality that creates a heroin liability. *There are too many marijuana users who do not graduate to heroin, and too many heroin addicts with no prior marijuana use, to support such a theory.* Moreover, there is no scientific basis for such a theory. (Task Force on Narcotics and Drug Abuse 1967, 220; emphasis added)

The Nixon Era: The War on Drugs 1.0

> America's public enemy number one in the United States is drug abuse. In order to fight and defeat this enemy, it is necessary to wage a new, all-out offensive.
>
> —RICHARD NIXON, "Remarks about an Intensified Program for Drug Abuse Prevention and Control"

Marijuana use in the United States continued to increase in the late 1960s and into the early 1970s; in 1967, only 5 percent of college students admitted to having tried the drug; by 1970, the figure was at 43 percent (Barcott 2015),[4] and marijuana arrests in the country increased from 119,000 in 1969 to 445,000 in 1974 (Fox, Armentano, and Tvert 2009). While many commentators in the United States and other countries in the 1960s were calling for softening drug laws, particularly with respect to marijuana, Richard Nixon was a strong opponent of marijuana; although the drug war had been launched much earlier in the United States, Nixon was arguably most responsible for intensifying the racial components of the war. In a conversation with his chief of staff, Bob Haldeman, in 1971, Nixon stated, "I want a strong statement about marijuana. . . . I mean one on marijuana that just tears the ass out of them" (quoted in D'Angelo 2015, 32). But perhaps even more important

---

4. Growing acceptance of marijuana in U.S. culture may have led to more students being honest about their use of the drug; thus, social desirability effects may explain part of this increase.

was the racist foundation of Nixon's views and efforts. In an interview with author/journalist Dan Baum in 1994, John Ehrlichman, Nixon's counsel and assistant for domestic affairs, revealed, "We knew we couldn't make it illegal to be either against the war or black, but by getting the public to associate hippies with marijuana and blacks with heroin, and then criminalizing them both heavily, we could disrupt those communities. We could arrest their leaders, raid their homes, break up those meetings, and vilify them night after night on the evening news. Did we know we were lying about the drugs? Of course we did" (quoted in Baum 2016). Nixon also added a touch of anti-Semitism to the mix, commenting that "every one of those bastards that are out for legalizing marijuana is Jewish. . . . What the Christ is the matter with the Jews?" (quoted in Dickinson 2016).

During the Nixon administration, the budget to fight the war on drugs increased from $41 million at the start of his presidency to nearly $800 million when he left office in 1974 (Martin and Rashidian 2014). And by issuing a 1973 executive order consolidating the Bureau of Narcotics and Dangerous Drugs, the Office of Drug Abuse Law Enforcement, and drug enforcement offices in the United States Department of Customs into the U.S. Drug Enforcement Administration (Elkins 2018), Nixon established an important organizational component of the drug war that continues to be influential to this day.

However, Nixon also held some mildly progressive views on the issue of drug addiction, telling Congress in 1969, "It has been a common oversimplification to consider narcotics addiction or drug abuse to be a law enforcement problem alone" (quoted in Martin and Rashidian 2014, 47). In fact, Nixon was the only president (to this day) to devote more federal funding to drug-use prevention and treatment than to law enforcement and the criminal justice system in fighting drugs.

The most significant and enduring development during the Nixon era was labeling marijuana as a Schedule I substance under the Controlled Substances Act of 1970—meaning the substance was illegal with no approved medical purposes. At the time, Congress acknowledged that it did not have sufficient information on marijuana for it to remain a Schedule I drug permanently, leading to the creation of a presidential commission (the Shafer Commission) to review the research evidence and recommend a long-term strategy for the drug (Zeese 2002).

Responses to Marijuana: Commissions and Reports

Britain: The Wootton Report

Similar to the situation in the United States, marijuana was not widely used in Britain prior to the 1960s. In 1945, there were only four convictions for offenses involving the drug in the entire United Kingdom, and not until 1950 were the number of prosecutions for cannabis (eighty-six) greater than the number for opium and other illegal drugs (Nutt 2012). However, prosecutions for marijuana offenses began to increase in the mid- to late 1960s, reaching 2,393 by 1967 (Advisory Committee on Drug Dependence 1968). Although data on the racial characteristics of cannabis users in Britain are not available for this period, there is some evidence that at the level of enforcement (and also similar to the situation in the United States in the twentieth and twenty-first centuries) there was considerable racial disparity in the processing of marijuana offenders in the United Kingdom. In 1963, of the 663 convictions for marijuana offenses in Britain, black offenders accounted for 367 (55 percent). Perhaps also reflecting increased levels of marijuana use in Britain, by 1967, of 2,393 convictions for marijuana, black offenders accounted for 656 (27 percent) (Advisory Committee on Drug Dependence 1968).

An editorial in the British medical journal the *Lancet* suggested that it might be worthwhile for Britain to consider removing cannabis from the country's list of dangerous drugs (where it had been placed in 1951) and "giving it the same social status as alcohol by legalizing its importation and consumption" (1963, 989). The editorial noted that the potential benefits of marijuana legalization included "allowing the wider spread of something that can give pleasure" and increased revenue for the government if marijuana sales were taxed. In addition, legalization could potentially reduce "interracial tensions," as well as intergenerational tensions, because "here it [marijuana] has been taken up by the younger members of society in which alcohol is the inheritance of the more elderly" (990).

In response to the apparent increases in the use of marijuana and other drugs in Britain, the British government appointed a parliamentary committee to study drug-dependence issues and to make policy recommendations. The Wootton Committee (formally the Advisory Committee on Drug Dependence), headed by sociologist/criminologist Barbara Wootton, began by framing the issue of drug use in the context of personal liberty: "There is considerable support today for John Stuart Mill's dictum that 'the only purpose for which power can be rightfully exercised over any member of a civilized community against his will is to prevent harm to others. His own good, either physical or moral, is not a sufficient warrant" (Advisory Committee on Drug Dependence 1968).

The 1968 Wootton report made a clear distinction between hard and soft drugs, a distinction that, similar to the situation in the United States, had previously not been acknowledged in British law (Lee 2012). While emphasizing that "the wider use of cannabis should not be encouraged . . . [it] is very much less dangerous than opiates, amphetamines, and barbiturates, and also less dangerous than alcohol." Rejecting the gateway drug theory (which the report referred to as "progression"), the committee wisely recognized the methodological challenges in studying the issue: "Hitherto discussion of the question of whether there is progression from cannabis to heroin has relied chiefly upon evidence from retrospective investigations of the previous habits of heroin users. In the nature of the case, such evidence can never be conclusive" (Advisory Committee on Drug Dependence 1968). It was further noted that there was nothing inherent in the "pharmacological properties of cannabis that led to its users trying other drugs"; however, because consumers had to purchase the drug in the "criminal underworld," they often had access to opiates and other hard drugs—it was the "personality of the user, rather than the properties of [marijuana] that is likely to cause progression to other drugs."

While acknowledging that a form of psychological dependence on marijuana may occur for some users, the Wootton report noted that "cannabis does not produce tolerance. . . . Unlike heroin, cannabis does not cause physical dependence and withdrawal effects when its use is discontinued." With respect to the purported relationship between marijuana use and involvement in crime, the report made an important distinction between users being arrested for violations of drug legislation and the actual commission of property or violent crimes: "Published statements on links between cannabis and crime tend to confuse the consequences of enforcing legal restrictions on non-conforming drug users with alleged criminogenic effects of cannabis smoking itself." The committee made a further important distinction between "social sharing" of marijuana and larger-scale trafficking in the substance: "The traditional view of supplier as large scale criminal is an oversimplification—in cannabis 'society' there is a regular give and take of the drug and many users are in a position to supply it, and do supply it, in very small quantities without real criminal intent."

The Wootton report concluded, "Having reviewed all the material available to us, we find ourselves in agreement with the conclusions reached by the Indian Hemp Drugs Commission . . . and the New York Mayor's Committee on Marijuana that the long-term consumption of cannabis in moderate doses has no harmful effects. . . . There is no evidence that in Western society serious physical dangers are associated with the smoking of cannabis. . . . All in all, it is impossible to make out a firm case against cannabis being potentially a greater personal or social danger than alcohol."

At the time of the Wootton report, Britain's 1965 Dangerous Drugs Act prescribed maximum penalties for any offense related to cannabis (and all prohibited drugs) in Britain: on summary conviction (roughly equivalent to a misdemeanor offense in the United States), a fine not exceeding 250 pounds or imprisonment for twelve months or both; and on indictment (roughly equivalent to a felony offense in the United States), a fine not exceeding 1,000 pounds and/or imprisonment for not more than ten years. Recognizing that these penalties were unduly harsh, the Wootton Committee recommended removing the possibility of imprisonment for possession of small amounts of cannabis and limiting fines to 100 pounds on summary conviction (Advisory Committee on Drug Dependence 1968).

The Netherlands: The Hulsman and Baan Commissions

The first drug law in the Netherlands was the Opium Act of 1919 (Korf, Wouters, and Benschop 2011), and laws criminalizing the possession of opium and cocaine were passed in 1928 to comply with the requirements of the 1925 Geneva Convention on Drugs. But law enforcement officials in the Netherlands in the 1930s through the 1960s generally did not focus on users of illicit drugs and even tolerated small-scale drug dealing (Davenport-Hines 2001). However, in response to increases in the use of cannabis and other drugs in the Netherlands in the 1960s, two drug policy commissions were created.

The Hulsman Commission (1968–1971) was set up by the Dutch National Federation of Mental Health Organizations with a mandate to "clarify factors associated with the use of drugs" and to "suggest proposals for a rational policy" (National Commission on Marihuana and Drug Abuse 1972). The commission was chaired by Louk Hulsman, a criminal law professor at Erasmus University in Rotterdam, and included law enforcement officials, alcohol-treatment experts, psychiatrists, a drug-use researcher, and a sociologist among its members.

The Hulsman Commission began with the premise that complete prohibition of illicit drug use may not be necessary—these substances could be used and controlled in a limited way, an idea that, at the time, "was just as unconventional as it is in many circles today" (Cohen 1994). As done in the 1968 Wootton report, the Hulsman Commission framed the issue of drug use in the context of personal liberties: "If an individual makes a choice that may be dangerous to herself as a private person, no one should deny her this right" (quoted in Cohen 1994). Also similar to conclusions in the Wootton report, the Hulsman Commission rejected the notion of marijuana as a gateway drug but recognized that "becoming a member of a . . . drug-use subculture may make a cannabis user familiar with the existence of other drugs" (quoted in Cohen 1994). This insight regarding the separation of drug markets and the demand and supply sides of these different markets, as well as more general principles of harm reduction, has informed Dutch drug policy since 1976, especially in the context of de facto cannabis legalization in the country (see Chapter 6 for a detailed discussion of this policy). In its conclusion regarding drug policy options, the Hulsman Commission recommended full decriminalization of marijuana possession: "Use of cannabis and the possession of small quantities should be taken out of the criminal law straight away. Production and distribution for the time being should remain within the criminal law but as a misdemeanor" (quoted in Cohen 1994).

The Dutch also established a state commission on drugs in 1968, which included some members of the Hulsman Commission, as well as officials from the Ministry of Justice and the Amsterdam chief of police (National Commission on Marihuana and Drug Abuse 1972). In 1970, Peter Baan, the chief inspector of mental health in the Netherlands, assumed the role of chair of the commission, and a final report was published in 1972 (Cohen 1994).

The Baan Commission suggested dividing drugs into categories with acceptable and unacceptable risks and described cannabis as a relatively benign substance with minimal health risks (National Commission on Marihuana and Drug Abuse 1972). However, the commission recommended against use of the criminal law even for drugs that were believed to pose unacceptable risks and suggested that the criminal justice system should be used as a mechanism to encourage heavy drug users to enter into treatment. Similar to the Hulsman Commission report, the Baan report rejected the idea of cannabis as a gateway drug but again recognized that laws banning marijuana expose cannabis users to individuals who have access to and use "heavier" substances (Cohen 1994).

Partially in response to the recommendations of these two commissions, the Dutch government considered legalizing cannabis in 1974 (Bewley-Taylor, Blickman, and Jelsma 2014) but ultimately adopted a policy of nonenforcement for violations involving the possession of marijuana. As Peter Cohen (1994) notes, in the larger context, at the end of the 1950s and into the 1960s, official policy in the Netherlands was to generally restrict the reach of law enforcement, to prevent violations of the law by enacting adequate social policies, and to avoid imprisonment of those who did not violate the law. The Netherlands effectively decriminalized marijuana possession in 1976.

Canada: The Le Dain Commission

> Any body of law that permits a man who is drunk to run down a kid in his car and then gets sent to jail for only three months when a kid can get two years for passing a joint to his friend is obviously a very stupid and indefensible law.
> —IAN CAMPBELL (member of Le Dain Commission), quoted
> in *Vancouver Sun*, "Pot Law Very Stupid, Indefensible"

From 1947 (the first year for which judicial statistics are available in Canada) until 1955 inclusive, there was a total of only sixteen convictions for marijuana possession under Canada's Opium and Narcotic Drug Act (marijuana was banned at the federal level in Canada in 1923). However, as was occurring in several other Western countries, marijuana use, and arrests for such use, began to increase during the mid- to late 1960s and into the 1970s—

there were 2,964 convictions for cannabis offenses in Canada in 1969 and 6,270 in 1970 (Mosher 1999).

Faced with these increases in marijuana and other drug use, and concerned that large numbers of middle-class youth were being incarcerated for the violation of marijuana laws, in 1969, the Canadian federal government appointed the Le Dain Commission, chaired by Gerald Le Dain (dean of the Osgoode Hall Law School in Toronto), to examine the nature of the drug situation in Canada and to make policy recommendations. This commission received more than 350 submissions, and about twelve thousand people attended and participated in hearings, including a number of prominent individuals such as John Lennon and Yoko Ono (in a private hearing) (Mosher 1999).

In the course of its investigations into drug issues in Canada, the Le Dain Commission reviewed the extant scientific evidence on marijuana and lamented the fact that, although there were approximately two thousand publications on cannabis, most of them did not meet the standards of scientific evidence and were "ill-documented and ambiguous, emotion-laden and incredibly biased" (Le Dain 1972). However, after reviewing the evidence, the commission members indicated that they agreed with the findings of the Indian Hemp Drugs Commission and the La Guardia Committee that the long-term consumption of marijuana in moderate doses had no harmful effects. They noted that the psychological effects of marijuana varied widely and were related to the dose, mode of administration, the personality and experience of users with cannabis and other drugs, and the setting in which the drug was consumed (Le Dain 1972). Providing an important insight regarding the ability of experienced users to titrate their dosage of marijuana (only consuming enough of the substance to achieve the desired psychoactive effects), the Le Dain Commission noted that hashish (which was becoming more popular in Canada in the early 1970s), while more potent than marijuana, was not necessarily more dangerous, because consumers "smoke to attain a certain effect or level of 'high' and adjust the dose according to the potency of substance used" (Le Dain 1972). The commission also noted that physical dependence on marijuana did not occur in users—that is, withdrawal symptoms did not occur following cessation of use. Interestingly, the Le Dain Commission also commented on marijuana's possible substitution effects (see detailed discussion of substitution effects in Chapter 3):"Many marijuana users claim that they have drastically reduced their consumption of alcohol, or quit it, since using cannabis" (Le Dain 1972).

The final Le Dain Commission report was published in 1972, with the recommendation that penalties for simple possession of cannabis should be eliminated (three members of the commission urged outright legalization of the substance) and that Canadian provinces should implement controls on the possession and cultivation of cannabis similar to those regulating the use of alcohol (MacLeod 2015). However, similar to the actions of the U.S. government in response to the recommendations of the Shafer Commission, rather than completely eliminate penalties for marijuana possession, the Canadian federal government created new, and less severe, sentencing options for drug-possession offenses (absolute and conditional discharges, which significantly reduced the number of drug offenders sentenced to incarceration) (Mosher 1999).

United States: Shafer Commission

> Marijuana's relative potential for harm to the vast majority of users and its actual impact on society does not justify a social policy designed to seek out and firmly punish those who use it.
> —NATIONAL COMMISSION ON MARIHUANA AND
> DRUG ABUSE, *Marihuana*

Officially known as the National Commission on Marihuana and Drug Abuse, the Shafer Commission was appointed by President Richard Nixon, with the primary purpose of considering the scheduling of marijuana, which had been placed in Schedule I of the Controlled Substances Act of 1970. The head of the commission, Raymond Shafer, was the former governor of Pennsylvania, a supporter of President Nixon, and a staunch Republican, "an old-fashioned moderate who believed in facts, evidence, and science" (Barcott 2015, 39). Prior to becoming governor, Shafer had served as a prosecutor, with a "law and order, drug warrior reputation" (Zeese 2002).

The Shafer Commission sponsored fifty research projects, conducted public opinion polls, consulted members of the criminal justice community, and took thousands of pages of testimony (Zeese 2002). Its final report, appropriately titled *Marihuana: A Signal of Misunderstanding*, was 1,184 pages long and called for a "more rational discussion of marihuana policy. . . . The time for politicizing the marihuana issue is at an end" (quoted in Lee 2012, 122). As Keven Zeese (2002) comments, "[The work of the Shafer Commission] is still the most comprehensive review of marijuana ever conducted by the federal government."

As did the Wootton report in Britain, and the Hulsman and Baan Commission reports in the Netherlands, the Shafer Commission report rejected the theory of marijuana as a gateway drug: "The fact should be emphasized that the overwhelming majority of marijuana users do not progress to other drugs" (quoted in Barcott 2015, 41). The commission similarly rejected the purported relationship between marijuana use and involvement in aggressive or violent acts: "Rather than inducing violent or aggressive behavior through its purported effects of lowering inhibitions, weakening impulse control and heightening aggressive tendencies, marihuana was actually found to inhibit the expression of aggressive impulses by pacifying the user" (National Commission on Marihuana and Drug Abuse 1972, 71–72).

The Shafer Commission found no evidence that marijuana use caused significant physical or psychological harm, nor was the substance physically addictive, and the commission further noted that "neither the marihuana user nor the drug itself can be said to constitute a danger to public safety" (National Commission on Marihuana and Drug Abuse 1972, 78). However, the commission did highlight several deleterious effects of marijuana *prohibition*, including selective enforcement and prosecution under existing marijuana laws and the creation of disrespect for the criminal law among youth. The commission recommended that state and federal laws be changed to decriminalize possession of marijuana for personal use, as well as distribution of small amounts of the drug:

> The criminal law is too harsh a tool to apply to personal possession [of marihuana] even in the effort to discourage use. . . . The actual and potential harm of use of the drug is not great enough to justify intrusion by the criminal law into private behavior, a step which our society takes only with the greatest reluctance. . . . Therefore, the Commission recommends [that the] possession of marihuana for personal use . . . no longer be an offense [and that the] casual distribution of small amounts of marihuana for no remuneration, or insignificant remuneration, . . . no longer be an offense. (140, 152)

As Lee (2012) notes, the Shafer Commission report simply confirmed the findings of several other reports on the topic of cannabis that had appeared earlier. In response to its primary mandate to make recommendations on the rescheduling of marijuana under the Controlled Substances Act, the commission concluded that rescheduling was not sufficient but that the drug should be completely decriminalized. However, the recommendations of the Shafer Commission were not sufficient to convince President Nixon to alter his stance on marijuana; he claimed to have read the report (this has been disputed), but it did not change his mind (Barcott 2015).

United States: Eastland Report

A less well-known U.S. government committee addressing drug issues in the 1970s, with a specific focus on marijuana, was chaired by Mississippi senator James O. Eastland. In 1974, this committee produced a report titled *The Marihuana-Hashish Epidemic and Its Impact on U.S. Security*, which presented findings that were in stark contrast to those of the Shafer Commission (and similar commissions in other countries discussed previously). Among other things, the Eastland report claimed that cannabis caused severe and

irreversible brain damage, damage to the reproductive system, and amotiva-
tional syndrome and induced "pathological forms of thinking resembling
paranoia" (United States Congressional Record 1974). Eastland traced the
"marihuana-hashish epidemic" to student protests at the University of California, Berkeley, in 1965, where "not only was pot smoking embraced as a
symbolic rejection of the establishment, but, together with the 'dirty speech
movement,' the right to smoke marijuana became an integral part of the
catalogue of demands of the uprising." Marijuana legalization was allegedly
being promoted by "clearly subversive groups," and the growing population
of marijuana users posed a "serious political danger because it makes them
susceptible to manipulation by extremists."

The Eastland report claimed that the marijuana "epidemic" was spreading into high schools and junior high schools and had even "invaded" grade
schools. It had also spread "into the ranks of professional society and of the
blue collar workers, so that all sectors of our society are today affected by the
epidemic." Portending impending disaster, the report stated, "If the cannabis epidemic continues to spread at the rate of the post-Berkeley period, we
may find ourselves saddled with a large population of semi-zombies." Not
surprisingly, the Eastland Committee was opposed to the decriminalization
of marijuana, commenting on the 1973 Oregon decriminalization legislation, "The approach [decriminalization] I submit, is altogether too permissive and just doesn't take into account the serious social damage done by
marihuana or the compelling need to protect society against the spread of
the habit. It doesn't take into consideration the basic fact that all drug addiction—including marihuana addiction, is like a contagious disease" (United
States Congressional Record 1974).

Australia: Baume Committee

Also faced with increasing levels of substance use (especially with respect to
youth cannabis use) in the 1960s and 1970s, the Australian Senate's Select
Committee on Drug Trafficking and Drug Abuse, recognizing that cannabis
was not a narcotic and not as harmful a drug as heroin or cocaine, recommended in 1971 that the substance be moved from Schedule I of the Single
Convention on Narcotic Drugs to a more appropriate schedule (Health
Commission of New South Wales 1973). A 1973 report by the Health Commission of New South Wales similarly concluded that marijuana was not a
particularly dangerous drug, found little relationship between cannabis consumption and crime, and found no evidence of physical dependence on the
substance among users. This report also rejected the gateway drug theory
but noted that cannabis users' association with social groups and subcul-
tures who use "stronger" drugs may expose them to such substances.

A more extensive examination of drug issues in Australia was undertaken by a committee appointed by the Australian Senate Standing Committee on Social Welfare in 1976, chaired by Dr. Peter Baume (Commonwealth of Australia 1977). Similar to the Canadian Le Dain Commission, the Baume Committee began its discussion of cannabis by noting that the scientific research literature on the substance "varies enormously in quality and interpretation. Both denigrators and advocates of cannabis have harangued, and continue to harangue, the public, law makers, and law enforcers. The result is a most difficult tangle of half-truths, fact and fiction" (Commonwealth of Australia 1977, 127).

With respect to the gateway drug theory, the Baume Committee cited the testimony of Dr. Neal Blewett, who noted that statistically, users of barbiturates were more likely to use harder drugs than were users of marijuana, but there were no assertions that barbiturates were gateway drugs (Commonwealth of Australia 1977). Blewett also noted that "neither in the biochemistry of marijuana, nor in its typical effects, is there any sign of a causal mechanism which might explain progress to hard drugs or propensity to crime. Rather, the reverse—for marijuana tends to inhibit aggression, and increased sensitization appears to develop with greater use" (quoted in Commonwealth of Australia 1977, 156).

In its conclusions, the Baume Committee emphasized that cannabis was not a narcotic and that the policies addressing use of the substance should be "based on harm, actual or potential, which may result from cannabis use rather than on judgements about the politics, sexual mores, dress, and vague hedonism of the youth culture" (Commonwealth of Australia 1977, 157). The committee recommended that possession of marijuana for personal use should not be defined as a crime, that fines of approximately $100 to $150 be imposed for possession, and that "no record of conviction kept by courts or police shall be used in subsequent proceedings or in relation to any application by the offender for employment" (165). Although the Australian federal government rejected many of the Baume Committee report's recommendations, its focus on harm reduction has had a lasting influence on Australian drug policy.

In summary, of the eight marijuana commissions that addressed the issue of physiological addiction to marijuana, seven concluded that it was not physiologically addictive. Of the ten commissions that addressed whether marijuana consumption leads to violence, nine indicated that the substance did not lead to crime. Of the eight commissions that considered whether marijuana was a gateway to the use of other (harder) drugs, all concluded that marijuana was *not* a gateway drug. Of the eleven commissions that addressed the relative harm of marijuana in comparison to other substances, all concluded that other drugs were more harmful than cannabis. Of the

TABLE 2.1: SUMMARY OF MARIJUANA COMMISSIONS

Name of commission	Marijuana addictive?	Crime/ violence?	Gateway?	Relative harm?	Recommendations, legality
Indian Hemp (1894)	NA	No	NA	Alcohol worse	Decriminalization/ regulation
Panama (1925, 1933)	No	No	NA	Opium, cocaine worse	NA
La Guardia (1944)	No	No	No	Others worse	NA
White House Advisory (1962)	No	No	NA	Others worse	Reduce penalties
Task Force (1967)	NA	NA	No	Others worse	NA
Wootton (1968)	No	No	No	Others worse	No incarceration
Hulsman (1968–1971)	NA	No	No	NA	Decriminalization
Baan (1968)	NA	NA	No	Others worse	Decriminalization
Le Dain (1972)	No	No	No	Others worse	Decriminalization
Shafer (1972)	No	No	No	Others worse	Decriminalization
Eastland (1974)	Yes	Yes	NA	Very harmful	Strengthen penalties
Baume (1977)	No	No	No	Others worse	Decriminalization

nine commissions that made recommendations regarding changes in the legality of the substance, only one (Eastland) recommended strengthening penalties for possession of marijuana. As Table 2.1 clearly demonstrates, the 1974 Eastland Commission was an outlier with respect to its conclusions regarding marijuana.

The Ford and Carter Eras: The Calm before the (Marijuana and Other Drug) Storm

In September 1975, President Gerald Ford (whose wife, Betty, battled addictions to alcohol and prescription drugs) created the Domestic Council Drug Abuse Task Force, chaired by Vice President Nelson Rockefeller, to examine the extent of drug abuse in the United States and recommend policies for addressing it. The members of this council included Robert DuPont, director of the National Institute on Drug Abuse, and John Bartle, previous administrator of the Drug Enforcement Administration—Raymond Shafer, primary author of the Shafer report, was an ex-officio member. The report from this council noted that marijuana was only a minor problem, attended by "relatively low social costs," and recognized that "not all drugs are equally dangerous. Enforcement efforts should therefore concentrate on drugs which have a high addiction potential" (quoted in Drug Enforcement Administration, n.d.). Although President Ford supported mandatory sentences for individuals trafficking in hard drugs, perhaps influenced by the findings of the report and also by the fact that his four sons admitted to smoking marijuana (*New York Times* 1974), he reportedly favored the legalization of marijuana (Stringer and Maggard 2016).

In 1977, President Jimmy Carter (whose wife, Rosalynn, disclosed that their three sons had smoked marijuana [*New York Times* 1976]) recommended that Congress eliminate the federal penalties for marijuana possession: "We can, and should, continue to discourage the use [of marijuana] but this can be done without defining the smoker as a criminal" (quoted in Mapes 2014b). Carter apparently had given careful consideration to the recommendations of the Shafer Commission before making these comments in 1977:

> Penalties against possession of a drug should not be more damaging to an individual than the use of the drug itself; and where they are, they should be changed. Nowhere is this more clear than in laws against possession of marijuana in private for personal use. . . . States which have already removed criminal penalties for marijuana use, like Oregon and California, have not noted any significant increase in marijuana smoking. The National Commission on Marijuana and Drug Abuse concluded five years ago that marijuana use should be decriminalized, and I believe it is time to implement those basic recommendations.

Carter's support of marijuana decriminalization led some to believe that "ending the federal war on pot seemed little more than a waiting game" (Dickinson 2013); needless to say, decriminalization of marijuana at the federal level did not occur although several states decriminalized the substance during this period. More generally, while the policies and actions of the Ford and Carter administrations generally did not intensify the drug war that had been declared by Richard Nixon, things would change significantly with the election of Ronald Reagan in 1980.

The Reagan Era: War on Drugs 2.0

> We're making no excuses for drugs—hard, soft, or otherwise. Drugs are bad, and we're going after them. As I've said before, we've taken down the surrender flag and run up the battle flag. And we're going to win the war on drugs.
> —RONALD REAGAN, quoted in Chris Elkins, "The Republican
>   Party Policies on Substance Abuse"

With his wife, Nancy (and her "Just Say No" and "If you're a casual drug user, you're an accomplice to murder" slogans), as the public face of antidrug efforts, drugs became a central focus of the Reagan administration, and the drug war was ramped up through several policies.[5] For example, although the Posse Comitatus Act of 1878 explicitly restricted U.S. military interference in local law enforcement, Reagan amended the act to permit military involvement in civilian law enforcement activities, particularly those related to the enforcement of drug laws (Martin and Rashidian 2014). In addition, during the Reagan presidency, the U.S. Army, Navy, and Air Force lent troops, facilities, and aircraft to support domestic drug law enforcement. As part of the 1984 Crime Control Act, Reagan also reintroduced mandatory minimum sentences for drug and other offenses that had largely been repealed during the Nixon administration (Martin and Rashidian 2014), and criminal and civil asset forfeiture programs, which allowed police departments to seize the assets of individuals involved in drug trafficking, were expanded and increased (Drug Enforcement Administration, n.d.).

Perhaps most (in)famously, after African American basketball player Len Bias (selected second overall in the 1986 National Basketball Association draft) died from an apparent crack cocaine overdose, Reagan warned about the "new epidemic of smokable cocaine, otherwise known as crack" (quoted in Beckett 2017). Congress subsequently passed the Anti–Drug Abuse Act of 1986, which created a 100:1 disparity in the amount of powder versus crack cocaine needed to trigger a five-year mandatory minimum sentence for possession. And although estimates suggest that roughly equal proportions of white and black Americans consumed crack cocaine, studies by the U.S. Sentencing Commission examining racial disparities in the application of this law found that more than 90 percent of federal prosecutions under the law involved black offenders (Gelacak 1997; see also Mosher and Akins 2014). It is also important to stress that the reinvigoration of the war on drugs during the Reagan era was also supported by Democrats: for example, Congressman Glen English of Oklahoma commented, "We in the Democratic Party realize that the war on drugs has to be fought like World War II—a complete and thorough effort, one dedicated to victory at any cost" (quoted in Hinton 2016, 310).

With respect to marijuana, while serving as governor of California in the 1960s, Reagan asserted that marijuana users were largely draft-dodging pro-communist Vietnam supporters (*Daily Kos* 2007). Later in his presidency, he claimed that "marijuana, pot, grass, whatever you want to call it, is probably the most dangerous drug in the U.S., and we haven't begun to find out all its ill effects" (quoted in Mapes 2014a).

---

5. Somewhat ironically, given her exhortations to people to "just say no" to drugs, Nancy Reagan was a chronic user of prescription tranquilizers and sleeping pills, as revealed in her daughter, Patti Davis's, autobiography (Lacher 1992; see also Lee 2012).

Reagan's drug czar was Carlton Turner, a biochemist who had previously been employed by the University of Mississippi, where he was growing research-grade marijuana under contract with the federal government (Barcott 2015). In October 1986, Turner told a *Newsweek* reporter that he believed that marijuana smoking might lead to homosexuality (Barcott 2015; Kastor 1986):[6] "Marijuana leads to homosexuality, the breakdown of the immune system, and ultimately, AIDS" (quoted in Legum 2014). While Turner later claimed that "I have never said marijuana will make you gay," he added that when he visited drug treatment centers housing individuals under eighteen years of age, approximately 40 percent of them had engaged in homosexual activity: "It seems to be something that follows along with their marijuana use" (quoted in Kastor 1986). Turner also believed that marijuana use was linked to "the present young-adult generation's involvement in anti-military, anti-nuclear power, anti-big business, anti-authority demonstrations" (quoted in Merritt 2004). Interestingly, almost thirty years after expressing these views, Turner was appointed chairman of Drug Free Florida, the main opposition group to that state's proposed medical marijuana legislation in 2014 (Legum 2014).

The George H. W. Bush Era

In a speech in 1989 announcing an additional $1.5 billion to address drug problems, which began with the statement, "All of us agree that the gravest domestic threat facing our nation today is drugs," President George

---

6. The theme that marijuana use led to homosexuality and aberrant sexual behaviors emerged in the early 1970s. One of the most interesting examples of this theme was an article written by psychiatrists Harold Kolansky and William Moore, published in the *Journal of the American Medical Association*. Kolansky and Moore studied thirty-eight individuals, most of whom smoked marijuana more than once per week, and reported that "these patients consistently showed very poor social judgment, poor attention span, poor concentration, confusion, anxiety, depression, apathy, indifference, and often slow and slurred speech" (1971, 489). Kolansky and Moore also noted that thirteen females in their study, aged thirteen to twenty-two, exhibited "an unusual degree of sexual promiscuity, which ranged from sexual relations with individuals of the opposite sex to relations with individuals of both sexes, and sometimes, individuals of both sexes at the same time" (490). In addition, Kolansky and Moore claimed that "shortly after a 14-year old boy began to smoke marijuana, he began to demonstrate indolence, apathy, and depression. Over a period of 8 months, his condition worsened until he began to develop paranoid ideas. Simultaneously, he became homosexual" (488).

And as late as 1999, the head of the U.S. Public Health Service argued that marijuana should not be prescribed to AIDS patients because these individuals would become "crazed" by the high they achieved from the drug and would be more likely to practice unsafe sex as a result (Manderson 1999).

H. W. Bush held up a plastic bag filled with a white substance and, apparently to emphasize the ubiquity of the drug problem, alleged that the crack cocaine had been purchased across from the White House:

> This is crack cocaine seized a few days ago by Drug Enforcement agents in a park just across from the White House. It could have easily been heroin or PCP. It's as innocent-looking as candy, but it's turning our cities into battle zones, and it's murdering our children. (Bush 1989)

However, it turned out that agents had lured an individual (who apparently did not even know the location of the White House) to the park just so the president could say the substance was purchased near the White House (Isikoff 1989). Perhaps more important, Bush's speech signaled an intensification of the war on drugs, proposing to build more prisons and jails and to increase interdiction efforts in source/producer countries. As was the case with President Reagan before him and future presidents, while Bush made reference to the need for drug treatment and prevention, the bulk of drug war funding under his administration was devoted to law enforcement and interdiction. And although Bush did not specifically mention marijuana in his speech, at least some of these funds were devoted to the enforcement of marijuana laws.

In his discussion of science abuse, Chris Mooney (2005) notes that a simple strategy used by the U.S. government that contributes to science abuse is to fill key federal administrative positions on the basis of ideology rather than genuine expertise in a particular domain. This strategy has certainly been used by the federal government in its appointment of directors (drug czars) of the ONDCP.

William Bennett, appointed during the presidency of George H. W. Bush, was the first *official* drug czar. Bennett, who had served as chairman of the National Endowment for the Humanities and later, secretary of education during the Reagan administration, apparently volunteered for the position. Similar to drug czars appointed in subsequent administrations, Bennett had extremist views on drugs and how to ameliorate drug problems in the United States and demonized not only drug traffickers but also those who used illegal drugs.

Bennett also convinced President Bush to expand the role of the U.S. military in the drug war, and Bush signed a directive to allow American soldiers to assist local military patrols in Colombia, Bolivia, and Peru in capturing drug traffickers (Kohn 1989). Bennett supported incarcerating parents and pregnant women who were drug users and evicting tenants from public housing based on the mere suspicion of drug use (Kohn 1989). Although Bennett resigned from the drug czar position in November 1990

(Savage 1990), he has continued to engage in antidrug crusades, including in a book published in 2015 and coauthored with Robert White, *Going to Pot: Why the Rush to Legalize Marijuana Is Harming America*, which we discuss in Chapter 5.

While the drug war certainly intensified during the administration of George H. W. Bush, not all of the drug policy developments during this period should be attributed exclusively to Republicans. Democrat Joe Biden (who chaired the Judiciary Committee and would later become vice president during the Obama administration) was also a prominent supporter of severe drug policies. While serving as chair of the Judiciary Committee, Biden recommended the creation of the national drug czar position, and among other things, he advocated for more severe sentences for drug offenders (On the Issues 2016).

The Clinton Era

While some may have expected marijuana and other drug policy reform to occur after the election of Bill Clinton as president in 1992, it could be argued that the opposite occurred—under his administration, the war on drugs was escalated (Lee 2012), with arrests for marijuana offenses increasing from 287,850 in 1991 to 723,627 in 2001 (Gettman 2009). In fact, the number of jail sentences meted out for marijuana offenses during Clinton's two terms in office was 800 percent higher than during the twelve years under Ronald Reagan and George H. W. Bush (Lee 2012). As Lee comments, Bill Clinton's (now famous) statement that he smoked marijuana but did not inhale "spoke volumes about the U.S. political establishment's inability or unwillingness to be truthful about cannabis" (2012, 234).

One of the most significant developments with respect to marijuana during the years of the Clinton administration was the legalization of medical marijuana in Arizona and California in 1996. Clinton administration officials quickly initiated efforts to thwart these initiatives; Attorney General Janet Reno indicated that physicians who prescribed marijuana to patients could lose their privileges and be excluded from Medicare and Medicaid reimbursement (Kampia 2011). But most relevant to developments in the continuing drug war in general, and the war on marijuana in particular, was the appointment of General Barry McCaffrey as Clinton's drug czar.

Unless one believes that there is no one better to lead a drug war than a general, President Clinton's choice of General Barry McCaffrey as drug czar may seem rather curious, as there is little evidence to suggest that McCaffrey possessed any particular knowledge of drug issues. Particularly notable with respect to his views on marijuana was McCaffrey's criticism of the Netherlands' de facto legalization of marijuana: "The Dutch experiment is not something we want to model. It's an unmitigated disaster" (quoted in J. Gray 2001).

McCaffrey made this statement prior to an eight-day trip to examine drug policies in European countries. Following his trip to the Netherlands, McCaffrey observed that all youth in Amsterdam's Vondel Park were "stoned zombies"; he also (incorrectly) asserted that "the murder rate in Holland is double that of the United States. . . . That's drugs" (quoted in Reinarman 2002, 127). In support of this claim (apparently using information from a briefing book prepared before his trip to Europe), McCaffrey noted that there were 17.58 murders per 100,000 population in the Netherlands, more than double the rate of 8.22 per 100,000 in the United States. However, the Dutch homicide rate cited by McCaffrey included both homicides and *attempted* homicides— the actual Dutch homicide rate was 1.8 per 100,000. When a Dutch official questioned McCaffrey's deputy regarding the citation of these incorrect statistics, he responded, "Let's say that's right. What you're left with is that they [the Dutch] are a much more violent society and more inept [at murder] and that's not much to brag about" (quoted in Reinarman 2002, 129).

McCaffrey's briefing book also contained misinformation on drug-use rates in the Netherlands, which was also invoked in his criticism of Dutch marijuana policy. Based on data from 1994, it was alleged that "30.2% of Dutch youths say they have tried marijuana, vs. 9.1% in the United States." However, the figure represented lifetime use of marijuana for sixteen- to nineteen-year-olds in Amsterdam but past-month (current) use by American youth. The actual figure for lifetime marijuana use for American youth, at 49.6 percent, was some 19 percent higher than the rate in the Netherlands (Peele, n.d.). In response to criticisms of the distortion of marijuana-use statistics, and in a comment eerily similar to that of some officials in the current Trump administration (who have a tendency to refer to "alternative facts"), McCaffrey claimed that "hard data are a matter of opinion" (quoted in Peele, n.d.)

The 1997 National Institutes of Health report (also known as the Institute of Medicine [IOM] report) on medical marijuana was the most comprehensive review of medical marijuana ever conducted up to that time. In an example of the distortion and dismissal themes of marijuana demonization, McCaffrey, who likely had not read the report, stated, "I think what the IOM report said was that smoked marijuana is harmful, particularly for those with chronic conditions" (quoted in Barcott 2015, 98). As Bruce Barcott observes, McCaffrey "suppressed the science to fit the policy" (2015, 99). And as has been the case with other drug czars, McCaffrey has continued to comment on developments in drug policies; in response to recreational marijuana legalization in Colorado and Washington State in 2012, he stated, "The opposition has gone silent. The politicians, police, judges know this is a bad policy, but they don't make a peep. We're going to end up with impaired surgeons and airline pilots. We're just accepting another drug of abuse" (quoted in Fisher 2014).

The George W. Bush Era

The administration of George W. Bush allocated more funds to the drug war (his funding request to Congress was $19 billion [G. W. Bush 2002], most of which was to be directed to interdiction and law enforcement rather than prevention and treatment) than any previous administration. Among other things, the 2000–2008 period of the Bush administration saw a "rapid escalation of militarization of domestic drug law enforcement," with more than forty thousand SWAT raids on homes and other establishments alleged to be involved in drug trafficking (Drug Policy Alliance, n.d.). Over the eight-year term of George W. Bush's administration, there were at least 260 raids of marijuana businesses, with eighty-four individuals prosecuted at an estimated cost of more than $180 million (D'Angelo 2015). This period also saw the expansion of drug testing in schools and the launch of a largely ineffective and, according to a 2006 Government Accountability Office report, counterproductive antidrug advertisement campaign that, following the terrorist attacks of September 11, 2001, attempted to link drug trafficking to terrorism (Mosher and Akins 2014). In a 2002 presidential address announcing his government's drug control strategy, Bush stated, "The drug trade supports terrorist networks. When people purchase drugs, they put money in the hands of those who want to hurt America. . . . When we fight drugs we fight the war on terror." Bush appointed John Walters as his drug czar, and Walters continued, and arguably even amplified, the distortion of information on drugs in general and marijuana in particular.

Similar to Barry McCaffrey, Walters was also vociferously opposed to medical marijuana. He and former drug czar William Bennett published an article in the *Weekly Standard* titled "Medical Reefer Madness," in which they rejected the very idea of marijuana being useful as medicine (Bennett and Walters 1996); at one point, Walters referred to medical marijuana as "medicinal crack" (T. Newman 2005). Walters also actively campaigned against proposed marijuana reform measures in several states (Montgomery and Whitlock 2003) and attempted to influence marijuana policies in other countries, such as Canada (Mosher and Akins 2014).

Walters also authored an article in the *Washington Post* titled "The Myth of 'Harmless' Marijuana," in which he claimed, among other things, that marijuana was addictive and "directly affects the brain," that "sixty percent of teens in drug treatment have a primary marijuana diagnosis" (conveniently ignoring the fact that the overwhelming majority of such youth were mandated to treatment after contact with the criminal/juvenile justice system), that the substance was linked to "tens of thousands of serious traffic accidents" each year, and that "medical marijuana initiatives are based on pseudoscience" (Walters 2002). In reference to the array of misinformation contained in Walters's *Washington Post* article, Keith Stroup and Paul

Armentano comment, "It is ironic that Drug Czar John Walters cites the movie *Reefer Madness* in his opinion/editorial. . . . Indeed, many of Mr. Walters more egregious claims about cannabis appear to have been lifted straight from the 1936 propaganda film" (2002, 223).

The Obama Era

> As has been well documented, I smoked pot as a kid, and I view it as a bad habit and a vice, not very different from the cigarettes I smoked as a young person up through a big chunk of my adult life. I don't think it's more dangerous than alcohol.
>
> —BARACK OBAMA, quoted in David Remnick, "Going the Distance"

When the Obama administration came into power in 2009, it vowed a commitment to evidence-based drug policies and to investing in drug treatment instead of incarceration. Among the more significant developments during the Obama administration with respect to general drug policy was the repeal of several mandatory minimum-sentencing laws and the passage of the Fair Sentencing Act in 2010, which increased the amount of crack cocaine required to meet the threshold for a mandatory drug trafficking sentence and removed the five-year minimum sentence for first-time possession of crack cocaine (Elkins 2018). Obama also commuted the sentences of several low-level drug offenders and, in July 2016, signed the Comprehensive Addiction and Recovery Act, which provided additional funds for prevention programs and expanded access to the opioid overdose medication naloxone for law enforcement and first responders (Dyer 2018). But as Tim Dickinson (2016) notes, "Despite strides toward a more sane national drug policy, the deeper infrastructure of the war on drugs remain[ed] fundamentally unaltered under Obama."

Obama appointed former Seattle police chief Gil Kerlikowske to head the ONDCP. In his role as drug czar, Kerlikowske promised to "end the war on drugs" (Graves 2014), and he announced that "[all] who have a substance abuse disorder should receive evidence-based treatment services . . . through an expansion of community addiction centers and the development of new medications and evidence-based treatments for addiction" (Office of National Drug Control Policy 2010). Shortly thereafter, the White House boasted of "relying on science and research to support our nation's drug control strategy" (Office of National Drug Control Policy 2011, 1). Given such views, some drug policy reformers were encouraged and thought that Kerlikowske's appointment as drug czar indicated a change from the previous federal government approach of emphasizing arrests and prosecutions to one focused on harm reduction, prevention, and treatment. However, during his opening remarks at the 2012 World Federation against Drugs Forum,

Kerlikowske seemed to hint that the Obama administration was only rhe-torically committed to harm-reduction drug policies: "Policies and pro-grams such as injection rooms [for intravenous drug users], drug distribu-tion efforts, and drug legalization should be opposed because they tolerate drug use and allow the debilitating disease of addiction to continue un-treated" (Kerlikowske 2012). In 2013, Kerlikowske referred to marijuana le-galization as an "extreme" approach and referenced the primacy of federal laws in relation to legalization: "No state, no executive, can nullify a statute that's been passed by Congress" (quoted in Hotakainen 2013a).

President Obama's public statements on marijuana, both prior to being elected and while in office, seemed to signal a change in the federal govern-ment's approach to the substance. While growing up in Hawaii, Obama be-longed to a group known as the "choom gang" ("choom" is a verb that means "to smoke marijuana") and (in contrast to President Clinton, who claimed he sampled marijuana but did not inhale) in 2006, Obama famously stated, "I inhaled frequently, that was the point" (quoted in Kaczynksi 2014). In 2004, while indicating he was not a supporter of marijuana legalization, Obama commented, "I think the war on drugs has been an utter failure" and, in 2007, indicated he "would not have the Justice Department prosecut-ing and raiding medical marijuana users. It's not a good use of resources" (quoted in Kaczynski 2014). But as Barcott comments, Obama essentially left marijuana law enforcement up to local U.S. attorneys, who "became de facto drug czars within their own jurisdictions" (2015, 65).

As noted previously, President Obama indicated that his administration would take a hands-off approach to medical marijuana, not intervening in states that had passed laws legalizing the substance (Egelko 2011). This stance was reflected in the 2009 Ogden memo from the federal Department of Justice stipulating that, as a general rule, prosecutors should not use re-sources to focus on "individuals whose actions are in clear and unambigu-ous compliance with existing state laws providing for the medical use of marijuana." However, the Ogden memo also noted that "Congress has de-termined that marijuana is a dangerous drug, and the illegal sale and manu-facture of marijuana is a serious crime and provides a significant source of revenue to large scale criminal enterprises, gangs, and cartels." The memo also listed conditions that may imply that medical marijuana providers were not in compliance with state laws, indicating possible "illegal drug traffick-ing activity of potential federal interest." These included (1) unlawful pos-session of firearms; (2) violence; (3) sales to minors; (4) financial and market-ing activities inconsistent with the terms, conditions, or purposes of state law, including evidence of money laundering activity and/or financial gains or excessive amounts of cash inconsistent with purported compliance with state or local law; (5) amounts of marijuana inconsistent with purported compliance with state or local law; (6) illegal possession or sale of other controlled substances; and (7) ties to other criminal enterprises (Ogden 2009).

While the Ogden memo seemingly signaled a decline in federal agencies' targeting medical marijuana, demonstrating the relative autonomy of federal government agencies and officials within those agencies, raids of medical marijuana facilities continued. Federal law enforcement officials, including Jeffrey Sweeting, a special agent in charge of the DEA's Denver office, and Melinda Haag, the U.S. attorney for the Northern District of California, publicly rejected the notion that they were required to consider state law in their actions against marijuana dispensaries (Sullum 2014). These agencies and individuals were abetted by a 2011 Justice Department memo that appeared to indicate a change in the approach recommended in the Ogden memo, which stated, "We maintain the authority to enforce [federal law] vigorously against individuals and organizations that participate in unlawful manufacturing and distribution activity involving marijuana, even if such activities are permitted under state law" (cited in M. Baker 2011).

This change apparently had an impact; a 2013 report by the medical marijuana advocacy group Americans for Safe Access suggested that by the summer of 2013, the DEA had conducted at least 270 raids on medical marijuana establishments during the Obama administration—twelve more than had occurred in the previous twelve years (Riggs 2013). D'Angelo (2015) estimates that these raids cost $300 million—50 percent more than was spent on such actions during the eight years of the George W. Bush administration. Another estimate suggests that between October 2011 and October 2012 alone, federal law enforcement officials closed at least six hundred medical marijuana dispensaries in California (Holden 2013).

Two of the most prominent raids in 2012 involved Oaksterdam University and Harborside Health Center in Oakland, which were among the most conspicuous and high-profile marijuana-related businesses in California. Before discussing these cases, it is important to note that the city of Oakland strongly supported marijuana patients and dispensaries—in 2004, the city granted permits to four dispensaries and passed Measure Z, which specified that investigations, arrests, and prosecutions for marijuana offenses committed by adults should be the lowest priority for local law enforcement (Thomas 2013a).

Oaksterdam University, founded by Richard Lee in 2007, was the first trade school in the United States focusing entirely on the cannabis industry—it offered classes on legal issues and politics surrounding marijuana, horticulture, and "cannabusiness" among other topics (Thomas 2013a). On April 2, 2012, agents from the U.S. Marshals Service, the DEA, and the Internal Revenue Service raided Oaksterdam (and the apartment and other businesses of Richard Lee) and seized several pounds of marijuana and other property (Kuruvilla 2014).

In July 2012, federal government agencies continued these activities in a raid on Oakland's Harborside Health Center (founded by Steve D'Angelo in 2006), the largest medical marijuana dispensary in California, with more than 220,000 registered patients (D'Angelo 2015). Around the same time, the U.S. attorney for the Northern District of California, Melinda Haag, initiated civil forfeiture proceedings against Harborside, essentially, as *Mother Jones* reporter Josh Harkinson (2015) argues, because, with estimated annual sales of $25 million, Harborside had "grown too big." In defending the actions against Harborside, Haag stated, "I now find the need to consider actions regarding marijuana superstores such as Harborside. The larger the operation, the greater the likelihood that there will be abuse of the state's medical marijuana laws, and marijuana in the hands of individuals who do not have a demonstrated medical need" (quoted in D'Angelo 2015, 155). Importantly, while the forfeiture complaint noted that Harborside was in violation of federal marijuana laws, it did not claim that the dispensary was in violation of California's medical marijuana law (Thomas 2013b).

As noted previously, the city of Oakland was supportive of medical marijuana patients and businesses, and in October 2012 the city sued the federal government in an attempt to prevent the Department of Justice from seizing Harborside's property, arguing that closing the dispensary would harm medical marijuana patients and force them to obtain marijuana through illegal sources (Reilly 2016). While a federal judge dismissed the city of Oakland lawsuit in February 2013, the city appealed, and in July of the same year, another judge ruled that Harborside could remain open while the litigation continued. The suit against Harborside was eventually dismissed in May 2016, prompting Steve D'Angelo to (perhaps prematurely) claim that this signaled "the beginning of the end of federal [marijuana] prohibition" (quoted in Downs 2016b).

Former Seattle police chief Norm Stamper commented on the actions of the Justice Department and DEA in the cases discussed previously (as well as numerous other raids): "Although President Obama has talked about states' rights to enact medical marijuana laws, his DEA has raided state-legal medical marijuana providers at a higher rate than the Bush administration" (quoted in Friedersdorf 2011). Even more critically, Rob Kampia (2011), director of the MPP) referred to Obama as the "worst" president in history when it comes to medical marijuana.

The Obama Administration's Response to the Legalization of Recreational Marijuana

Following the legalization of recreational marijuana in Colorado and Washington State in 2012, in an interview with Barbara Walters, President Obama stated, "We've got bigger fish to fry. . . . It would not make sense for us to see a top priority as going after recreational users in states that have determined that it's legal" (quoted in Memmott 2012). In a later 2014 interview with David Remnick of the *New Yorker*, Obama emphasized the social and racial injustices associated with marijuana prohibition: "Middle class kids don't get locked up for smoking pot and poor kids do and African-American and Latino kids are more likely to be poor, and less likely to have the resources and support to avoid unduly harsh penalties. . . . We should not be locking up kids or individual users for long stretches of jail time when some of the folks who are writing these laws have probably done the same thing."

But several commentators have noted that Obama did little to further the cause of the liberalization of marijuana laws, and certain high-ranking officials within his administration apparently did not share his views on marijuana. For example, Attorney General Loretta Lynch was publicly opposed to marijuana legalization, and when asked to comment on Obama's remark that marijuana is not more dangerous than alcohol, Lynch replied, "Well, I certainly don't hold that view and don't agree with that view of marijuana as a substance" (quoted in Labak 2015).

Similarly, during a House Judiciary subcommittee hearing in 2012, Michelle Leonhart (who had served as director of the DEA during the George W. Bush administration and was reappointed to the position by Obama) refused to say whether marijuana was safer than crack (Arit 2015). She also criticized Obama's statement that marijuana was safer than alcohol and said (apparently referring to the legalization of recreational marijuana in Washington, D.C.) that the "lowest day of her 33 years in law enforcement was when a hemp flag flew over the nation's capital" (Arit 2015). In her confirmation hearings, Leonhart indicated that the DEA would continue to enforce federal drug laws in states that had legalized medical marijuana, and she oversaw the raids of several dispensaries during Obama's first term (Arit 2015).

After revelations that DEA agents in Colombia had engaged in sex parties with prostitutes (and also likely due to her disagreement with Obama regarding marijuana), Leonhart was eventually forced to resign as director of the DEA in May 2015 (Arit 2015; J. Davis 2015). After Leonhart's resignation, Chuck Rosenberg was appointed head of the DEA. Rosenberg once referred to medical marijuana as "a joke" (Ingraham 2016b) and, after initially stating that marijuana was "probably not" as dangerous as heroin, a week later conceded that "heroin is clearly more dangerous than marijuana" (quoted in Ferner 2016). But as Ethan Nadelmann commented with respect to Rosenberg's statement, "It's sort of remarkable that a DEA chief simply saying heroin is more dangerous than marijuana could actually make news" (quoted in Ferner 2016). The director of federal policies for the MPP, Dan Riffle, added, "In other news, the sky is blue" (quoted in Ferner 2016).

After Obama's first drug czar, Gil Kerlikowske, was appointed commissioner of U.S. Customs and Border Protection in March 2014, Michael Botticelli (who had struggled with his own addiction problems) became director of the ONDCP. Botticelli conceded that "I do think it's somewhat of a fair criticism that the government hasn't fully supported research to really investigate what's the potential therapeutic value [of marijuana]" (quoted in Wallace 2016b). However, in earlier comments at congressional hearings in February 2014, he demonstrated reluctance to distinguish between marijuana and harder drugs, commenting that "totality of harm" associated with marijuana indicated it was a dangerous drug, even though it was not associated with deaths (Sullum 2014). This prompted Oregon state representative Earl Blumenauer to suggest to Botticelli, "If a professional like you cannot answer that meth is more dangerous than marijuana, which every kid on the street knows, every parent knows, if you can't answer that, maybe that's why we're failing to educate people about the dangers. I don't want kids smoking marijuana . . . [but] how do you expect high school kids to take you seriously? You, sir, represent part of the problem" (quoted in Ellison 2015b).

In conclusion, we discuss two important marijuana policy developments at the federal level, which have proven to have lasting impacts on the federal government's approach to marijuana. In 2013, the Department of Justice issued the Cole memorandum (many provisions of which were similar to the Ogden memo) to provide further guidance regarding marijuana regulation. The memorandum begins by noting that "Congress has determined that marijuana is a dangerous drug and that illegal distribution and sale of marijuana is a serious crime that provides a significant source of revenue to large scale criminal enterprises, gangs, and cartels."

Eight "enforcement priorities" were listed in the Cole memorandum: (1) preventing the distribution of marijuana to minors; (2) preventing revenue from the sale of marijuana going to criminal enterprises, gangs, and cartels; (3) preventing the diversion of marijuana from states where it is legal under state law in some form to other states; (4) preventing state-authorized marijuana activity from being used as a cover or pretext for the trafficking of other illegal drugs or illegal activity; (5) preventing violence and the use of firearms in the cultivation and distribution of marijuana; (6) preventing drugged driving and the exacerbation of other adverse public health consequences associated with marijuana use; (7) preventing the growing of marijuana on public lands and attendant public safety and environmental dangers posed by marijuana production on public lands; and (8) preventing marijuana possession or use on federal property.

The Cole memorandum further specified that "the enforcement of state law by state and local law enforcement and regulatory bodies should remain the primary means of addressing marijuana-related activity" (Cole 2013). Further, and importantly, the memo allowed for considerable law enforcement and prosecutorial autonomy and discretion in enforcing mari-juana legislation, stating that the memorandum was "solely a guide. . . . Nothing herein precludes investigation or prosecution, even in the absence of any one of the factors listed above, in particular circumstances where investigators and prosecution otherwise serves an important federal inter-est." Further clarifying this point, in testimony before the Senate Judiciary Committee, Deputy Attorney General James Cole indicated that the federal government would focus on interstate trafficking in marijuana: "We are not giving immunity. We are not giving a free pass. We are not abdicating our responsibility" (quoted in Bewley-Taylor, Blickman, and Jelsma 2014, 54).

An additional important development with respect to marijuana regula-tion during the Obama administration was passage in the House of Repre-sentatives (by a vote of 219–189) of the Rohrabacher-Farr amendment to a government spending bill in 2014. Under this legislation, the Department of Justice was prohibited from using federal funds to "prevent states from im-plementing their own state laws that authorize the use, possession, or culti-vation of medical marijuana" (Ingraham 2015b). The amendment was inter-preted by advocates and legislators on both sides of the issue as preventing the DEA from raiding and attempting to shut down medical marijuana dis-pensaries that were acting in compliance with laws in their state. However, a leaked Justice Department memo indicated a different interpretation—it claimed that the amendment prevented taking enforcement actions only against actual states but not against individuals or businesses involved in the medical marijuana industry (Ingraham 2015b). Justice Department officials told federal prosecutors that despite the congressional ban on federal inter-ference with state medical marijuana laws, criminal charges could still be filed against medical marijuana users and providers. Patty Merkamp Stem-pler, head of the Department of Justice's appellate section, informed the prosecutors that the Rohrabacher-Farr amendment "addresses actions di-rected against states, not individuals" (quoted in Egelko 2015).

In supporting the reauthorization of the Rohrabacher-Farr amendment in 2015, cosponsor Representative Sam Farr (Democrat, California) stated, "With a clear voice we have once again said to the Department of Justice: Stop wasting our tax dollars and attacking patients. Let's spend those funds more wisely going after real criminals, and not sick people" (quoted in Baca 2015c). Dana Rohrabacher (2016) issued a press release on his website, stat-ing, "If the protection afforded by our amendment were to expire, it would amount to an unconscionable infliction of punishment, by their own gov-ernment, on these unfortunate Americans—many of whom would turn down the vicious path of opioid addiction as an alternative." Representative Jared Polis (Democrat, Colorado) added, "The federal government should not be swooping into Colorado to decide how to regulate marijuana any more than they should be swooping into Louisiana to tell them how they should regulate crawfish" (quoted in Baca 2015c).

As we discuss in further detail in Chapter 7, in January 2018, Attorney General Jeff Sessions rescinded the Cole memorandum (Zapotosky, Horwitz, and Achenbach 2018), which may lead to federal intervention in states that have legalized recreational marijuana.

3

Marijuana

The Plant and Its Acute and Chronic Effects,
Addictive Potential, and Medicinal Applications

> As a scientist and educator, I am worried that our illogical,
> unscientific scheduling of marijuana is costing us credibility
> with young people and with those seeking treatments for a
> variety of conditions. . . . It's time we lessened the outsized
> influence of a law-enforcement agency on medical decisions
> and started to rebuild our credibility as scientists on the issue
> of marijuana.
> —CARL HART, "The DEA's Decision to Keep Pot Restrictions
>   Perpetuates Hypocrisy"

In addressing ongoing debates about marijuana, this chapter discusses issues that are directly relevant to marijuana's classification as a Schedule I drug. Recall that under the Controlled Substances Act, a Schedule I drug is one that "has a high potential for abuse, has no medical use in the United States, and has a lack of accepted safety for use under medical supervision" (Drug Enforcement Administration 2005). Marijuana shares its Schedule I status with drugs such as heroin and LSD, while drugs such as methamphetamine and cocaine are classified in the less restrictive Schedule II. Given these justifications for a drug's scheduling, we discuss the scientific evidence with respect to marijuana's relative harms and benefits across a variety of domains: its acute (including psychoactive) and chronic effects, its addictive potential, and its medicinal uses. We also address the emerging scientific evidence suggesting that marijuana can serve as a substitute for more harmful drugs (in particular, opioids). In addition, because several opponents of marijuana law reform have claimed its use leads consumers to progress to the use of harder, more dangerous drugs, we also address the timeworn and stubbornly enduring gateway drug theory.

In considering the results of studies reported here, it is important to stress that there is a great deal that we do not know about marijuana, especially with respect to its long-term effects. Most studies rely on the self-reporting of marijuana use by subjects—in many cases requiring subjects to recall their use of the drug many years prior to the question being asked rather than using more objective measures; it is therefore difficult to measure how much and how often they consumed the drug and how it was administered. Studies also vary widely concerning the ability to control for confounding factors in explaining marijuana's effects. A final, and arguably the most significant, problem regarding research on marijuana is the complex process that researchers must navigate to conduct their studies as a result of marijuana's Schedule I classification, which limits both the number of studies and quality of research on the substance.

In assessing marijuana's classification, this chapter, which by necessity is somewhat technical, draws extensively on a recent report by the National Academies of Science, Engineering, and Medicine (NASEM) (2017), *The Health Effects of Cannabis and Cannabinoids: The Current State of Evidence and Recommendations for Research*. This report reviewed approximately ten thousand scientific studies on marijuana; while concluding that cannabis had public health risks, it also documented several medicinal uses of the substance and noted that its Schedule I classification impedes research on both the benefits and relative risks/harms of marijuana. We also review the scientific research on the harms and risks associated with marijuana in comparison to those of other psychoactive substances, both legal (i.e., alcohol, tobacco, prescription opioids) and illegal (i.e., heroin, cocaine, methamphetamine). Considered in totality, the scientific evidence simply does not justify marijuana's placement in Schedule I of the Controlled Substances Act; in fact, many argue that it should be completely removed from the act (Drug Policy Alliance 2013). We begin by reviewing some basic but important information regarding the cannabis plant and its constituent chemicals.

Cannabis: The Plant and the Chemicals

The terms "marijuana" and "cannabis" are used interchangeably and refer to a preparation of the materials of cannabis plants for various means of consumption. Although smoking is the most common route of administration, or method by which the drug is taken into the body, marijuana can also be eaten or drunk in various foods and beverages, vaporized, and taken topically via balms, lotions, and oils. Marijuana is a psychoactive drug, meaning it has properties that act on the central nervous system and affect perception and cognition.

The primary psychoactive ingredient in marijuana is delta 9-tetrahydrocannabinol (THC), which is concentrated in the resin of cannabis plants. Because the resin (and thus THC) concentration is highest in the flowering tops of buds of the plant, this part of the plant has the strongest psychoactive effect and is most commonly sought after by recreational users seeking intoxication (National Academies of Science, Engineering, and Medicine [NASEM] 2017). Although an extensive discussion of the chemical constituents of marijuana is outside the scope of this book, some coverage of this issue is necessary to understand the hundreds of strains of marijuana and their consequent effects. We offer a brief and simplified discussion of this later.

Cannabinoids are chemicals unique to the cannabis plant. How many cannabinoids exist remains debated, but the number is at least sixty, and recent research puts it at more than one hundred (NASEM 2017). THC is the most well-known cannabinoid, and its content is highest in the *Cannabis sativa* subspecies, so these are the plants most commonly cultivated by recreational growers and commercial producers providing marijuana for intoxication purposes (Atakan 2012). Cannabidiol (CBD) is the cannabinoid most well known for its therapeutic/medicinal effects, and CBD content is generally higher in the *Cannabis indica* subspecies (NASEM 2017). The relative balance of THC and CBD (and, to a lesser extent, other cannabinoids) in the particular strain of marijuana is essential to understanding both its medicinal and psychoactive effects, as these two cannabinoids have similar effects in some ways but opposite (or nearly opposite) effects in other ways (see Atakan 2012 for a review). For example, CBD is considered nonpsychoactive and can actually counter the psychoactive effects of THC (Lee 2012). The various strains of cannabis are typically categorized into three broad phenotypes, although not a perfect classification: THC type, or "drug-type" with high THC and low CBD; CBD type with the inverse ratio of THC to CBD content; and a hybrid type with more moderate levels of each cannabinoid (Galal et al. 2009; NASEM 2017).

Consequently, in our discussion of the effects of marijuana, we focus primarily on the THC type, typically sought by recreational users attempting to achieve intoxication. Later, in our discussion of medical effects, we include other cannabis types—the CBD and lower-THC hybrid types. In the medical context, the type of marijuana can vary, as particular medical conditions may respond better or worse to various strains of marijuana with different ratios of THC to CBD.

The Psychoactive Effects of Marijuana

The psychoactive effects of all drugs can vary significantly from person to person, the setting in which the drug is consumed, and many other factors not related to the chemical properties of the substance itself (Pollan 2001). In the case of marijuana the effects (and especially the negative side effects that sometimes result from recreational use) may vary by route of administration and the potency (level of THC) in the marijuana product consumed. With respect to the subjectivity of the psychoactive experience, much research has shown that there is a learned component to psychoactive drug use. Drugs do not create uniform experiences, and novice users must learn to interpret the effects of drugs, recognize these effects as characteristics of "being high," and (typically) interpret these effects as pleasurable for drug use to continue (Becker 1963). As Howard Becker comments:

> Marihuana-produced sensations are not automatically or necessarily pleasurable. The taste for such an experience is a socially acquired one, not different from acquired tastes for oysters or martinis. The user feels dizzy, thirsty; his scalp tingles; he misjudges time and distances. Are these things pleasurable? He isn't sure. If he is to continue marijuana use, he must decide that they are. (1963, 53)

The usual effects of marijuana when consumed recreationally include mild euphoria, increased sociability (talkativeness, laughter), altered perceptions of time and distance, and heightened responses to certain stimuli, such as music. Many users report feelings of relaxation "or experiencing a pleasurable 'rush' or 'buzz' after smoking cannabis" (NASEM 2017, 53), with a period of tranquility following this initial period. Short-term memory is often adversely affected, as is reaction time and psychomotor performance (an important effect that may impair an individual's ability to operate a motor vehicle). Users may also experience a moderate increase in heart rate, a reddening of the eyes, and dryness in the mouth and eyes. Paranoia, anxiety, and panic attacks may also be experienced by *some* users, particularly when very high blood levels of THC are reached (NASEM 2017). Hallucinations are also possible, but these have been reported only at very high levels of THC intoxication (Earleywine 2002; NASEM 2017), and they are more likely to arise as a consequence of consumption of edible and other high-potency cannabis products rather than smoking (Grotenhermen 2007).

Marijuana Assessed across Indicators of Drug-Related Harm

All drugs, regardless of their legal status, have potentially beneficial and potentially harmful effects. Some drugs are clearly riskier than others, but the harms associated with drug use are much more related to patterns of use (i.e., larger doses, highly repetitive dosing, certain routes of administration) than to the particular type of drug per se. The risks posed by psychoactive drugs are typically assessed across six domains of potential harm—behavioral toxicity, acute toxicity, chronic toxicity, tolerance potential, physical dependence potential, and reinforcement potential (the last three comprise different domains of the addictive liability of a drug).

Behavioral Toxicity of Marijuana

The first domain of potential drug harm, behavioral toxicity, is the most subjective of the six. Due to their psychoactive effects, all drugs have the potential to cause harm in society, as drug users may harm people, either intentionally or accidentally, while under the influence (Hart and Ksir 2015). Behavioral toxicity is more subjective in terms of its assessment than the other domains of harm because many factors other than the pharmaceutical properties of the drug can and do influence drug-related harm. These additional factors include the context and setting of drug use; biological, psychological, and social variables related to the user; the potency and quantity of the drug that is taken; and the manner (route of administration) in which it is taken. Behavioral toxicity is usually assessed by considering the common result of a "typical" dose in a recreational context and the associated risk to the individual and society. In terms of behavioral toxicity, marijuana is quite mild compared to other psychoactive drugs, in part because marijuana is typically not aggression inducing, particularly when contrasted with alcohol, which is involved in a large percentage of violent crimes perpetrated each year (Bureau of Justice Statistics 2010). In fact, much research has found marijuana to reduce the likelihood of violence (Hoaken and Stewart 2003), findings that have been replicated in state-level analysis of those states that recently legalized medicinal and/or recreational marijuana. A 2016 CATO Institute report, *Dose of Reality: The Effect of State Marijuana Legalizations* (Dills, Goffard, and Miron 2016), included an analysis of crime data from major cities in states that had legalized marijuana. The report concluded that legalization had no discernible effect on the violent or property crime rates in states that had legalized.

Acute Toxicity of Marijuana

The second indicator of drug-related harm, acute toxicity, addresses adverse health effects that arise almost immediately after ingestion of a drug, such as fatal overdose or a psychotic reaction (Hart and Ksir 2015). In terms of acute toxicity, the risks of marijuana are mild compared to those of most recreationally used psychoactive drugs. The most serious consequence of drug use—fatal overdose—is for all intents and purposes impossible through marijuana use. There has never been a fatal overdose attributed to the use of marijuana (however, opioids were involved in 33,091 fatal overdoses in 2015) (Centers for Disease Control 2017a), and even the DEA, in a 2017 report, has acknowledged that "no deaths from overdose of marijuana have been reported."

In laboratory settings the risk of fatal overdose is assessed via a drug's therapeutic ratio, which is the ratio of the amount of the substance needed to generate a therapeutically useful effect (e.g., pain relief, appetite stimulation) relative to the amount of the drug necessary to cause death in half of the laboratory animals studied. Drugs that depress the central nervous system, meaning those that affect respiration (e.g., alcohol, sedatives, and narcotic drugs such as OxyContin and heroin) are the most dangerous in this regard and can cause death at therapeutic ratios of five to one to ten to one, or at least five to ten times the level taken to achieve a therapeutic effect. Conversely, the therapeutic ratio of marijuana is estimated to be *forty thousand to one* (Gahlinger 2001). Thus, for a fatal overdose from marijuana to occur, a 160-pound person would require all the THC in approximately 900 one-gram joints consumed in a relatively short period of time (Earleywine 2002).

While fatal overdose is therefore not a risk posed by marijuana, negative consequences associated with marijuana "overdose" (consuming a greater amount of the substance than intended) are found in some users. Anxiety and panic attacks, especially among novice users, often accompany marijuana overdose and are the most common cause for a visit to a hospital emergency room following marijuana use (Hesse 2016c). Episodes of marijuana-induced psychosis that mimic more complex long-term schizophrenic disorders have been identified following marijuana overdose, but these episodes nearly always resolve after blood THC levels subside (Grotenhermen 2007). Finally, some research suggests that, although it is extremely rare, marijuana use may be linked to schizophrenia/chronic psychosis (NASEM 2017). As this is a chronic rather than an acute/temporary condition, it is discussed in the context of chronic toxicity.

Chronic Toxicity of Marijuana

The third indicator of drug-related harm, chronic toxicity, addresses the adverse health effects associated with long-term use of a particular drug (Hart and Ksir 2015). Marijuana use does pose a number of risks in terms of chronic toxicity. However, it is useful initially to place the relative risk of marijuana in perspective by comparing its chronic toxicity to that of other commonly used drugs. In comparison to the most commonly used recreational drug, alcohol, the chronic health effects of marijuana are extremely mild. Alcohol is one of the most harmful drugs, legal or illegal, both in terms of acute and chronic toxicity. An average of six people a day die of alcohol poisoning in the United States (Centers for Disease Control 2015). Alcohol is associated with several diseases and causes of mortality, including numerous forms of cancer, heart diseases, high blood pressure and stroke, and cirrhosis of the liver and other liver diseases, as well as dementia and multiple mental health problems. Annually, this results in an estimated eighty-eight thousand premature deaths and 2.5 million years of life prematurely lost in the United States (Centers for Disease Control 2016). Even more problematic in terms of chronic toxicity is the use of tobacco, which in the United States is the leading cause of preventable death. It is the cause of approximately one in every five deaths, resulting in an estimated 480,000 premature deaths annually, mostly as a result of cancer, heart disease, and chronic obstructive pulmonary disease (Centers for Disease Control 2017b). Globally, tobacco use is related to more than one in every ten deaths, killing an estimated six million people annually, with a premature loss of more than 150 million years of potential life (Britton 2017).

Although the chronic toxicity of marijuana is low when compared to that of alcohol and tobacco, there is evidence of a connection between marijuana and a number of chronic diseases. Despite these disease-specific connections, the association between marijuana use and early death from all causes continues to be debated, with various reports and systematic reviews finding either no association (Calabria et al. 2010) or some association (Degenhardt et al. 2013; Imtiaz et al. 2016). With respect to this issue, the NASEM report concluded that there was "insufficient evidence to support or refute a statistical association between self-reported cannabis use and all-cause mortality" (2017, 218).

In terms of specific chronic diseases, the ONDCP has cited research by University of California, Los Angeles School of Medicine professor Dr. Donald Tashkin in claims on its website and in advertisements that marijuana use causes lung cancer. While Tashkin had previously warned that this relationship exists, in two more recent studies, he concluded that there was no evidence of a causal relationship between long-term marijuana use and lung cancer. In a study presented at a meeting of the American Thoracic Society in 2006, Tashkin and his colleagues interviewed 611 lung cancer patients, 601 patients with cancer in the head or neck region, and 1,040 healthy controls (all subjects were under the age of sixty). The researchers found that 80 percent of those with lung cancer and 70 percent of those with other cancers had smoked tobacco, and approximately half of the subjects in both groups had consumed marijuana. However, after statistically controlling for a number of other variables (most important, tobacco, alcohol, and other drug use), Tashkin and his colleagues found that there was no relationship between marijuana use and cancer (Biello 2006). In discussing the results of this study, Tashkin told a *Washington Post* reporter that the findings were "against our expectations. We hypothesized that there would be a relationship between marijuana use and lung cancer, and that the association would be more positive with heavier use. What we found instead was no association at all, and even a suggestion of a protective effect" (quoted in Kaufman 2006). In a publication focused on the same issue, Tashkin further noted that "habitual use of marijuana alone does not appear to lead to significant abnormalities in lung function when assessed either cross-sectionally or longitudinally.... In summary, the accumulated weight of evidence implies far lower risks for pulmonary complications of even regular heavy use of marijuana compared with the grave pulmonary consequences of tobacco" (2013, 239).

A more recent study by a group of researchers at Toronto's Mount Sinai hospital, led by Li Rita Zhang, examined the marijuana smoking habits of 2,159 individuals with confirmed lung cancer and 2,895 healthy controls. When the tobacco use of the subjects was statistically controlled for, the researchers found "little evidence of an increased risk for lung cancer, among habitual or long-term cannabis smokers, although the possibility of potential adverse effects for heavy consumption cannot be excluded" (Zhang et al. 2015, 894).

In summing up the research on the relationship between marijuana use and lung cancer, it is safe to conclude that most studies have not found that smoking marijuana causes lung cancer (Casarett 2015; NASEM 2017). Tashkin believes this is largely due to the anti-inflammatory properties of THC and CBD and asserts, "The bottom line is that there isn't really any good evidence of an increased risk of cancer and the pulmonary risks can be dialed down pretty close to zero with the use of [cannabis] vaporizers" (quoted in Casarett 2015, 176). The lack of a relationship between marijuana consumption and lung cancer could also be related to the fact that the typical marijuana smoker does not ingest as much smoke and related chemicals as the typical tobacco smoker does.

However, there is some evidence that smoking marijuana can increase the risk of chronic pulmonary disorder, even when controlling for possible tobacco use by individuals. The 2017 NASEM report also found smoking marijuana to be associated with a worsening of other respiratory symptoms (although not asthma) and frequent bronchitis, although these conditions were found to generally disappear with the cessation of cannabis smoking. The report also found insufficient evidence to connect (or to refute a connection of) marijuana use to a number of other cancers.

Heart and Stroke Risk
A 2017 study found that marijuana use increased the risk of stroke by 26 percent and heart failure by 10 percent (American College of Cardiology 2017; Bennett and Woodward 2017). The study, conducted by cardiologist Aditi Kalla and colleagues, examined more than twenty million records of patients ages eighteen to fifty-five who were discharged from hospitals in 2009 and 2010 and found that individuals who used marijuana had a higher risk of stroke, coronary artery disease, and sudden cardiac death. However, the risk of developing these conditions was very small, and the lead author of the study suggested the findings should not preclude marijuana from being legalized or prescribed (Bennett and Woodward 2017).

However, the findings of the Kalla study are in direct contrast to two other recent studies examining the same issue. The first, published in February 2017 in the *American Journal of Public Health*, which followed over five thousand subjects for more than twenty-five years found no association between marijuana consumption and cardiovascular disease: "Compared with no marijuana use, cumulative lifetime and recent marijuana use showed no association with incident CVD (cardiovascular disease), stroke, or ischemic attacks, coronary heart disease, or CVD mortality" (Reis et al. 2017). Another longitudinal study from Sweden that followed 49,231 Swedish males born between 1949 and 1951 until they were sixty years of age found "no evident association between cannabis use in young adulthood and stroke, including strokes before 45 years of age. Tobacco smoking, however, showed a clear, dose-response association with stroke" (Falkstedt et al. 2017).

Schizophrenia/Psychosis

> Attempts to prove that marijuana will make you crazy have a long and undignified history in the debate over legalization. You seem crazy when you smoke marijuana, anti-potters decided, so it must make you crazy in a clinical way, such as (most notably and scariest) schizophrenia.
> —JAKE ELLISON, "Study"

Arguably the strongest evidence for a serious, chronic condition linked to the use of marijuana is for schizophrenia and chronic psychosis. However, this research is exceedingly complex, with multiple potential causal paths, each of which may have some validity. These causal ordering complexities are characteristic of the larger field of research on the association between mental illness broadly defined and many different forms of drug use (including alcohol). The complexity of these issues should be apparent, because one of the reasons people take marijuana and other psychoactive drugs is to produce a change in their mental state, and these changes "are a bit akin to being psychotic—they include distortions of perception . . . as well as the way one thinks" (Nutt 2009, 4). When these changes to the mental state remain after the effects of the drug have worn off (which is very rare), researchers are tasked with determining if the lasting changes in mental state would have emerged regardless of the drug use, which presents considerable challenges.

The condition of overlapping mental health and substance abuse disorders also affects significant numbers of people, with recent data indicating almost eight million American adults have such "co-occurring" disorders (Substance Abuse and Mental Health Services Administration 2015). As summarized in the 2017 NASEM report, the primary hypothesized explanations for the high co-occurrence of substance abuse and a serious mental illness (which also apply to the relationship between marijuana use and schizophrenia) include the following:

1. Substance use may be a potential risk factor for developing mental health disorders. Given the overlap in associated neurochemical substances (dopamine, serotonin), specific neurobiological altera-

tions due to drug use may have resulting effects on the neural processes regulating mental health.

2. Mental illness may be a potential risk factor for developing a substance abuse disorder. Research suggests that individuals who are at risk for a mental health disorder, or those who experience subclinical symptoms, may be more likely than others to use drugs as a form of self-medication.

3. An overlap in predisposing factors (e.g., genetic vulnerability, environment) may contribute to the development of both substance abuse and a mental health disorder. Several studies suggest that the development of mental health disorders and substance abuse disorders may be a symptomatic outcome of preexisting neurobiological abnormalities.

With these caveats and causal ordering issues made clear, people who smoke marijuana are significantly more likely than people who do not smoke marijuana to have schizophrenia (McLoughin et al. 2014), as well as other serious mental illnesses (NASEM 2017). Some estimates have put the risk of experiencing a psychotic-like episode at 2.6 times greater for individuals who smoke marijuana than for those who do not (Nutt 2009). Generally, psychotic symptoms (including schizophrenia or schizophrenia-like conditions) induced by cannabis intoxication last only for the duration of the intoxication (and thus would be considered an acute rather than chronic effect) but in some cases have been found to persist for days (Barrus et al. 2016; Hudak, Severn, and Nordstrom 2015) or to persist as a long-lasting condition. These adverse outcomes appear to be most common among heavy marijuana users and those who use high-THC products such as concentrates and edibles. The NASEM report concluded that there is "substantial evidence of a statistical association between cannabis use and the development of schizophrenia or other psychoses" (2017, 295).

As alluded to earlier, and as is the case in other domains, the issue of causality is important to consider in discussing the relationship between marijuana use and schizophrenia. A 2014 study by Robert Power and colleagues based on a sample of 2,082 individuals, while noting the link between marijuana use and schizophrenia, cautioned that it was not clear whether the observed relationship was due to cannabis directly increasing the risk of psychosis or whether the same genes that increase the risk of psychosis may also increase the risk of marijuana use. Power and colleagues concluded that "[our] findings suggest that part of the association between schizophrenia and cannabis use is due to shared genetic aetiology."

Also with respect to the relationship between marijuana use and schizophrenia, the NASEM report conceded that it did not consider ecological data in assessing the relationship. Basic trend data indicate that as the rates of marijuana use were rapidly increasing through the 1970s and 1980s in many countries, including the United States and Great Britain, rates of schizophrenia remained relatively stable. For example, a retrospective analysis of Great Britain's General (medical) Practice Research Database, covering the 1996 to 2005 period (a period of substantial increases in marijuana use in Great Britain), found that the incidence and prevalence of schizophrenia and psychoses were either stable or declining over this period (Frisher et al. 2009; see also Nutt 2009). There are societies that have been introduced to marijuana over the last fifty years but in which the incidence of schizophrenia has remained stable (Kirkbride et al. 2012; NASEM 2017).

When assessing the possible relationship between marijuana use and schizophrenia, it is also important to consider that the measurement/diagnosis of schizophrenia and related psychotic conditions may have changed over time and that schizophrenia is quite rare, affecting approximately 1 percent of the population (Hickman et al. 2009; Szalavitz 2010). Thus, to measure the purported connection between marijuana use and schizophrenia, large-scale data, including valid measurements of drug use and mental illness, are needed. One such study examining the British population concluded that to prevent a single case of schizophrenia, it would be necessary to stop twenty-eight hundred heavy cannabis users among young men and more than five thousand heavy cannabis users among young women. Among light cannabis users, the authors concluded that it would be necessary to stop more than ten thousand young men and almost thirty thousand young women to prevent one case of schizophrenia (Hickman et al. 2009).

To conclude, based on the available research on the topic, it appears that a relationship between marijuana use and schizophrenia may in fact exist, but it is a very weak relationship and may follow one of several causal paths, each of which may have some validity. For example, marijuana use may (1) cause schizophrenia in non-predisposed individuals; (2) trigger schizophrenia but only among those who are already genetically predisposed to the disease; (3) exacerbate the symptoms of schizophrenia in those who have the disease; (4) be more common among those with schizophrenia, as patients believe that marijuana may be useful in relieving symptoms associated with schizophrenia, consistent with the self-medication hypothesis; or (5) be caused by some preexisting factors that also caused both the marijuana use and the individuals' schizophrenia/mental illness (Bostwick 2012; NASEM 2017).

Addiction (Tolerance, Dependence, and Craving)

A major concern with psychoactive drug use is dependence, more commonly referred to as addiction. In simple terms, addiction refers to an individual's inability to stop a behavior when that behavior is causing problems

(Weil and Rosen 1998). Although almost any behavior can be rewarding and thus potentially addictive (gambling, sex, video games, eating, and even tanning can all be addicting, and none involve the ingestion of a drug) (see Mosher and Akins 2014), drugs are particularly risky with respect to the development of dependence. Marijuana use certainly qualifies as a rewarding behavior, but compared to that of most commonly used psychoactive drugs its addictive liability is fairly modest.

Addiction is a complex process that can take several forms. Psychoactive substances typically induce pleasant feelings, and over time the body and mind adjust to these feelings, often causing people to seek out the drug (or behavior) and its associated sensations (Cami and Farre 2003). Although the language used to describe the processes linked to addiction varies somewhat across scientific discipline, and is evolving with the collective understanding of addiction, three essential terms in addiction science are "physical dependence," "psychological dependence" (or craving), and "tolerance." Some drugs have much greater addictive liability than others primarily because of how they are characterized across physical dependence potential, psychological dependence potential, and tolerance potential. Physical (or physiological) dependence refers to the potential of a drug to generate a withdrawal syndrome, which is a predictable set of symptoms that emerge when drug use is discontinued after a significant period of time. Typically, the symptoms and feelings associated with withdrawal are the opposite of those that characterize the use of the drug (Nutt 2012).

Some withdrawal symptoms, such as those associated with depressant drugs (e.g., alcohol, certain sedatives) and opiates (e.g., heroin, OxyContin) are quite dramatic, resembling a severe case of the flu (or worse, death is possible as a consequence of withdrawal from severe alcoholism) (Gahlinger 2001). Other types of drugs have withdrawal symptoms that are more muted, with agitation, sleeplessness, and symptoms resembling those of mental illness such as depression (this form of withdrawal is more typical of certain stimulant drugs, such as cocaine). Typically, drugs that do not produce some form of measurable physical withdrawal syndrome are not regarded as addictive.

Although at one time marijuana was not considered to be physically addictive, some argue that it may be characterized by mild physical dependence. The symptoms characterizing withdrawal for marijuana users (not surprisingly, these are far more likely to be experienced by heavy marijuana smokers who attempt to quit cold turkey) include decreased appetite, insomnia, and mood changes (Nutt 2012).

Physical dependence on drugs arises in part because users develop tolerance to some forms of drugs. There are many forms of tolerance, but most basically tolerance occurs when repeatedly doing something changes the way a person reacts to it (Nutt 2012). With most forms of tolerance the body adapts to repeated drug use so that the same dose of a drug produces less of the desired effect, often prompting users to take greater amounts or higher doses of the substance. Some drugs generate extreme levels of tolerance—for instance, heroin users may be routinely taking an amount that would kill them as a novice user, and "alcoholics consume several times the volume of alcohol that would put non-alcoholics in a coma" (Nutt 2012, 140).

The tolerance potential of marijuana compared to that of other drugs is not severe, but it does occur. A recent experimental study on this issue documented that with chronic, moderate cannabis use, the availability of cannabinoid receptor 1 (the receptor that is triggered in the brain by THC, inducing the psychoactive effects of marijuana) decreases in most brain regions (D'Souza et al. 2016). However, this pattern begins to reverse itself after two days of abstinence from marijuana, and after four weeks the levels of the receptor are almost back to normal (meaning tolerance has been almost completely eliminated) (D'Souza et al. 2016).

Drugs may also result in "psychological dependence," a term that is sometimes used interchangeably with "craving." Behavioral psychologists have pointed out that repetitive and positively reinforced behaviors such as drug use are often accompanied by a desire (or craving) to be reexperienced (Cami and Farre 2003). But anything that is positively reinforced may generate craving; thus, non-drug behaviors like gambling, sex, and eating may also trigger craving and, through this, addiction to the behavior in question. Psychological dependence is typically determined according to the criteria set forth in the *Diagnostic and Statistical Manual of Mental Disorders* (currently DSM-V-TR), published by the American Psychiatric Association (2013). There is no question that psychological dependence can be extremely powerful; it is believed to be the primary cause of relapse—a resumption of drug use after a significant period of abstinence (Cami and Farre 2003). However, it should be noted that although the DSM dependence standards are widely applied, experts debate their utility, and the standards have also been criticized as "medicalizing" everyday behavior and broadening clinical criteria to the point that it becomes meaningless (Urbina 2012).

Marijuana use is a reinforcing behavior, and the DSM-V-TR recognizes "cannabis use disorder" (CUD), but the potential for psychological dependence on marijuana is again far less than that of alcohol, the opiates, or powerful stimulants (Gahlinger 2001). It is estimated that the lifetime risk of developing dependence among those who have ever used cannabis is 9 percent but 32 percent for nicotine, 23 percent for heroin, 17 percent for alcohol, and 11 percent for stimulants (Hall 2015). In short, with respect to its addictive potential, marijuana is simply not as dangerous as other psychoactive substances such as alcohol, tobacco, opiate drugs, and stimulants.

In assessing the relative harms of marijuana compared with those of other psychoactive substances, it is worth considering the results of a study coauthored by David Nutt, British psychiatrist and former chair of the British Advisory Committee on the Misuse of Drugs, that was published in the British medical journal the *Lancet*. David Nutt and colleagues asked drug experts to rank twenty commonly used drugs on sixteen measures of harm. Drugs were ranked with respect to the damage caused to the users' health; their addictive/dependency potential; and their effects on families, communities, and society in general (including economic costs and their relationship to crime). Under this ranking, alcohol was deemed by far to be the most harmful drug, followed by heroin, crack cocaine, methamphetamine, cocaine, tobacco, and amphetamines—cannabis was ranked eighth on the list, with a significantly lower total harm score than that of other substances (Nutt et al. 2007). Although referring to scheduling under the British Misuse of Drugs Act (not the U.S. Controlled Substances Act), Nutt and colleagues conclude, "Overall, there was a surprisingly poor correlation between drugs' class according to the Misuse of Drugs Act and harm score" (2007, 1050).

Marijuana as a Gateway Drug

The gateway drug theory can be summarized as an ounce of truth and a pound of bull. Yes, most people who use heroin and cocaine used marijuana . . . first. But the vast majority of people who use marijuana never progress to using other illicit drugs, or even to becoming regular marijuana consumers.

—Ethan Nadelmann, "Fears of Marijuana's Gateway Effect
Vastly Exceed the Evidence"

As Chapter 2 notes, the contention that marijuana is a gateway (or stepping-stone) drug first gained prominence in the 1950s. While this theory has been widely rejected, including by virtually all of the various government reports on marijuana and by most scientific research on the issue, it is still an enduring theme emphasized by marijuana prohibitionists/demonizers. The gateway theory/hypothesis asserts that the use of a substance (and interestingly, it is almost always marijuana—not other "entry-level" substances, such as tobacco and alcohol; Nadelmann 2016) will cause its users to go on to the use of harder drugs such as cocaine, heroin, or methamphetamine.

There are numerous examples of the invocation of the gateway drug hypothesis to justify marijuana prohibition. For example, at a hearing of the Senate drug caucus in April 2016, implicitly referencing the gateway drug theory, Senator Chuck Grassley (Republican, Iowa) claimed that the lax enforcement of existing marijuana laws was a major cause of the prescription opioid and heroin epidemics in the United States: "Our country is in the middle of an epidemic of addiction focused on heroin and prescription opioids . . . and just last year the Centers for Disease Control found that people who are addicted to marijuana are three times more likely to be addicted to heroin" (quoted in Ingraham 2016k).

Similarly, Robert DuPont, the first director of NIDA and currently the president of the Institute for Behavioral Health, wrote an editorial in 2016 in the *New York Times* supporting the gateway drug theory: "There is ample evidence that early initiation of drug use primes the brain for enhanced later responses to other drugs. Like nearly all people with substance abuse problems, most heroin users initiated their drug use in their early teens." While conceding that "this does not mean that everyone who uses marijuana will transition to heroin and other drugs," DuPont further asserted, "People who use marijuana also consume more, not less, legal and illegal drugs than people who do not use marijuana." Apparently not recognizing that prescription drugs are legal (and ignoring the much greater devastation associated with these substances), DuPont concluded, "We are at a crossroads. Legalizing marijuana will have lasting effects on future generations. Establishing marijuana as a third [presumably in addition to tobacco and alcohol] legal drug will increase the national drug abuse problem, including expanding the opioid epidemic." This statement of course ignores the evidence (discussed later) that marijuana may be a substitute for opiates and other drugs.

In examining the empirical support (or lack thereof) for the gateway drug theory, it is initially important to examine its theoretical logic. As Denise Kandel (2003) notes, the gateway theory is based on three interrelated principles. First, the notion of "sequencing" implies that there is a fixed relationship between two drugs, such that the use of one substance is initiated before the other. Second, "association" implies that the initiation of the use of one drug increases the likelihood that use of the second substance will be initiated. Finally, the notion of "causation" suggests that the use of one substance actually *causes* use of the second drug.

A 1994 report by the Center on Addiction and Substance Abuse was one of the first to provide statistical evidence in support of the gateway drug theory (cited in Zimmer and Morgan 1997). This report alleged that marijuana users were eighty-five times more likely than non–marijuana users to have used cocaine, with the figure being derived from respondents' reports of lifetime use of marijuana and cocaine in the 1991 National Household Survey on Drug Abuse. However, in an interesting use of statistics, to obtain the figure of eighty-five, the study divided the proportion of marijuana users who had *ever* tried cocaine (17 percent) by the percentage of cocaine users who had *never* tried marijuana (0.02 percent). In other words, the risk factor is large not because a large proportion of marijuana users tried cocaine but because very few people try cocaine without trying marijuana first. In their critique of this report, Lynn Zimmer and John Morgan (1997) note that a similar relationship exists between other kinds of common and uncommon activities/behaviors that tend to be related to one another. For example, most people who ride motorcycles, which is a relatively rare activity, have also ridden a bicycle, which is of course a fairly common activity. It is also likely that motorcycle riding among those who have never ridden a bicycle is quite rare. Thus, we (hopefully) would not suggest that bicycle riding caused motorcycle riding. In addition, just as the majority of people who ride bicycles do not become future motorcycle riders, the majority of marijuana users do not proceed to cocaine (or other hard-drug) use.

While it is important to question the logic of the gateway drug theory, it is equally important to examine empirical research on the issue. A longitudinal study of 311 monozygotic (identical) twins in Australia found that individuals who had used cannabis by the age of eighteen had odds of other illegal drug use and/or clinical diagnoses of alcohol dependence and drug abuse that were 2.1 to 5.2 times higher than those of their identical twin who did not use marijuana before the age of eighteen (Lynskey et al. 2003). While on the surface this study would appear to provide support for the gateway theory, the authors themselves did not conclude that they had provided incontrovertible truth. Michael Lynskey and colleagues suggested that if the association between early use of marijuana and the use of other illegal drugs is causal, the particular mechanisms by which this association occurs are not entirely clear. But the most likely mechanism is that experience with and access to marijuana can provide users with access to other illegal substances through contact with individuals who deal in such drugs.

Research conducted by Andrew Morral, Daniel McCaffrey, and Susan Paddock (2002) used data from the National Household Survey on Drug Use (now called National Survey on Drug Use and Health) conducted between 1982 and 1984 to assess the validity of the gateway drug theory. These authors note that the associations between marijuana and hard-drug use likely result from differences in the age at which young people have opportunities to use marijuana and hard drugs and differences in individuals' willingness to try any type of drug. Simply put, marijuana is usually the first illegal drug used by young people because it is more widely available than other illicit drugs. As Morral, McCaffrey, and Paddock conclude, "Although marijuana gateway effects may truly exist, available evidence does not favor the marijuana gateway effect over the alternative hypothesis that marijuana and hard drug initiation are correlated because both are influenced by individuals' heterogeneous liabilities to try drugs" (2002, 1501).

As alluded to previously, the small association between marijuana and hard-drug use may also be partially explained by the fact that until recently the legal status of marijuana (in most countries and states) requires users to purchase it in illicit markets where they may also be offered other drugs. Here it is worth considering the situation in the Netherlands, where marijuana has been sold in coffee shops since the 1990s but where rates of hard-drug use are significantly lower than those in the United States (Zimmer and

Morgan 1997; see also Mosher and Akins 2014). A government report from the Netherlands noted, "If young adults wish to use soft drugs . . . they should not be exposed to the criminal subculture surrounding hard drugs. Tolerating relatively easy access to quantities of soft drugs for personal use is intended to keep the consumer markets for soft and hard drugs separate, thus creating a social barrier to the transition from soft to hard drugs" (quoted in Zimmer and Morgan 1997, 53).

Probably the most convincing evidence against the gateway drug theory is that by the early 2000s, approximately eighty-three million people in the United States had tried marijuana at some point in their lives but had never used hard drugs. Data from the U.S. National Household Survey on Drug Use reveal that if individuals had ever tried marijuana in their lifetimes, their chance of using marijuana and other illegal drugs in the previous month was 1 in 7 for marijuana, 1 in 12 for any other illegal drug, 1 in 50 for cocaine, and 1 in 677 for heroin (Earleywine 2004). A National Academy of Sciences report suggested, "There is no evidence that marijuana serves as a stepping stone [or gateway] on the basis of its particular drug effect" (Joy, Watson, and Benson 1999). Similarly, the 2017 NASEM report, while concluding that there was some evidence that marijuana use is related to developing dependency on other substances, found no support for the traditional gateway argument that marijuana causes users to seek out harder drugs. In short, and as several commentators have argued, it is marijuana *prohibition*, not the substance itself, that functions as a gateway to the possible use of harder drugs (Fox, Armentano, and Tvert 2009), and thus a potential benefit of marijuana legalization is the separation of soft- and hard-drug markets.

Medical Marijuana

> Of all the tragic consequences of marijuana prohibition, none is as tragic as the denial of medicinal marijuana to those who need it.
> —KEITH STROUP, "NORML's Testimony on Medical Marijuana before Congress"

As discussed in Chapter 2, cannabis has been used as a medicine for approximately five thousand years, and more than one hundred articles on its therapeutic effects were published in medical and scientific journals between 1840 and 1900. As Lester Grinspoon (1998), Professor Emeritus of Psychiatry at Harvard University, commented, "In the 19th century, physicians knew more about marijuana than contemporary doctors do." In the 1800s, among other uses, cannabis was recommended as an appetite stimulant, muscle relaxant, analgesic sedative and anticonvulsant, and even as a treatment for opium addiction (Grinspoon 1998). Cannabis was listed as a recognized medicine in the U.S. Pharmacopeia from 1850 until 1942 and could be purchased at local pharmacies in several states (Davenport-Hines 2001). During this period, major U.S.-based pharmaceutical companies, including Lilly, Burroughs Wellcome, and Parke-Davis, produced a variety of cannabis-based products (Brecher 1972).

While opponents of medical marijuana frequently invoke the claim that there is a lack of clinical trials demonstrating the effectiveness of the substance in treating a variety of ailments and that anecdotal evidence is not sufficient to justify the use of marijuana for medicinal purposes, Grinspoon (1998) notes that anecdotal evidence is the source of a great deal of knowledge about drugs: "Controlled experiments were not needed to recognize the therapeutic potential of barbiturates, aspirin, insulin, penicillin or lithium." Importantly, Grinspoon adds that anecdotal evidence in support of cannabis's medicinal applications would be a problem only if it were a dangerous drug.

In recent years, as evidence has accumulated and dozens of studies on the medical benefits of marijuana have been published, the claims of certain government officials and other medical marijuana opponents that the drug has no medical benefits are increasingly indefensible and incredibly naïve. Reports by the National Institutes of Health (NIH) and the Institute of Medicine in the late 1990s have acknowledged that cannabis and its constituents have clinical utility (National Institutes of Health 1997). A publication from the National Academy Press noted that "accumulated data indicate a therapeutic potential for cannabinoid drugs, particularly for symptoms such as pain relief, control of nausea and vomiting, and appetite stimulation" (Joy, Watson, and Benson 1999, 3). The report also emphasized that with the exception of harms associated with administering marijuana via smoking, the adverse effects of the substance "are within the range of effects tolerated for other medications" (4).

Organizations supporting the use of medical marijuana in the late 1990s included the American Public Health Association, the Federation of American Scientists, the Physicians' Association for AIDS Care, the Lymphoma Association of America, and the National Association of Prosecutors and Criminal Defense Attorneys (Zimmer and Morgan 1997). And although the AMA has not publicly supported medical marijuana (a stance the organization first took in the 1940s), in the 1990s, both the *New England Journal of Medicine* (*NEJM*) and *JAMA* published articles in support of medical marijuana. Jerome Kassirer, writing in *NEJM*, stated, "I believe that federal marijuana policy that prohibits patients from alleviating suffering by prescribing marijuana for seriously ill patients is misguided, heavy-handed, and inhumane. . . . It is also hypocritical to forbid physicians to prescribe marijuana while permitting them to use morphine and meperidine to relieve extreme dyspnea and pain" (1997, 366). In *JAMA*, Lester Grinspoon and James Bakalar called for a "reconsideration" of marijuana as medicine: "It is time for physicians to acknowledge more openly that the present classification [of marijuana as a Schedule I drug] is scientifically, legally, and morally wrong" (1995, 1876).

In recent years, support for medical marijuana has also gone "mainstream," with the popular Dr. Sanjay Gupta, a medical correspondent for CNN who in 2009 had written an article in *Time* magazine titled "Why I Would Vote No on Pot," publicly apologizing for misleading his viewers when he claimed that marijuana had no medical uses. Gupta (2013) revealed that he changed his position after expanding his knowledge of the medical marijuana literature and was influenced by the "loud chorus of patients whose symptoms improved on cannabis." Later, Gupta made Charlotte Figi, a Colorado child who suffers from Dravet syndrome (discussed later) the subject of his first marijuana documentary, *Weed*, which appeared on CNN in 2013.

Medical Marijuana Uses

In 2017, a 395-page report published by NASEM analyzed approximately ten thousand published studies on marijuana. Among other findings, the report found strong evidence that marijuana is effective in treating chronic pain for adults and is useful in treating nausea, vomiting, and weight loss in cancer patients and muscle spasticity in patients with multiple sclerosis. The report also identified moderate supporting evidence (meaning that there were very few or no opposing findings in the literature) that marijuana is effective as a sleep aid for people whose sleep problems originate from sleep apnea, chronic pain, fibromyalgia, and multiple sclerosis. Limited evidence (meaning mixed findings but most studies favoring one conclusion or very few [or only one] quality studies) was found indicating that marijuana is useful in increasing appetite and weight among those suffering from HIV/AIDS, lessening the symptoms of Tourette's syndrome, assisting those with social anxiety, and providing better outcomes following a traumatic brain injury or intracranial hemorrhage. At the same time, the NASEM report noted that there was not sufficient scientific evidence to conclude that marijuana is effective in treating glaucoma and epilepsy, both conditions for which it is frequently used (however, see our discussion of more recent studies on the use of marijuana for treating epilepsy).

Nausea, Vomiting, and Weight Loss Associated with Cancer and HIV/AIDS

There is some evidence that suggests that cannabinoids and the endocannabinoid system may act to regulate cancer (NASEM 2017; Rocha et al. 2014). The anticancer properties of cannabinoid compounds have been studied for a wide range of cancers, including prostate, colon, pancreatic, breast, cervical, leukemia, stomach, skin carcinoma, lymphoma, Hodgkin's, liver, and lung (Lee 2012; see also Casarett 2015). Evidence of the effectiveness of marijuana in treating these cancers is promising, but there remains a paucity of high-quality research on this issue (once again, in part due to marijuana's Schedule I status). This has prompted the National Academy of Sciences, Engineering, and Medicine to conclude that further clinical research on the potential anticancer properties of cannabinoids is needed, but presently "there is insufficient evidence to support or refute the conclusions that cannabinoids are an effective treatment for cancer" (NASEM 2017, 91).

While the jury thus remains out on whether the use of marijuana is effective as a direct treatment for cancer, evidence is strong that the substance can serve as an effective treatment for nausea, vomiting, and associated weight loss that accompanies chemotherapy (NASEM 2017). Hundreds of thousands of Americans undergo chemotherapy every year (there are currently more than 15.5 million cancer survivors in the United States) (American Cancer Society 2017), and studies have found that 70 percent of these patients experience nausea and vomiting, with 40 percent of the patients responding poorly to standard antiemetic drugs (Lee 2012). Oral preparations of THC have been used and found to be effective for the treatment of chemotherapy-related nausea and vomiting for more than thirty years (NASEM 2017).

Similarly, research has found marijuana to be an effective treatment for decreased appetite and weight loss experienced by those undergoing treatment for HIV/AIDS (NASEM 2017). Research has also found that smoked marijuana relieves both acute and chronic neuropathic pain and improves mood and mental functioning in those undergoing treatment for HIV/AIDS (Abrams et al. 2007; Ellis et al. 2009).

Epilepsy and Dravet Syndrome

Epilepsy is a chronic neurological disorder that is most distinguished by recurrent and unprovoked seizures. It affects approximately 2.75 million Americans, and roughly one-third of people with epilepsy will continue to experience seizures despite medical treatment (Mohanraj and Brodie 2006; NASEM 2017). Those afflicted with treatment-resistant epilepsy face multiple indicators of mortality, and some forms of treatment-resistant epilepsy are especially problematic. One of these is Dravet syndrome, a rare form of epilepsy that begins in the first year of life and causes a wide variety of serious health problems in addition to frequent and prolonged seizures. Approximately 15 percent to 20 percent of people (mostly children) with Dravet syndrome die as a result of SUDEP (sudden unexpected death in epilepsy), prolonged seizures, and seizure-related accidents and infections (Dravet Syndrome Foundation, n.d.).

There are currently no approved treatments in the United States for Dravet syndrome, although high-CBD-content marijuana is used by a growing number of people to treat various forms of epilepsy, including Dravet syndrome (recall that Dr. William O'Shaughnessy reported on the utility of treating an infant's seizures with cannabis as early as the 1830s). Although systematic reviews of the efficacy of cannabis for the treatment of epilepsy have found the available research insufficient to reach strong conclusions (in large part, the paucity of research is due to restrictions imposed by the Schedule I status of the drug), there are extensive anecdotal reports of treatment efficacy with cannabis, and some recent studies have reported promising results.

For example, in a 2017 study published in *NEJM*, Orrin Devinsky and colleagues randomly assigned 120 children and young adults with Dravet syndrome who had experienced drug-resistant seizures to receive either a cannabidiol-based oral solution or a placebo and measured the subjects' frequency of seizures over a fourteen-week period, which they compared to a four-week baseline period. The authors found that the average number of convulsive seizures decreased from 12.4 to 5.9 per month for subjects receiving the cannabidiol solution and from 14.9 to 14.1 seizures per month for those receiving the placebo. Although this study was funded by the British company GW Pharmaceuticals (which manufactures the prescription synthetic cannabis product Sativex), the results suggest that cannabis products may be useful in treating Dravet syndrome.

Another randomized, double-blind, placebo-controlled study of 225 people (average age of sixteen) with Lennox-Gastaut syndrome (also a severe form of epilepsy that begins in childhood) published on the American Academy of Neurology website in 2017 found that taking a liquid form of cannabidiol reduced seizures by at least 50 percent in 40 percent of the subjects.

While the extant empirical research is insufficient to justify strong conclusions about the efficacy of marijuana/cannabinoids to treat epilepsy, the extensive anecdotal evidence has prompted countless families with children suffering from epilepsy to relocate to places where they can legally access medical marijuana treatment—there are even reports of "international medical marijuana refugees" who travel across national borders to provide their children with access to the substance (Levin 2016). Nicole Mattison, outreach director for the Colorado Springs–based nonprofit organization Realm of Caring, which provides support for families using CBD therapy, knows of approximately four hundred families who have moved to Colorado for medical cannabis (Levin 2016).

Post-traumatic Stress Disorder

Post-traumatic stress disorder (PTSD) is a mental health problem that may develop after an individual experiences or witnesses a life-threatening event "like combat, a natural disaster, a car accident, or sexual assault" (National Center for Post-traumatic Stress Disorder 2018, 3) or other traumatic life experiences such as childhood abuse or learning about the death of a loved one. The symptoms of PTSD can include an experience of reliving the event (referred to as "flashbacks"), avoiding stimuli that remind the person of the traumatic event, depression, anxiety, and emotional numbness—these symptoms may have a delayed onset and can appear and reappear over time (National Center for Post-traumatic Stress Disorder 2018).

Research has consistently demonstrated that the human endocannabinoid system plays a major role in PTSD (people with the condition have greater availability of cannabinoid type 1 than others do), and those with PTSD are far more likely to use marijuana than those who do not suffer from PTSD (Bonn-Miller and Rousseau 2017). The association between marijuana use and PTSD is complex—research in this area considers issues such as whether the use of marijuana puts one at increased risk of developing PTSD (there is no evidence), whether marijuana use can exacerbate the symptoms of PTSD (there is some limited evidence), and whether marijuana can be an effective treatment of PTSD (there is some evidence) (NASEM 2017).

Although there are numerous anecdotal reports of marijuana being an effective treatment for the symptoms of PTSD, primarily because marijuana is classified as a Schedule I substance, rigorous scientific research on this topic is limited (Bonn-Miller and Rousseau 2017). However, a few studies on the issue have been published, and a clinical trial with a proposed seventy-six subjects, which will be conducted by the Multidisciplinary Association for Psychedelic Studies (MAPS) and Dr. Sue Sisley is in its initial stage. A systematic review of thirty-one studies already published that examined the effect of marijuana for the treatment of various mental health problems found the substance to be potentially useful for the treatment of PTSD (Walsh et al. 2017). And in a study using psychometric data on PTSD symptoms involving eighty patients who had applied to the New Mexico medical cannabis program over the 2009–2011 period, George Greer, Charles Grob, and Adam Halberstat (2014) reported a more than 75 percent reduction in PTSD symptoms when patients were using cannabis than when they were not. While noting that theirs was not a clinical, placebo-controlled study of the issue, Greer, Grob, and Halberstat commented, "The finding that the use of cannabis can reduce symptoms of PTSD is consistent with preclinical evidence showing that the endocannabinoid system is involved in the regulation of emotional memory" (2014, 76).

Perhaps the most rigorous study on the efficacy of marijuana for treating PTSD is a randomized, double-blind, placebo-controlled study on Canadian military personnel who had experienced trauma-related nightmares (Jetly et al. 2015). This research found that nabilone (a synthetic cannabinoid that mimics THC) was effective in reducing nightmares among these subjects and in improving their global clinical state and general well-being.

The use of cannabis for treating PTSD is particularly relevant for military veterans in the United States. The Department of Veterans Affairs estimates that approximately 31 percent of Vietnam War veterans, 10 percent of Gulf War (Desert Storm) veterans, 11 percent of those who served in Afghanistan, and 20 percent of Iraqi war veterans are afflicted with PTSD (*Medline Plus* 2009). And as a result of PTSD and other mental and physical health issues, an average of twenty-two U.S. military veterans commit suicide every day (Hobbs 2015). However, under current law in the United States (again, because marijuana is a Schedule I drug), Veterans Administration (VA) doctors cannot prescribe marijuana as treatment for PTSD, even for veterans who reside in states where medical marijuana is legal (Wax-Thibodeaux 2014). In addition, possession and/or use of marijuana is prohibited at all VA medical centers, locations, and grounds. VA pharmacies will not fill prescriptions; nor will the VA pay for medical marijuana prescriptions, and veterans who are currently employed by the agency are subject to drug testing (including for marijuana) under their terms of employment (U.S. Department of Veterans Affairs 2018). But as one veteran commented, "It's not about getting stoned, it's about getting help. The VA doesn't have any problems with giving us addictive pharmaceutical drugs by the bagful" (quoted in Wax-Thibodeaux 2014).

Several individuals and organizations have challenged the VA's policies regarding veterans' use of medical marijuana. For example, the veterans' support group Twenty22many (the group took its name from the statistic concerning the number of U.S. veterans who commit suicide every day), formed by army combat veteran Andrew Collins, is focused on reducing suicide rates among veterans through the use of medical marijuana (Hobbs 2015). The organization Hero Grown (formerly Grow for Vets) (n.d.) "assist[s] veterans, first responders and their families with the use of cannabis as a safe alternative to deadly prescription drugs." And in 2017, the American Legion, which represents more than two million veterans in the United States, adopted a resolution recommending that the federal government allow VA doctors to discuss and recommend medical marijuana in states where the substance is legal (Wentling 2017; see also Angell 2017).

As of early 2017, twenty states and Washington, D.C., listed PTSD as a qualifying condition for medical marijuana (Wallace 2017a), and there are signs that the federal government and VA stances on marijuana for veterans may be softening somewhat. Although the legislation did not go into effect, in May 2016, the U.S. House of Representatives (by a vote of 233–189) and the Senate (by a vote of 89–9) both voted to allow doctors affiliated with the VA to discuss medical marijuana as an option for treatment with their patients under the Veterans Equal Access Act (Wentling 2017). The bill was introduced by Representative Earl Blumenauer of Oregon, who argued, "A lot [of veterans] are suffering from PTSD, chronic pain, traumatic brain injury, and these are all conditions that have been shown to respond to medical marijuana" (quoted in Reilly 2016). The bill was reintroduced in 2017, but a full vote on the measure was blocked by the House of Representatives Rules Committee chairman (Strekal 2017). However, the new VA secretary in the Trump administration, David Shulkin (a trained physician who previously served as the VA's undersecretary of health in the Obama administration), has indicated a willingness to allow medical marijuana for veterans experiencing PTSD. "Right now, federal law does not prevent us at VA to look at that as an option for veterans. . . . I believe that everything that could help veterans should be debated by Congress and medical experts and we will implement that law" (quoted in Fabian 2017).

Chronic Pain and Marijuana as a Substitute for More Harmful Drugs

> The DEA's refusal to remove marijuana from Schedule I is, quite frankly, mind-boggling. It is intellectually dishonest and completely indefensible. Not everyone agrees that marijuana should be legal, but few will deny that it is less harmful than alcohol and many prescription drugs. It is less toxic, less addictive, and less damaging to the body.
> —MASON TVERT, quoted in Abby Haglage, "The DEA Just Blew It on Pot"

Although as discussed previously, there is no evidence for the so-called gateway effect of marijuana, there *is* emerging evidence of an anti-gateway effect in that people are substituting marijuana for more harmful and addictive drugs, particularly opioids and alcohol. In large part this substitution appears to have occurred because marijuana is an effective treatment for chronic pain (NASEM 2017). Chronic pain is a condition that, in the more traditional medical model, particularly in the United States, is typically treated with prescription opioids, which leads to addiction and overdose for significant numbers of individuals. While constituting about 4.4 percent of the world's population, Americans consume approximately 80 percent of the world's opiate painkiller supply (Gusovsky 2016). Between 1999 and 2014, there were more than 165,000 prescription opioid overdose deaths in the United States (Hsu 2016), and in 2015 alone, more than 33,000 people in the United States died of opioid overdoses (including synthetic/prescription opioids, as well as street drugs such as heroin)—translating to a rate of 10.4 deaths for every 100,000 people (Ingraham 2016p). This is almost triple the rate for murder and nonnegligent manslaughter of 3.5 per 100,000 in 2015 (Federal Bureau of Investigation 2017b). There is mounting evidence that a partial solution to this opioid epidemic may be more widespread use of medical cannabis.

A study by Marcus Bachhuber and colleagues (2014) found that, between 1999 and 2010, states that permitted the use of medical marijuana had an average of about 25 percent fewer opioid overdose deaths each year than states where medical marijuana use was not allowed. While this research does not necessarily prove that access to medical cannabis led directly to fewer opioid-related deaths, the authors speculated that in states where access to medicinal marijuana is legal, people taking prescription opiates to relieve pain may take lower doses of these drugs, making overdose less likely. They conclude, "If the relationship between medical cannabis laws and opioid analgesic mortality is substantiated in further work, enactment of laws which allow for use of medical cannabis may be advocated as part of a comprehensive package of policies to reduce the population risk of opioid analgesics" (1672). In an accompanying editorial on the Bachhuber and colleagues' article, opioid abuse researchers Marie Hayes and Mark Brown added, "The striking implication is that medical marijuana laws, when implemented, may represent a promising approach for stemming runaway rates of non-intentional opioid analgesic-related deaths. If true, this finding upsets the apple cart of conventional wisdom regarding the public health implications of marijuana legalization and medicinal usefulness" (2014, 1674).

Another study, using data on all prescriptions filed by enrollees in Medicaid Part D (a federal government program that subsidizes the cost of prescription drugs for Medicare beneficiaries) over the 2010–2013 period, found a significant decline in the use of prescription drugs for which marijuana could serve as an alternative in states where medical marijuana laws had been implemented (Bradford and Bradford 2016). As a control, the researchers conducted an analysis of drugs for which marijuana is not generally recommended (blood thinners, antiviral drugs, and antibiotics)—there was no change in the number of prescriptions issued for these substances after the passage of medical marijuana laws. Most important in the context of the potential for medical marijuana to ameliorate the prescription opioid epidemic, the typical physician in medical marijuana states prescribed 1,826 fewer doses of painkillers to Medicaid Part D subscribers in a given year. The authors concluded that state medical marijuana programs saved Medicare approximately $165 million in 2013 (Bradford and Bradford 2016). As Christopher Ingraham (2016i) points out, while one limitation to this study is that it examined only Medicare Part D spending (which applies only to seniors), previous studies have shown that the elderly are particularly reluctant to use medical marijuana, so the overall effect of medical marijuana laws on all prescriptions may be even greater. There is also more specific evidence to suggest that marijuana is being used as an alternative to opioid painkillers by a significant number of elderly Americans, and the drug has emerged as a potential alternative for the undertreatment of pain for dying patients (Hu 2017; Kaskie et al. 2017).

Ashley Bradford and David Bradford (2017) subsequently applied a similar analysis to (general) Medicaid (which covers low-income people of all ages) prescriptions and found that in states allowing for medical marijuana, prescriptions for antinausea drugs decreased by 17 percent; prescriptions for antidepressant drugs decreased by 13 percent; those for seizure and psychosis drugs declined by 12 percent; and most relevant with respect to evidence for a possible substitution effect, prescriptions for painkillers declined by 11 percent. Noting the significance with respect to potential health-care cost savings, Bradford and Bradford comment, "If all states had had a medical marijuana law in 2014, the savings for fee-for-service Medicaid would have been approximately $1.1 billion" (2017, 5). Underscoring the significance of these two studies by Bradford and Bradford, Ingraham (2017d) comments, "The Bradfords' data only include prescriptions made under Medicare and Medicaid, but given the totality of their evidence it seems reasonable to assume that similar patterns hold true for patients on private insurance plans."

In February 2017, an additional study provided evidence of possible substitution effects. Yuyan Shi (2017) examined state-level annual administrative records of hospital discharges over the 1997–2014 period, focusing on the rate of hospitalizations involving marijuana and opioid dependence and abuse and opioid overdoses. Shi found that medical marijuana legalization was associated with a 23 percent reduction in hospitalizations related to opioid dependence/abuse and a 13 percent decrease in opioid pain reliever overdose.

While a growing number of studies have focused on the impact of medical marijuana legalization on opioid-related deaths, a study published in November 2017 examined the impact of recreational cannabis legalization on such deaths. Melvin Livingston and colleagues (2017) analyzed monthly counts of opioid (both pharmaceutical and nonpharmaceutical) deaths in Colorado from January 2000 through December 2015 and found that after the state legalized recreational marijuana, opioid-related deaths decreased by 6.5 percent (a reduction of 0.7 deaths per month) in the following two years.

Additional evidence regarding possible substitution effects of marijuana comes from studies using individual-level data. For example, Amanda Reiman (2009) collected survey data from 350 subjects at the Berkeley Patients Group, a medical marijuana dispensary in the San Francisco Bay Area. Although the findings must be treated with some caution because the data on subjects' drug use were self-reported, Reiman found that medical marijuana patients had been using cannabis as an alternative for alcohol, prescription, and illicit drugs. More specifically, 40 percent of the sample reported using cannabis as a substitute for alcohol; 26 percent, as a substitute for illicit drugs: and 66 percent, as a substitute for prescription drugs. More recently, in a December 2016 study published in the *Clinical Journal of Pain*, Simon Haroutounian and colleagues followed a group of 176 chronic pain patients (an admittedly small sample size) in Israel and found that 44 percent of them stopped taking prescription opioids within seven months of starting the use of medical marijuana. And in a study published in the *Journal of Psychopharmacology*, Brian Piper and colleagues (2017) found that patients ($n = 1,513$) with legal access to medical marijuana via dispensaries in New England reduced their use of opioids, as well as antidepressant and anti-anxiety drugs. While the concerns regarding the use of self-reported data need to be kept in mind, 77 percent of the patients in this study indicated they had reduced their use of opioids, and 42 percent also reported reducing their consumption of alcohol.

Recognition that cannabis can be a substitute for opioid drugs has led Massachusetts senator Elizabeth Warren to write a letter to the director of the Centers for Disease Control urging the agency to devote resources to studying the issue (Ingraham 2016q). In Canada, an editorial in the *Journal of the Canadian Public Health Association* suggested that deaths from opiates in that country could be reduced if physicians were more willing to prescribe marijuana to those experiencing chronic pain (Lake, Kerr, and Montaner 2015).

Despite the strong evidence that marijuana can be used as an effective and comparatively safe treatment for chronic pain (NASEM 2017) and thus a potential substitute for prescription opioids, of states with medical marijuana legislation, Connecticut, Illinois, New Jersey, and New York do not include chronic pain as a qualifying condition, apparently because of concerns that this condition is overly broad and could lead to more widespread and possibly inappropriate use of cannabis (Vestal 2017). It is certainly true that marijuana will not be a replacement for opioids in all medical situations, but even the most severe critics of medical marijuana legalization would likely concede that cannabis is much safer than opioids with respect to the risk of addiction and fatal overdoses (Hsu 2016).

In addition to research suggesting that marijuana can serve as a substitute for opioid drugs, there are indications that it may be useful in the treatment of addiction to stimulants. Stephanie Oliere and colleagues noted that the endocannabinoid system is involved in the neurobiological process related to stimulant addiction and concluded that "cannabinoids modulate the brain reward systems closely involved in stimulant addiction, and provide further evidence that the cannabinoid system could be explored as a potential drug discovery target for treating addiction across different classes of stimulants" (2013, 1). Although not specifically focused on the issue of cannabis as a substitute for stimulants, M. Paola Castelli and colleagues (2014) found that delta-9-tetrahyrdrocannabinol can attenuate the neurotoxic effects of methamphetamine. And a 2017 Canadian study that followed 122 crack cocaine users in Vancouver for three years found that these individuals consumed crack less frequently when they were also consuming cannabis (Socias et al. 2017). Even though this study also relied on self-reports of the subjects, it is consistent with the results of an earlier study of twenty-five crack users in Brazil, two-thirds of whom were able to stop consuming crack while using cannabis and who reported that the use of cannabis had reduced their cravings for crack (Labigalini, Rodrigues, and Da Silveira 1999).

There is also mounting evidence to suggest that marijuana may be a substitute for alcohol. While these studies are subject to the limitations associated with subjects' self-reporting of behaviors, a 2013 Canadian study of 404 medical marijuana patients in the province of British Columbia found that 41 percent of the patients stated they used marijuana as a substitute for alcohol (35 percent used it as a substitute for other drugs; and 68 percent, for prescription drugs) (Lucas et al. 2013). The same researchers in a 2016 study published in the journal *Drug and Alcohol Review* (Lucas et al. 2016) found that 52 percent of medical marijuana users reported consuming less alcohol while taking medical marijuana, while 80 percent reported substituting marijuana for painkillers and 32.6 percent, for other illicit substances.

Interestingly, the fact that marijuana may be a substitute for alcohol has been implicitly (and in some cases, explicitly) acknowledged by beer and alcohol companies. For example, in its 2018 10-K filing (a report required by the U.S. Securities and Exchange Commission that gives a comprehensive summary of a company's financial performance) the Molson Coors Brewing Company, based in Denver, Colorado, and Montreal, Canada, noted, "Although the ultimate impact is currently unknown, the emergence of legal cannabis in certain U.S. states and Canada may result in a shift of discretionary income away from our products or a change in consumer preferences away from beer" (quoted in Wallace 2018).

Based on several measures of harm, marijuana's classification as a Schedule I drug is simply indefensible. There is also clear and convincing scientific evidence that the substance has several medical applications and that it can serve as a safer substitute for more harmful drugs. Unfortunately, certain government agencies and marijuana prohibitionists have completely ignored these findings (while at the same time invoking a number of demonization themes) in their opposition to marijuana law reform.

4

Marijuana Demonization Themes

> Drug war propaganda causes a systematic reduction in
> people's ability to think intelligently about drugs.
> —BRUCE ALEXANDER, *Peaceful Measures*

In the drug policy arena, both historically and in the present era, scientific evidence seems to be only loosely related to how policies are made—instead, these policies are largely based on ideology (Netherland 2016). Although he was focused on Republican legislators, and more specifically, the George W. Bush administration, in his book *The Republican War on Science*, Chris Mooney (2005) introduces the concept of "science abuse," which he defines as "any attempt to inappropriately undermine, alter, or otherwise interfere with the scientific process, or scientific conclusions, for political or ideological reasons." Science abuse has long been a characteristic of U.S. government agencies' and other marijuana prohibitionists' approach to marijuana and other drugs.

In this chapter, we examine and deconstruct a number of themes emphasized by individuals and organizations opposed to the liberalization of marijuana laws. In no particular order, these themes include the claim that marijuana use can lead to cognitive deficits/IQ decline; that marijuana legalization (both medicinal and recreational) will lead to increases in youth use and the related issue that marijuana, especially edible cannabis products, poses more general threats to children, including neglect by their parents; and that marijuana legalization will lead to an increase in automobile accidents and traffic fatalities, one of the most prominent and debated themes. Space considerations preclude a discussion of the less prominent themes that marijuana production and cultivation cause damage to the environment (Drug Enforcement Administration 2014; Mills 2012; Oregon State Police

2017) and poses particular threats to pets (Brulliard 2016; Drug Enforcement Administration 2014; Meola et al. 2012) and wildlife (Ingraham 2015a).

Since approximately the 1930s, several strategies have been employed in the demonization of marijuana, such as deception, decontextualization (for example, a failure, or choice, to consider the harms of marijuana in the context of harms associated with other substances and/or behaviors), denial that cannabis has any benefits, distraction, and distortion. Some demonizers also sprinkle in a touch of faulty logic, as well as creative (or perhaps naïve) mathematics, and cherry-pick anecdotes to emphasize the dangers of marijuana. In our examination and deconstruction of these demonization themes, we are not trying to minimize the real harms that may be related to marijuana. However, in many cases, the claims are not sufficiently contextualized and are grossly distorted. Marijuana has existed and has been used for thousands of years. *Legalization did not create marijuana.*

Cognitive Deficits/IQ Decline

> The assertion that marijuana makes you crazy has a long, unscientific history. Documenting physical changes in the brain caused by cannabis is the holy grail of the war on marijuana.
>
> —JAKE ELLISON, "Why Anti-pot Crusaders Need Marijuana to Change the Brain"

One of the more prominent themes in the demonization of marijuana is the drug's alleged influence on cognitive functioning and IQ decline, particularly among youth who begin using it at an early age. Considerable attention was devoted to a 2012 study by Madeline Meier and colleagues, which until then was claimed to be the largest and most complete study of the relationship between marijuana use and IQ decline; the study was widely cited in numerous media sources, most of which asserted that it provided definitive proof that marijuana use negatively impacted IQ. However, there is considerable disagreement regarding whether the decline in IQ reported in this study (and several others) was a direct result of marijuana use or instead attributable to confounding factors and methodological problems—in addition, several other studies on this issue have not reported similar results.

The Meier (2012) research used subjects from the Dunedin (New Zealand) twin cohort, in a prospective longitudinal study of 1,037 individuals who were followed from birth (in 1972–1973) to age thirty-eight. The researchers found that persistent marijuana use was associated with neurophysiological decline and that this impairment was concentrated among users who initiated cannabis use during adolescence. More frequent use of the substance was associated with greater cognitive decline, and ceasing use of cannabis did not fully restore neurophysiological functioning among the early-onset users. However, Ole Rogeberg (2013) notes that the methodology of the Meier study was flawed and that the causal claims made were premature. He cites a Canadian study of cannabis exposure on IQ changes from ages nine to twelve to ages seventeen to twenty that included subjects from a less socioeconomically diverse sample (unlike in the Dunedin twin cohort, most subjects in the Canadian study were middle class), which reported no permanent effects of marijuana consumption on IQ (Fried et al. 2002). The study noted, "We conclude that marijuana does not have a long-term negative impact on global intelligence" (2002, 891). Rogeberg also conducted a simulation of the Meier study that included measures of socioeconomic status and concluded that "Meier et al.'s estimated effect of adolescent-onset cannabis use on IQ is likely biased, and the true effect could be zero. It would be too strong to say that the results have been discredited, but fair to say that the methodology is flawed and the causal inference drawn from the results premature" (2013, 4253). Or to put it simply, "The New Zealand data on cannabis use and IQ is consistent with confounding by socioeconomic status: those who smoked would have ended up with lower IQs anyways" (Starling 2016, 17).

The Meier and colleagues' (2012) study contained methodological problems in that it included no breakdown of the frequency of consumption or the amount of cannabis consumed by subjects, and, similar to that of many other longitudinal studies, the measure of use was via subjects' self-reports, which may have been subject to memory problems.

In another study (funded by the NIDA) widely cited in print, television, and online media, Jodi Gilman and colleagues (2014) claimed that "casual" marijuana use resulted in abnormalities in the nucleus accumbens and amygdala regions of the brain. This study was based on a comparison of twenty marijuana users who consumed marijuana for an average of 3.8 days per week, smoking an average of 11.2 joints per week, to a control group of twenty-five nonusers. The Gilman study concluded, "The results of this study indicate that in young, recreational marijuana users, structural abnormalities in gray matter density, volume, and shape of the nucleus accumbens and amygdala can be observed" (2014, 5537).

While the authors of this article should be commended for pointing out that their sample size was small and that causation could not be implied because it was a cross-sectional study, several media sources apparently missed those important caveats and neglected to mention (or understand) other weaknesses in the Gilman (2014) study. For example, in response to the findings, the online media source *Science Daily* (2014) ran a headline, "Brain Changes Associated with Casual Marijuana Use in Young Adults: More 'Joints' Equal More Damage." Another online article, from Fox News with the headline "Casual Marijuana Use Linked with Brain Abnormalities," similarly overstated the results of this study in claiming that "for the first time ever, researchers at Northwestern University have analyzed the relationship between casual use of marijuana and brain changes—finding that young adults who used cannabis *just once or twice per week* showed significant abnormalities in two important brain structures" (Grush 2014; emphasis added). The anti-marijuana group Smart Approaches to Marijuana (SAM) (2014) also misinterpreted the results of the Gilman study, claiming that it was "especially important because it shows even casual, recreational users are not immune from developing brain abnormalities."

There are several problems with the Gilman and colleagues' (2014) study. Most obvious is the small sample size; and suggesting that an average of 11.2 joints smoked per week is typical of recreational marijuana use seems problematic. In addition, while the data are included in the tables in the article, the authors did not emphasize in the text of the piece that the twenty marijuana users consumed an average of 5.09 alcoholic drinks per week, almost double the control group's average of 2.64; it is thus possible that the negative effects on brain structures may have been caused by alcohol consumption. Noting that even if the findings reported by the Gilman study are robust, they say nothing about behavioral outcomes. The prominent Columbia University drug researcher Carl Hart commented, "I'm disappointed that scientists are still able to publish high-profile papers that only look at neuroimaging without a behavioral endpoint. . . . There are structural differences between men and women in certain areas, we don't say this means women are impaired" (quoted in Szalavitz 2014).

A study examining the association between cumulative lifetime cannabis use and cognitive performance in middle age, involving 3,385 Americans over a twenty-five-year period, found that individuals who consumed greater amounts of marijuana had deficits in verbal memory, processing speed, and executive function (Auer et al. 2016). However, after excluding subjects who were currently using marijuana and statistically adjusting for potential confounding factors, Reto Auer and colleagues found that marijuana use was associated only with deficits in verbal memory. However, as Christopher Ingraham (2016c) points out, it is not possible to determine whether heavy marijuana use *causes* deficits in an individual's short-term memory from this study because the people with cognitive impairment could be more prone to use marijuana heavily.

Far less media attention was paid to three studies published between 2013 and 2016 that did not support the claim that marijuana use negatively impacts cognitive performance. The 2013 study by Sarah Bava and colleagues examined forty-one adolescents with extensive marijuana- and alcohol-use histories and fifty-one youth with minimal, if any, substance-use histories (the sample size is also small in this study). This study followed the youth for an eighteen-month period and found that teenagers who consumed five or more drinks at least once a week evidenced reduced white matter brain tissue health, while the level of marijuana use—up to nine times per week over the period—was not related to changes in brain tissue health. In fact, these authors found that cannabidiol may actually have neuroprotective effects.

A study of 2,235 British youth found that, after statistically adjusting for factors such as maternal health, the subjects' mental health symptoms, behavioral problems, and cigarette and alcohol use, individuals who had used cannabis fifty times or more by the age of fifteen "did not differ from never-users on either IQ or educational performance" (Mokrysz et al. 2016, 159). Although this study looked only at individuals with low to moderate levels of cannabis use, the authors concluded that "these findings suggest that adolescent cannabis use is not associated with IQ or educational performance, once adjustment is made for potential confounds" (159).

A study by Nicholas Jackson and colleagues (2016), published in the *Proceedings of the National Academy of Sciences*, examined the association between marijuana use and changes in intellectual performance in two longitudinal studies of twins. The authors note that, if marijuana use is a direct cause of neurocognitive decline, it would be expected that (1) the use of marijuana would precede poor cognitive functioning; (2) a dose-response relationship would exist between marijuana use and IQ decline—that is, individuals who consume more marijuana would show greater cognitive declines; and (3) the association between marijuana use and cognitive decline would persist after adjusting for genetic influences and factors related to family upbringing (Jackson et al. 2016).

In the Jackson study, measures of IQ were administered to subjects at ages nine to twelve (prior to their involvement with marijuana) and again at ages seventeen to twenty; marijuana consumption was self-reported by subjects at each point of cognitive assessment and also during the intervening period. The researchers found that marijuana users had lower IQ test scores than nonusers and evidenced a statistically significant decline in intelligence between preadolescence and adolescence. However, there was no evidence of a dose-response relationship between the frequency of marijuana use and IQ decline. In addition, and most important, marijuana-using twins did not show a significantly greater decline in IQ than their nonusing siblings: "children who are predisposed to intellectual stagnation in middle school are on a trajectory for future marijuana use" (Jackson et al. 2016). While the caveats regarding self-reporting of marijuana use apply to this study as well, the researchers concluded, "The evidence from these two samples suggests that observed declines in measured IQ may not be a direct result of marijuana exposure but rather attributable to familial factors that underlie both marijuana initiation and low intellectual attainment" (e500). In short, the causal-order issue is important to consider; instead of marijuana use possibly making youth less intelligent, it is at least plausible that young people who are not as intelligent or have problems in school are more prone to try marijuana (Ingraham 2016j).

More recently, several media sources in the United States and Canada have made reference to a Dutch study on the effects of a change in marijuana policy on the academic performance of college students in Maastricht, Holland (Marie and Zolitz 2015, 2017), with headlines such as "New Study Links Marijuana Usage to Decreased Academic Success" (C. Burke 2017) and "These College Students Lost Access to Legal Pot—and Started Getting Better Grades" (Humphreys 2017). Keith Humphreys (2017), professor of psychiatry and behavioral sciences at Stanford University, wrote an article in the *Washington Post*, referring to the Maastricht study as "the most rigorous study yet on the effects of marijuana legalization. . . . It provides highly credible evidence that marijuana legalization will lead to decreased academic success." Rosalie Pacula, senior economist and codirector of the Rand Drug Policy Drug Research Center (who is thanked in the acknowledgments section of the Marie and Zolitz [2017] paper), added that the study provided evidence on the effects of marijuana legalization that is "much better than anything done so far in the United States" (quoted in Humphreys 2017). With all due respect to Humphreys and Pacula (and others who are unaware of the methodological weaknesses and other problems with this study), it is not clear that they actually read the study, or if they did so, they did not read it carefully.

The 2015 Olivier Marie and Ulf Zolitz study, which originally appeared as a discussion paper for the Institute for the Study of Labor in Bonn, Germany—a later identical paper was published in the *Review of Economic Studies* (Marie and Zolitz 2017)—involved analyses of students' performance (dropouts, grades, and passed courses) at Maastricht University following a change in the city of Maastricht's policy regarding cannabis sales. As we discuss in more detail in Chapter 6, beginning in the mid-1990s, and apparently intensifying in the 2000s, Maastricht (as well as several other cities in the Netherlands) was experiencing a considerable amount of "marijuana (and other drug) tourism" from other European countries (particularly Belgium, France, Luxembourg, and Germany), leading to public nuisance problems. In October 2011, under pressure from local government authorities, the Maastricht Association of Cannabis Shop Owners implemented a new policy that allowed individuals of only certain nationalities to purchase cannabis on their premises. More specifically, because individuals from France and Luxembourg were identified as the "most nuisance-prone" population, cannabis sales to these individuals were prohibited (but sales to Dutch, Belgian, and German citizens were still allowed) (Marie and Zolitz 2017). This situation provided an opportunity to conduct a "natural experiment" by comparing the outcomes for students of different nationalities and those no longer permitted to purchase cannabis at coffee shops before and after the policy change.

   Marie and Zolitz (2015, 2017) thus examined the records (course drop-outs and grades and whether students passed the course) of 4,419 individual students and found that "on average, students were 5.4% more likely to pass courses when they were banned from entering cannabis shops" (2017, 1212). "After the policy introduction, non-DGB (Dutch, German, Belgian) students appear to *suddenly* perform *substantially* better than their DGB peers" (1221; emphasis added). This difference does not in and of itself seem inordinately large and certainly does not warrant the claims of Humphreys (2017) and others regarding the study's significance and importance. In addition, and digging deeper into the article, in footnote 12 Marie and Zolitz (2017) note that they had access to student outcomes before and after the policy change for 236 non-Dutch/German/Belgian students.[1] Given that the authors report that students in this group were 5.4 percent more likely to pass courses, it would appear that the policy change "led" to thirteen students who could no longer purchase cannabis at coffee shops passing their courses. But even more important, a serious methodological flaw in the Marie and Zolitz (2015, 2017) study is that the authors did not have access to the *actual levels of cannabis use* by students (neither in the group who had been denied access to the substance via coffee shops nor in the larger group of students who still had such access). To their credit, the authors recognize this potential weakness but attempt to argue that it is actually a strength, since "observing that student achievement is affected by cannabis regulations is perhaps more policy-relevant than documenting changes in cannabis consumption itself, since it might be irrelevant how much cannabis individuals smoke if it does not lead to important negative externalities for society" (Marie and Zolitz 2017, 1234). The authors are perhaps also correct (although their claims are somewhat overstated) in asserting that "our results quite clearly show that students who lost the right to buy cannabis legally experienced important performance improvements relative to their peers who could still enter cannabis shops" (1228), but this is *all* their results show. It is more than a stretch to argue that this study provides prima facie evidence of the negative impact of marijuana legalization in general on cognitive performance, as many of the commentators discussed previously have suggested.
   While we share the concerns regarding the potential negative effects of early-onset and heavy cannabis use by adolescents, marijuana demonizers and several in the media have overstated this relationship. As Maia Szalavitz (2014) comments, "Does this imply that marijuana is completely benign and everyone should smoke all day, every day? Of course not! But what it does mean is that, as we consider policy changes like legalization, we need a far

---

   1. An additional, related problem is that the ban on sales applied only to nonresidents; students from any country who had an address in the Netherlands were not affected (Toine Spappens [professor at Tilburg University], personal correspondence, August 1, 2017).

more skeptical and intelligent press" (and, we might add, more skeptical and intelligent legislators and others, some of whom have a decided tendency to misinterpret and/or overstate the findings of certain studies). Szalavitz continues, "Marijuana itself may or may not impair cognition—but discussions of marijuana policy clearly do so, in a way that is detrimental to our political health." It is also important to distinguish between youths' simple experimentation with marijuana and other psychoactive substances and heavy use. A considerable amount of research has found that experimentation with marijuana can be part of a normal maturational process.

Increases in Youth Use of Marijuana?

> We had predicted based on changes in legalization, culture in the U.S. as well as decreasing perceptions among teenagers that marijuana was harmful [and] that [accessibility and use] would go up. But it hasn't gone up.
> —NORA VOLKOW (director of NIDA), quoted in Christopher Ingraham, "One Big Thing Marijuana Opponents Warned You About Is Definitely Not Happening"

One of the primary claims of opponents of marijuana legalization has been that legalization will inevitably lead to increases in use of the substance (we address the issue of increases in adult use in Chapter 1); of particular concern is that youth use will increase. As George Murkin (2016) comments, "The fear that drug use will increase following any move away from a punitive approach is the most frequently raised and politically potent of all the objections to reform."

In considering the results of the studies on increases in use that we review, we stress that far too many marijuana legalization opponents (including special interest groups, federal and state government and criminal justice system officials, reporters/journalists, and some academics) almost seem unaware that marijuana has existed and has been consumed by people well before medical and recreational legalization of the substance. We also stress that, while legalization of recreational marijuana officially occurred in Colorado and Washington in 2012, retail sales of the substance did not commence until January 1, 2014, in Colorado, and July 8, 2014, in Washington State. As Mark Kleiman and other drug policy experts have pointed out, the results of studies of trends in cannabis use must be interpreted with caution, as the effects of legalization on youth and adult use may not have had sufficient time to manifest. Finally, it is necessary to be cognizant of the inherent weaknesses in survey methodology (e.g., sampling error, response bias) more generally in considering the results of these studies (Mosher, Miethe, and Hart 2011). In the specific case of marijuana consumption, legalization itself, which signals an increased social acceptability of the drug, may influence survey respondents' tendencies to more truthfully report use of the drug. Thus, an increase in self-reported use of marijuana over time may simply reflect changes in respondents' reporting tendencies.

It is also important to distinguish between casual use/experimentation and heavy use of psychoactive substances among youth. Some studies have suggested that experimentation with alcohol, marijuana, and other drugs is in fact a normal part of adolescence. For example, Michelle Englund and colleagues (2013) studied 159 teenagers who were born as first children in low-income families and found that those who experimented with alcohol and other drugs were more likely to obtain higher education and had more stable romances in early adulthood than those who abstained. Although the sample size in this study is small, the researchers concluded, "Overall, the results of this study suggest that experimentation with substances may not only be normative in adolescence but also predictive of developmental competence in early adulthood." Similarly, a 1999 SAMHSA report concluded that not all young people who experiment with alcohol and other drugs develop clinical problems and that "some degree of experimentation with drugs is technically normative." The report further noted that "the formidable task faced by every adolescent—to become an independent and responsible adult—is undertaken with strategies that may include experimentation, risk-taking, limit testing, and questioning of established rules and authority. Experimentation with substances may be among these usually functional strategies, despite the potential harms and hazards associated with this behavior."

In considering trends in youth use of psychoactive drugs more generally, the 2015 Monitoring the Future Survey, an ongoing national survey of the "behaviors, attitudes and values of American secondary school students, college students and young adults" conducted by the Institute for Social Research at the University of Michigan (Monitoring the Future 2016), found that past-year use of drugs other than marijuana for eighth-, tenth-, and twelfth-grade students was at the lowest level in the forty years that the survey has been conducted (Schulenberg et al. 2017). The SAMHSA National Survey on Drug Use and Health (NSDUH) provides further evidence of these general declines in youth substance use. The 2015 NSDUH found that 4.2 percent of youth ages twelve to seventeen had smoked cigarettes in the past month (but 10.8 percent had done so in 2005), while past-month alcohol use in the same group had decreased from 16.5 percent in 2005 to 9.6 percent in 2015 (Substance Abuse and Mental Health Service Administration 2016). According to the Monitoring the Future Survey, consumption of marijuana by eighth- and tenth-graders has declined nationally in the past decade, while slightly increasing for twelfth-graders (Schulenberg et al. 2017).

We now turn to the specific research on trends in youth cannabis use following marijuana legalization. Drawing on state-level NSDUH data for the years 2002–2009, Sam Harper, Erin Strumpf, and Jay Kaufman (2012) found that the legalization of medical marijuana was associated with a slight *reduction* in marijuana use among twelve- to seventeen-year-olds. The researchers argue that their results are consistent with an unmeasured confounding explanation—that is, states differ on many variables that are not easily measured in standard social surveys. Once they statistically controlled for these unmeasured state characteristics that did not change over time, there was no evidence that the passage of medical marijuana legislation increased reported youth use of marijuana or use by any other demographic group.

Research by D. Mark Anderson, Benjamin Hansen, and Daniel I. Rees (2012) similarly examined the relationship between the passage of medical marijuana laws and marijuana consumption among high school students, using data from national- and state-level Youth Risk Behavior surveys (conducted by the Centers for Disease Control) for the years 1993–2009. These authors reported that legalization of medical marijuana was not associated with an increase in use by youth, and several of their estimates indicated that marijuana use actually declined with the passage of such laws. They concluded, "Our results are not consistent with the hypothesis that the legalization of medical marijuana caused an increase in the use of marijuana [or other substances] among high school students" (18). Esther Choo and colleagues (2014), also using data from the Youth Risk Behavior surveys but focusing on the years 1991–2011, similarly found no statistically significant differences in youth marijuana use after the passage of medical marijuana laws.

Deborah Hasin and colleagues (2015), in a study published in the journal *Lancet Psychiatry*, used data from the Monitoring the Future surveys over a twenty-four-year period to study the effects of medical marijuana laws on youth consumption. Statistically controlling for individual-, school-, and state-level factors, the researchers found that in states with medical marijuana laws, there was no difference in adolescent marijuana use before or after the passage of such laws. They concluded, "Our study findings suggest that the debate over the role of medical marijuana laws in adolescent marijuana use should cease, and that resources should be applied to identifying the factors that do affect risk" (2015, 602). An accompanying editorial to their article in *Lancet Psychiatry* commented, "The growing body of research that includes this study suggests that medical marijuana laws do not increase adolescent marijuana use, and future decisions that states make about whether or not to enact medical marijuana laws should at least be partly guided by this evidence" (Hill 2015, 573). In reaction to such findings, and somewhat curiously (representing a prime example of the denial demonization strategy), an article published in *JAMA Pediatrics*, while acknowledging that none of the states with medical marijuana laws evidenced a significant increase in adolescent marijuana use within two to three years of the passage of the laws, claimed, "It is simply unreasonable to speculate that a policy that increases the use of marijuana by adults would not also increase adolescent use" (S. Levy 2013, 600).

More recent studies on youth marijuana use have focused on the states of Colorado and Washington, where recreational marijuana was legalized in 2012. For example, the 2015 Healthy Kids Colorado Survey found that 21.2 percent of teenagers in the state reported past-month marijuana use; however, and importantly, the rate of use had not increased significantly since legalization in 2012 and the beginning of retail sales in 2014. The 2013 results from the same survey found that 19.7 percent of Colorado teenagers reported marijuana use in the previous month (Ingold 2016). A study using state-level data from the NSDUH found that 18.35 percent of Colorado youth aged twelve to seventeen had used marijuana in the past year in 2014–2015, a statistically significant *decrease* from the 20.81 percent of youth who reported past-year use of the drug in 2013–2014 (Ingold 2016).

In response to the results of the 2015 Healthy Kids Colorado Survey, critics argued that the sample was biased because more than half of the students selected for the survey chose not to participate. Critics also noted that school-based surveys are problematic because frequent users of marijuana are either skipping school or have dropped out (Evans 2016). While these critiques are not without merit, unless those making them can demonstrate that there had been increases in nonparticipation of students in these surveys over time, the critiques are essentially irrelevant. Additional skepticism regarding the results of surveys showing no change in youth use after the legalization of recreational marijuana was offered by Gina Carbone, a representative of Smart Colorado, a group concerned with the impact of marijuana legalization on youth. Carbone claimed that earlier results from the Healthy Kids Colorado Survey indicating no increases in youth use after legalization of recreational marijuana in the state were not valid because the survey measured use among youth in areas where there had been little to no commercialization of marijuana (McGhee 2014). Others, such as marijuana legalization opponent Dr. Dean Lenoue, a psychiatrist in Aurora, Colorado, felt that the most disturbing aspect of the survey results was that the percentage of teenagers who indicated that marijuana use was risky declined from 54 percent in 2013 to 48 percent in 2015 (Evans 2016).

A 2016 study published in *JAMA Pediatrics*, using Monitoring the Future survey data, found that, while there was no change in marijuana consumption among youth in Colorado over the 2010–2014 period, youth in the eighth and tenth grades in Washington State were more likely to use the substance since legalization and that there had been greater increases in the proportion of youth in the state than youth in other states who believed that marijuana does not pose a great health risk (Cerda, Wall, and Feng 2017).

However, the study found no increase in marijuana consumption among twelfth-graders in Washington State, and the increases for eighth-graders (2 percent) and tenth-graders (4 percent) were relatively modest. In interpreting these increases, while providing no data to support their claims, Magdalena Cerda, Melanie Wall, and Tianshu Feng suggest that legalization may have increased the availability of marijuana: "increasing adolescent access to marijuana indirectly through third-party purchases" and/or that "legalization could have decreased the price of marijuana in the black market" (2017, e5). While such an explanation may seem plausible, it is by no means clear why the same argument apparently did not apply to both youth in Colorado and twelfth-graders in Washington State (where there was no increase in use). While the researchers do not specifically address these problems with their argument, they suggest that no increase in marijuana consumption by youth in Colorado occurred because several years of medical marijuana sales in the state had already led to changes in youth use (although Washington State legalized medical marijuana in 1998, and Colorado, in 2000). The authors attribute the absence of an increase in consumption by twelfth-graders in Washington State to the fact that twelfth-graders were old enough to have already formed attitudes related to marijuana use before it was legalized in 2012.

In addition to studies focused on trends in self-reported marijuana use, researchers have addressed changes in youths' perception of the dangers associated with use of the substance and their intentions to use it in the future. The previously mentioned 2016 study by Cerda and colleagues found that, in Washington State over the 2010–2015 period, the percentage of youth who believed marijuana use would result in physical or other harms declined by 14.2 percent among eighth-graders (from 74.9 percent in 2010 to 60.7 percent in 2015) and 16.2 percent among tenth-graders (from 62.8 percent in 2010 to 46.6 percent in 2015). They note that, in states that did not legalize recreational marijuana use, perceived harmfulness declined by 4.9 percent and 7.2 percent among eighth- and twelfth-graders, respectively. However, differences in the perceived harmfulness of marijuana among twelfth-graders in Washington State and among youth in any grade in Colorado over the 2010–2015 period were not statistically significant.

Some commentators have expressed alarm over these changes in perception (see, for example, Evans 2016). However, youth perceptions of harm from marijuana consumption began declining well before legalization. Further, it seems reasonable to conclude that teenagers are simply being rational in their responses; while marijuana use certainly involves risks, especially for young people, in comparison to risk of harms resulting from the use of other psychoactive substances (including alcohol and many prescription drugs, in particular, prescription opioids), marijuana use is simply not that risky. It is also likely the case that the normalization of marijuana through the legalization of medical and recreational marijuana has contributed to these declines in youth perceptions of harm.

Studies showing declines in the perceived harmfulness of marijuana among youth also need to be interpreted with caution, especially because attitudes expressed in surveys do not inevitably lead to behaviors; young people viewing marijuana as less harmful (again, partially as a result of its normalization with legalization) does not necessarily mean that they will use it. While it is important to keep in mind the caveats regarding attitudes not necessarily resulting in these behaviors, in the 2014 Monitoring the Future survey, 52 percent of teenagers said they would not try marijuana even if it was legally available, and only 7.7 percent said they would use marijuana more frequently than they currently did if it was legally available (Meza 2015).

It is clear that there is little, if any, evidence of a strong relationship between legalization of medical and recreational marijuana and youth use. As *Washington Post* columnist Christopher Ingraham (2016h) comments, "There is a simple reason why legalization is not affecting teen use—adolescents already report that marijuana is widely available. The kids who want to smoke it are probably already doing so, and legalization will do little to change that." Unfortunately, in some of the reports and comments regarding the issue of increases in youth use invoked by marijuana demonizers in campaigns to oppose legalization, commentators have misinterpreted (or conveniently ignored) the results of scientific studies on the issue.

One final thing should be noted in this context. The results of some survey data indicate that it is at least possible that the lack of an increase and, in some cases, decreases in youth marijuana use under legalization may result because the substance has been more difficult for youth to obtain. We are aware that a few more years of data are needed before making any firm conclusions on this issue, and it is difficult to obtain accurate information on the extent of the marijuana black market, but data from the Washington State Healthy Youth Survey indicate that youth in all grades report that marijuana has been more difficult to obtain under legalization. More specifically, in 2010, 16.5 percent of twelfth-grade students in Washington indicated that marijuana would be "very hard" to obtain; by 2016, this had increased to 18.6 percent. Among tenth-grade students the percentage reporting that marijuana would be "very hard" to obtain increased from 27.8 percent in 2010 to 33.7 percent in 2016.[2] It is also interesting to consider data from the Washington State Liquor and Cannabis Control Board's (LCB) compliance checks (in which an "investigative aide" aged eighteen to twenty attempts to purchase cannabis using their real identification; separate checks are conducted for liquor and tobacco) to ensure that retail marijuana stores are not

---

2. The Healthy Youth Survey results are available at http://www.askhys.net.

selling the substance to individuals under the age of twenty-one. Of the 1,749 compliance checks conducted by the LCB between July 2014 and June 2017, 144 (8.2 percent) marijuana retailers sold cannabis to underage people (Washington State Liquor and Cannabis Board 2017b).[3] And it appears as though compliance rates are improving—of 635 compliance checks conducted in the first six months of 2017, 36 (5.7 percent) retailers sold marijuana to underage people (Washington State Liquor and Cannabis Board 2017b). While there is obviously still a need for improvement in compliance, it is notable that the compliance rates for retail marijuana stores in Washington State are in fact higher than those for outlets selling alcohol and tobacco. Again, while we are not suggesting by any means that legalization has led to the demise of the black market in marijuana in Washington State, collectively these data suggest the possibility that the lack of significant increases (and in some groups, decreases) in youth marijuana use may be related to the fact that the substance has become more difficult for them to obtain.

As Mason Tvert, former communications director for the MPP comments, "Every time a state considers rolling back marijuana prohibition, opponents predict it will result in more teen use. Yet the data seems to tell a very different story. The best way to prevent teen marijuana use is education and regulation, not arresting responsible adult consumers and depriving sick people of medical marijuana" (quoted in Nelson 2016).

More General Threats to Children

In Chapter 2, we note that a prominent justification for the passage of the 1937 Marihuana Tax Act was the alleged threat the substance posed to children, which has proved to be an enduring and one of the most widely cited themes in opposition to marijuana law reform. In addition to the issue of legalization's allegedly inevitable effect of increasing youth use of marijuana, we have seen the marshaling of data documenting increases in children's visits to emergency rooms as a result of exposure to cannabis products (often involving edibles) and similar data from poison control systems.

In an article published in the *New York Times*, titled "After 5 Months of Sales, Colorado Sees the Downside of a Legal High," Jack Healy (2014a) noted that nine children had been admitted to Children's Hospital Colorado in the first five months of 2014 "after consuming marijuana, six of whom got critically sick. In all of 2013, the hospital treated only eight such cases." Healy

---

3. Data from the Washington State Healthy Youth survey provide additional evidence that sales to individuals under the age of twenty-one are not a major problem in the state. In 2016, 0.2 percent of twelfth-graders and 0.1 percent of tenth-graders reported that they "bought marijuana from a store."

implies that this increase (which, if projected across the year, would possibly constitute more than a doubling of such exposures in 2014 than in 2013) was attributable to marijuana legalization but does not define what constitutes "critically sick." In the articles from George Wang and colleagues (Wang et al. 2011; Wang, Roosevelt, and Heard 2013; Wang et al. 2016) on pediatric cannabis exposures to which Healy is apparently referring, the authors did not indicate that the effects on youth were particularly serious—for example "the majority of patients had central nervous system effects such as lethargy or somnolence with respiratory insufficiency as the most serious problem" (Wang, Roosevelt, and Heard 2013).

In three studies published over the 2011–2016 period, the results of which were widely circulated in the media, Wang and colleagues focused on increases in pediatric admissions to emergency departments and reports to poison control centers resulting from marijuana exposure in Colorado. In the first study, published in the *Journal of Child Abuse and Neglect*, Wang and colleagues (2011) performed a retrospective review of electronic health records from the October 2009 to March 2010 period and found that five children under the age of five had been admitted to Children's Hospital Colorado for marijuana exposure. In a similar, and also widely cited study, George Wang, Genie Roosevelt, and Kennon Heard (2013) examined pediatric marijuana exposures before and after the 2009 change in the Justice Department's policy instructing federal prosecutors not to focus on medical marijuana users and suppliers if they were complying with state laws. The researchers note that between January 1, 2005, and September 30, 2009, no patients younger than twelve were admitted to the Children's Hospital Colorado for marijuana exposures; however, between October 1, 2009, and December 31, 2011, fourteen such patients were admitted. The authors attributed this increase to the decriminalization of marijuana, as well as the availability of edible marijuana products that are attractive to children.

In a later study, Wang and colleagues (2016) reported that eighty-one patients were evaluated at Children's Hospital Colorado and that the state's Regional Poison Control Center received 163 marijuana exposure cases of children under the age of ten between January 1, 2009, and December 31, 2015. The authors note that the average rate of marijuana visits to Children's Hospital Colorado increased from 1.2 per 100,000 population two years prior to legalization in the state to 2.3 per 100,000 two years after legalization. However, they also note that, of the 163 pediatric marijuana exposure cases from the Regional Poison Control Center, "most (45) children had either no (28%) or minor 75 (46%) effects. Eighteen children (11%) experienced moderate effects, and 4 (3%) had major effects. An additional 20 children (12%) had minimal effects, effects were not followed, or were unrelated" (Wang et al. 2016, 34). The authors also indicate that there was one reported death in an eleven-month-old, although they do not specify the mechanisms through which exposure to cannabis *caused* this death. To their credit, the authors acknowledge that "these unintentional exposures represent a small fraction of the total pediatric ingestions and exposures presenting to the emergency department and regional poison control centers. In 2014, Poison Control Centers reported 1,031,927 [total] exposures in children younger than 6 years" (e4). In addition, and importantly, the researchers note that the increase may simply be a reporting increase—that is, parents may be more willing to take their children who have been exposed to marijuana products to emergency departments and/or poison control centers because the normalization and legalization of marijuana may have led to increases in people telling the truth.

In a fourth study focusing on pediatric marijuana exposures, using data from the National Poison data system, Bridget Onders and colleagues (2016) found that, over the 2000–2013 period, 1,969 children under the age of six had been reported for marijuana exposures. The authors also asserted that the annual rate of such exposures had been increasing, particularly in states where medical marijuana had been legalized prior to 2000. While we are not trying to minimize the potential negative effects of children's exposure to marijuana, such exposures occur at an overall rate of 5.9 per million children. In addition, the data on pediatric marijuana exposures need to be placed in the context of exposures to other drugs (and potentially dangerous household products). A study published in *JAMA Pediatrics* (Gaither et al. 2016) found that between 1997 and 2012, 13,052 children were hospitalized as a result of poisonings from opioid prescriptions, and, in contrast to the situation with marijuana exposures (where there were no deaths), 176 of the children exposed to opioids died. And to further contextualize the 1,969 exposures to marijuana reported in Onders and colleagues (2016), it is worth noting that in 2014 alone, there were 150,530 reported exposures of children under the age of six for "cosmetics and personal care products," as well as 48,215 for vitamins, and 45,915 for antihistamines (Poison Control 2015).

As Tabatha Southey (2017) comments, "Most homes are brimming with things that are potentially dangerous to children, from sharp knives to prescription pills, and we encourage, warn, educate, and take legal action but also trust parents to put these things where their children can't get them. We should keep doing that." Or, as Bob Eschino, president of Incredibles, the largest producer of edible cannabis products in Colorado suggests, "You don't keep your Vicodin out on the counter, you don't leave loaded guns around. . . . You don't leave these things that are dangerous to your children out. So we have to educate (parents) to make sure these products stay safe and secure" (quoted in Jacquie Miller 2017). In short, unintentional ingestion of cannabis by children is extremely more rare than ingestion of other, often more toxic products (Subritzky, Pettigrew, and Lenton 2016).

Marijuana Edibles

One of the most prominent recent themes in marijuana demonization has been the focus on edibles (which, in Colorado, made up 45 percent of legal sales in 2014) (Steffen 2014). Edibles push two buttons, the first and most prominent being the threat they pose to children and that they may constitute a gateway: "health officials are concerned that edible marijuana could become an on-ramp for pre-teens and teenagers to regular marijuana use" (Deam 2014). Edible cannabis products, which pose several risks to consumers, including "overintoxication" (MacCoun and Mello 2015), are also being transported across state lines, and part of the problem is that in nonlegal recreational states, there is far less likely to be a public education campaign addressing the potential dangers associated with consumption of these products (Saint-Louis 2015).

Two iconic cases from Colorado are illustrative of the demonization surrounding edible cannabis products. Richard Kirk purchased karma kandy orange ginger, which contained ten servings of THC (Steffen 2015), from a retail marijuana store in Denver, began "raving about the end of the world" (Healy 2014a), and eventually shot and killed his wife. In Kirk's criminal trial, his attorneys indicated that he would plead not guilty by reason of insanity due to "cannabis intoxication," which they alleged had triggered his psychotic episode.

In the spring of 2016, Kristine Kirk's parents and sister, on behalf of the sons of Richard and Kristine Kirk, filed a lawsuit against Gaia's Garden LLC, the company that had manufactured the cannabis product Kirk had consumed, and Nutritional Elements Inc., the store where Kirk purchased the candy. The suit claimed that these companies had recklessly and purposefully failed to warn Kirk about the potency of the candy and its effects (Steffen 2016). According to the suit, without proper information about potency and effects, consumers can "readily be misled into believing that they need to eat more of the product to feel its effects without realizing the zone of danger they are entering that could result in catastrophic effects" (Steffen 2016).

A second prominent Colorado case involved nineteen-year old college student Levy Thamba, who jumped to his death from the fourth floor of a Denver hotel after eating a marijuana-laced cookie in April 2014. According to the police report, Thamba initially consumed only a single piece of the cookie (as directed by the sales clerk he purchased it from), but approximately thirty to sixty minutes later, not experiencing any effects, he consumed the rest of the cookie (Hancock-Allen et al. 2015). During the ensuing two hours, Thamba, who had never consumed marijuana before, "began acting strangely hostile, tearing around the room and pulling pictures from the wall" (Deam 2014).

Bruce Barcott notes that the Kirk and Thamba cases, which have been widely cited in the popular media as reflective of the dangers of cannabis edibles, are classic examples of confirmation bias: "For those who saw marijuana legalization as a foolish experiment bound to unleash harm on society, the Thamba and Kirk cases exactly confirmed their suspicions. Those were only two cases though, tens of thousands of people purchased and consumed state legal cannabis [in Colorado] in the first six months of 2014. There had been zero overdose deaths and two tragic fatalities linked to the use of pot" (2015, 239).

Perhaps the best-known case involving marijuana edibles was that of *New York Times* columnist Maureen Dowd. On a trip to Denver in June 2014, Dowd reports that she consumed a "caramel chocolate flavored candy bar" (a cannabis edible) and, after feeling no effects for an hour, ordered dinner from room service and consumed some wine. "But then, I felt a scary shudder go through my body and brain. I barely made it from the desk to the bed where I lay curled up in a hallucinatory state for the next eight hours. I was thirsty but couldn't move to get water. I strained to remember where I was or even what I was wearing. . . . As my paranoia deepened, I became convinced that I had died and no one was telling me." While Dowd's consumption of the cannabis edible may have been the cause of these effects, we might also question whether the simultaneous consumption of wine had some impact.

The Dowd column sparked several interesting reactions and responses—some rather comical, some serious. Comedian Bill Dixon tweeted, "Every story about edible weed: 1. Not high. 2. Not high. 3. Still not high. 4. Not high. 5. Please drive me to the emergency room" (quoted in Widdicombe 2017). David Bienenstock (2014), former editor of the marijuana-focused magazine *High Times*, wrote a rebuttal to Dowd's article, titled "Maureen Dowd Freaked Out on Weed Chocolate Because She's Stupid." He questioned why Dowd would "walk into a retail marijuana store to purchase and consume a drug for the first time but asks no questions of the state-licensed store employees who've been trained to offer their advice. Who does no research regarding a proper dosage of THC for a novice user, the amount of time the drug will take before you begin to feel its effects, or even the overall potency of the product she selected—which might have been listed on the label, though she neglects to say."

On a more serious note, the Dowd column also led to positive outcomes concerning the safety of edibles. Not long after the column was published, the MPP began an advertising campaign, including billboards, that used Dowd's likeness and warned people to be cautious with edibles, with the slogan "with edibles, start low and go slow" (Baca 2014). In addition, in 2015 in Colorado, a stop sign symbol with the letters "THC" was placed on all edible products, and dispensaries initiated a "First Time 5" poster campaign to advise edible users to consume only a five-milligram half dose of an edible to ensure that they do not become overintoxicated (Wyatt 2015). Andrew Freedman, Colorado's director of marijuana coordination, noted that the Dowd column "was our best possible public-education campaign" regarding overconsumption of edibles (quoted in Widdicombe 2017). Or, as Barcott comments, "For all the ridicule she endured, the *Times* columnist did the cannabis industry an enormous service. She forced it to confront a crisis that too many pot people wanted to ignore" (2015, 271).

The Role of Marijuana Legalization in Potential Increases in Automobile Accidents and Traffic Fatalities

> Either everyone else is driving a hell of a lot safer to compensate for the stoned drivers, or marijuana legalization hasn't really had any effect on traffic safety. After all, legalization didn't invent cars and driving; stoners didn't all walk to Woodstock and Haight-Ashbury. . . . You're probably more likely to find married gays or lesbians dying in car wrecks these days now that gay marriage is legal. It doesn't mean that legalizing gay marriage has led to more traffic deaths.
> —RUSS BELVILLE, "Kevin Sabet Is Misleading You Again
>   about Marijuana Legalization"

Another major theme of marijuana demonization emphasized by individuals and organizations opposing legalization is the alleged role of marijuana in automobile accidents and traffic fatalities. While there is a widespread belief that marijuana consumption has serious negative effects on driving performance, there is still considerable dispute in the (ever-expanding) scientific literature on this issue (given the dozens of studies on this issue, our review here is not intended to be exhaustive). In fact, even the National Highway Traffic Safety Administration (NHTSA) has noted that "some [THC-intoxicated] drivers may actually be able to improve performance for brief periods by overcompensating for self-perceived impairment" (2014, 11). And, as we emphasize with respect to other demonization themes, it is critically important to remain aware that people, including people who operate automobiles, have consumed marijuana for decades, regardless of the legal status of the substance.

Research on the relationship between marijuana consumption and driving generally involves two types of studies: simulator studies examining the effects of consumption on driving performance in laboratory-type situations and aggregate-level epidemiological (also referred to as "case-control") studies assessing the impact of changes in marijuana laws (both medical and recreational) on automobile collisions and traffic fatalities.

A study sponsored by the American Automobile Association (AAA) used data from two sources: 602 drivers arrested for impaired driving in which only THC was present, along with a sample of 349 drug-free controls, in which full records of subjects' performance on drug recognition exams/ field sobriety tests were available (from the states of Minnesota, Pennsylvania, and Washington); and 4,799 drivers arrested for impaired driving who tested positive for one or more cannabinoids and for whom demographic information and toxicology testing results were available (Logan, Kacinko, and Beirness 2016).

Examining the drug recognition experts data, Barry Logan, Sherri Kacinko, and Douglas Beirness (2016) found that 55.5 percent of the drug-free subjects were able to successfully complete the walk-and-turn test, while only 6 percent of those who tested positive for marijuana were able to do so. In the one-leg stand test, 67.2 percent of drug-free subjects completed with no errors, while only 24 percent of marijuana-positive drivers were able to do so. On the finger-to-nose test, 49.2 percent of drug-free drivers performed without errors, but only 5.2 percent of those who tested positive for cannabis. While the failure rates on these tests for subjects who were allegedly sober are in and of themselves interesting (and underscore the more general problems with field sobriety tests, sometimes referred to as "failure-designed," in detecting impairment) (Mosher and Akins 2014), the data appear to indicate that cannabis-positive drivers are more likely to show signs of impairment.

Logan, Kacinko, and Beirness's analysis of the arrest data indicated that drivers arrested for impaired driving who tested positive for one or more cannabinoids had a median THC content of four nanograms/milliliter of blood, meaning that half of those placed under arrest had blood concentrations of four nanograms/milliliter of blood or lower (below the five nanograms/milliliter of blood legal standard for cannabis impairment adopted in Washington State and Colorado). These results led the researchers to conclude, "Based on this analysis, a quantitative threshold for per se laws following cannabis use cannot be scientifically supported" (2016, 3). However, and importantly, only 23 percent of drivers charged with driving under the influence were positive *only* for cannabinoids—alcohol was present in 59 percent of these drivers, and other drugs, in 33 percent.

There is no doubt that marijuana consumption can affect an individual's ability to operate a motor vehicle. However, and although this may be surprising to some, the results of simulation studies of the effects of marijuana on driving have been mixed. For example, Andrew Sewell, James Poling, and Mehmet Sofuoglo, in a review of experimental/simulator studies on marijuana's effect on driving, note that experienced marijuana smokers who drove on a course showed "*almost no* functional impairment under the influence of marijuana, except when it is combined with alcohol" (2009, 186; emphasis in original). In contrast to drivers under the influence of alcohol, who have a tendency to underestimate their degree of impairment and drive more aggressively, drivers who use marijuana tend to overestimate their degree of impairment and engage in compensatory strategies such as driving slower and increasing their following distances (Neavyn et al. 2014; Sewell, Poling, and Sofuoglo 2009). A more recent report by the NHTSA noted that "subjects dosed on marijuana showed reduced mean speeds, increased time driving below the speed limit and increased following distance during a car following task. Alcohol, in contrast[,] was associated with higher mean speeds (over the speed limit) [and] greater variability in speed" (Compton 2017, 11).

Case-control studies examine the contribution of drugs to collisions by comparing collision-involved drivers to those who were not involved in collisions, a method generally preferable because it can eliminate potential sources of bias in estimating the collision risk associated with drug use (Compton and Berning 2015). A study using this method conducted by the U.S. Department of Transportation compiled data on crash-involved and non-crash-involved drivers over a twenty-month period in Virginia Beach, Virginia (a total of three thousand crash-involved drivers and six thousand who were not involved in collisions). THC was detected in 7.6 percent of the crash-involved drivers and 6.1 percent of those in the comparison group, while alcohol was found in 5.0 percent of drivers involved in crashes and 2.7 percent of the control group. While these data would seem to point to a relationship between marijuana consumption and involvement in collisions, the authors note that there are important caveats: "Caution should be exercised in assuming that drug presence implies driver impairment. Drug tests do not necessarily indicate current impairment [and] in some cases, drug presence can be detected for a period of days or weeks after ingestion" (Compton and Berning 2015), which particularly applies to marijuana.

A 2016 AAA study examined the relationship between marijuana use and impaired driving using a census of all motor vehicle crashes on public roads in Washington State over the 2010–2014 period that resulted in a death within thirty days of the collision, focusing on the presence and concentration of THC in drivers involved in such collisions (Tefft 2016b). Statewide, 3,031 drivers were involved in fatal collisions over this period, an estimated 303 (10 percent) of whom had detectable levels of THC in their blood at or shortly after the time of the crash. Of the 303 drivers who tested positive for THC, only about one-third (34 percent) had neither alcohol nor other drugs in their blood, 39 percent had detectable alcohol in addition to THC, 16.5 percent had other drugs in addition to THC, and 10.5 percent had both alcohol and other drugs in their system in addition to THC (Tefft 2016b). Thus, in this study (as in several others examining the issue) it is difficult to disentangle the effects of marijuana, alcohol, and other drugs on involvement in fatal crashes. And while some media and government sources have used this

AAA study (as well as the 2016 Logan, Kacinko, and Beirness report discussed previously) to claim a strong relationship between marijuana consumption and involvement in fatal collisions, Brian Tefft was much more cautious in his conclusions: "The results of this study do not indicate that drivers with detectable levels of THC in their blood at the time of the crash were necessarily impaired by THC or that they were at fault for the crash" (2016b, 1).

In contrast to the results of some of the studies discussed earlier that indicate that marijuana consumption can increase the risk of involvement in collisions or traffic fatalities, a recent 2016 study by researchers at Columbia University, published in the *American Journal of Public Health*, used data from the NHTSA's Fatal Analysis Reporting System (FARS) for the years 1985–2014 (Santaella-Tenorio et al. 2016). Although the researchers did not include data on actual marijuana consumption by drivers, they found an 11 percent *reduction* in traffic fatalities in states that had enacted medical marijuana laws; they also found that the presence of medical marijuana dispensaries correlated with fewer fatalities. While the authors of this study were not able to rule out other plausible causal explanations for the reduction (for example, the severity of laws related to driving under the influence, the characteristics of transportation infrastructure, and/or the quality of health care in states with and without medical marijuana laws), they speculated it might be related to a substitution effect. This argument was supported by the fact that the fatality reductions were greatest among drivers in the fifteen to forty-four age group, who may be substituting cannabis for alcohol (Kunkle 2016).

In considering the results of aggregate-level studies on the relationship between marijuana consumption and involvement in collisions or traffic fatalities, we must take into account the relationship between risky driving-related behaviors, marijuana consumption, gender, and age. Richard Compton and Amy Berning (2015) note that in general, male drivers are more likely to be involved in collisions than female drivers, and younger drivers have higher crash risks than do older drivers. And given that males and younger people are more likely to consume both alcohol and marijuana, these demographic factors may explain some of the increased risk of collision associated with drug use. In fact, in Compton and Berning's study, once these factors were statistically controlled for, there was no relationship between the presence of THC and collision risk. Similarly, a 2017 study by the American Automobile Association Foundation for Traffic Safety found that millennials (ages nineteen to twenty-four) were more likely than any other age group (including teenage drivers) to engage in behaviors such as exceeding the speed limit by ten to fifteen miles per hour, running a red light when they could have stopped, reading or sending text messages while driving, and smoking marijuana within an hour of driving (7 percent of the sample)

(T. Johnson 2017). Each of these behaviors increases the probability of being involved in a collision.

More generally, the Norwegian economist Ole Rogeberg has reanalyzed several of the aggregate-level studies on the relationship between marijuana consumption and driving and noted, "Using cannabis and driving under the influence are behaviors that are more common among young adults and males, groups with higher crash risks irrespective of use. Estimated odds ratios (of crash risk) typically decline substantially after adjustments for such factors" (Rogeberg and Elvik 2016, 1356). Based on their meta-analysis, Ole Rogeberg and Rune Elvik estimate that marijuana use increases the risk of automobile collisions by 20 to 30 percent, certainly not insignificant but a far cry from the more alarmist and outlandish claims regarding this relationship.

Aggregate-level data from Colorado and Washington State also do not support the argument that marijuana legalization in these states has caused a significant increase in traffic fatalities. While the caveat that there have been approximately only three years of retail marijuana sales in these states must be taken into account; in both states, the traffic fatality rate has remained fairly stable compared to the period prior to marijuana legalization and is lower in each state than it was ten years previously. According to the Colorado State Patrol, the number of driving-under-the-influence arrests by their agency decreased by 18 percent over the 2014–2015 period (from 5,546 in 2014 to 4,546 in 2015), with only 8 percent of these arrests involving marijuana as the only drug (Drug Policy Alliance 2016b).

In Washington State, seventy-two drivers who were involved in fatal collisions in 2014 tested positive for THC alone (or in combination with alcohol and/or other drugs), but there were only forty-four such cases in 2010. However, only twenty of the drivers testing positive in 2014 were positive for THC only (the number was nine in 2010) (Drug Policy Alliance 2016b). While this increase is obviously statistically significant, by itself it does not indicate that more people were driving while *impaired* by marijuana nor that the fatalities that did occur were *caused* by marijuana-impaired drivers. Instead, the statistical increase may be related to changes in the screening and data-reporting methods and procedures after legalization in Washington State. Prior to the passage of I-502, law enforcement agencies in the state did not routinely conduct tests to determine whether THC was present in drivers involved in fatal crashes—such information had to be retroactively collected and manually obtained. Such methods are subject to high error rates and lead to problems in comparing the "real-time" THC tests that were increasingly used after legalization (Drug Policy Alliance 2016b).

In Oregon, a report by the Oregon State Police noted that "historically, an annual average of two percent of Oregon's traffic fatalities were associated solely with cannabis: this rate has not changed significantly since legalization" (2017, 5), although sales of recreational marijuana in the state did not begin until October 1, 2016, and close to one-third of fatal crashes in the state are not subject to toxicology screening.

The two most recent studies on the relationship between marijuana consumption and involvement in collisions and fatalities, published in 2017, offered contrasting conclusions. The first, published in the *American Journal of Public Health*, used FARS data to determine the annual number of fatal motor vehicle collisions between 2009 and 2015 in Colorado, Washington, and eight comparison states (Aydelotte et al. 2017). The authors compared yearly changes in crash fatality rates (per billion vehicle miles traveled) using what is known as a "difference in differences" approach and found that after the legalization of recreational marijuana, while the rates increased, they were not significantly different from those in the comparison states that had not legalized (there were 0.2 extra fatalities per billion miles traveled, equating to 77 additional traffic fatalities, or 2.7 percent of the 2,890 total fatalities) (see also Wallace 2017k). The researchers concluded, "Three years after recreational marijuana legalization, changes in motor vehicle crash fatality rates for Washington and Colorado are not statistically different from those in similar states without recreational marijuana legalization."

A second study, sponsored by the Insurance Institute for Highway Safety (IIHS) in 2017, found that insurance claims as a result of collisions in Colorado, Oregon, and Washington State were 2.7 higher than those in neighboring states (Idaho, Montana, Nevada, Utah, and Wyoming) in the three years since legal sales of recreational marijuana began. However, in contrast to the Aydelotte (2017) study, the IIHS study was not peer reviewed and was unable to demonstrate that marijuana legalization was a direct cause of the increase in insurance claims. The Aydelotte study also focused on collisions that resulted in fatalities, while the IIHS study examined collisions more generally (Ingraham 2017e). Noting these problems and other weaknesses of the study, the trade group Cannabis Business Alliance (which obviously has its own biases) claimed it was "just another attempt to incite reefer madness" (quoted in Wallace 2017k).

Unfortunately, although perhaps not surprisingly, the mainstream media, as well as some law enforcement organizations (see our discussion of the Washington State HIDTA report in Chapter 5) have not exercised caution in reporting on the relationship between marijuana consumption and involvement in collisions and/or traffic fatalities; there are several examples of the use of anecdotal cases to "prove" the relationship and a tendency to ignore important details and misinterpret the results of studies. For example, in a case in Colorado in which a man who had double the legal limit of marijuana in his system crashed into two police cars, both the police incident report and the media coverage failed to mention that the individual also had a blood alcohol content of .268—more than three times the legal limit (Balko

2014a). In this case, we might question whether the marijuana or the alcohol "caused" the collision. Similarly, reporting on a case from Washington State, an article in the *Seattle Post-Intelligencer*, titled "Charge: High Driver Killed Teen Pedestrian," noted that the driver was "high on marijuana and prescription painkillers" when he drove into the teenager and that he "let his Nissan pickup truck drift over the fog line as he answered his ringing mobile phone" (Pulkkinen 2013). Once again, we can question whether being high on marijuana, being high on prescription painkillers, or answering his mobile phone (or, more likely, some combination of the three) was the *cause* of this fatal accident.

To sum up the research on the relationship between cannabis consumption and involvement in collisions or traffic fatalities, it is safe to say that collectively, the results of both driving simulator–type studies and aggregate-level studies indicate some effects, although they are not inordinately large. Staci Hoff, research director for the Washington State Traffic Safety Commission, noted that there was "obvious bias in the published research [on the relationship between marijuana consumption and involvement in collisions,] offering erroneous conclusions while downplaying the significant study limitations" (personal communication, September 18, 2017).[4] More important, Hoff noted that recent studies have demonstrated that the level of THC in the blood is not necessarily related to impairment: "I.e., some subjects with greater than 15 ng/ml of THC in the blood exhibit no signs of driver impairment whereas a subject with no measurable THC but known to have recently used do exhibit signs of driver impairment. . . . We must also consider and be honest regarding the frequent occurrence of other substances known to cause driver impairment, such as alcohol."

It is also important to consider the crash risks associated with marijuana consumption in the context of other behaviors that contribute to automobile accidents. Most obvious here are traffic fatalities related to alcohol consumption, although there are problems with how these are measured (see Mosher and Akins 2014); an estimated 10,265 people died in alcohol-impaired driving collisions in 2015 (making up 29 percent of all traffic-related deaths in the United States in that year) (Centers for Disease Control 2017a). There is also the growing problem of traffic fatalities related to distracted driving—in 2015, according to the National Safety Council, distracted driving, largely from cell phone use and texting, caused 3,477 traffic deaths (Lindblom 2017).

Other conditions that can negatively affect driving ability include a lack of sleep—an AAA Foundation for Traffic Safety report in 2016 found that 35 percent of people get fewer than the needed seven hours of sleep, and 12

---

4. Dr. Hoff has generously provided permission for us to quote her; however, we stress that this does not constitute an endorsement of our views on the relationship between cannabis consumption and driving or other views expressed in this book.

percent indicated they slept for five hours or less (Tefft 2016a). Using data from the National Motor Vehicle Crash Causation Survey, the AAA study found that driving with four to five hours' sleep was equivalent to having a blood alcohol content at or above 0.08, while the crash risk associated with having less than four hours' sleep was equivalent to a blood alcohol content of 0.12 to 0.15 (Tefft 2016a). Another AAA study found that road debris was a factor in an estimated yearly average of 50,658 police-reported crashes and 125 deaths in the United States over the 2011–2014 period (Tefft 2016c).

While we are by no means suggesting that marijuana does not have harmful effects, much of the discussion of these harms (which all too commonly neglect the fact that the substance existed before legalization) has been overstated, misinterpreted, and insufficiently contextualized in relation to other, more serious harms. As we show in the next chapter, several of these marijuana demonization themes have been emphasized by those opposed to the reform of marijuana laws.

5

Marijuana Demonization

Agents and Agencies

I n Chapter 4, we address the themes emphasized by those opposed to marijuana law reform in attempts to demonize the substance. In this chapter, we examine the most prominent agents and agencies of demonization, which include federal government agencies such as the ONDCP, the DEA (including its actions and operations), and to a somewhat lesser extent, the NIDA. At the state and local levels, although there is by no means consensus among members of these professions, the most notable demonizers are certain law enforcement organizations (in particular, largely state-based but also federally funded High Intensity Drug Trafficking Areas [HIDTAs]) and officials, as well as criminal justice system officials more generally. We include a critical discussion of several reports produced by these agencies, as well as specific actions they have taken with respect to marijuana. Many of these reports distort the extant science on marijuana, cherry-pick information from sources that are consistent with their anti-marijuana philosophy, and conveniently ignore the findings of studies that are not consistent with their prohibitionist arguments.

We also briefly consider opposition to marijuana legalization as manifested in the (sometimes implicit) positions of large pharmaceutical companies, as well as beer and alcohol producers/distributors and professional medical associations. Finally, we discuss the views (and misinformation propagated by) the most prominent anti-marijuana legalization organization in the United States, SAM, and its president, Kevin Sabet, as well as recent contributions to the debate over marijuana legalization offered by former drug czars John Walters and William Bennett.

The Office of National Drug Control Policy

The ONDCP was established under the provisions of the Anti–Drug Abuse Act of 1988 during the Reagan administration, and initially the head of the agency was a cabinet-level appointment. In considering the actions of the ONDCP and statements of drug czars with respect to marijuana and other drugs, it is important to note that, under the ONDCP Reauthorization Act of 1998, the director of the ONDCP "shall ensure that no federal funds appropriated to the Office of National Drug Control Policy shall be expended for any study or contract relating to the legalization (for a medical use or any other use) of a substance listed in Schedule I of the Controlled Substances Act and take such actions as necessary to oppose any attempt to legalize the use of a substance (in any form) listed in Schedule I" (White House 1998). Given these provisions, while the actions of the ONDCP we discuss are perhaps not excusable, they are understandable—the organization is specifically charged with taking the responsibility to oppose the legalization of any Schedule I drug, including marijuana.

In addition to the views of individual drug czars we discuss in Chapter 2, the ONDCP has also produced a number of publications characterized by misleading, and in some cases, outright false claims: for example, the agency's *National Drug Control Strategy* report, in which it is claimed that the agency's stance is "an approach rooted in scientific research on addiction" (2014, 1). Among other misleading statements, the report refers to the alleged impact of marijuana use on young people's academic performance: "Studies have shown that among youth who earn mostly D's and F's in school, 66% had used marijuana" (7). In considering this claim, it is important to note that the original study to which the ONDCP is referring is by the Centers for Disease Control (CDC), which used data from the 2009 National Youth Risk Behavior Survey and cautioned against inferring causality from these data: "These associations [between marijuana consumption and grades] do not prove causation. Further research is needed to determine whether low grades lead to health risk behaviors, health risk behaviors lead to low grades, or some other factors contribute to both these outcomes." Also notable from the CDC study, and conveniently neglected in the ONDCP's reference to it, is that 21 percent of the students with A grades had *never* used marijuana, as had 37 percent of those with grades of B.

Similar to other federal government agency reports on the alleged evils of marijuana, the 2014 ONDCP *National Drug Control Strategy* tends to attribute outcomes that are the result of marijuana prohibition to the existence of the substance itself, for example, in noting that there were more than ten thousand guns seized from marijuana cultivation sites in 2012. Even assuming the number of guns seized is accurate, it is questionable whether marijuana cultivators would require such protection if the substance was legal. The report also emphasizes environmental threats and threats to wildlife, including diversion of water resources, the clearing of native bush, and use of banned pesticides: "At a marijuana cultivation site, law enforcement officials discovered poisoned hot dogs hung from fishing hooks. Approximately 10 meters away, law enforcement found a dead adult male fisher, a rare forest carnivore declared a candidate species for listing under the Endangered Species Act" (43).

Considering the report in its totality, as the drug law reform advocacy group Stop the Drug War (2014) comments, the report "appears not only wedded to marijuana prohibition, but even disturbed that Americans now think pot is safer than booze. The Drug Czar's Office is still tone deaf when it comes to marijuana policy. It appears to be addicted to marijuana prohibition."

Drug Enforcement Administration

Arguably the most prominent agency promoting marijuana demonization in the United States is the DEA, which has manifested this demonization in both rhetoric and action. The DEA was created by President Richard Nixon through an executive order in 1973 with the mission of establishing "a single unified command to combat an all-out global war on the drug menace" (Drug Enforcement Administration, n.d.). When it was first created, the DEA had 1,470 special agents and a budget of less than $75 million—the agency grew quickly to 2,135 special agents and a budget of $141 million by 1975. Housed under the Department of Justice, today the DEA has nearly 5,000 special agents and a budget of $2.03 billion.

The DEA has engaged in obstructionist activities with respect to rescheduling marijuana. After DEA administrative law judge Francis Young recommended moving cannabis to Schedule II of the Controlled Substances Act in 1988, DEA administrator Jack Lawn overruled the decision. Lawn asserted that there were no medicinal benefits associated with smoking marijuana and that scientific studies did not support the claims that marijuana was useful in the treatment of cancer or glaucoma. And while acknowledging that some studies had found that THC had some effect in easing nausea and vomiting, the DEA and Lawn noted that pure THC was already available in the form of Marinol (synthetic marijuana) (Drug Enforcement Administration, n.d.).

Robert Bonner, appointed to the DEA administrator position by George H. W. Bush in 1990, also considered rescheduling marijuana, relying on a five-point test, which includes these criteria (clearly not mutually exclusive): (1) the drug's chemistry must be known and reproducible; (2) adequate safety studies must have been performed on the drug; (3) there must have been adequate and well-controlled studies proving the drug's efficacy; (4) the drug's medicinal value must be accepted by qualified experts; and (5) the scientific evidence of the drug's safety and efficacy must be widely available (Drug Enforcement Administration, n.d.). Perhaps not surprisingly, Bonner concluded that marijuana did not meet all five criteria and refused to re-schedule the substance. However, given marijuana's classification as a Schedule I drug, which seriously limits scientific research on its effectiveness, satisfying these five criteria is virtually impossible.

Similar to the ONDCP, the DEA has produced several reports, most of which are available online, on the effects and problems associated with various psychoactive substances, including marijuana. The DEA's 2014 publication *The Dangers and Consequences of Marijuana Abuse* includes references to what at first glance may appear to be an impressive list of research studies, until one realizes that the authors of this report essentially cherry-picked studies that are consistent with the agency's anti-marijuana ideology. The report contains 212 footnotes to support its claims, although many of these involve the same source cited several times, and most do not in fact refer to original scientific studies and research. The report criticizes the use of anecdotes by supporters of marijuana legalization, but the report is itself full of anecdotes.

In the introduction to *The Dangers and Consequences of Marijuana Abuse*, the DEA notes that its responsibility concerning marijuana is clearly defined in federal law, "but our responsibility is to go further—to educate you about marijuana with facts and scientific evidence" (2014, 2). The report further argues that the legalization of marijuana will "come at the expense of our children and public safety. It will create dependency and treatment issues, and open the door to other drugs, impaired health, delinquent behavior, and drugged drivers. This is not the marijuana of the 1970s, today's marijuana is far more powerful" (6).

With respect to the alleged relationship between cannabis consumption and mental health problems, the DEA report evidences struggles with an understanding of the tenets of causality, noting that "people with mental illness are seven times more likely to use marijuana weekly than people without mental illness" (2014, 9). While such correlations between marijuana consumption and the incidence of "mental illness" may exist, most studies on this issue are unable to determine if mental illness preceded cannabis use, or vice versa. Also in reference to the mental health theme, the report quotes a British psychiatrist who argued that at least 10 percent of the people with schizophrenia in Britain would not have developed the illness if they had not used cannabis: "by his estimate, 25,000 individuals have ruined their lives because they smoked cannabis" (12). In considering this claim, it is again important to emphasize that it is very difficult to prove that marijuana consumption causes schizophrenia. The disease typically manifests in the late teens and early twenties, which is also the age group most likely to use cannabis. Schizophrenia is also more common among those in lower socioeconomic status groups and individuals who have experienced childhood trauma, both of which are associated with high levels of drug use (including cannabis) and addiction (Nutt 2012). In addition, at the aggregate level, the incidence of schizophrenia in the general population in Britain (and the United States) has been declining (Drug Policy Alliance 2016a). In Britain, where users have consumed high-potency "skunk" marijuana for at least ten years, there has been no increase in the incidence of schizophrenia (Starling 2016).

The DEA's report also emphasizes the role of marijuana in the commission of crime and violence, although in most of the anecdotal examples included, the authors appear to confuse the effects of prohibition with the effects of marijuana. For example, the report refers to several cases in the state of Massachusetts, including the fatal shooting of a twenty-one-year-old male in a Harvard University dormitory—allegedly in a "hit to rob him of his pot and cash"; the murder of a seventeen-year-old in Callahan State Park (Massachusetts), who was lured by two men seeking revenge in a fight over marijuana; and the "massacre" of four people in Mattapan, including a twenty-one-year-old woman and her two-year-old son "over a pot-dealing turf dispute" (Drug Enforcement Administration 2014, 29).

To further emphasize the marijuana-causes-violence theme, the DEA report refers to an Australian study that allegedly found that marijuana users "can be as aggressive as crystal methamphetamine users" (Drug Enforcement Administration 2014, 11). In this case, the report did not cite the original Australian study but a *Sydney Morning Herald* article that made reference to the study. Although we were unable to find this Australian study, the *Sydney Morning Herald* article notes that the researchers used data from visits to hospital emergency rooms in Sydney and found that "cannabis users are as aggressive as crystal methamphetamine users, with almost 1 in 4 men and 1 in 3 women [who appeared at emergency rooms as a result of marijuana consumption] being violent toward hospital staff or injuring themselves after acting aggressively" (Benson 2008).

In reading *The Dangers and Consequences of Marijuana Abuse* in its totality, one can legitimately question whether the authors (and the DEA) are aware of numerous studies that refute most of their marijuana demonization claims.

A more recent, and decidedly alarmist report, titled "Residential Marijuana Grows in Colorado: The New Meth Houses?," noted that "marijuana grows often cause extensive damage to the houses where they are maintained and are increasingly the causes of house fires, blown electrical transformers, and environmental damage. Much like the 'meth houses' of the 1990s, many of these homes may ultimately be rendered uninhabitable" (Drug Enforcement Administration 2016). Although providing no evidence for this claim, the report alleges that "as a result of Colorado's medical and recreational marijuana laws, the system is exploited by traffickers who operate large marijuana grows that supply out of state markets."

A 2014 report, "The DEA," by the Drug Policy Alliance lists several of the DEA's failings with respect to cannabis and other drugs. These include "failing to act in a timely fashion," especially with respect to marijuana rescheduling petitions (Drug Policy Alliance 2014, 2). Somewhat amazingly, the DEA took sixteen years to issue a decision in the first marijuana rescheduling petition, five years for the second, and nine years for the third, five years for the fourth, and five years for the most recent petition, filed in 2011 by Governors Christine Gregoire of Washington State and Lincoln Chaffee of Rhode Island. Of course, in each of these cases, the DEA refused to reclassify marijuana—it remains a Schedule I drug. The agency has also created a "regulatory Catch-22" by asserting that there is insufficient scientific evidence to support the medical use of marijuana, while simultaneously acting (in concert with the NIDA) to impede research by delaying and in many cases rejecting researchers' applications to obtain supplies of marijuana (Drug Policy Alliance 2014b, 2).

Actions/Operations of the DEA

> The DEA relies on marijuana being outlawed so they can justify invading peoples' privacy, using asset forfeiture laws to steal property, buying fancy toys, and requesting multi-million dollar budgets every year. You think they are just going to let all that go? They can't even admit that marijuana is less harmful than heroin.
>
> —NGAIO BEALUM, "Stoned Rabbits Are the Anti-marijuana
>   Movement's Weakest Ploy Yet"

In addition to the rhetoric of DEA administrators and misinformation included in several of their reports, the agency also has a long history of taking questionable actions in furthering the drug wars, with marijuana being a primary focus of these activities. For example, in February 2003, under a 1994 statute making it a crime to sell drug paraphernalia, the DEA launched Operation Pipe Dream, a countrywide crackdown on paraphernalia used to consume marijuana (water pipes, bongs, etc.). In this operation, which cost an estimated $12 million (*Huffington Post* 2013), approximately two thousand federal agents raided more than one hundred homes and businesses and arrested fifty-five people. Among the arrestees was Tommy Chong (famous for his roles in movies such as *Up in Smoke*), whose Los Angeles home was surrounded by SWAT team helicopters and who was sentenced to nine months in prison, fined $20,000, and had to forfeit $120,000 in assets for distributing bongs and marijuana pipes online (Lee 2012).

After the legalization of medical marijuana in California in 1996, the DEA conducted several raids of marijuana dispensaries in the state. And such actions continued in the 2010s—for example, in Seattle in the spring of 2013, a series of letters from the DEA led to the closure of several medical marijuana stores. One such letter, sent to landlords whose properties were being used as marijuana dispensaries, stated:

> Using this [*sic*] premises for the distribution of marijuana, or to fa-
> cilitate the unlawful trafficking in a controlled substance, is violative
> of the federal law. As owner of this [*sic*] premises, please take note
> that federal trafficking laws operate independently of Washington
> controlled substance laws. If your above-identified premises is [*sic*],
> indeed, being used to facilitate drug trafficking in violation of federal
> law, your property is subject to forfeiture. . . . Furthermore, you may
> be subject to criminal prosecution. (Quoted in Ellison 2013)

In June 2016, Cannacraft, a northern California cannabis producer and distributor, was raided by approximately one hundred federal and local law enforcement officers, who claimed that the process the company used to make marijuana products was dangerous and illegal. Raids at the company's headquarters and four other facilities resulted in the seizure of $5 million in equipment, inventory, and cash (Fuller 2016b).

Another costly and arguably wasteful DEA activity involves the eradication of marijuana crops—in 2016, the budget for this program totaled $18 million (Atkins 2017). The DEA initiated this program in 1979, with only California and Hawaii participating at the time, but by 1982, twenty-five states had joined in. In their original justification for this program, the DEA noted, "In addition to cultivating an illegal drug that contributed to wholesale abuse, marijuana growers presented other problems to law enforcement and the environment. They encroached on national forests and threatened innocent people. To protect their marijuana crops, many growers equipped their marijuana patches with booby traps, trip wires, and explosives. Marijuana growers also threatened the environment by using pesticides, building harmful dams for irrigation, and cutting down trees" (Drug Enforcement Administration, n.d.).

Christopher Ingraham (2015c) asserts that in the mid-2000s, the majority of "marijuana" plants eradicated under this program were in fact "ditchweed," and in 2015, the DEA spent $73,000 to eradicate marijuana plants in Utah but did not find a single plant (Ingraham 2016c). And even though marijuana is legal in Washington State, it was the fourth-largest recipient of

DEA eradication funds (at $760,000) in 2016—each plant destroyed in the state costs $26.49 (Atkins 2017). In what Ingraham (2016d) refers to as a "stunning abuse" of the marijuana eradication program, in September 2016, Massachusetts State Police and the National Guard sent a helicopter and several police vehicles to an eighty-one-year-old Amherst woman's house to eradicate a single marijuana plant (the woman was apparently growing it to deal with glaucoma and arthritis).

In the fall of 2016, a group of eight members of Congress sent a letter to the Government Accountability Office, questioning whether the cannabis eradication program should continue to receive funds: "While the DEA's cannabis eradication/suppression program has been in effect for three decades, given the recent trend in state laws to legalize and decriminalize the production, distribution, or consumption of marijuana calls into question the necessity of such a program" (quoted in Atkins 2017).

Agents of Demonization

The National Institute on Drug Abuse

> Consider what American science might look like if all research were run like marijuana research is being run now. Suppose the Institute for Creation Science were put in charge of approving paleontology digs and the science of human evolution. Imagine what would happen to the environment if we gave coal and oil companies the power to block any climate research they didn't like.
> —JOHN SCHWARZ (physicist at the California Institute of
>   Technology), quoted in Nicole Flatow, "Caltech Physicist"

The NIDA was established in 1974 as part of the federal government's response to issues of alcohol and other drug abuse and mental health problems. The agency's website states, "Our mission is to advance science on the causes and consequences of drug use and addiction and to apply that knowledge to improve individual and public health" (National Institute on Drug Abuse, n.d.). Given some of the views and actions of NIDA that we discuss, one might question this claim.

NIDA plays an indirect role in marijuana demonization through its funding of research on the substance. Thus, Sanjay Gupta (2013) estimates that only about 6 percent of current studies on marijuana in the United States investigate the benefits of marijuana, while the rest are focused on examining harms: "That imbalance paints a highly distorted picture" (see also Lee 2012). Or, as Bruce Barcott and Michael Scherer (2015) comment, "The U.S. leads the world in studies of marijuana's harm, but we're net importers of data dealing with its healing potential."

An additional and related problem with NIDA is that the agency has generally refused to provide medical marijuana researchers with the high-potency marijuana they require to further clarify the drug's benefits and its associated problems. Under the government's marijuana research program, researchers who want to study marijuana's effects must obtain their supplies of the drug from the University of Mississippi's cannabis production facility. According to its website, the strongest marijuana NIDA has available is 10 percent THC—far below the average THC content of the marijuana that is commonly being used in the United States (in Colorado, for example, the average marijuana flower product for sale at retail outlets averages 17.1 percent THC) (Hesse 2016b). The problem here is not only that research on marijuana loses its validity because it does not reflect the reality of what is happening in the real world; it also prevents marijuana researchers from being a watchdog of the legal marijuana industry (preventing research on the use of contaminants, the effects of higher-potency marijuana, including edibles, etc.) (Hesse 2016b). A prime example of the ongoing problems with NIDA's marijuana supply comes from a study of the potential benefits of marijuana for treating PTSD in veterans. Sue Sisley, the lead researcher in this study, reports that the marijuana she received from NIDA looked like "green talcum powder. . . . It didn't resemble cannabis. It didn't smell like cannabis" (quoted in Hellerman 2017). In addition, some of the samples contained mold, and others did not match the potency Sisley had requested.

NIDA has also been involved in spreading misinformation about drugs in general and marijuana in particular, including in drug "prevention" programs supported by the agency and the Partnership for a Drug Free America (now known as the Partnership for Drug Free Kids). For example, a NIDA document, "Marijuana: Facts Parents Need to Know," reads like a primer on how to tell if your child is an adolescent. Among the signs that NIDA claims, under the subheading "How Can I Tell If My Child Has Been Using Marijuana?," may indicate that a child is using marijuana are "changes in [the] child's behavior, such as not brushing hair or teeth, skipping showers, changes in mood . . . a change in friends . . . changes in grades . . . changes in eating or sleeping habits, and . . . hav[ing] unexplained lack of money or extra cash on hand" (National Institute on Drug Abuse 2018, 21).

Dr. Nora Volkow, who has been the director of NIDA since 2003, has taken something of a head-in-the-sand approach to marijuana, claiming that she has not consumed the substance but was "curious" about the drug. Volkow indicated that she was "terrified about anything that would interfere with my cognitive capacity. I don't like to contaminate my perception of the world, I have too much respect for my brain" (quoted in Marcus 2014). Volkow is also apparently unaware that pharmaceutical drugs (many of which cause far more damage than marijuana) are legal in the United States, commenting, "The legalization process generates a much greater exposure of people and hence of negative consequences that will emerge. And that's why I always say 'Can we as a country afford to have a *third* legal drug? Can we?'" (quoted in Marcus 2014; emphasis added). Here, it is worth stressing that alcohol and tobacco are legal drugs that cause a considerable amount of harm, but so too are pharmaceutical drugs—in particular, prescription opioids, which are associated with *far* more harm than marijuana.

Nora Volkow and colleagues (2014) published an article in the *New England Journal of Medicine* on the adverse effects of marijuana use that was somewhat balanced but still emphasized many of the same themes we have seen from other marijuana demonizers: the substance is addictive, causes brain damage, is related to mental illness, and has negative effects on school performance and "lifetime achievement." These authors also emphasize the theme of "this is not your father's marijuana," asserting, "The increase in potency [of marijuana] over time also raises questions about the current relevance of findings in older studies on the effects of marijuana use, especially studies that assessed long-term outcomes" (2222).

While we would agree with concerns regarding the potential negative effects of higher-potency marijuana, some research indicates that experienced marijuana users typically titrate their doses (Fox, Armentano, and Tvert 2009). A British study of 247 regular marijuana users found that individuals would adjust the size of the joints they rolled (and consumed) based on the marijuana product's THC content—users with higher-potency marijuana tended to roll smaller joints, and vice versa (cited in Casarett 2015). Interestingly, titration was recognized as far back as the La Guardia report, where it was noted, "A confirmed marijuana user can readily distinguish the quality and potency of various brands, just as the habitual cigarette or cigar smoker is able to differentiate between the qualities of tobacco" (Mayor's Committee on Marihuana 1944), and it was also mentioned in the Canadian government's Le Dain Commission report (see Le Dain 1972).

More recently however, NIDA has shown signs of softening its stance on cannabis. In August 2016 (ironically, around the same time that the DEA announced that marijuana would remain a Schedule I drug), NIDA posted a report on its website, noting that "in a recent study [Jackson et al. 2016] sponsored by NIDA and the National Institute of Mental Health, teens who used marijuana lost IQ points relative to their non-using peers. However, the drug appeared not to be the culprit" (Grabus 2016). Instead, the NIDA report pointed out, youth who used marijuana saw IQ decline because they had experienced adverse familial influences that led to declines in their motivation to learn and predisposed them to involvement in delinquency and deviant behaviors, including substance use. Further indication that NIDA was softening its stance is revealed in what Tom Angell (2017) of the organization Marijuana Majority refers to as "subtle" changes to information on marijuana that appears on the agency's web page. These changes include "paring back the rhetoric about cannabis's supposed potential to cause addiction and overdose" and downplaying the assertion that marijuana is a gateway drug.

Law Enforcement

> It is difficult to get a man to understand something when his salary depends on not understanding it.
> —UPTON SINCLAIR, *I, Candidate for Governor*

In discussing the role of certain law enforcement agencies and officials in marijuana demonization, it is important to stress that these agencies have a vested interest in marijuana remaining illegal, because to a certain extent, their funding depends on it. More widespread legalization of marijuana could potentially lead to significant reductions in federal grants, which are an important source of funding for many law enforcement agencies (Balko 2014b). More specifically, it has been pointed out that grant programs such as the Department of Justice Byrne Justice Assistance Grants, which provide funding for communities to target their "most pressing local" crime needs (National Criminal Justice Association Center for Justice Planning, n.d.), may lead police departments to pursue low-level drug offenses, including marijuana possession. Performance measures used to determine which departments receive grants and whether the grants are renewed are based on factors such as the number of arrests (Balko 2014b). As we note in Chapter 1, data on marijuana arrests indicate that such arrests are fairly easy for police to make.

Perhaps the iconic example of marijuana demonization comes from the Rocky Mountain HIDTA's 2015 report *The Legalization of Marijuana in Colorado: The Impact.*[1] This report of more than 160 pages, which one commentator referred to as "apocalyptic" (Adams 2016), is full of graphs and tables and engages in several strategies to distort the facts surrounding marijuana and the effects of marijuana legalization in Colorado.[2] Much of the data presented in the report is not sufficiently contextualized; historical

---

1. The HIDTA program was created by Congress under the Anti–Drug Abuse Act of 1988 to "provide assistance to federal, state, local, and tribal law enforcement agencies operating in areas determined to be critical drug-trafficking regions of the United States." As of 2016, there were twenty-eight HIDTAs, which covered close to 66 percent of the U.S. population (White House 2016). HIDTAs are a component of the White House's National Drug Control Strategy and thus are mandated to oppose any drug legalization efforts. As Russ Belville (2015) comments, HIDTAs are also bureaucracies that require "finding failure in legalization to maintain [their] budgets."

2. Several of the misleading claims and statistics contained in this report were removed after widespread criticism. However, we include them here because many of the original claims were cited in media sources and by marijuana legalization opponents.

goalposts that serve to inflate claims are used, and percentage figures are frequently reported without base numbers. And importantly, similar to several other reports on the effects of marijuana legalization, the Rocky Mountain HIDTA report seems oblivious to the fact that, while recreational marijuana was legalized in Colorado in 2012, retail sales of the drug did not begin until January 2014. As Mason Tvert, then associated with the MPP, commented about this report, "[It was] prepared by an organization that campaigned against the initiative to regulate marijuana in Colorado, and its head was a spokesperson and financial donor for that political campaign. Moreover, it's an organization who has a vested financial interest in keeping marijuana illegal in as many states as possible" (quoted in Adams 2016).

One of the major arguments of antilegalization groups and individuals is that marijuana legalization will lead to increases in youth use of the substance. The Rocky Mountain HIDTA report notes, "In 2013, 11.16 percent of Colorado youth ages 12 to 17 were considered current marijuana users compared to 7.1% nationally." Colorado ranked third in the nation with respect to this metric and was "56 percent higher than the national average" (2015, 2). However, the report conveniently neglects to mention that youth marijuana use in Colorado has been higher than that in other states for several years. In 2008–2010, the rate of youth marijuana use in Colorado was 13.25 percent, but the national rate was 8.61 percent, representing a difference of 54 percent. As Russ Belville (2015) comments, "Colorado has always had greater teen usage rates than the nation as a whole. Reforming marijuana laws doesn't lead to greater marijuana use; places with greater marijuana use demand reforms of marijuana laws." In addition, the authors of the Rocky Mountain HIDTA report chose not to include the results of the Healthy Kids Colorado Survey in considering trends in youth use "because of changes in sample size." It turns out that the change in sample size for the survey was an increase in the number of subjects—in almost all evaluations of the validity of survey data, a larger sample size is desirable. However, it appears the real reason the Healthy Kids Colorado data were not included in the report on the impacts of legalization is that they did not show increases in youth use.

Referring to data indicating that marijuana was being transported out of the state of Colorado (and thereby feeding the black market in those states), the HIDTA report notes that "U.S. mail parcel interceptions of Colorado marijuana, destined to 38 other states, increased 2,033 percent from 2010–2014. Pounds of Colorado marijuana seized in the U.S. mail, destined for 38 other states, increased 722 percent from 2010–2014" (Rocky Mountain High Intensity Drug Trafficking Area [HIDTA] 2015, 4). (Recall that legal sales of recreational marijuana did not commence in Colorado until January 1, 2014.) And as if this were not enough, the report further notes that from 2006 to 2008, compared to 2013 to 2014, the average number of seized parcels containing Colorado marijuana destined for outside the United States increased more than 7,750 percent (124). While all these percentage increases may seem impressive and, of course, cause for alarm, they are somewhat less so when one looks at the fine print and the raw numbers. Unfortunately, no raw data on the actual number of parcels seized are provided for the 2006–2008 period in the report, although the number of parcels seized in 2009 was zero and increased to 320 in 2014. The report includes a graph depicting "Colorado Emergency Department Rates that *Could be Related* to Marijuana," which increased from 873 in 2013 to 1,039 in 2014 (79; emphasis in original). The use of the term "rates" in the title of the graph seems curious and inappropriate (given that the graph includes the number of visits, not rates per population), and it is similarly curious that such data on visits that "could be" related to marijuana are even relevant.

The HIDTA report also claimed that crime in the city of Denver increased 12.3 percent over the 2010–2014 period, implying that this increase was solely due to marijuana legalization. However, other official crime reports suggest that these claims are inaccurate—for example, the Denver Police Department found that marijuana legalization had *not* had a significant impact on major crimes (N. Phillips 2016). Additionally, the report claims (quoting a Colorado Springs Police Department report) that "the legalization of marijuana is fueling a sex tourism industry in Colorado. 'Several victims were brought to Colorado specifically because of the availability of marijuana and the state being "4-20 friendly"'" (Rocky Mountain HIDTA 2015, 112). Marijuana legalization was also allegedly leading to an increase in homelessness in Colorado, "with the appeal of legal marijuana being a factor" (5). While acknowledging that "there are no records on how many homeless people came to Colorado because of 'legal weed,'" the report alleges that "homeless centers are seeing an influx, straining their ability to meet the need" (146).

With respect to another major marijuana demonization theme—that legalization will lead to an increase in automobile collisions and traffic deaths—the original version of the HIDTA report claimed, "Researchers found that marijuana users are 25 times more likely to be in an accident than those that did not use the drug. By comparison, drunk drivers are four times more likely to crash than sober drivers" (2015, 30). As journalist Russ Belville (2015) of the *Huffington Post* notes, the study being referred to was a NHTSA study that stated that there was a 1.25 odds-risk ratio for THC-positive drivers compared to sober drivers, which means that there was a 25 *percent* greater risk of involvement in a collision (which is obviously a much lower risk than the 400 percent greater risk for drunk drivers cited in the same study). The authors of the Rocky Mountain HIDTA report (either knowingly or unknowingly) reported the 25 percent greater risk as a 25 *times* greater risk. (A later version of the report was modified to delete this claim.)

The Rocky Mountain HIDTA report further claims that marijuana-related traffic deaths in Colorado increased 32 percent and that approximately 20 percent of all traffic deaths were marijuana-related compared to only 10 percent less than five years ago (2015, 14). However, these data seem somewhat less alarming when one considers that the 32 percent increase in marijuana-related traffic deaths was actually an increase from seventy-one to ninety-four deaths (Otinger 2015). In addition, and as is the case for other claims of increases in marijuana-related traffic deaths after legalization, the data do not allow for a determination of whether marijuana consumption *caused* the collision and subsequent death.

In addition to the questionable presentation of statistics, the Rocky Mountain HIDTA report also includes numerous anecdotes in support of the alleged deleterious effects of marijuana legalization. One of the more amusing anecdotes, apparently employed to emphasize the threat marijuana legalization poses to Colorado youth, claimed that marijuana was being used as a "pickup tool" by some youth. One boy, while in class and trying to pick up girls, "offered to share marijuana edibles . . . to three girls in his class while asking for their phone numbers" (2015, 45). Comments from school resource officers included, "Many kids come back from lunch highly intoxicated from marijuana use. The halls reek of pot, so many kids are high that it is impossible to apprehend all but the most impaired" (48). Security officers in one school "noticed an increased traffic flow to and from [the] restroom and found the weed and soon after the violators" (50).

Of course, negligent and evil parents are also implicated in many of the cases of youth use. The report notes that a school resource officer reported that the father of two boys at a high school, who held a medical marijuana card, was having them both "smoke a bowl" before school: "He thought it would make their school day easier" (Rocky Mountain HIDTA 2015, 50). Another elementary school official commented that there had been an increase in the "number of parents showing up to school high" (51).

Additional anecdotes included in the report make reference to people doing crazy things while under the influence of marijuana. For example, it is noted that Dr. Chris Colwell, the chief of emergency medicine at Denver Health Medical Center, says that several times each week, he and his staff see people who have consumed marijuana and are acting suicidal. "He states that they have to be restrained to ensure they are not a danger to themselves or other people. [He] recalls one example in which a man dressed as Super Man ingested marijuana edibles and then jumped off a balcony as if he could fly" (Rocky Mountain HIDTA 2015, 70).

In considering this report and its various misleading and outlandish claims, it is important to note that, as Chapter 6 discusses in more detail, several of the "facts" derived from it have been cited by other marijuana prohibitionists and in antilegalization campaigns in other states. For example, in October 2016, a letter written by Denver District Attorney Michael Morrisey was sent to the "No on 64" antilegalization campaign in California. Among other things, and while not elucidating the specifics of the causal relationships, Morrisey argued that homicide, motor vehicle thefts, robberies, and even sexual assaults had increased in Colorado—all of this was alleged to be *caused* by marijuana legalization. Several of the claims made in the Rocky Mountain HIDTA report have also been cited by Kevin Sabet of SAM in support of his assertions that marijuana legalization in Colorado has been a disaster (Belville 2015). And most recently, as we discuss in Chapter 7, in a letter to Colorado governor John Hickenlooper expressing concerns about marijuana legalization in that state, Attorney General Jeff Sessions made extensive reference to the report.

Although much more balanced in general than the 2015 Rocky Mountain HIDTA, a 2016 report by the Northwest HIDTA on the impact of marijuana legalization in Washington State also contains several alarmist and misleading statements. For example, the report notes that Washington State's medical marijuana law specified the number of plants that could be grown by providers but not their size. As a result, "norms for the state soon entailed marijuana plants in the form of trees rather than small bushes. . . . Law enforcement has encountered single plants that generate several pounds per harvest." A picture beside this statement shows a large, treelike marijuana plant, with the caption "This photo provides an example of what a *typical* outdoor marijuana plant looks like" (Northwest High Intensity Drug Trafficking Area [HIDTA] 2016, 17; emphasis added).

With respect to youth use of marijuana in Washington State since legalization, the Northwest HIDTA report notes that Washington State Healthy Youth Survey data indicate a decline in use for eighth- and tenth-grade students over the 2010–2014 period, while rates of use for sixth- and twelfth-grade students were unchanged. However, similar to the use of anecdotes in the Rocky Mountain HIDTA report, the Northwest HIDTA report notes, "One of the elementary schools in the Seattle School District reported that a 5th grade student had brought a marijuana infused candy bar to school to share with fellow students" (2016, 64).

The Northwest HIDTA report also includes data and comments on apparent increases in marijuana-related cases of driving under the influence (DUI) in Washington State, using the tactic of reporting large percentage increases to emphasize the alleged seriousness of the problem. It notes that the Spokane Valley Police Department recorded eight marijuana-related DUIs in 2012 but forty in 2014, a "400% increase" (Northwest HIDTA 2016, 85). And in Spokane Valley "youth marijuana DUIs have been increasing *exponentially*. In 2012, Spokane Valley had only one youth test confirmed for active THC. In 2014, the number was 18, a 1700% increase in three years" (85; emphasis added). To further emphasize the marijuana DUI problem, the report includes six anecdotes of "news articles related to Washington State roadways on marijuana use" (90)—only one of which, the case from Granger, provides objective data (actual marijuana blood content) for the drivers involved.

- Skagit County, May 2014: A nineteen year-old driver under the influence of marijuana and *alcohol* killed three in a head on collision.
- Vancouver, October 2014: A driver who smoked marijuana three hours before driving hit four trick-or-treaters, killing one seven year-old. Two women, one being the seven year-old's mother, and the other child, a six year old, were injured.
- Puyallup, November 2014: A nineteen year-old ran a stop sign and hit a local pastor killing him as he rode his bike. The driver admitted to smoking marijuana before the crash.
- Ephrata, February 2015: Officers pulled over a twenty-three year old driver with a felony record and an eleven year-old passenger, the driver's niece. The officer noticed the impairment of the driver in regard to which the driver admitted to smoking marijuana earlier. Officers found a 9mm pistol in the glove compartment with ammunition.
- Granger, May 2015: A twenty-five year old man killed his wife and injured his three year old daughter in an accident. . . . The driver's blood content for marijuana was 23 ng/ml—far above the 5 ng/ml limit.
- Olympia, July 2015: A twenty-six year old driver under the influence of marijuana was reported to be exceeding speeds over 100mph before he crashed into the back of a woman's car. The woman's car then rolled into a ditch where she died. The passenger in the driver's car was also injured. (90–91; emphasis added)

In addition to reports on the evils associated with marijuana legalization by law enforcement organizations, individual law enforcement officers have offered critical comments in response to legalization. For example, in response to reports that recreational marijuana legalization in Washington State was freeing up police resources and leading to significantly fewer arrests, Mitch Barker, executive director of the Washington State Association of Sheriffs and Police Chiefs, in an example of reducing arguments to the absurd, commented, "I can't fault their logic. If we took speeding off the book, that would free up time. The question we have to look at is, is it good public policy? My sole concern is that when you expand access to marijuana for adults, you expand access for underage people" (quoted in G. Johnson 2014a). Barker's comment is also reflective of the tendency of some law enforcement officials to make it seem as though "legalization invented marijuana" (Ellison 2014a).

Bill Bratton, a prominent law enforcement official who twice served as police commissioner in New York City (1994–1996 and 2014–2016), as well as in Boston and Los Angeles, has also been a vocal marijuana demonizer. Bratton held a press conference in the spring of 2015 in which he blamed occasional marijuana use and sales of the drug for an increase in murders in New York City. Further, in a 2016 radio interview, Bratton stated, "Interestingly enough, here in New York City, most of the violence we see, violence around drug trafficking, is involving marijuana, and I have to scratch my head as we're seeing more states wanting to legalize marijuana" (quoted in K. Shapiro 2016a). In essence, and similar to other law enforcement officials, even if these doubtful claims regarding the role of marijuana in generating violence were true, Bratton is actually presenting an argument *for* legalization as an argument against it—marijuana-related violence in New York City (the actual extent of which is unknown) is a predictable outcome of the black market.

One of the more comical examples of law enforcement officials' concerns regarding the liberalization of marijuana laws is that of Michael Pristoop, chief of police in Annapolis, Maryland. Testifying against two marijuana-related bills before Maryland's Judicial Proceedings Committee, Pristoop indicated that he had uncovered a news article reporting that thirty-seven people in Colorado had overdosed on the same day the state legalized marijuana. Unfortunately for Pristoop, the story he referred to had been made up by the *Daily Currant*, an online comedy magazine (Kunkle 2014).

However, not all law enforcement and criminal justice system officials are opposed to the liberalization of marijuana laws (or drug laws more generally). For example, a group known as Law Enforcement Against Prohibition (now known as Law Enforcement Action Partnership [LEAP]) has been critical of U.S. drug laws since its formation in 2002 and endorsed several marijuana law reform initiatives in 2016. LEAP (2016a) is committed to "ending decades of failed marijuana policies that have damaged the lives of countless Americans and their families, slowed the justice system at every level, and eroded trust between communities and police."

Several prominent individual law enforcement officials have also spoken out against the drug war and advocated for drug law reform. Over two decades ago, former Kansas City and San Jose police chief Joseph McNamara spoke out against the widespread corruption created by the drug war: "We are familiar with the perception that the first casualty in any war is truth. Eighty years of drug war propaganda has so influenced public opinion that most politicians believe they will lose their jobs if opponents can claim they are soft on drugs" (Buckley 1996). Similarly, Norm Stamper (2005a, 2005b), who served as chief of the Seattle Police Department for six years, wrote a book and an op-ed that appeared in the *Los Angeles Times* and several other newspapers, in which he argued, "It's time to accept drug use as a right of adult Americans, treat drug abuse as a public health problem, and end the madness of this unwinnable war."

Agents of Opposition

Big Pharma and the American Medical Association

Although not as prominent or vocal in their opposition to marijuana law reform, large pharmaceutical companies have generally been opposed to marijuana legalization and have worked behind the scenes to influence public opinion on the issue. These companies have lobbied federal agencies to prevent marijuana law reform, have funded studies by anti-marijuana researchers, and have provided funding to anti-marijuana legalization groups such as the Anti-Drug Coalition of America (Ingraham 2016i). For example, Insys Therapeutics, a company that manufactures painkillers and is also developing a drug based on a synthetic version of THC, contributed $500,000 to the anti-marijuana legalization campaign in Arizona (Ingraham 2016a). With further marijuana law reform on both the medical and recreational side, pharmaceutical companies are likely to experience decreases in sales of their products. As Doug Fine notes, the dilemma faced by Big Pharma with respect to marijuana is that "a plant that's relatively easy to grow in your backyard can prove an impediment to shareholder value if your business model calls for patenting much more expensive, usually much less effective, synthesized or derivative pills" (2012, 27–28).

The AMA, while supporting additional clinical research on marijuana's possible medicinal benefits, has continued to take an official stance opposing recreational and medical marijuana legalization—a position that first emerged in the 1940s. One could speculate that at least some of this opposition is related to the fact that doctors are influenced by large pharmaceutical companies, who provide them with several financial benefits (including gifts, meals, tickets to major sporting and entertainment events, and in some cases, lavish trips) (Mosher and Akins 2014) in an attempt to influence the doctors to prescribe their products. More specifically, a recent study published in the *American Journal of Public Health* found that over the August 2013 to December 2015 period, a total of 375,266 nonresearch opioid payments were made to more than sixty-eight thousand physicians (representing one in twelve physicians in the United States), with a total amount of more than $46 million distributed (Hadland, Krieger, and Marshall 2017). While the authors of this study did not track whether physicians given these payments actually recommended opiates to their patients, they suggest that their findings "should prompt an examination of industry influences on opioid prescribing" (Hadland, Krieger, and Marshall 2017, 1493).

Members of the American Psychiatric Association (APA) have also been skeptical of medical marijuana, with Dr. Timothy Jennings, a "prominent Tennessee psychiatrist," stating, "Medical marijuana for treatment of psychiatric problems is no better than prescribing cigarette smoke to treat lung disease" and that "psychiatry is positioned with a unique opportunity to stand up and oppose the latest chicanery to be promoted as 'medicine'—medical marijuana" (quoted in Bennett and White 2015, 56). Jennings believes medical marijuana is a fad that has no scientific merit and compares it to the practice of intentionally bleeding patients to drain away "evil humors" (News Medical 2013). While we are not suggesting that Jennings's views are representative of those of all psychiatrists, the official position of the APA (2013) on medical marijuana is that there is "no current scientific evidence that marijuana is in any way beneficial for the treatment of any psychiatric disorder. In contrast, current evidence supports, at minimum, a strong association of cannabis use with the onset of psychiatric disorders." The APA statement adds that medical treatment "should not be authorized by ballot initiatives" and "no medication approved by the FDA is smoked." Is the APA not aware of the numerous studies documenting marijuana's medicinal benefits?

While the AMA and APA are still opposed to marijuana legalization, there are signs that other professional medical-related organizations are changing their stance toward the issue. For example, the California Medical Association (CMA), which represents more than forty-one thousand physicians in the state, has publicly supported marijuana legalization. This organization first endorsed marijuana legalization in a white paper in 2011 that focused on social justice issues. The paper noted that marijuana prohibition diverted limited economic resources to the justice system, resulted in the destruction of family units when marijuana users were incarcerated, and disproportionately affected members of minority groups. In a February 2016 press release in support of marijuana legalization in California, the CMA stated, "CMA does not as a matter of policy encourage the use of marijuana and discourages smoking. But, ultimately, its members believe that the most effective way to protect the public health is to tightly control, track, and regulate marijuana and to comprehensively research and educate the public on its health impacts, not through ineffective prohibition."

The motto of the organization Doctors for Cannabis Regulation (DFCR) states, "Because you don't have to be pro-marijuana to oppose its prohibition." On its website, DFCR notes that (according to a 2014 Medscape poll of physicians) a majority of American doctors believe that marijuana should be legalized and that "cannabis prohibition clearly causes more harm than good."[3] In support of legalization, DFCR focuses on harm reduction and public health principles (Ingraham 2016l) and emphasizes on its website that

---

3. See the DFCR home page, at https://dfcr.org.

(1) use of cannabis by healthy adults is generally benign; (2) cannabis is less harmful for adults than alcohol and tobacco; (3) while the substance can be harmful to minors, prohibition has not prevented them from accessing marijuana; and (4) "the burden of cannabis prohibition falls disproportionately upon communities of color and the nation's poor." An article by David Nathan, H. Westley Clark, and former U.S. surgeon general Jocelyn Elders, published in the *American Journal of Public Health*, notes that marijuana prohibition "has done more harm to public health than marijuana itself" (2017, 1746) and that DFCR advocates for the legalization of cannabis rather than decriminalization "because effective regulation requires legalization" (1747).

While not supporting full legalization, the American Academy of Pediatrics (AAP) (2015) recommends that marijuana should be decriminalized and reclassified from Schedule I to allow for additional research on its medical benefits. In defense of its recommendation that marijuana be rescheduled, Seth Ammerman, a clinical professor in pediatrics and member of the AAP's national committee on substance abuse, commented, "A Schedule I listing means there's no medical use or helpful indications, but we know that's not true because there has been limited evidence showing [marijuana] may be helpful for certain conditions in adults" (quoted in Reiman 2015b). The AAP (2015) also recommends allowing some children access to cannabinoids more immediately: "Given that some children who may benefit from cannabinoids cannot wait for a meticulous and lengthy research process, the Academy recognizes some exceptions should be made for compassionate use in children with debilitating or life-limiting diseases."

The American Public Health Association (APHA), while not necessarily supporting marijuana legalization, issued a policy statement in November 2014 that implicitly criticized marijuana prohibition and calls for "a public health approach to regulating and controlling commercially legalized marijuana and urges that regulation of legalized marijuana be viewed as a public health priority. Regulation will provide oversight of a market that is currently uncontrolled and can help address the unforeseen effects of marijuana legalization" (Reiman 2015b).

A final indication that the views of influential medical organizations on marijuana may be changing is evidenced in comments by U.S. surgeon general Dr. Vivek Murthy in February 2015 on *CBS This Morning*: "We have some preliminary data showing that for certain medical conditions and symptoms, marijuana can be helpful. I think we have to use that data to drive policymaking" (quoted in Davies 2015).

Beer and Alcohol Distributors

Although they are somewhat under the radar, beer and alcohol distributors have made financial contributions to anti-marijuana legalization campaigns in several states, largely because they see legalized marijuana as a threat to their sales. For example, the Beer Distributors Political Action Committee, consisting of sixteen beer distributors in the state of Massachusetts, donated $25,000 to the antilegalization group Campaign for a Safe and Healthy Massachusetts in 2016 (although this is obviously not a large amount of money, it was the third-largest financial contribution the antilegalization group received) (Wallace 2016c). The Boston Beer Company (the parent company of Samuel Adams) informed its investors that "laws that allow the sale and distribution of marijuana" might "adversely impact the demand for beer" (quoted in Wallace 2016c). Similarly, the Brown-Forman Company (producers of Jack Daniels Tennessee whiskey and Finlandia vodka) noted in its annual report to the Securities and Exchange Commission that "consumer preferences and purchases may shift due to a host of factors, many of which are difficult to predict, including . . . the potential legalization of marijuana use on a more widespread basis" (quoted in Wallace 2016c). It is significant that the Nevada Resort Association (the main lobbying group for the state's casino industry) (Rindels 2016) supported the antilegalization campaign in the state of Nevada; and Sheldon Adelson, CEO of the Las Vegas Sands Casino company, contributed $2 million to the antilegalization campaign in Nevada and $500,000 to the antilegalization campaign in Arizona (Ingraham 2016a). Although we do not have definitive evidence of their motivation in doing so, it is possible that the financial support of the gambling/casino industry was related to the fact that marijuana legalization might negatively impact their alcohol sales. As Mason Tvert, then associated with the MPP, commented, "If you like drinking alcohol and playing blackjack at the casino, Mr. Adelson wants you to be his guest. If you prefer to consume marijuana while playing video games in the privacy of your home, Mr. Adelson wants you to be in jail" (quoted in Ingraham 2016a).

Agencies of Demonization: SAM

> The marijuana industry is taking cues from big tobacco . . . downplay the risks, encourage heavy use [and] start 'em young.
> —KEVIN SABET, quoted in Jeff Mapes, "The Rise of a Drug
>   from Outlaw Status to Retail Shelves"

The most prominent anti-marijuana legalization group in the current era is SAM, headed by Kevin Sabet, who worked in the Clinton, Bush, and Obama administrations as a researcher at the ONDCP. Bruce Barcott has referred to Sabet as a "spin doctor" (2015, 240) whose claims "simply don't correspond with the facts on the ground, no matter how much he wanted them to be true" (171).

SAM's main focus appears to be the (as yet unsubstantiated) claim that large-scale commercialization of the marijuana industry is inevitable. For example, in response to a proposal by Republican senator Rand Paul of Kentucky and Democratic senators Cory Booker of New Jersey and Kirsten Gillibrand of New York to decriminalize the use of medical marijuana by moving the substance to Schedule II of the Controlled Substances Act, Sabet commented that the proposed bill "is like using a sledgehammer to crack a nut. . . . We should not open the floodgates to Big Marijuana so that businesses can sell pot for profit to people with a headache" (quoted in Halper 2015). Similarly, in response to the proliferation of billboards advertising marijuana businesses in Portland, Oregon, after the state voted to legalize recreational marijuana in 2014, Sabet commented, "Joe Camel normalized cigarette smoking, especially for young people. The Marlboro man normalized cigarettes for an entire generation. Marijuana wants to follow suit. Normalization is the cornerstone of that" (quoted in McGreal 2016).

Other leaders (although far less vocal than Kevin Sabet) of SAM include Patrick Kennedy, who has admitted addictions to alcohol and prescription painkillers (Jaffe 2016). Although he had voiced approval of marijuana for medical purposes, he announced in 2013 that "I now stand corrected by science" (quoted in Hotakainen 2013b). Echoing the themes of other marijuana demonizers, Kennedy, who asserted that SAM was a "truth-telling organization," claimed that research proved marijuana is a gateway drug, that it can induce psychosis, and that it can lead teenage consumers to lose IQ points (Hotakainen 2013b). SAM's advisory board also includes former George W. Bush's speechwriter (and current *Atlantic* magazine senior editor) David Frum and former drug czar Barry McCaffrey.

We were unable to uncover information on how SAM is funded, but Belville notes that a majority of the organization's advisory board are affiliated with drug rehabilitation/treatment companies, who receive over half of their referrals for individuals who have marijuana as their primary drug of choice. "Plus, marijuana is so non-addictive that these 'addicts' can easily stop, boosting the success of Big Rehab" (Belville 2015). We later deconstruct some of the more questionable claims made by SAM and Kevin Sabet.

Challenging one of the main themes of marijuana law reform proponents—that current laws result in far too many arrests, Sabet (2013a) asserted that "private, personal use of marijuana is rarely pursued by law enforcement" but in the following paragraph notes that "about 700,000 arrests are made yearly for marijuana possession." As we note in Chapter 1, it seems that seven hundred thousand arrests is not a trivial number. And whether or not individuals arrested for marijuana offenses end up in prison, their arrests show up on background checks when individuals are applying to rent apartments or obtain jobs and are "often treated by society as de facto markers of guilt" and constitute a "scarlet letter" (James 2016).

In an example of distortion that borders on the comical (or what might be referred to as "magic with math"), Sabet apparently sent a tweet to journalist Russ Belville of the *Huffington Post*, in which he stated, "Wow, two out of five high school students statewide [in Washington State] report getting their pot from dispensaries" (Belville 2013). Belville checked the data Sabet was referring to and found that it pertained to Seattle youth (not youth in the entire state of Washington). But more important (or perhaps he was being more deceitful or was just unaware), Sabet had basically added up the percentages of youth from the ninth through twelfth grades who reported that they had obtained their marijuana at a dispensary (3.8 percent of ninth-graders, 8.5 percent of tenth-graders, 12.0 percent of eleventh-graders, and 14.9 percent of twelfth-graders) to obtain the figure of 40 percent (actually, 39.2 percent). Sabet has also claimed that "marijuana addicts 1 out of every 6 children who *try* the drug" (2013a; emphasis added)—a claim that is simply not supported by scientific studies.

Reacting to a federal study indicating that marijuana use by youth in Colorado was highest among all states in 2014, Sabet commented, "In Colorado especially, big marijuana has been allowed to run wild, and it appears that kids are paying the price more than any other state in the country" (quoted in Nicholson 2015). Of course, this comment conveniently neglected the fact that Colorado has had among the highest rates of youth marijuana use for several years. It also neglected the fact that while Colorado's youth usage rates were relatively stable (even with recreational legalization)—in 2013–2014, 12.6 percent of twelve- to seventeen-year-olds in Colorado reported past-month marijuana use, which had increased from 11.2 percent in 2012–2013—the increase in use was not statistically significant (Baca 2015e).

In early 2017, in response to marijuana law reform initiatives in Vermont and Rhode Island, SAM initiated a new campaign, "Are We Sure?" (n.d.a, n.d.b). In reference to Senate Bill 16 in Vermont, which would expand the state's medical marijuana program, an online SAM publication offered the same timeworn arguments: the bill was "designed to create a powerful marijuana industry in Vermont that uses the same deceptive tactics as the tobacco industry." The document also repeated the same (largely false) claims that under legalization in Colorado, marijuana-related traffic deaths had increased, that youth drug use was increasing in the state, and that there had been an increase in crime in Denver (also false, and even if it were true, it is not specified how this alleged crime increase was related to marijuana legalization). Rejecting claims that marijuana tax revenues had been used to increase school funding in Colorado, the Are We Sure? document cites the superintendent of Cherry Street School in Greenwood Village, Colorado, who stated, "So far the only thing that legalization of marijuana has brought to our schools has been marijuana" (quoted in Are We Sure?, n.d.b). While the superintendent is entitled to his opinion, and SAM is similarly entitled to cite him, it is notable that a minimum of $40 million per year from wholesale marijuana taxes in Colorado are devoted to the state's Building Excellent

Schools Today program (Rittiman 2016). In fact, as of July 2017, $117.9 million of the total $506 million collected by the state of Colorado since the beginning of recreational marijuana sales in January 2014 had been used to fund school construction projects, with an additional $5.7 million dedicated to the Public School Fund, $5.8 million for drop-out and bullying prevention programs, and $4.5 million to increase the number of health professionals in schools (VS Strategies 2017).

Some might suggest that SAM's views are unimportant and would be ignored by most rational people. However, Sabet (n.d.) has a regular blog on the *Huffington Post*; has been widely cited in numerous media sources, many of which do not properly deconstruct his often outlandish claims; and according to his website, Sabet has "given over 100 guest lectures at major universities." Sabet and SAM have also been very active in antilegalization campaigns. He testified before the U.S. Senate Judiciary Committee and the House and Senate Judiciary Committee in Oregon State in January 2013 (as the state was debating marijuana legalization) (Sabet 2013b). In its opposition to the recreational marijuana legalization initiative (Initiative 71) in Washington, D.C., a 2014 *Washington Post* editorial cited SAM's findings regarding the "negative consequences of legalization in Colorado."

More recently, SAM (2017) issued the ten-page "Status Report on State Compliance of Federal Marijuana Enforcement Policy," which noted, "Unfortunately, since Colorado and Washington became the first states to legalize the recreational sale of marijuana in 2012, evidence has emerged that regulations intended to control the sale and use of marijuana have failed to meet the promises made by advocates for legalization." This status report emphasizes the same timeworn themes evidenced in other publications by SAM, including allegations that there have been increases in marijuana-impaired driving and increases in youth use of the substance. Although acknowledging that "it is not possible to link legalization to a direct change in crime rates," the report claims that Colorado's crime rate has increased. "There has been an increase in rape, murder, robbery, and auto thefts." Somewhat more curiously, but apparently to assert that racial disparities in the enforcement of marijuana laws will be exacerbated with legalization, the report refers to a publication by Colorado's public safety agency that indicated that marijuana-related arrests for black and Hispanic youth increased by 58 percent and 29 percent, respectively, while arrest rates for white youth declined by 8 percent. Perhaps most reflective of SAM's lack of attention to details and facts that do not fit with their ideology, the status report makes several references to a 2017 report by the Oregon State Police that had suggested that marijuana legalization in that state was fueling increases in the transportation of black-market marijuana to other states. This report was publicly discredited by the superintendent of the Oregon State Police himself, who noted in a letter to Attorney General Jeff Sessions that the report was "not a published report and is regrettably utilized to represent Oregon's efforts and compliance surrounding marijuana enforcement" and that it included many "subjective or invalidated sources" (Hampton 2017).

Other than ignoring the results of scientific studies that are inconsistent with their marijuana prohibitionist ideology and distorting the findings of other studies, it is not entirely clear what SAM's approach to marijuana actually is. Its "Mission and Vision" statement hints at support of marijuana decriminalization: "We believe in an approach that neither legalizes, nor demonizes, marijuana"; "reject dichotomies—such as 'incarceration versus legalization'"; and "champion smart policies that decrease marijuana use—and do not harm marijuana users and low-level dealers with arrest records that stigmatize them for life" (Smart Approaches to Marijuana, n.d.b), SAM seems unwilling to specifically state that it supports decriminalization.

Revenge of the Drug Czars: William Bennett and John Walters

> With marijuana we have inexplicably suspended all the normal rules
> of reasoning and knowledge.
> —WILLIAM BENNETT AND ROBERT WHITE, *Going to Pot*

Former drug czars William Bennett and John Walters have also been active in responding to marijuana legalization. After being ousted from his position as drug czar after the election of President Obama, in a 2014 *Weekly Standard* article, John Walters criticized Obama's "hands-off" stance toward the legalization of recreational marijuana in Colorado and Washington: "The president is cutting the legs out from every parent and schoolteacher and clergyman across the country who is trying to steer kids away from illegal drugs." And in reference to Obama's comments on marijuana to *New Yorker* reporter David Remnick (in which he claimed that the substance was no more dangerous than alcohol), Walters somewhat ironically stated (given his own history of distortion on the issue), "Obama's remarks to Remnick point to the powerful role of ignorance and distortion."

Walters is currently chief operating officer and director of political studies for the Hudson Institute, an organization that "seeks to guide public policy makers and global leaders in government and business through a vigorous program of publications, conferences, policy briefings, and recommendations" (Hudson Institute, n.d.). In February 2017, David Murray, Brian Blake, and John Walters published an article on the Hudson Institute website criticizing marijuana legalization, which included many of the same false claims of other marijuana demonizers. The article included links to "research" supporting many of its claims, including the assertion that "the impact of the 'gateway' effect has been substantiated in multiple research reports," with a link to a single, one-page slide from an apparent Power-

Point presentation and a two-page report from the *Live Science* website. The slide's graphics state that "7 out of 10 ten nonmedical users [of drugs] combine Rx opioids with other substances," and of these, "58.8% co-ingested" marijuana. As is common with those asserting that marijuana is a gateway drug, there is no consideration (or apparently, even an understanding) of causality.

According to these authors marijuana legalization is even responsible for problems in hiring workers in fields including engineering, construction, and trucking. In the case of trucking (with a link to an article from truck inginfo.com; see Fulton 2015), they assert that "[marijuana] legalization has made an already critical shortage of drivers even worse" because several current and prospective truck drivers are testing positive for marijuana (Murray, Blake, and Walters 2017). And similar to the assertions in the Rocky Mountain HIDTA report, citing an article from the Colorado anti-marijuana group Parents Opposed to Pot, Murray, Blake, and Walters assert that in Pueblo, Colorado, "a large influx of homeless, seeking marijuana access, are creating tent cities."

Perhaps not surprisingly, Murray, Blake, and Walters (2017) attribute the host of marijuana-related problems in the United States to the Obama administration, which "suspend[ed] the enforcement of multiple federal laws." Among the solutions to these problems offered by these authors are the establishment of "federal drug prevention efforts of proven effectiveness, such as a national anti-drug media campaign" and "random student drug testing"—both of which have proven to be ineffective and even counterproductive (Mosher and Akins 2014). Proposing a decidedly business-oriented solution to marijuana problems, and perhaps unaware that the prescription opioid epidemic they refer to in their article was at least partially caused by the unscrupulous actions of large pharmaceutical companies, Murray, Blake, and Walters (2017) further suggest that the marijuana problem could be attenuated by suing marijuana businesses: "The willful production, distribution, and commercial sale of addictive, health-destroying products should be limited or penalized through lawsuits."

One of John Walters's colleagues at the Hudson Institute, Robert White, coauthored with William Bennett in 2015 *Going to Pot: Why the Rush to Legalize Marijuana Is Harming America*. Similar to other antilegalization tomes, this book is full of misinformation and half-truths. Although the authors decry the use of anecdotes by supporters of marijuana legalization, each chapter of the book contains at least one "Dear Bill" anecdote (which range in length from one-half to one and one-half pages), which Bennett reports he received via e-mail or from people calling into his national talk show. The first of these "Dear Bill" messages concludes with the statement, "Anyone who believes that marijuana is harmless is like inviting your wife to have a boyfriend and believing things will be better in your marriage" (2).

In discussing the Rocky Mountain HIDTA report, we note that a great deal of the misleading information contained in the report has appeared in other sources arguing against marijuana law reform. Bennett and White's 2015 book includes many false claims that are lifted from that report and several charts and graphs that were apparently directly copied from it (see, for example, pages 41, 43, 74, and a six-page insert between pages 76 and 77).

In dismissing the supporters of marijuana legalization, Bennett and White (2015) (ironically) claim that advocates of legalization have "come to their conclusions . . . because of an absence of information and through a series of misunderstandings," some of which "have been the result of deliberate falsehoods promulgated by interest groups" (2015, 82). Dismissing legalization supporters as a bunch of stoners, Bennett and White add, "Some have resulted from arguments that contravene conventional wisdom and common sense, but are seized upon by *those who would rather get high* than critically think about the negative results of their positions or desires. Some simply do not know history very well, or are misinformed about the potency of today's marijuana" (82–83; emphasis added).

In a somewhat indirect reference to the theory of marijuana as a gateway drug, perhaps not aware that these individuals died as a result of opiate use, Bennett and White comment, "Take a look at some of the national and international talents we have recently lost to substance abuse problems: Just to name a handful, Whitney Houston, Michael Jackson, Amy Winehouse, Heath Ledger, Cory Monteith, and Philip Seymour Hoffman" (2015, 114). Later in the book, we find that the real culprit in these deaths was marijuana: "Recall the list of famous actors and musicians who recently died from drug overdoses that we mentioned earlier? Heath Ledger started with marijuana. Whitney Houston started with marijuana. Cory Monteith started with marijuana. Amy Winehouse started with marijuana. . . . Where there are other drugs, there is usually marijuana—as was found in Michael Jackson's bedroom, and as was found in Philip Seymour Hoffman's heroin dealer's home" (151, 153).

Further, dismissing arguments that marijuana enforcement in the United States has been costly and referring to the 2013 American Civil Liberties Union report's finding that enforcing marijuana laws costs between $1.2 billion and $1.6 billion annually, Bennett and White engage in a rather strange form of contextualization, noting that the amount "is about one-seventh to one-half what the U.S. pays to the United Nations. Understood another way, it is approximately the amount of the additional net worth Warren Buffett obtained in one day in March" (2015, 93). Similar to other marijuana prohibitionists, Bennett and White apparently believe that the hundreds of thousands of marijuana arrests each year are not relevant to consider in the debate on legalization and, similar to John Walters, Kevin Sabet, Jonathan Caulkins, and other demonizers, emphasize that those arrested for marijuana offenses are rarely sentenced to prison. "Is there any crime committed in America for which the number of violators leads to the argument that the law should be dispensed with? Or rather, does the number of violators lead one to the argument that the enforcement of the law should be stronger" (169).

Much of the final chapter of *Going to Pot* consists of a critique of a *New York Times* editorial (2014) that advocated for marijuana legalization. Bennett and White (2015) engage in a point-by-point critique of the arguments made in the editorial, while frequently referencing *Times* columnist Maureen Dowd's article on her experience with edible marijuana. "As for moderate use of marijuana not appearing to pose a risk for adults, why did the *Times* not consult its own pages and employees?" In a more specific reference to the Dowd column, Bennett and White comment, "The editors of the *Times* not only ignored modern science and research, they ignored the recent writing of their longest-standing op-ed contributor, Maureen Dowd" (2015, 168).

Bennett and White also do not approve of medical marijuana; in reference to Sanjay Gupta's (2013) article in support of medical marijuana, the authors note, "Dr. Gupta's article is mostly anecdotal. . . . That said, almost every study we have found on the medicinal effects of marijuana is anecdotal" (2015, 58). Statements such as these reveal that Bennett and White have simply not taken the time to actually consult the scientific literature on medical marijuana (or perhaps are not interested in doing so).[4]

Perhaps not surprisingly, Bennett and White long for the good old days of the Ronald Reagan and George H. W. Bush administrations (as noted, Bennett served as secretary of education in the Reagan administration and drug czar in the George H. W. Bush administration), claiming that drug use in the United States had been "halved" between 1979 and 1992. Apparently unaware that the anti-marijuana advertisement campaign spearheaded by the Partnership for a Drug Free America and the ONDCP was not successful in reducing youth drug use, Bennett and White state, "Let us bring back the ads detailing the dangers of marijuana, but with all the improved graphics and technology that are not at our disposal" (2015, 121).

Many of the marijuana demonization themes we discuss in this chapter have surfaced in debates over legalization of the substance in several states, which we address in Chapter 6.

---

4. Interestingly, however, Bennett and White indicate that they do support synthetic/chemical forms of marijuana for medicinal purposes and claim that "the vast majority of [medical marijuana] purchases have nothing to do with medication and are entirely geared toward getting high from the smoked and eaten product rather than obtaining it from the regimented and truly prescribed medicinal form [Sativex and Marinol] of it" (2015, 64).

6

Medical and Recreational Marijuana Legalization Policies

We now trace the evolution of medical and recreational marijuana legalization in the United States, as well as recreational legalization in the three countries that have or were about to legalize as of 2018. We begin by providing a discussion of the organizations that have driven marijuana policy reform in the United States. Most marijuana policy change in America has been grassroots or "bottom up," driven disproportionately by reform-minded organizations such as the Drug Policy Alliance (DPA; formerly the Lindesmith Center), the National Organization for the Reform of Marijuana Laws (NORML), and the Marijuana Policy Project (MPP). These groups have worked to place policy reform measures on the ballot, ultimately resulting in changes in the law.

Largely as a result of these efforts, as of mid-2018, nine states and the District of Columbia have legalized recreational marijuana (with only Vermont the result of legislative action rather than a ballot measure), and thirty states and D.C. allow medical marijuana. Conversely, recreational marijuana legalization in other countries has been "top down," driven by actors in the national government rather than voters. We provide an overview of the three countries that have federally legal recreational marijuana: the Netherlands (technically de facto legalization), Canada, and Uruguay. We address these policy experiments in marijuana legalization, both in the United States and abroad, examining the nuances of various legalization schemes, including limitations on possession amount and type, allowance for home cultivation of marijuana, taxation designed to regulate the substance and fund other governmental needs, vertical integration of cannabis businesses, and the varying paths taken to legalization. We conclude with a summary of what has been learned from these policy experiments in recreational marijuana legalization. Of most importance, rates of use of the drug have not significantly changed, in large part because marijuana was widely available prior to legalization; and extensive revenue, formerly untaxed and collected by illegal enterprise, has come under government control. Observing these outcomes, we can conclude that additional U.S. states and some foreign countries seem poised to legalize in the near future.

The Organizations behind Change in Marijuana Laws

As we note in Chapter 1, there are several forces that have been driving changes in marijuana legislation over the past few decades. Organizations such as the DPA, NORML, and the MPP have played major roles in shaping reform, both through financial contributions to medical and recreational marijuana legalization campaigns and in debunking several of the myths surrounding marijuana in their print and online publications.

Drug Policy Alliance

The DPA is primarily funded by Hungarian-born billionaire philanthropist George Soros (as well as fellow billionaires Peter Lewis, chairman of the Progressive Insurance Foundation, and John Sperling, founder of the University of Phoenix, both of whom have used marijuana for medicinal purposes), who became involved in the drug reform movement because of his concerns over racial justice and civil liberties (Halper 2014). In 1994, Soros funded the Lindesmith Center, which was headed by former Princeton University political science professor Ethan Nadelmann and named after Alfred Lindesmith, who challenged the criminalization of drugs in the United States beginning in the 1940s. The Lindesmith Center promoted harm-reduction drug policies and an end to the racially discriminatory drug policies in the United States. In 2000, the Lindesmith Center merged with the New York–based Drug Policy Foundation (founded in 1987 by Arnold Trebach, a professor at American University, and Kevin Zeese, a lawyer and political activist) to create the DPA (Lee 2012). The mission of the DPA (2014a) is to "end the drug war, which means treating drug use and addiction as health issues, not criminal ones. It means not arresting people for possessing or using any drug, absent harm to others."

The Lindesmith Center, Nadelmann, and later the DPA played key roles in the legalization of medical marijuana in California in 1996 and in several other states. In the summer of 1997, Nadelmann, to whom *Rolling Stone* magazine has referred as "the real drug czar" (Dickinson 2013), convinced Soros,

Lewis, and Sperling to fund an $8 million partnership to support medical marijuana ballot initiatives in six states. They selected states in which public opinion polls indicated there was at least 60 percent support for medical cannabis, there was a motivated group of activists, and the state was not so large that the campaign would be too expensive: Alaska, Colorado, Maine, Nevada, and Oregon (Martin and Rashidian 2014). In discussing the successes of marijuana legalization campaigns, Nadelmann (who stepped down from his position as head of the DPA in early 2017) noted that "some of it was just being disciplined about our messaging. Some was managing tensions between a professional campaign and grassroots activists" (quoted in Michaelson 2017).

National Organization for the Reform of Marijuana Laws

NORML was founded in 1970 by attorney Keith Stroup, a public interest lawyer who had worked with Ralph Nader at the National Commission on Product Safety in the 1960s (Roffman 2014). The organization's original advisory board included prominent pediatrician Benjamin Spock, former deputy director of the Bureau of Narcotics and Dangerous Drugs John Finlater, and Harvard Medical School professor Lester Grinspoon (Lee 2012). Stroup served two terms as executive director of NORML (1970–1978 and 1994–2005), and in contrast to some other marijuana activists Stroup made it clear that the government should continue to discourage the use of marijuana but should not impose criminal penalties for personal use (Payne 2013).

After the 1972 Shafer Commission recommended the decriminalization of personal possession and consumption of marijuana, NORML played a significant role in the passage of marijuana decriminalization measures in eleven states between 1973 and 1978 (Payne 2013) and has continued its activism in marijuana law reform efforts to this day. NORML's (2013) mission is to "move public opinion sufficiently to legalize the responsible use of marijuana by adults, and to serve as advocates for consumers to assure they have access to high quality marijuana that is safe, convenient, and affordable." The organization has several dozen chapters in the United States, as well as in a number of other countries.

Marijuana Policy Project

The MPP has also played a prominent role in advancing marijuana law reform in the United States. This nonprofit organization, based in Washington, D.C., was established in 1995 by Rob Kampia, Chuck Thomas (both of whom had previously been affiliated with NORML but were fired by NORML director Richard Cowin after infighting within the organization), and Mike Kishner. The stated aims of the MPP (n.d.) are to (1) increase public support for nonpunitive, noncoercive marijuana policies; (2) identify and activate supporters of nonpunitive, noncoercive marijuana policies; (3) change state laws to reduce or eliminate penalties for medical and nonmedical use of marijuana; and to (4) gain influence in Congress. More generally, the MPP supports taxing and regulating cannabis in a way similar to how alcohol is taxed and regulated and believes that the treatment for problem marijuana users should be noncoercive with the goal of reducing harm.

The MPP (n.d.) was actively involved in ballot initiatives to legalize recreational marijuana in Colorado (2012); Alaska (2014); and Maine, Massachusetts, and Nevada (2016) and also assisted in the 2016 campaign in California. The group remains actively involved in efforts to implement and expand medical marijuana legislation in many states that either ban or restrict it.

Medical Marijuana Legislation

Given the large number of states that have legalized medical marijuana and significant differences in policy that characterize various states, it is beyond the scope of this chapter to provide in-depth analysis of each medical marijuana policy. We provide key details of each policy in Table 6.1. However, with respect to the idea that medical marijuana legislation is gateway legislation (Balko 2014b), in the context of our discussion of recreational marijuana legalization, we document how the path to recreational marijuana legalization was, in many cases, facilitated by medical marijuana legalization.

As Table 6.1 shows, there is substantial policy heterogeneity evidenced across states with legalized medical marijuana. For example, why is home cultivation of cannabis allowed in some states and not in others? In the twenty-nine states that have legalized medical marijuana, Connecticut, Delaware, Florida, Illinois, Maryland, New Hampshire, New Jersey, New York, Ohio, and Pennsylvania do not allow home cultivation. Why are some states highly restrictive in qualifying conditions and others much more permissive? Why do some states allow for a (sometimes very) large amount of marijuana to be possessed while others are far more restrictive? For states with more permissive medical marijuana policies that have not legalized recreationally, it is fair to question whether this more permissive approach to medical marijuana presages recreational legalization to come.

Legalization of Recreational Marijuana in the United States

Kenneth Leon and Ronald Weitzer identify a number of factors that predict "vice legalization" (2014, 196) and that serve as useful heuristics in discussing the path to recreational marijuana legalization covered in the following discussion: for example, (1) significant numbers of people engage in the vice, with many of them having "conventional lifestyles"; (2) there is evidence that legalization will produce less harm than criminalization; (3) production and

TABLE 6.1: SUMMARY OF MEDICAL MARIJUANA LEGISLATION

State	Statute and year enacted	First enacted via ballot or legislative action?	Estimated no. of patients	Limits on possession amount	Dispensaries allowed?	Private cultivation allowed?	Qualifying conditions
California	Prop. 215 (1996)	Ballot	1,078,795	None specified	Yes	Yes	Any debilitating illness where the medical use of marijuana has been "deemed appropriate and has been recommended by a physician"
Alaska	Measure 8 (1998); SB 94 (1999)	Ballot	1,178	1 oz.	Yes	Yes	Cachexia, cancer, chronic pain, glaucoma, HIV/AIDS, multiple sclerosis (MS), nausea, seizures
Oregon	Oregon Medical Marijuana Act (1998); SB 161 (2007)	Ballot	61,839	24 oz.	Yes	Yes	Alzheimer's, cachexia, cancer, chronic pain, glaucoma, HIV/AIDS, nausea, persistent spasms, PTSD, seizures, other conditions subject to approval
Washington	Initiative 692 (1998); SB 5798 (2010); SB 5073 (2011)	Ballot	20,000	3 oz. or 21 g of concentrates	Yes	Yes	Cachexia, cancer, Crohn's disease, glaucoma, hepatitis C, HIV/AIDS, intractable pain, persistent muscle spasms/spasticity, nausea, PTSD seizures, traumatic brain injury, any "terminal or debilitating condition"
Washington, D.C.	Initiative 59 (1998); L18-0210 (2010)	Ballot	5,219	2 oz.	Yes	Yes	Any "debilitating condition" as recommended by a D.C. licensed doctor
Maine	Question 2 (1999); LD 611 (2002); Question 5 (2009); LD 1811 (2010); LD 1296 (2011)	Ballot	46,423	2.5 oz.	Yes	Yes	Alzheimer's, ALS, cachexia, cancer, chronic pain, Crohn's disease, epilepsy, glaucoma, hepatitis C, HIV/AIDS, Huntington's disease, inflammatory bowel disease, MS, nail-patella syndrome, nausea, Parkinson's disease, PTSD
Colorado	Amendment 20 (2000)	Ballot	94,577	2 oz.	Yes	Yes	Cachexia, cancer, chronic pain, chronic nervous system disorders, glaucoma, HIV/AIDS, nausea, persistent muscle spasms, PTSD, seizures

State	Statute	Type	Patients	Possession Limit			Conditions
Hawaii	SB 862 (2000)	Legislative	17,018	4 oz.	Yes	Yes	ALS, cachexia, cancer, chronic pain, Crohn's disease, epilepsy, glaucoma, HIV/AIDS, lupus, MS, nausea, persistent muscle spasms, PTSD, rheumatoid arthritis, seizures
Nevada	Question 9 (2000); NRS 453A; NAC 453A	Ballot	27,952	2.5 oz. and/or a maximum allowable quantity of edibles and marijuana-infused products as established by regulation	Yes	Yes	AIDS, cachexia, cancer, glaucoma, PTSD, persistent muscle spasms or seizures, other conditions subject to approval
Maryland	HB 702 (2003); SB 308 (2011); HB180/ SB580 (2013); HB1101-Ch 403 (2013); SB 923 (2014)	Legislative	19,450	Thirty-day supply (edibles ineligible)	Yes	No	Cachexia, anorexia or wasting syndrome, chronic pain, nausea, seizures, severe or persistent muscle spasms
Montana	Initiative 148 (2004); SB 423 (2011); Initiative 182 (2016)	Ballot	17,819	1 oz. for those with a provider; four plants, four seedlings and the usable marijuana associated for those without a provider	Yes (reinstituted 2016)	Yes (see limits on possession)	Cachexia or wasting syndrome, cancer, chronic pain, Crohn's disease, glaucoma, HIV/AIDS, nausea, seizures, severe or persistent muscle spasms
Vermont	SB 76 (2004); SB 7 (2007); SB 17 (2011); H.511 (2018)	Legislative	4,438	2 oz.	Yes	Yes	Any patient receiving hospice care, cachexia or wasting syndrome, cancer, Crohn's disease, glaucoma, HIV/AIDS, MS, Parkinson's disease, seizures, severe or chronic pain, severe nausea
New Mexico	SB 523 (2007)	Legislative	45,347	8 oz. (over ninety-day period)	Yes	Yes	ALS, anorexia/cachexia, arthritis, cancer, cervical dystonia, chronic pain, Crohn's disease, epilepsy, glaucoma, hepatitis C, HIV/AIDS, hospice patients, Huntington's disease, intractable nausea/vomiting, MS, nausea, painful peripheral neuropathy, Parkinson's disease, PTSD, spinal cord damage

(continued)

TABLE 6.1: SUMMARY OF MEDICAL MARIJUANA LEGISLATION (*continued*)

State	Statute and year enacted	First enacted via ballot or legislative action?	Estimated no. of patients	Limits on possession amount	Dispensaries allowed?	Private cultivation allowed?	Qualifying conditions
Rhode Island	SB 791 (2007); SB 185 (2009)	Legislative	19,161	2.5 oz.	Yes	Yes	Alzheimer's, cachexia, cancer, chronic pain, Crohn's disease, glaucoma, hepatitis C, HIV/AIDS, nausea, persistent muscle spasms, PTSD, seizures, other conditions subject to approval
Michigan	Proposal 1 (2008)	Ballot	218,556	2.5 oz.	Yes	Yes	Alzheimer's, ALS, cachexia or wasting syndrome, cancer, chronic pain, Crohn's disease, glaucoma, HIV/AIDS, nail-patella syndrome, nausea, PTSD, seizures, severe and persistent muscle spasms
New Jersey	SB 119 (2009)	Legislative	10,332	2 oz. (per month)	Yes	No	ALS, cancer (includes associated chronic pain and/or severe nausea), Crohn's disease, glaucoma, HIV/AIDS (includes associated chronic pain and/or severe nausea), inflammatory bowel disease, MS, muscular dystrophy, PTSD, seizures or spasticity, any terminal illness if a doctor has determined the patient will die within a year
Arizona	Proposition 203 (2010)	Ballot	125,991	2.5 oz.	Yes	Yes, if residence is farther than twenty-five miles from a state-licensed dispensary	Alzheimer's, ALS, cachexia or wasting syndrome, cancer, chronic pain, Crohn's disease, glaucoma, hepatitis C, HIV/AIDS, nausea, persistent muscle spasms, PTSD, seizures

State	Bill (Year)	Enactment	Number	Possession Limit			Qualifying Conditions
Delaware	SB 17 (2011)	Legislative	1,407	6 oz.	Yes	No	Alzheimer's, ALS, cachexia, cancer, chronic pain, HIV/AIDS, intractable epilepsy, nausea, PTSD, seizures, severe and persistent muscle spasms
Connecticut	HB 5389 (2012)	Legislative	22,411	One-month supply	Yes	Yes	ALS, cachexia, cancer, cerebral palsy, complex regional pain syndrome, Crohn's disease, cystic fibrosis, epilepsy, glaucoma, HIV/AIDS, intractable spasticity, irreversible spinal cord damage with objective neurological indication of intractable spasticity, MS, Parkinson's disease, postsurgical back pain with chronic radiculopathy, post laminectomy syndrome, severe psoriasis and psoriatic arthritis, sickle cell disease, terminal illness requiring end-of-life care, ulcerative colitis, uncontrolled intractable seizure disorder, other conditions may be approved by the Department of Consumer Protection
Massachusetts	Question 3 (2012)	Ballot	35,412	10 oz. (every two months)	Yes	Yes	ALS, cancer, Crohn's disease, glaucoma, hepatitis C, HIV/AIDS, MS, Parkinson's disease, other conditions as determined in writing by a qualified patient's physician
Illinois	HB 1 (2013)	Legislative	21,800	2.5 oz. (every two weeks)	Yes	No	Thirty-six qualifying medical conditions
New Hampshire	HB 573 (2013)	Legislative	2,089	2 oz.	Yes	No	Twenty-seven qualifying medical conditions
Minnesota	SF 2471 (2014)	Legislative	5,137	Thirty-day supply	Yes, sales limited to liquid extracts	No	ALS, autism, cancer/cachexia, glaucoma, HIV/AIDS, intractable pain, PTSD, seizures, severe and persistent muscle spasms, terminal illness, Tourette's syndrome

(continued)

TABLE 6.1: SUMMARY OF MEDICAL MARIJUANA LEGISLATION (*continued*)

State	Statute and year enacted	First enacted via ballot or legislative action?	Estimated no. of patients	Limits on possession amount	Dispensaries allowed?	Private cultivation allowed?	Qualifying conditions
New York	A 6357 (2014)	Legislative	31,166	Thirty-day supply, only nonsmokable products	Yes	No	ALS, cancer, chronic pain, epilepsy, HIV/AIDS, Huntington's disease, inflammatory bowel disease, MS, neuropathies, Parkinson's disease, spinal cord damage
Arkansas	Issue 6 (2016)	Ballot	539	Details pending	Yes, not operational as of writing	No	Alzheimer's, ALS, cachexia or wasting syndrome, cancer, chronic or debilitating disease, Crohn's disease, fibromyalgia, glaucoma, hepatitis C, HIV/AIDS, intractable pain, MS, peripheral neuropathy, PTSD, seizures, severe arthritis, severe nausea, severe and persistent muscle spasms, Tourette's syndrome, ulcerative colitis, any condition or its treatment approved by the Department of Health
Florida	Amendment 2 (2016)	Ballot	26,968	CBD-specific law: except for terminally ill patients, patients may possess strains with 10% or more CBD and no more than 0.8% THC	Yes	No	Cancer, muscle spasms, seizures, terminal illness with less than twelve months to live
North Dakota	Measure 5 (2016)	Ballot	0	3 oz., or 2,000 mg of THC concentrate, or a combination of these totaling no more than 2,000 mg THC in a thirty-day period	Yes, not operational as of writing	No	Agitation from Alzheimer's or related dementia, ALS, cachexia or wasting syndrome, cancer, chronic or debilitating disease, Crohn's disease, fibromyalgia, glaucoma, hepatitis C, HIV/AIDS, intractable nausea, MS, PTSD, seizures, severe and persistent muscle spasms, severe debilitating pain, spinal stenosis

State	Bill		Number	Delivery			Conditions
Ohio	HB 523 (2016)	Legislative	0	Details pending	Yes, not operational as of writing	No	AIDS, Alzheimer's, ALS, cancer, chronic traumatic encephalopathy, Crohn's disease, epilepsy or seizure disorders, fibromyalgia, glaucoma, hepatitis C, inflammatory bowel disease, MS, pain that is either chronic and severe or intractable, Parkinson's disease, positive status for HIV, PTSD, sickle cell anemia, spinal cord disease or injury, Tourette's syndrome, traumatic brain injury, ulcerative colitis
Pennsylvania	SB 3 (2016)	Legislative	10,135	Thirty-day supply, cannabis-infused pills, oils, ointments, tinctures, or liquids only	Yes	No	ALS, autism, cancer, Crohn's disease, epilepsy, glaucoma, HIV/AIDS, Huntington's disease, inflammatory bowel disease, intractable seizures, intractable spasticity, MS, neuropathies, Parkinson's disease, PTSD, sickle cell anemia, severe, chronic or intractable pain, terminal illness (defined as twelve months or fewer to live)
West Virginia	SB 386 (2017)	Legislative	0	Thirty-day supply of cannabis-infused products (herbal cannabis disallowed)	Yes, not operational as of writing	No	ALS, cancer, Crohn's disease, epilepsy, HIV/AIDS, Huntington's disease, intractable seizures, MS, neuropathies (chronic nerve pain), Parkinson's disease, PTSD, severe, chronic, or intractable pain, sickle cell anemia, spinal cord damage, terminal illness

Sources: National Conference of State Legislatures 2018; National Organization for the Reform of Marijuana Laws 2018.

distribution of the vice can be controlled by government authorities; (4) decriminalization or legalization of the vice in question is supported by law enforcement, prominent politicians/legislators, and/or business leaders; and (5) decriminalization/legalization can produce significant revenues for governments (197). Success of vice legalization also depends on the status of supporters and opponents, the extent and content of media coverage and editorials regarding the issue, timing (whether the legalization initiative is proposed in a national or midterm election), federal government threats to intervene to prevent the initiative, and campaign spending by advocates and opponents of the proposed legislation. Leon and Weitzer make the important point more specific to marijuana legalization measures that, given that younger voters are more likely to support reform of marijuana laws, the age distribution of voters in a particular election can affect the outcome of legalization measures.

In the sections that follow, we review the paths to recreational marijuana legalization in nine U.S. states (Colorado, Washington, Oregon, Alaska, California, Nevada, Massachusetts, Maine, and Vermont) and the District of Columbia, as well as in three other countries (the Netherlands, Canada, and Uruguay). Drawing on Leon and Weitzer's factors predicting vice legalization, we summarize the various paths to recreational marijuana legalization taken by these state and national actors, with particular attention paid to whether the legislation was enacted via ballot or legislative action, the specifics of the legislation (such as possession amounts allowed and whether private cultivation is allowed), the political actors and constituencies representing the pro and con sides of the legalization effort, and the pricing and taxation regulations designed to regulate the substance and fund other public needs, including those related to the potential harm generated by marijuana (see Table 6.2). As noted earlier, some have referred to medical marijuana legalization as gateway legislation (Balko 2014b), and for many states this seems to have been the case. In those states where the path to legalization was preceded by recreational decriminalization and/or medical marijuana legalization, we document this and note the importance of these steps toward the eventual legislation that legalized recreational marijuana.

Colorado Legislation

The Path to Legalization

In 1975, Colorado became one of the first states to decriminalize marijuana possession, with possession of up to one ounce downgraded to a petty offense with a $100 fine. In November 2000, under the Medical Use of Marijuana Act (Amendment 20, which passed with 54 percent of voters in support) medical marijuana was legalized in the state (Dills, Goffard, and Miron 2016).

Under Colorado's medical marijuana legislation, patients with a medical marijuana registry card or their primary caregivers were allowed to possess

TABLE 6.2: SUMMARY OF RECREATIONAL MARIJUANA LEGISLATION

Location	Year passed	Enacted via ballot or legislative action?	Limits on possession amount	Private transfer of small amount allowed?	Private cultivation allowed?	Taxation	Notes
Colorado	2012	Ballot (Amendment 64)	1 oz., twenty-one and older	Yes, up to 1 oz. for no remuneration allowed	Yes, up to six plants (maximum of three mature)	At minimum (additional local taxes may apply) 15% excise tax, 15% state retail marijuana sales tax, plus licensing and application fees	New system began July 1, 2017
Washington	2012	Ballot (Initiative 502)	1 oz., twenty-one and older	No, felony offense	No, felony offense	37% excise tax	Initially 25% tax on producers, processors, and retailers; in 2015, revised to present status under Senate Bill 512
Oregon	2014	Ballot (Measure 91)	1 oz., twenty-one and older	Yes, up to 1 oz., homegrown only, for no remuneration	Yes, up to four plants	17% state tax, with local governments eligible to add up to 3% additional sales tax	Up to 8 oz. allowed in home if homegrown
Alaska	2014	Ballot (Measure 2)	1 oz., twenty-one and older	No; misdemeanor offense	Yes, up to six plants (maximum of three mature)	Tax of $50 per ounce levied when marijuana is sold or transferred from a cultivation facility to a dispensary	Based on an Alaska Supreme Court decision, possession of up to 4 oz. in the home protected under right to privacy
Washington, D.C.	2014	Ballot (Initiative 71)	2 oz., twenty-one and older, in primary residence	Yes, up to 1 oz. for no remuneration	Yes, up to six plants (maximum of three mature)	N/A, sales and dispensaries not permitted	
California	2016	Ballot (Proposition 64)	1 oz. or 8 g of concentrated cannabis, twenty-one and older	No, gift of 28.5 g or less is an infraction subject to fine of $100	Yes, up to six plants	15% excise tax on cannabis retail sales and a cannabis cultivation tax of $9.25 per ounce of flowers and $2.75 per ounce of leaves	Additional local and state taxes ranging from 7.75% to 9.75% can be levied adding up to what is predicted to be an effective tax rate of approximately 45%

(continued)

TABLE 6.2: SUMMARY OF RECREATIONAL MARIJUANA LEGISLATION (*continued*)

Location	Year passed	Enacted via ballot or legislative action?	Limits on possession amount	Private transfer of small amount allowed?	Private cultivation allowed?	Taxation	Notes
Nevada	2016	Ballot (Question 2)	1 oz. and/or 3.5 g of concentrate, twenty-one and older	Yes, up to 1 oz. for no remuneration	Yes, for those residing twenty-five miles or more from a marijuana retailer, up to six plants	15% excise tax on first wholesale sale and 10% retail excise tax	Medical marijuana cardholders exempted from second tax
Massachusetts	2016	Ballot (Question 4)	1 oz., up to 5 g of concentrate, twenty-one and older	No, not classified, penalty discretionary and specific to amount (zero to two years of incarceration and $500–$5,000 fine)	Yes, up to six plants per person at primary residence, with a cap of twelve plants total at said residence	10.75% excise tax, state sales tax of 6.25%, and localities may levy an additional 3%	Up to 10 oz. in the home is allowed
Maine	2016	Ballot (Question 1)	2.5 oz. of marijuana, or up to 2.5 oz. of marijuana and marijuana concentrate with no more than 5 g of concentrate, twenty-one and older	No, misdemeanor offense	Yes, up to six flowering marijuana plants, twelve immature plants, and unlimited seedlings	10% sales tax	Additional 10% sales or additional 10% excise being considered as of 2018
Vermont	2018	Legislative Action (H.511)	1 oz., twenty-one and older	No, misdemeanor offense if up to 0.5 oz, felony offense if above 1 oz.	Yes, adult cultivation of up to six plants (two mature, four immature)	Tax rate not yet established, no established dispensaries as of 2018	

Country	Year	Method	Possession	Sharing	Cultivation	Tax	Notes
Netherlands	1976	Legislative Action	5 g, eighteen and older (maximum purchase from coffee shops is 5 g per day)	No	No	None, income tax levied on coffee shop revenue generated, but no additional tax on cannabis as it is not "fully" legal	Although typically referred to as legalization, the policy is more factually one of de facto legalization (see text discussion); generally police will only seize the plants, not prosecute, if there are no more than five plants being grown
Uruguay	2013	Legislative action	40 g per month, eighteen and older	No	Yes, adult cultivation of up to six plants with a limit of 480 g per year	No additional (value-added) tax	Users must choose one of three methods of obtaining the drug: homegrown, purchase via a pharmacy, or as a member of a cannabis club (the latter option could be viewed as "sharing")
Canada	2018	Legislative action	30 g of dried cannabis or equivalent in nondried form, eighteen and older	Yes, up to 30 g of dried cannabis or equivalent in nondried form may be shared with adults	Yes, up to four cannabis plants	Tax rate not yet established, no established dispensaries as of 2018	Concentrates are to be made available no more than twelve months following enactment of proposed legislation

Sources: Scarboro 2017; Mogensen 2017; Colorado Department of Revenue 2018.

up to two ounces of usable marijuana and to grow no more than six marijuana plants (three or fewer of those plants could be mature) (Sensible Colorado, n.d.). The state's medical marijuana legislation has been characterized by considerable controversy since its enactment, largely because there were no stipulations in the 2000 legislation regarding the number of patients caregivers could serve. In the early 2000s, several caregivers began to supply marijuana to large numbers of patients, creating concerns that medical marijuana was being commercially distributed. This led to the Colorado Department of Public Health and Environment establishing an informal rule limiting caregivers to providing medical marijuana to no more than five patients. The marijuana advocacy group Sensible Colorado (n.d.) successfully sued the state over this provision, and as a rewsult, caregivers were allowed to provide medical marijuana to an unlimited number of patients.

The state of Colorado continued its attempts to further regulate the medical marijuana industry, and in 2010, the legislature passed two medical marijuana bills—Senate Bill 109 and House Bill 1284. Senate Bill 104 stipulated that medical marijuana patients must have a bona fide relationship with doctors who approved them for medical marijuana—doctors were required to have completed a full assessment of the patient's medical history, to consult with the patient regarding the condition that led the individual to seek marijuana, and to be available for follow-up care (Ingold 2010).

Colorado House Bill 1284 created strict regulations for medical marijuana businesses, stipulating that dispensaries must be licensed at both the state and local levels, and also allowed local governments to prohibit dispensaries or marijuana-growing operations within their jurisdictions (Ingold 2010). Individuals who had recently been convicted of a felony offense, or at any time for a drug-related felony, were prohibited from operating a medical marijuana dispensary, and dispensaries were also required to grow at least 70 percent of the marijuana they sold to customers. House Bill 1284 also created new regulations for primary caregivers, who under the legislation could serve no more than five patients and grow no more than six plants per patient (Ingold 2010).

Legalization: Amendment 64 (2012)

> Supporters of legalization [in Colorado] outplanned, outspent, and outfoxed marijuana opponents. They capitalized on years of groundwork to reframe the legal debate about marijuana. They even anticipated their opposition's arguments and moves so effectively, they could frequently rebut endorsements for the "No on 64" campaign by announcing endorsements of their own on the same day.
>
> —JOHN INGOLD, "The Inside Story of How Marijuana Became Legal in Colorado"

The legalization of recreational marijuana in Colorado was an incremental process, with its key emphasis being that marijuana was a safer drug than alcohol. In 2005, a group known as SAFER (Safer Alternative for Enjoyable Recreation) initiated a marijuana legalization movement on the campuses of Colorado State University and the University of Colorado Boulder on the platform of marijuana's safety in comparison to that of alcohol. Also in 2005, SAFER ran an initiative in the city of Denver proposing to eliminate all penalties for adult possession of up to one ounce of marijuana—54 percent voted in favor of the initiative (Fox, Armentano, and Tvert 2009, 112). The fact that then Denver mayor (and later, Colorado governor) John Hickenlooper was a beer brewer and brew pub owner provided SAFER with an opportunity to emphasize their "marijuana is safer than alcohol" theme. As Mason Tvert, founder of SAFER and former director of communications for the MPP in Colorado commented, "He [Hickenlooper] was the greatest foil ever for a marijuana reform campaign" (quoted in Lizza 2013). SAFER posted a banner outside Hickenlooper's office with the question, "What is the difference between the mayor and a marijuana dealer?" The answer, which appeared on the banner, was "Mayor Hickenlooper deals a more dangerous drug" (Fox, Armentano, and Tvert 2009, 139).

SAFER was instrumental in getting Question 44, known as the Alcohol-Marijuana Equalization Initiative, on the 2006 Colorado ballot. Although the measure was ultimately opposed by 56 percent of Colorado voters (Dills, Goffard, and Miron 2016), SAFER viewed this as part of the incremental process toward marijuana legalization: "Accepting defeat as a likely outcome, SAFER's goal was to use the campaign to generate, on a very limited budget, widespread media coverage containing the 'marijuana is safer than alcohol' message" (Fox, Armentano, and Tvert 2009, 141).

In 2012 recreational marijuana was legalized in Colorado after the passage of Amendment 64, Use and Regulation of Marijuana, with 54.8 percent of Coloradoans voting in favor (*Denver Post* 2012). A factor that likely contributed to its passage was that 2012 was a presidential election year—"basically, pot rode Obama's coattails"; exit polls showed that 68 percent of those who voted for Obama also approved marijuana legalization (Obama won 51.5 percent of the popular vote in Colorado in 2012) (Ingold 2012).

While the main thrust of the Colorado marijuana legalization campaign focused on the theme that marijuana was a less harmful drug than alcohol, other proponents emphasized social justice issues. For example, Bruce Madison, a former associate director at the University of Colorado School of Medicine, commented, "As physicians, we have a professional obligation to do no harm. But the truth is that the Colorado marijuana laws do just that, by wasting millions of dollars in a failed war on marijuana, by ruining thousands of lives by unnecessary arrest and incarceration, and by causing the deaths of hundreds of people killed in black market criminal activities" (quoted in Horwitz 2012). Interestingly, and in contrast to the failed 2010 recreational marijuana legalization measure in California and Washington

State's successful marijuana legalization initiative in 2012, representatives of Colorado's medical marijuana industry were mostly supportive of Amendment 64 (Leon and Weitzer 2014)—likely because these businesses would have priority in applying for licenses to sell recreational marijuana.[1] Other supporters of Amendment 64, who collectively raised $3.5 million (the opposition campaign raised only $707,000), included the Campaign to Regulate Marijuana like Alcohol, the MPP, the Colorado branch of the National Association for the Advancement of Colored People (NAACP), Progressive Insurance founder Peter Lewis, and Colorado Republican congressman Tom Tancredo (Leon and Weitzer 2014).

An important opponent of the legislation was Colorado governor John Hickenlooper, who stated at the time, "Colorado is known for a lot of things—marijuana should not be one of them" (quoted in Hudak 2014, 5). Additional opposition to Amendment 64 came from Smart Colorado (whose motto was "protecting youth from marijuana"), law enforcement organizations, the *Denver Post*, Denver mayor Michael Hancock, and Kevin Sabet of SAM. The opposition arguments emphasized that the passage of Amendment 64 would increase marijuana's availability to youth, tourists would flock to Colorado to consume marijuana, and the federal government would intervene if the legislation passed (Leon and Weitzer 2014).

There are several interesting aspects of Colorado's Amendment 64, some of which we touch on here. For example, the legislation created a seed-to-sale tracking system, which tracks every plant in every cultivation facility with a computerized barcode system that is accessible to regulators (Hudak 2014). And in stark contrast to the provisions of Initiative 502 in Washington State (discussed later), Colorado's law created a vertically integrated structure, whereby "cultivation, processing, and manufacturing and retail sales must be a common enterprise" (Hudak 2014, 9). It was believed that the tracking of marijuana plants and vertical integration of the industry would limit diversion of legal marijuana and provide greater enforcement capacity for regulators (Hudak 2014). However, one (perhaps unintended) consequence of vertical integration is that it may be facilitating increased corporatization and consolidation of the marijuana industry in Colorado, which has been one of the primary criticisms of marijuana legalization by opponents such as SAM.

Under Colorado's recreational marijuana legalization measure, there was a 2.9 percent state sales tax on medical and retail marijuana, a 10 percent state retail marijuana sales tax, and a 15 percent state retail marijuana excise

---

1. The Colorado legislation (in contrast to provisions in Initiative 502 in Washington State) required that in the initial period of legalization, all retail marijuana businesses seeking licenses must come from, or be part of, the existing medical marijuana businesses in the state (Hudak 2014).

tax (as well as marijuana business application and license fees). However, as of July 1, 2017, the 2.9 percent state sales tax was removed for retail marijuana sales, and the state retail marijuana sales tax was increased from 10 percent to 15 percent (Colorado Department of Revenue 2018).

In response to challenges and problems associated with the legalization of recreational marijuana in Colorado, there have been several alterations to the law—over the 2015–2016 period alone, there were 141 regulatory changes in Colorado's marijuana laws (Hutchinson 2016). And while certainly not all residents of Colorado would agree, based on the results of public opinion polls, it appears that the legalization of marijuana in the state has been a success. A 2016 poll of registered voters in the state conducted by the MPP found that only 36 percent supported repeal of Amendment 64, only 39 percent indicated that marijuana legalization had been bad for the state generally, and 61 percent suggested the law had had a positive impact on the state's economy (Baca 2016a).

Washington State Legislation

The Path to Legalization

Washington State first considered the legalization of marijuana in 1971, when a bill was introduced in the legislature. Although this bill did not pass, in the same year, the legislature changed the offense of possession of less than forty grams of marijuana to a misdemeanor (Roffman 2014). Medical marijuana was legalized in Washington State in 1988, when voters approved Initiative 692, the Medical Use of Marijuana Act, with 59 percent of voters in favor of the measure. Initiative 692 passed in thirty of the thirty-nine counties in the state (P. McCarthy 2016) and allowed qualifying patients a sixty-day supply of marijuana. However, the law did not specify the quantity of marijuana that would constitute a sixty-day supply, and it was not until 2008, under House Bill 6032, that the amount allowed was specified as twenty-four ounces of usable marijuana and up to fifteen plants for home cultivation (Northwest High Intensity Drug Trafficking Area 2016). In addition, although I-692 allowed for the use of medical marijuana in Washington State, it did not provide for any regulation, and in contrast to medical marijuana legislation in other states, Washington did not have a database of registered patients (Wilson 2014).

Additional laws relating to medical marijuana were passed in Washington State in 2007 and 2010, and in 2011, Senate Bill 5073 passed, which established a regulatory system to license the production and distribution of medical marijuana, allowed for patient home grows and collective gardens, and created a voluntary patient registry (Washington State Senate, n.d.). However, the provisions of the bill relating to licensing and regulation were vetoed by Washington governor Christine Gregoire because of concerns regarding the possible federal prosecution of state employees involved in the actions required to license cannabis production and medical dispensaries. In fact, it was not until 2015, some seventeen years after the legalization of medical marijuana in Washington State, that the state legislature enacted specific licensing requirements for medical marijuana (Senate Bill 5052). Among other provisions, this legislation required retailers selling recreational marijuana to obtain a medical endorsement to sell medical-grade marijuana and replaced collective gardens and medical marijuana dispensaries with small-scale patient cooperatives that were required to register with the state's Liquor and Cannabis Board. The legislation also required that stores seeking medical endorsements had to employ at least one "consultant" who would receive twenty hours of training to advise patients in selecting cannabis products for medical use—these consultants are also responsible for enrolling medical users in a state database (Washington State Senate, n.d.). Individuals who enroll in the medical marijuana patient database are exempt from paying sales tax (approximately 8.4 percent) on the products purchased and are also allowed to "grow six plants by default in the system" and up to fifteen plants if authorized by their health-care practitioner (Washington State Department of Health, n.d.). While Washington State officials predicted that up to 90,000 people would enroll in the patient database, apparently because of concerns about having their names in the registry, only 23,997 were enrolled as of July 2017 (Harshman 2017).

Legalization: Initiative 502 (2012)

In November 2012, Washington State legalized marijuana through Initiative 502, Marijuana Legalization and Regulation, which was supported by 55.7 percent of voters. I-502 authorized possession of one ounce or less of cannabis for individuals twenty-one years of age and older (Washington State Senate, n.d.), but in contrast to the recreational legalization measure that passed in Colorado in the same year, Washington did not allow home cultivation (in fact, growing one's own plants remains a felony).[2] I-502 also established a regulatory structure for the licensing and taxation of marijuana production and distribution; however, Washington State's legal marijuana industry is not vertically integrated, meaning that businesses holding retail licenses are prohibited from involvement in production and processing (Darnell and Bitney 2017). The legislation initially imposed a 25 percent tax on producers, processors, and retailers, but in 2015, under Senate Bill 5121, the taxation system was changed so that a single 37 percent tax was levied on marijuana purchases. Because Washington State, unlike Colorado, did not

---

2. Under a bill proposed in 2017, Washington residents would be allowed to grow up to six plants (and in residences with more than one adult, up to twelve plants). As of 2018, the proposed legislation has not passed but remains under consideration.

have an established and regulated system of medical marijuana dispensaries, a lottery was created for recreational licenses. More than twenty-one hundred applications for the 334 available licenses were received,[3] and in seventy-eight cities and counties, there were more applicants than available licenses (G. Johnson 2014b)—in those jurisdictions, a lottery system was used to determine who would be granted licenses.

In contrast to the successful 2012 proposal in Colorado (which emphasized the relative harms of alcohol and marijuana) the pro-I-502 campaign in Washington State focused on social justice issues, reporting that between 1986 and 2012, there had been more than 241,000 marijuana possession arrests in Washington State, with African Americans and Latinos being much more likely to be arrested for the offense. Marijuana enforcement efforts were said to have cost the state $306 million over this period (Leon and Weitzer 2014). A significant influence on "New Approach Washington" (the official name of the campaign) was Tonia Winchester, the deputy campaign director and former prosecutor in the central Washington city of Wenatchee. Winchester questioned why a large proportion of individuals she was prosecuting on marijuana charges were Latino and African American, when the majority of users of the substance were white (Hari 2015).

Alison Holcomb, the primary architect of the pro-I-502 campaign, crafted the initiative to focus on mainstream voters in the state, so the initiative was relatively conservative and attempted to address the most salient voter concerns, such as restrictions on driving under the influence of marijuana, in-home cultivation, and the prevention of youth use (Martin and Rashidian 2014). The campaign did not stress that cannabis was good (or "better" than alcohol, as did Colorado's Amendment 64) but emphasized that current cannabis laws were creating several social harms, so supporters of I-502 argued that marijuana should be legalized not because it is safe but because it is dangerous—individuals who deal drugs in the streets do not check identification to make sure buyers are old enough (Hari 2015).

Echoing these sentiments, the *Seattle Times* published an editorial in 2012 supporting I-502, beginning, "The question for voters is not whether marijuana is good. It is whether prohibition is good." The piece went on to note, "If marijuana killed people, or if smoking it made people commit violence and mayhem, prohibition might be worth all its bad effects. But marijuana does not kill people; there is no lethal dose." With respect to concerns about possible increases in youth use under legalization, the editorial made the important point that marijuana prohibition did not result in youth being unable to access marijuana: "Parents may ask whether I-502 will make

---

3. When Washington State's medical marijuana system was "merged" with the recreational system in July 2016, the number of available licenses was increased from 334 to 556 (Camden 2015).

marijuana more available to their teenage children. The answer is to compare marijuana with beer. For teenagers, both are illegal—and available. But which is more easily available, the one that is banned or the one that is regulated? For more than 40 years, the one more easily available to teenagers has been the one that is banned."

Major supporters of the legalization included former federal prosecutor John McKay (who authored an opinion-editorial in support of the measure in the *Seattle Times*), Seattle city attorney Pete Holmes (N. Shapiro 2012), Seattle mayor Michael McGinn and the city council (Garber and Miletich 2011; Martin 2012), and international travel guide Rick Steves (N. Shapiro 2012). In support of I-502, Steves commented, "I'm a hardworking, church-going, child-raising, taxpaying citizen. If I want to go home and smoke a joint and stare at the fireplace for two hours, that's my civil liberty" (quoted in Martin 2015).

Other supporters of the legislation included televangelist Pat Robertson, the NAACP, the American Civil Liberties Union of Western Washington, and the DPA, which contributed more than $715,000 to the pro-I-502 campaign (Carson 2012). Another notable supporter of I-502 was King County sheriff Steve Strachan, a former Drug Abuse Resistance Education (DARE) officer, who commented, "With alcohol being highly regulated, we're able to have a little more discussion about it" (quoted in Westneat 2012). Strachan acknowledged that the DARE program had "overblown the dangers of pot" and that its mixing of messages about marijuana with "truly dangerous" hard drugs was "incredibly unhelpful" (quoted in Holden 2012). Even the Children's Alliance, a "non-partisan child advocacy organization," came out in support of I-502 because of its concern about racial bias in the enforcement of marijuana laws and the effect of such bias on minority youth (N. Shapiro 2012).

Major opponents of I-502 included those involved in medical marijuana businesses and Governor Christine Gregoire, who was primarily concerned about possible federal government intervention if the state legalized recreational marijuana (Leon and Weitzer 2014). The two candidates for Washington governor in 2012, Republican Rob McKenna (former state attorney general) and Democrat Jay Inslee, were also opposed to the measure (O'Neill 2012).

Oregon Legislation

The Path to Legalization
In 1973, Oregon became the first state to decriminalize marijuana; individuals possessing up to one ounce of the drug were subject to a $100 fine. An early study on the effects of decriminalization of marijuana in the state, con-

ducted by the legislative research service of the Oregon State Assembly and presented in 1974, concluded that there were no major negative effects of decriminalization and that it had removed small-scale users and possessors of marijuana from the criminal justice system, allowing criminal justice system officials in the state to concentrate on more serious matters (Legislative Research Bureau 1974). Thirteen years after the state decriminalized marijuana (in 1986) a marijuana legalization measure appeared on the Oregon ballot, with the measure failing by a vote of 74 percent opposed to 26 percent in favor (Bewley-Taylor, Blickman, and Jelsma 2014). In 1997, Oregon legislators attempted to recriminalize marijuana and Governor John Kitzhaber signed legislation making incarceration a possible penalty for possession of less than one ounce, but activists in the state forced a referendum on marijuana recriminalization, and the measure was defeated by a margin of two to one (Dills, Goffard, and Miron 2016).

In 2012 recreational legalization of marijuana was proposed with Measure 80, the Oregon Cannabis Tax Act Initiative, but failed with 54.3 percent of Oregon voters opposed. The text of the measure made several (many would say accurate) assertions, including that cannabis was not a gateway drug, that its users were less likely to commit violent acts and engage in criminal acts than alcohol users, that use of the substance did not impair psychomotor functions, and that cannabis use "does not constitute a public health problem of any significant dimension" (Oregon Secretary of State 2012, 53).

Similar to what occurred with California's 2010 Proposition 19, the three largest newspapers in Oregon (the [Portland] *Oregonian*, the *Eugene Register-Guard*, and the *Salem Statesman-Journal*) joined Governor John Kitzhauber, the Oregon Sheriffs' Association, and the Oregon District Attorneys' Association as the main opponents to Measure 80 (Leon and Weitzer 2014).

Legalization: Measure 91 (2014)

Recreational marijuana was legalized in Oregon in November 2014 with voter approval of Measure 91, the Control, Regulation, and Taxation of Marijuana and Industrial Hemp Act. The measure was supported by 56.1 percent of Oregon voters, with votes in favor of the measure particularly high in counties within the major metropolitan area of Portland—in one precinct support for the measure was at 89.9 percent (Mapes 2014a). The most significant provisions of the new law included allowing adults over twenty-one to possess one ounce of dried marijuana outside the home and up to eight ounces of marijuana inside their home and to grow up to four marijuana plants; the Oregon Liquor Commission (OLC) was assigned the responsibility of regulating sales of the substance (League of Oregon Cities 2016). Possession and home cultivation became legal on July 1, 2015, and sales through existing medical dispensaries began on October 1 of the same year. Sales from OLC-approved recreational dispensaries commenced in January 2016 (Marijuana Policy Project 2017).

When sales by OLC-approved recreational marijuana retailers began, all transactions were subject to a 17 percent state tax (local governments could add up to 3 percent additional sales tax).[4] The tax revenue generated from sales was to be allocated (after covering OLC oversight costs) to the Common School Fund (40 percent), Mental Health Alcoholism and Drug Services Account (20 percent), local law enforcement (20 percent), and state police (15 percent), with the remaining 5 percent allocated to the Oregon Health Authority for drug prevention and treatment services (Marijuana Policy Project 2017).

As has been the case in other states that have legalized marijuana, Oregon legislators have responded to problems with the legislation, and it has essentially been in a virtually constant state of flux. Subsequent protocols put into effect by the OLC have addressed some of the regulatory gaps in the original legislation, including those addressing "testing, packaging, labeling, advertising, waste and implementing a seed-to-sale tracking system" (League of Oregon Cities 2016, 8). Additional rules that went into effect in January 2017 increased the amount of marijuana flower consumers could purchase (from one-quarter ounce to one ounce); stipulated that individual edible cannabis products be limited to five milligrams of THC per serving (half of what is allowed in Colorado and Washington and a reduction from the previous limit of fifteen grams); and lowered the state tax on marijuana from 25 percent to 20 percent (Crombie 2017a). More important, this legislation specified that medical marijuana dispensaries in the state could no longer sell recreational marijuana and provided that certified medical marijuana patients do not have to pay retail sales tax on cannabis products. Businesses selling only medical marijuana were regulated by the Oregon Health Authority, while the OLC assumed control over recreational sales (Crombie 2016c). As a result of this change, the number of medical marijuana dispensaries registered with the state's Health Authority decreased from 425 in October 2016 to 115 in March 2017. As of the same date, the OLC had approved 365 licenses for recreational marijuana statewide, approximately three-quarters of which were also approved to sell medical marijuana (Marum 2017). As of early 2017, the city of Portland, with a population of approximately 630,000, had forty-one stores selling recreational marijuana (Crombie 2017a), and billboards advertising these stores proliferated in the city.

---

4. Recreational marijuana sales at medical marijuana dispensaries were initially taxed at 25 percent, until recreational sales from medical dispensaries were prohibited in 2017 (Oregon Department of Revenue 2018).

Alaska Legislation

The Path to Legalization

Alaska is a generally conservative state but also has a strong libertarian tradition and a very interesting and complicated history with respect to marijuana legislation. Marijuana possession has been effectively legal in the state since 1975, when the Alaska Supreme Court, basing its decision on unique privacy protections in the state constitution, ruled that possessing small amounts of marijuana in one's own home was not illegal (Dickinson 2012). This decision is traced to the case of *Ravin v. State* (1975), involving Irwin Ravin, an attorney who set himself up to be arrested so that he could challenge the constitutionality of the existing marijuana law in Alaska. Ravin was pulled over for a broken taillight and, knowing he had marijuana in his pocket, refused to sign the citation so he would be searched and arrested for marijuana possession (J. Burke 2010). At the time Ravin's law partner, Robert Wagstaff, was the Alaska representative for NORML. After Ravin's arrest he and his partner had the client they needed (i.e., Ravin) to challenge Alaska's marijuana law, and NORML paid for the expert witnesses necessary for Ravin's defense (Lippman 2014). In rendering its decision on this case, the Alaska Supreme Court indicated that privacy concerns provided a fundamental right to Alaskans to possess small amounts of marijuana in their home, but individuals were not entitled to possess marijuana outside the home or to possess it in amounts that would suggest an intent to sell the drug (Lippman 2014). The court further stated that after reviewing the medical evidence regarding the potential health problems associated with marijuana use, there was insufficient evidence to generate "widespread concern" (Lippman 2014). The *Ravin* decision set the stage for many subsequent privacy rights cases addressing the legality of marijuana possession in Alaska (J. Burke 2010).

Also in 1975, just a week prior to the *Ravin* decision, the Alaska legislature decriminalized marijuana, making it the second state to do so (after Oregon in 1973). The juxtaposition of slightly different interpretations of the law between the courts and legislature regarding the legal status of marijuana provided a complex legal situation that remained largely unresolved until full legalization of recreational marijuana occurred in 2014 (Edge and Andrews 2014). Under the 1975 Alaska decriminalization measure, the maximum penalty for marijuana possession was $100 for up to an ounce in public or for any amount in one's home—the fine option was removed from the legislation in 1982 (Dills, Goffard, and Miron 2016).

In 1989, a statewide petition began the process toward recriminalization of marijuana in Alaska, and the substance was officially recriminalized in 1990, when voters approved Measure 2, the Alaska Marijuana Criminalization Initiative, by a 54 percent majority (Edge and Andrews 2014). Measure

2 prohibited marijuana possession, even in one's home (again, the constitutionality of this was questionable due to the *Ravin* precedent—essentially the legislature and the Alaska Supreme Court held different interpretations of what was and was not legal), with penalties extending up to ninety days in jail and a $1,000 fine (Dills, Goffard, and Miron 2016). Measure 2 was met with a variety of appeals and finally struck down in 2003.

In 2000 and 2004, ballot measures to fully legalize marijuana in Alaska were considered, but both failed, with the measures opposed by 59 percent of voters in 2000 (Dills, Goffard, and Miron 2016) and 56 percent in 2004 (Dickinson 2012). A study funded by a group backing the 2004 initiative, Alaskans for Rights and Revenues, concluded that the prohibition of marijuana cost the state between $25 million and $30 million (Edge and Andrews 2014). In 2006, Governor Frank Murkowski (drawing on claims that the more potent marijuana available then than in the 1970s made the substance more dangerous) signed into law House Bill 149, making possession of one to four ounces of marijuana in public a misdemeanor punishable by up to a year in jail and possession of more than four ounces a felony (Edge and Andrews 2014). Shortly after this legislation was passed, the American Civil Liberties Union challenged it on the grounds that it violated the privacy clause of the Alaska constitution as interpreted by *Ravin* (Brandeis 2012). However, when the matter reached the Alaska Supreme Court, the court essentially punted on the issue, concluding that "the matter was not ripe for review" (Brandeis 2012, 198), a decision that was essentially a win for marijuana advocates, especially with respect to possession of marijuana in the home.

Legalization: Measure 2 (2014)

In 2014, a third ballot initiative to legalize marijuana in Alaska was put forth, and this time it passed, with 53 percent of voters supporting Measure 2 (Dills, Goffard, and Miron 2016). Proponents of marijuana legalization in Alaska included libertarians and certain Republicans who support privacy rights in the state's constitution (Dischner 2015). Under Alaska's marijuana legalization measure, similar to the situation in other states that have legalized recreational marijuana, local communities can choose not to allow sales of the substance within their jurisdictions.

Alaska regulators were also attentive to the issue of public consumption of marijuana, in recognition of the fact that the state attracts large numbers of tourists (particularly from cruise ships). The agency constructing the rules for Alaska's recreational marijuana industry (the Alcohol and Marijuana Control Office, housed under the state's Department of Commerce, Community, and Economic Development) decided to allow individuals to consume marijuana in some of the retail outlets selling the drug (Bohrer 2015). The proposed consumption areas within these stores were required to be separated from the rest of the establishment by secure doors, and items consumed at the store could not be removed (Bohrer and Thiessen 2016). However, public consumption of marijuana in Alaska remains prohibited and is punishable by a fine of up to $100 (Chokshi 2015).

Alaska's legalization measure allows individuals to possess up to one ounce of marijuana in public (because of the *Ravin* decision possession of up to four ounces in the home is considered "protected conduct" under the state's right-to-privacy protections) and to grow up to six plants in their home, and it initially permitted adults to gift an ounce of marijuana to another person (Chokshi 2015), though with the opening of retail stores in November 2016, gifting was made illegal. Alaska also created a regulatory board to monitor the industry and oversee the tax of $50 per ounce levied when marijuana is sold or transferred from a cultivation facility to a dispensary (Dills, Goffard, and Miron 2016). As in other states that have legalized recreational marijuana, the rollout of regulatory guidelines and availability of the substance at retail outlets have taken some time. The state approved industry regulations for the sale of marijuana in February 2016, and prospective dispensary owners were then able to apply for a business license. As of early 2018, sixty-four retail marijuana stores were listed as active (but not necessarily operating) by the Alaska Department of Commerce, Community, and Economic Development, with fifteen stores open for business in Anchorage (the state's largest city, with a population of approximately three hundred thousand) (Carvajal and Sullivan 2018).

Washington, D.C., Legislation

The Path to Legalization

Perhaps more than in any other recreationally legalized location, social justice issues have been at the forefront of marijuana policy reform in Washington, D.C. Marijuana arrests by the Metropolitan Police Department in Washington, D.C., increased from 334 in 1968 to 3,002 in 1975, the bulk of which were arrests of African Americans (James Forman 2017). Marijuana arrests were viewed by some in D.C. as issues of civil rights and racial justice, and a proposal to decriminalize marijuana in the district was first considered in 1975. David Clarke, a civil rights lawyer who was elected as one of the original members of the Council of the District of Columbia (after D.C. gained home rule in 1974), proposed eliminating incarceration as a possible penalty for possession of less than one ounce of marijuana (James Forman 2017). At the time, possession of marijuana in D.C. had the same maximum penalty as sale of the drug—one year in prison and a $1,000 fine.

In his book *Locking Up Our Own*, Yale Law School professor James Forman, a former public defense lawyer in D.C., documents the role of African American politicians and law enforcement officials in facilitating policies and procedures that led to mass incarceration (and its attendant gross racial disparities) in the United States. Forman also notes that one reason proposed legislation to decriminalize marijuana in 1975 in D.C. failed was that the bill's two primary sponsors were white. He also notes that most opposition to marijuana decriminalization came from the black community, including religious leaders. One black opponent commented, "It would seem to me to be a social crime to depenalize marijuana so as to make it possible for more black children who cannot think already to keep them from thinking" (quoted in Forman 2017, 38).

In 1998, Washington, D.C., voters approved Initiative 59, the Legalization of Marijuana for Medical Treatment Initiative, with 69 percent in favor (Altieri 2013). However, implementation of this measure was delayed by passage of the Barr amendment in Congress, which prohibited the city government from using funds to implement the legislation. Somewhat amazingly, this amendment delayed the start of the medical marijuana program in D.C. until 2009, and it was not until 2013 that customers began purchasing medical marijuana at dispensaries (Altieri 2013).

Legalization: Initiative 71 (2014)

In the November 2014 elections Washington, D.C., legalized recreational marijuana with Initiative 71, the Legalization of Possession of Minimal Amounts of Marijuana for Personal Use Act of 2014. As alluded to previously, the issue of legalization was primarily framed as a racial justice issue (Calabria 2016). Similar to what had occurred in New York and several other large U.S. cities, marijuana arrests in D.C. had increased significantly from the mid-1990s to the 2010s, with attendant racial disproportionality. In 1995, there were 1,850 arrests for marijuana possession in the District; by 2011, the number of arrests topped 6,000, with more than 90 percent involving African Americans (Zukerberg 2013)—this represented a larger percentage of arrests of African Americans for marijuana possession than in any other major U.S. city (Fisher, Davis, and Stein 2015).

Despite opposition from several members of Congress, Washington, D.C., voters approved Initiative 71, with 70.6 percent of voters in favor. Under the legislation, individuals over the age of twenty-one can possess up to two ounces of marijuana, can grow up to six cannabis plants (with three or fewer being mature), and can transfer without payment up to one ounce of marijuana to another individual over the age of twenty-one (Calabria 2016).

As had happened with previous marijuana reform initiatives in D.C., the federal government has continued to engage in obstructionist tactics to prevent the full implementation of legalization. This is facilitated by the unique legislative status of the District (because D.C. is the capital of the United States, the Constitution grants Congress exclusive jurisdiction over the District). As an example of the obstructionist tactics employed, conservative

Republicans in the House of Representatives barred the local government from using tax revenues to create regulations for marijuana legalization, including where and how the substance would be sold (A. Davis 2016). So marijuana legalization in D.C. is perhaps the most curious of all legalized locales—most tellingly, even though the substance is legal, an individual cannot buy or sell marijuana in D.C. (Gurciullo and Mawdley 2015). An additional issue is that because the substance is still banned under federal law, individuals possessing and/or consuming marijuana on the mall, several parks, and almost every traffic circle in the city can receive up to one year in prison, as these locations are under the jurisdiction of the federal government. Partially in response to this absurd situation a number of "gray-market" companies have emerged that deliver various products to a person's home, along with marijuana—the purchasers receive the marijuana after buying one of these other products (Hendrix 2017). These companies are exploiting the provision in the legislation that allows for the transfer of marijuana without payment.

In addition to many in Congress, among individuals and organizations opposed to Initiative 71 was the *Washington Post*, which published an editorial in 2014 titled "D.C. Voters Should Reject the Rush to Legalize Marijuana." In defense of the *Post*'s opposition to Initiative 71, the editorial noted that the AMA did not support legalization and that "the active ingredient in marijuana has been linked to memory problems, impaired thinking and weakened immune systems, not to mention it acts as a gateway to more dangerous drugs." Apparently, at least some of the "facts" about marijuana cited in the *Post* editorial were taken from SAM, as the authors commented, "Smart Approaches to Marijuana has catalogued the negative consequences of legalization in Colorado."

California Legislation

The Path to Legalization

Although the measure failed with only 33 percent of voters in support, California was the first state in which a recreational marijuana legalization measure appeared on the ballot (Proposition 19 in 1972) (Romero 2016). The state decriminalized marijuana under the 1976 Moscone Act, which reduced the penalty for possessing less than one ounce of marijuana from a felony to a misdemeanor, punishable by a $100 fine (Lee 2012). And in 1996, with the passage of Proposition 215, California became the first state to legalize cannabis for medical purposes.

The medical marijuana campaign and its ultimate success in California occurred because of strong grassroots organizing by individuals such as medical cannabis and LGBT rights activist Dennis Peron (who in 1992 established the Cannabis Buyers Club, the first medical marijuana dispensary, in San Francisco in response to the AIDS epidemic). With colleagues in San Francisco, Peron drafted a medical marijuana initiative in 1995 and turned to Ethan Nadelmann of the Lindesmith Center for financial assistance in qualifying Proposition 215 for the ballot. Nadelmann enlisted the assistance of a prominent political consultant/strategist, Bill Zimmerman, to organize the signature gathering and media campaigns for the measure (Dickinson 2013). As Nadelmann told *Rolling Stone* reporter Tom Dickinson in 2013, part of the goal of the Proposition 215 campaign was to "change the public face of the marijuana consumer" from the stereotype of a "17-year old high school dropout with dreadlocks to a middle-aged cancer patient braving chemo." Zimmerman added, "We sought two goals: Legalizing medical marijuana in the short run, but preparing for a broader effort in the long run" (quoted in Gardner 2015).

Virtually all individuals and organizations in the California law enforcement community opposed Proposition 215, and California attorney general Dan Lungren (who also helped draft the state's controversial Three Strikes law), announced a narrow interpretation of the legislation that encouraged law enforcement to continue arresting, and district attorneys to continue prosecuting, individuals for cultivating marijuana (Gardner 2015). Following the passage of Proposition 215, California law enforcement agencies assisted the DEA and other federal government agencies in pursuing cannabis growers and medical dispensaries in the state.

In November 2010, a proposal to legalize recreational marijuana, known as Proposition 19, the Regulate, Control, and Tax Cannabis Act, was included on the ballot in California. Major supporters of this measure (who collectively spent $4.5 million on the campaign) included the American Civil Liberties Union, the MPP, the DPA (and George Soros), and LEAP (Leon and Weitzer 2014). Opposition to Proposition 19 included the California Chamber of Commerce, the four leading newspapers in the state (the *Los Angeles Times*, the *San Diego Union Tribune*, the *San Jose Mercury News*, and even the more liberal *San Francisco Chronicle*), Governor Arnold Schwarzenegger, both candidates for 2010 governor (Democrat Jerry Brown and Republican Meg Whitman), and California's two U.S. senators (Barbara Boxer and Dianne Feinstein) (Leon and Weitzer 2014). And as would happen with the 2016 marijuana legalization measure in California, among the major financial contributors to the campaign against Proposition 19 were beer and alcoholic beverage distributors (Egan 2010).

Similar to the themes expressed in other antilegalization campaigns, Proposition 19 opponents emphasized concerns over increases in youth use of marijuana and in individuals driving under the influence of cannabis if legalization occurred. In addition, related to Leon and Weitzer's (2014) suggestion that the threat of federal intervention can impact the outcome of legalization measures, U.S. attorney general Eric Holder announced that the federal government would vigorously enforce federal marijuana laws in California, regardless of whether the measure passed.

Likely in reaction to the results of some public opinion polls that suggested Proposition 19 would pass, Governor Arnold Schwarzenegger signed a law just weeks prior to the vote reducing the penalty for marijuana possession to the equivalent of a traffic ticket: a $100 fine and no allowance for jail time. This strategy was important, as one of the key arguments of supporters of Proposition 19 was that California's marijuana laws were costly in terms of enforcement and prosecution (Lagos 2010).

Although Proposition 19 was ultimately defeated (46.5 percent in favor and 53.5 percent opposed), younger voters were more likely to favor legalization, and 65 percent of voters in San Francisco approved the measure ("Prop 19" 2010). In addition, a poll conducted after the election found that 50 percent of voters believed marijuana should be legal but voted against the measure because of issues related to details of the regulations (Bewley-Taylor, Blickman, and Jelsma 2014): as the *Los Angeles Times* (2016) suggested, "not necessarily because it [marijuana legalization] was a bad idea, but because it was a poorly drafted mess that would have created a regulatory nightmare." The percentage of California voters who supported Proposition 19 perhaps presaged the success of subsequent marijuana legalization measures over the 2012–2016 period both in California and in other states.

Legalization: Proposition 64 (2016)

Supporters of marijuana legalization in California continued to organize and refine their strategies, and in 2016 Proposition 64, the Adult Use of Marijuana Act, was approved by just more than 57 percent of California voters. Partially because proponents of legalized recreational marijuana in California were able to learn from some of the mistakes made by Colorado and Washington in their legalization measures, the legislation in California was much more comprehensive and included several progressive clauses. Under the provisions of Proposition 64, individuals are allowed to possess up to one ounce/28.5 grams of marijuana for personal use and grow up to six plants (as long as the plants are "shielded from the public view") (Fuller 2016a). Taxes under the legislation include a 15 percent state excise tax on retail sales and cultivation taxes of $9.25 per ounce of flower and $2.75 per ounce of trim/leaves. There are also local and nonexcise state taxes that range from 7.75 to 9.75 percent, an effective tax rate of roughly 45 percent, which is more than twice the rate in Oregon and Alaska (Mogensen 2017). Smoking marijuana in public is prohibited, with violators subject to a $100 fine. Cannabis products must be packaged in child-resistant containers, and the drug cannot be advertised along interstate highways or state highways that cross the border of another state (McGreevy 2016c). Sales of recreational marijuana via dispensaries commenced on January 1, 2018.

Among the major supporters of Proposition 64 was Sean Parker, founder of the online music service Napster. Parker contributed $8.5 million to the "Yes on Proposition 64" campaign—he saw marijuana prohibition as a social justice issue and claimed to have no interest in the commercial marijuana industry (McGreevy 2016a). Dana Rohrabacher, a Republican congressman from Orange County (who has also influenced marijuana-related legislation at the federal level), also supported the measure: "I can't think of a bigger waste of government money than to try to use it to control the private lives of adults. . . . The forest service and other key government agencies are being defunded to maintain a war on drugs that is philosophically wrong" (quoted in La Ganga 2016). The "Yes on Proposition 64" campaign was also endorsed by former San Francisco mayor and current California lieutenant governor Gavin Newsom and the state's branch of the NAACP (Romero 2016).

Reversing its opposition to the 2010 legalization measure, the editorial board of the *Los Angeles Times* came out in support of Proposition 64 in 2016, emphasizing the potential public health and social justice benefits: "The Proposition deserves a 'yes' vote. It is ultimately better for public health, for law and order and for society if marijuana is a legal, regulated, and controlled product for adults." The passage of the law would "deal a blow to the illegal market. . . . For decades, drug enforcement—and particularly the enforcement of marijuana laws—has disproportionately affected African-Americans and Latino men."

Importantly, the California Medical Association (CMA), representing more than forty thousand physicians in the state, also supported Proposition 64. Although emphasizing that it was not encouraging marijuana use, the CMA commented, "The most effective way to protect public health is to highly control, track, and regulate marijuana and to comprehensively research and educate the public on its health impacts, not through ineffective prohibition" (quoted in Staggs 2016b).

The "No on Proposition 64" campaign in California enlisted the assistance of Colorado officials in opposition to legalization in their state. In a letter sent to the "No on 64 Campaign and SAM [Smart Approaches to Marijuana] Action," in October 2016, Denver district attorney Mitchell Morrissey made a number of misleading and outlandish claims regarding the effects of marijuana legalization in Colorado. These included assertions that traffic-related marijuana deaths, marijuana-related emergency room visits, and marijuana-related calls to poison control centers in the state had increased significantly since legalization. While not elucidating the specifics of the causal relationship, Morrissey also argued that homicides, thefts, motor vehicle thefts, robberies, and even sexual assaults had increased statewide and in specific cities in Colorado after legalization—all of these negative outcomes, he implied, were due to marijuana legalization.

Additional opposition to Proposition 64 included the group California Citizens against Legalizing Marijuana, who argued, "This is not about a war on drugs—it's a battle to protect the human brain, the mind, our future, our kids" (quoted in Fuller 2016a). Not surprisingly, opposition also came from some law enforcement and criminal justice groups, including the California Police Chiefs' Association, the Los Angeles Police Protective League, and the California Correctional Supervisors' Association (K. Shapiro 2016b). More specifically, to counter the social justice theme of marijuana legalization supporters, Jennifer Tejada, chair of the California Police Chiefs' Law and Legislative Committees, attempted to refute claims that individuals were being incarcerated for marijuana offenses: "Go to any county jail and find someone who is in there for possession of pot. It hasn't happened in decades" (quoted in Fuller 2016a). While data on the number of individuals incarcerated for marijuana offenses in California are not readily available, it seems unlikely that there were no such cases, especially given that between 2006 and 2015 there were close to five hundred thousand marijuana arrests in the state, including more than one hundred thousand for felonies (Jolene Foreman 2016). Of course, the primary reason for law enforcement groups' opposition to marijuana legalization is fairly simple to understand—these organizations realize several benefits from drug wars (Fang 2016), especially with respect to revenue generation.

California governor Jerry Brown (who also opposed Proposition 19 in 2010) expressed concern that passage of Proposition 64 would increase the number of "stoners" in California with resultant negative effects in the state: "All of a sudden, if there's advertising and legitimacy, how many people can get stoned and still have a great state or a great nation? The world's pretty dangerous, very competitive. I think we need to stay alert, if not twenty-four hours a day, more than some of the potheads might be able to put together" (quoted in Associated Press 2014).

A notable consequence of the passage of Proposition 64 is that it allows individuals who have previously been convicted of marijuana crimes to apply for resentencing or expungement of their records (the California legislation is unique with respect to this provision) and reduced all previous marijuana-related felonies to misdemeanors, which could possibly apply to those sentenced under California's Three Strikes law (Abcarian 2016). The legislation also reduced the penalties for marijuana charges for juveniles, virtually eliminating the possibility of incarceration for such offenses (Way 2017); minors who are found in possession of marijuana will be required to complete four hours of a drug education or counseling program and up to ten hours of community service (McGreevy 2016c). Proposition 64 also added certain protections for medical marijuana patients in the state involved in child custody cases. Although the exact numbers are not known, it is estimated that hundreds of parents in California have had their children removed by state authorities as a result of their use of medical marijuana; Proposition 64 requires justification beyond a parent's mere status as a medical marijuana patient for their children to be removed (Staggs 2016c).

Nevada Legislation

The Path to Legalization
Nevada approved medical marijuana in 1998 and 2000, but, similar to the situation in other states, the legislation did not include provisions that would allow for the establishment of a system to sell or distribute the substance—these were not established until 2013 (Sonner and Rindels 2015). One of the unique features of the Nevada medical marijuana program is that it allows registered patients from other states to purchase the substance in Nevada (E. Gray 2015); given the large number of tourists who visit Nevada each year, this provision has likely benefited the sales of medical marijuana dispensaries in the state.

Prior to 2016, Nevada had considered marijuana legalization four times. While the 2002 legalization measure was opposed by 61 percent of Nevada voters, a similar measure in 2006 garnered somewhat less opposition, with 56 percent of voters opposed. In both 2013 and 2015, the Nevada legislature considered, but ultimately rejected, marijuana legalization.

Legalization: Ballot Question 2 (2016)
In November 2016, 54.5 percent of voters supported Ballot Question 2, the Regulation and Taxation of Marijuana Act, which allowed adults over twenty-one years of age to possess up to one ounce of marijuana or 3.5 grams of marijuana concentrate. Although the legislation allows for home cultivation of up to six marijuana plants per person (and up to twelve per household) (Cano and Sonner 2017), one of the more curious aspects of the Nevada legislation is that it prohibited home cultivation of marijuana anywhere within twenty-five miles of a licensed dispensary, possibly rendering home growing illegal in up to 90 percent of the state (Hughes 2016). The legislation also bans smoking cannabis in public places (including along the strip and in casinos in Las Vegas), with violations of this provision potentially resulting in a $600 fine. The Nevada legislation imposes a 15 percent excise tax on the first wholesale and a 10 percent retail excise tax, with an exemption for medical marijuana patients (State of Nevada Department of Taxation 2018), and existing medical marijuana dispensaries were given an eighteen-month monopoly on recreational sales, while alcohol distributors were provided an eighteen-month monopoly on distribution of the substance.

The pro–marijuana legalization campaign in Nevada included several of the same themes from successful legalization campaigns in other states, emphasizing that marijuana is safer than alcohol, legalization would reduce the black market for the drug, and legalization would benefit the state's economy (Rindels 2016).

Opponents of the measure included the group Protect Nevada's Children, Democratic senator Harry Reid, and, interestingly, the Nevada Resort Association (the main lobbying group for the state's casino industry) (Rindels 2016). While the casino industry's opposition to marijuana legalization may seem curious, it is of course possible that its concerns were related to the fact that legalization might negatively impact alcohol sales.

Among the four states that legalized recreational marijuana in the 2016 legislation, Nevada was the only one in which recreational marijuana was available for sale before the date stipulated in the legislation. The Nevada State Department of Taxation (the primary regulatory body overseeing marijuana legalization in the state) began accepting applications for licenses to sell recreational marijuana in May 2017 (Noon 2017), and sales began on July 1 of the same year (well ahead of the January 1, 2018, deadline for sales to begin). In the first few days of sales, marijuana dispensaries reported more than forty thousand transactions involving recreational marijuana (Westervelt 2017), and within two weeks Nevada Republican governor Brian Sandoval called for a state of emergency due to a lack of marijuana supply in retail outlets (Fuller 2017c).

As of September 2017, Nevada had thirty-one licensed retail marijuana stores, ninety-two cultivation operations, sixty-five manufacturers, and thirty-one distributors (with 80 percent of the total licensed facilities located in Las Vegas and Clark County) (Sonner 2017). Data released by the Nevada Department of Taxation indicated that cannabis dispensaries in the state sold $27.1 million worth of marijuana in July 2017 (significantly higher than the $14 million in Oregon and Colorado and $3.8 million in Washington State in those states' first month of legal sales), providing $3.68 million in tax revenues to the state (Sonner 2017).

Massachusetts Legislation

The Path to Legalization
Massachusetts decriminalized possession of marijuana in 2008, replacing criminal penalties for possession of less than one ounce of the substance with a system of civil penalties, and in 2012, a medical marijuana measure was approved by voters in the state (Joshua Miller 2016). The medical marijuana legislation (Question 3), passed with 63 percent of voters in favor, eliminated all criminal and civil penalties for patients diagnosed with "a debilitating medical condition." As in many states, access to marijuana met with many delays, and it took nearly three years for the state to open the first dispensaries (Dumcius 2018b). Massachusetts allows individuals to purchase

up to ten ounces every two months, an amount that is arguably the most permissive (in terms of weight, not in terms of qualifying conditions) nationally.

Legalization: Ballot Question 4 (2016)

Massachusetts legalized recreational marijuana in 2016 after 53 percent of Massachusetts adults voted in favor (a 240,000-vote margin) of Question 4, the Massachusetts Marijuana Legalization Initiative. Under the provisions of the legislation, adults age twenty-one and older can possess up to one ounce of marijuana (while inside their homes, possession of up to ten ounces is allowed), and an individual can grow up to six cannabis plants for personal use (and up to twelve plants per household if more than one adult lives on the premises). Public consumption of marijuana remains illegal under the measure, and possession of any amount of marijuana on school grounds remains illegal (Salsberg 2016). Retail sales were scheduled to begin in Massachusetts by July 1, 2018, but as of August 2018, sales had not yet begun (Dumcius 2018a, 2018b). One of the more controversial aspects of the legislation is that it initially imposed only a 3.7 percent excise tax on sales, far below the national average.

Major opposition to Massachusetts recreational legalization measure was presented by the Catholic Church, doctors and business groups, law enforcement, and high-level state officials (Joshua Miller 2016). In March 2016, the governor of Massachusetts (Charlie Baker), the state's attorney general (Maura Healey), and the mayor of Boston (Martin J. Walsh) wrote an editorial in the *Boston Globe* arguing against legalization, in which they recited the same timeworn (and largely disproven) themes of other marijuana prohibitionists. Referring to the Rocky Mountain HIDTA report we discuss in Chapter 5, the group argued that "where marijuana is legal, young people are more likely to use it," and "the science shows that regular marijuana users . . . are more likely to try dangerous drugs." Echoing the main theme of the anti-marijuana legalization group SAM, they noted, "The financial backers of legalization are not neighborhood leaders, medical professionals, or grassroots activists. They're big business and investors."

In hearings held in early 2017, Massachusetts legislators considered the specific regulations that would apply to recreational marijuana sales. As noted, one of the more controversial aspects of the Massachusetts legislation is that it imposes an excise tax of only 3.7 percent on retail marijuana sales, the lowest nationally, raising concerns about whether the tax would generate sufficient revenue to cover the costs of regulating marijuana in the state (Salsberg 2017). Partially in response, in July 2017 (and in a move similar to what happened in Maine) Governor Baker signed legislation that increased the maximum effective tax rate on retail sales of marijuana to 20 percent (a 10.75 percent excise tax, the state sales tax of 6.25 percent, and an additional tax of up to 3 percent that localities may add [WCBV News 2017]). The bill also stipulated that cities and towns whose voters approved marijuana legalization could prohibit marijuana stores only within their jurisdictions if a majority of voters approved of such bans, while allowing local governing bodies themselves to ban shops in cities and towns that voted against the measure.

Maine Legislation

The Path to Legalization

Maine has a long history of progressive marijuana policy. The state was among the first to decriminalize, doing so in 1975, when the state made possession of small amounts of the drug punishable by no more than a fine. In 1999 Maine became the fifth state to legalize medical marijuana, but legal acquisition of the drug was not provided for under the legislation (Shepherd 2016). This was addressed in 2009 when 58 percent of Maine voters passed Question 5, which made Maine one of the first states to provide medical marijuana dispensaries (Haskell 2009). Then in 2013, voters in Portland, Maine's most populous city, passed a local law, legalizing the possession of small amounts of the drug, followed in the next year by voters in the adjacent city of South Portland (Marijuana Policy Project 2018). This set the stage for the voters to consider statewide legalization in 2016.

Legalization: Ballot Question 1 (2016)

In Maine, the 2016 marijuana legalization ballot measure, known as Question 1, the Marijuana Legalization Measure, was narrowly approved (with 51.3 percent of voters in support, a margin of just under four thousand votes). Marijuana became officially legal in Maine on January 30, 2017, and under the specifics of the legislation individuals twenty-one years of age and over are allowed to possess up to 2.5 ounces of marijuana and can grow six mature and twelve immature cannabis plants (although the substance cannot be grown where it is visible to others or accessible by anyone under the age of twenty-one) (Maine State Legislature 2018; see also Graham 2017). Interestingly, the stipulations on cultivation require that each plant have a name tag that includes the grower's name and Maine driver's license or alternative identification number. And although public consumption of marijuana could result in a $100 fine, the law also allows for state-licensed clubs where individuals can consume marijuana (Graham 2017). As in many states, retail sales of recreational marijuana in Maine have experienced delays prior to implementation; such sales were expected to begin in summer of 2018 but will likely be postponed to 2019. The legislation also provided the state with regulatory power on retail outlets and cultivation and provides for a 10 percent sales tax on marijuana products (Shepherd 2016), but as of mid-2018, legislators in Maine have proposed various revisions to taxation in the original legislation, including adding a 10 percent wholesale/excise tax or an additional 10 percent on the sales tax, making it 20 percent (Overton 2017).

Among those opposing the legislation was Maine Republican governor Paul LePage, who has referred to marijuana as "deadly" and in a radio interview in late December 2016 asserted that the state's constitution stipulated that ballot referendums are "recommendations that the legislature doesn't have to enact" (quoted in Villeneuve 2016), an interpretation that Maine constitutional experts disputed. LePage also expressed concern over the "unintended consequences" of marijuana legalization and indicated he needed legal advice and possibly $5 million to implement the law. While LePage eventually signed the bill in early 2017, he also called for a moratorium on marijuana sales, and the legislature passed a bill that would delay retail sales until 2018.

Barely one month after Question 1 passed in Maine, more than thirty municipalities in the state were considering imposing moratoriums on retail sales, and eleven communities had passed legislation imposing six-month moratoriums on sales (Villeneuve and Whittle 2016). While these moratoriums are reflective of the continuing controversies surrounding marijuana legalization, it is not entirely clear what they will accomplish. As David Boyer, campaign manager for "Yes on 1," commented, "These towns have their head in the sand if they think they're stopping marijuana from being sold by putting a moratorium on marijuana. Marijuana's being sold in every town in this state" (quoted in Villeneuve and Whittle 2016).

Vermont Legislation

The Path to Legalization
Somewhat ironically, the "Green Mountain State" didn't decriminalize marijuana until 2013, becoming the seventeenth state to do so. The legislation ended criminal penalties for possession of up to an ounce of marijuana or five grams of hashish, replacing them with a fine of $200 for a first offense and $500 for subsequent offenses (Clarke 2013). Vermont legalized medical marijuana in 2004, allowing for possession of up to two ounces and/or the cultivation of one mature and two immature plants, though this was expanded to two mature and seven immature plants in 2007 (National Organization for the Reform of Marijuana Laws 2018). The Vermont House approved a measure to legalize marijuana in 2017, but Governor Phil Scott vetoed it (McCullum 2017). However, Governor Scott indicated that although he had serious problems with the legislation he vetoed, he was not in principle opposed to legalization and was willing to work with lawmakers to craft an alternative legalization measure. This came to fruition in 2018.

Legalization: H.511 (2018)

Perhaps presaging things to come in other states, Vermont became the first state to legalize recreational marijuana via legislative action rather than the ballot. As noted previously, recreational legalization campaigns in the United States have been exclusively bottom up, driven by political activism and voter-approved initiatives that state government officials are then tasked with implementing. Governor Scott signed H.511 into law on January 22, 2018, a revised version of the bill he had previously vetoed, making Vermont the ninth U.S. state to legalize recreational marijuana. The legislation allows individuals twenty-one and older to possess up to an ounce of marijuana and allows for home cultivation—an individual can possess up to two mature and four immature plants (Zezima 2018). Notably, however, the legislation does not provide guidelines for how marijuana will be legally sold, regulated, and taxed. As of mid-2018, an advisory board has been tasked with providing recommendations to Governor Scott on the specifics of the regulatory framework. The legislation also provided enhanced penalties for selling marijuana to people under twenty-one or for enabling consumption for people under twenty-one and made it a crime to use marijuana in a vehicle with a child present (Zezima 2018). Public consumption of marijuana is also prohibited, but there are only civil penalties, with a $100 fine for a first offense.

Among those who opposed Vermont's measure was Kevin Sabet, who as the founder SAM has opposed all marijuana legalization measures. However, even Sabet acknowledged that Vermont's legislation has some merit, noting that it is "a heck of a lot better" than other state legalization measures (Zezima 2018).

Policy Heterogeneity and Local Variation

> America's legal cannabis industry has grown into a patchwork Frankenstein monster.
>
> —ALEX HALPERIN, "Canada's Legal Weed"

As we have discussed, and as Tables 6.1 and 6.2 reveal, there is considerable variation in the specifics of recreational and medical marijuana laws across states that have passed such laws. And importantly, even in states where the legalization of recreational marijuana is in place, reflecting continuing political divisions over the policies, there is considerable local variation.

In Colorado, Amendment 64 allowed individual towns and cities to decide whether to permit retail sales of marijuana within their boundaries, and several jurisdictions, including the state's second-largest city, Colorado Springs, and the popular ski resort town of Vail, imposed bans (Aguilar 2016). According to Vail's mayor Dave Chapin, the town banned marijuana sales to protect its brand as a ski vacation destination: "The Vail brand is a very valuable brand, and a lot of that brand is families. We weighed the value of that (potential) tax revenue against the value of the brand" (quoted in Aguilar 2016). Of course, the ban in Vail does not prevent tourists from purchasing marijuana only a few miles away in Eagle County, which has several marijuana shops (Aguilar 2016).

Similarly, in Washington State, the language of I-502 does not prohibit local bans on marijuana sales. While 55.7 percent of voters approved I-502, the majority of voters in nineteen of Washington State's counties voted against the measure (Dilley et al. 2017), so it is perhaps not surprising that several local jurisdictions have implemented bans on marijuana businesses. In response to a query by Washington State Liquor and Cannabis Control Board chair Sharon Foster regarding whether local governments were prevented by state law from prohibiting state-licensed marijuana producers, processors, or retailers within their jurisdiction, Washington State attorney general Bob Ferguson (2014) acknowledged that "we are mindful that if a large number of jurisdictions were to ban licenses, it could interfere with the [I-502] measure's intent to supplant the illegal market." However, Ferguson added, "Under Washington law, there is a strong presumption against finding that state law preempts local ordinances. . . . Local governments have broad authority to regulate within their jurisdictions, and nothing in I-502 limits that authority with respect to marijuana businesses." Confirming Ferguson's interpretation, as of early 2015, all five Washington State courts that had heard challenges to local bans agreed that these can be imposed (Ferguson 2015). As a result, as of June 2016, six of Washington's counties, and 54 of 152 cities with populations of three thousand or more had implemented local bans on retail cannabis sales, covering approximately 30 percent of the state's population (Dilley et al. 2017).

Although cities have allowed retail sales within the boundaries of these counties, large Washington State counties such as Pierce (the second largest, with a 2016 population of 843,945), and Clark (the fifth largest, with a 2016 population of 459,495), originally banned recreational marijuana sales. Clark County commissioner Tom Mielke, while admitting that he had not read the I-502 rules, justified the moratorium by claiming that he was concerned about (unspecified) unintended consequences of allowing marijuana stores in the county (Graf 2014). However, in Clark County, the local newspaper of record, the *Columbian* (2014), recommended that the county commissioners rescind the ban. As of mid-2018, the ban on marijuana sales in Clark County had not been rescinded, although there were thirteen retail marijuana stores within the county's boundaries (Washington State Liquor and Cannabis Board 2017b).

While the ban on marijuana sales in Clark County is still in place, Pierce County executive Pat McCarthy vetoed Pierce County's ban in June 2016, commenting, "I am vetoing this ordinance because my job as an elected of-ficial requires me to advance the will of the people who voted in 2012 [54 percent approved the legalization], in a comprehensive election, to legalize recreational marijuana" (quoted in Grimley 2016).

It is by no means clear what legislators are trying to accomplish in enacting these local bans. Are they unaware that residents of their jurisdictions are able to travel (in many cases short distances) to purchase marijuana? Do they believe that, because they have imposed these bans, people who are interested in consuming marijuana will not do so? In a letter to Pierce County Council chair Doug Richardson, Executive Pat McCarthy (2016) noted that banning the sale of marijuana "piecemeal throughout the state defeats one of the most important goals of I-502: that is, eradication of the black market. Effective regulation, licensing, and enforcement of marijuana is the best tool we have for keeping marijuana out of the hands of young people."

Local variation in the implementation of marijuana policies has also oc-curred in Oregon. Under Measure 91 (passed in 2014), the state gave cities and counties until December 2015 to either prohibit or allow marijuana pro-duction and sales within their jurisdiction (Berg 2017). As of spring 2016, more than one hundred cities in Oregon had banned sales, with most of these jurisdictions in the eastern part of the state (Selsky 2016). The mayor of Pendleton (which imposed a ban), in the north-central part of the state, told a reporter, "When it comes to a lot of our laws, they are determined by a couple of counties and Portland. We are used to that, so what we have to do is buck up and figure out what we are going to do" (quoted in Crombie 2015).

As noted previously, one of the more problematic aspects of local bans is that they increase the probability that black markets for marijuana will con-tinue in communities (especially more rural, isolated ones) that prohibit sales. As Alison Holcomb, the main architect of the Washington State I-502 campaign, told the King County Council, "Every city and county that has put itself above the law, above the vote of the people [by prohibiting mari-juana sales] has done nothing more than funnel money into the illicit market but also into the hands of the privileged few who have managed to secure a state license" (quoted in Young 2016).

Recreational Marijuana Legislation in Other Countries

The Netherlands

Consistent with policies that apply to the regulation of a wide range of social issues—including homosexuality, abortion, and euthanasia—the Nether-lands has among the most progressive drug policies in the world (R. Baker

2002). As Cyrille Fijnaut and Brice De Ruyer note, for years "Dutch cannabis policy has been an important point of reference in the international discussion about the policy that should be pursued regarding the use of cannabis" (2015, 1). Following the specific recommendations of the Baan Commission (see discussion in Chapter 2), the country officially decriminalized marijuana possession in 1976 through revisions to the Opium Act, which distinguishes between Schedule I drugs (viewed as posing "unacceptable" risk), and Schedule II ("soft") drugs (with marijuana being placed in the latter category) (Korf, Wouters, and Benschop 2011). However, as Dirk Korf, Marije Wouters, and Annemieke Benschop note, "De facto decriminalization [in the Netherlands] had set in earlier, as local authorities began tolerating 'house dealers' at youth centers in the early 1970s," and this led to the current coffee shop model, which began in the 1980s.

In 1976, the Netherlands adopted a policy of nonenforcement for violations involving the possession of small amounts of marijuana, but technically, individuals in the Netherlands can still be sent to jail for as long as one month for marijuana possession (G. Smith 2002). However, under Dutch drug legislation, individuals are allowed to buy and sell small amounts of marijuana for personal use, and the cultivation of up to five plants for personal use, though technically illegal, is tolerated (Blickman and Jelsma 2009). While the Dutch policy toward marijuana is commonly referred to as legalization, it is more appropriate to call it de facto legalization (MacCoun and Reuter 2001).

Partially as a result of the de facto legalization of cannabis in the Netherlands, as of the early 2000s, estimates indicated that there were between twelve hundred and fifteen hundred "coffee shops" in the country that had emerged to provide cannabis products to consumers (Fijnaut and De Ruyer 2015). Contrary to the view often promoted by American drug enforcement officials (see the discussion of President Clinton's drug czar General Barry McCaffrey in Chapter 2), in principle these coffee shops are tightly controlled. Consumers can purchase cannabis in establishments that meet the following criteria: (1) no overt advertising of cannabis products, (2) no sales or consumption of hard drugs on the premises, (3) no nuisance or disturbance, (4) no customers under the age of eighteen, and (5) no purchase of more than five grams per day (Chatwin 2003). In the view of city leaders in Amsterdam, the coffee shop idea was successful: "The coffee shop concept was an expedient: it managed the inevitability of soft drugs; it contained their use; it provided for a measure of control. Technically, pot was still illegal, but provided coffee shops didn't advertise and didn't permit hard drug use, gedogen [tolerance] ruled" (Shorto 2013, 301).

However, the central paradox of Dutch cannabis policy is that, while the coffee shops themselves are legal, they are reliant on illegal markets to supply them with cannabis—this is known as the "backdoor problem." As Bill Griffin (2016) appropriately analogizes, "Imagine if buying a loaf of bread was tolerated and shops were allowed to make and sell bread, but no one was allowed to supply them with flour."

As Fijnaut and De Ruyer note, organized crime is an important player in cannabis and other drug markets in the Netherlands; there was and continues to be large-scale illegal indoor and outdoor cultivation of cannabis, and "large numbers of foreign tourists have traveled to the Netherlands to provide themselves with drugs in the coffeeshops and nearby illicit points of sale" (2015, 92). Drug tourism began to increase, leading to public nuisance problems (beginning as early as 1993 in southern border cities such as Maastricht, which is located in one of the European Union's largest metropolitan areas and had twenty-eight coffee shops at the time, and in Amsterdam) (Fijnaut and De Ruyer 2015). By 2009, partially in response to the marijuana tourism problem, 77.1 percent of the municipalities in the Netherlands prohibited marijuana-selling coffee shops within their jurisdictions (Korf, Wouters, and Benschop 2011).

In the late 2000s, national politicians in the Netherlands began to frame the drug tourism problem as a nationwide threat, and in 2012, a measure was passed to limit admissions to coffee shops only to people who had a club pass—these *wietpasses* were issued only to Dutch residents. This development was not without controversy, as there were concerns that those who would not want to officially register as members of a cannabis club would turn to the black market to obtain the substance (Fijnaut and De Ruyer 2015); this could also weaken the separation of drug markets and possibly make harder drugs more easily available to marijuana users (Korf, Wouters, and Benschop 2011). Several coffee shop owners actively resisted this policy, particularly in Amsterdam,[5] where in addition to emphasizing the potential black-market problems, owners expressed concerns that the law would compromise their customers' privacy and impose what might amount to a discriminatory ban on foreign tourists.

There have also been significant changes with respect to coffee shops in Amsterdam, with the number of such establishments declining from approximately 350 in 1995 to 167 as of early 2017 (S. N. 2017). The *wietpass* legislation was never enforced in Amsterdam (or in other major cities in the northern part of the Netherlands) (Fijnaut 2014), at least partially because the city was exempted from enforcing the law on the condition that coffee shops within 250 meters of schools be closed (Haines 2017). This measure, which was ostensibly aimed at deterring young people from using marijuana, affected at least twenty-eight establishments in the city (including

---

5. Approximately one-third of the remaining coffee shops in the Netherlands are in Amsterdam, about half of which are located in the city center. Only 5 percent of the country's population live in Amsterdam (Korf, Wouters, and Benschop 2011).

Mellow Yellow,[6] the oldest coffee shop in Amsterdam, which opened in 1967) (Haines 2016). However, there were concerns regarding the potential unintended consequences of this legislation. Because it will lead to an even fewer number of shops serving more customers, marijuana consumers may be pushed to the black market, and couriers who deliver cannabis to the coffee shops (where there is a limit of five hundred grams of cannabis they can have in their establishments) may be more vulnerable to robberies (S. N. 2017).

Taxation of cannabis is somewhat complicated in the Netherlands due to the de facto legalization model. Cannabis is not assigned an additional value-added tax in the Netherlands because sales of the substance are not fully legal. Coffee shops themselves are legal, however, and pay tax on their cumulative profits. Estimates indicate that the Dutch government generates roughly 400 million euros (approximately $495 million) in tax revenue annually from the coffee shops (Grund and Breeksema 2013).

Canada

Canada has among the highest rates of reported marijuana use of any Western country: according to a 2012 survey by Health Canada, 41.5 percent of Canadians reported lifetime marijuana use (Wente 2015). Similar to the situation in the United States, since the late 1960s and continuing into the current era, approximately two-thirds of drug arrests in Canada have involved cannabis, and of those, approximately three-quarters are possession offenses. In fact, in the late 1990s and into the 2000s, the arrest rate per capita for marijuana offenses in Canada was actually higher than in the United States (Fischer et al. 2003). However, an important difference between Canada and the United States in responding to drug offenses is manifested in sentencing practices. While sentences for drug offenses in the United States are generally quite severe, in Canada in 2007, 43 percent of all drug-related adult court cases and 51 percent of all drug-related juvenile cases were stayed, withdrawn, or dismissed (Dauvergne 2009). An additional and important key difference between Canada and the United States is that, with respect to drug (and all criminal) legislation, policies are determined exclusively at the federal level.

Canada's prohibition of marijuana at the federal level in 1923 predated the U.S. Marihuana Tax Act by fourteen years, and the country has a long history of punitive marijuana (and other drug) laws. Canada's 1961 revised Narcotic Control Act allowed for a maximum of seven years' imprisonment

---

6. Mellow Yellow was located 230 meters from a hairdressing school (S. N. 2017), most of whose students were eighteen or older (Haines 2016). Coffee shop owners in Amsterdam also questioned why pubs and bars that were within 250 meters of a school were not forced to close (Haines 2017).

for possession of certain drugs, including marijuana, and life imprisonment for most trafficking offenses (Mosher 1999). As noted previously, while recommendations to decriminalize marijuana were made by the 1972 Le Dain Commission and despite Prime Minister Pierre Trudeau's statement in 1976 that he would legalize marijuana, the Canadian law dealing with marijuana was not substantially altered until 1996. Under that year's Controlled Drug and Substances Act, individuals possessing thirty grams of marijuana or one gram of hashish or less were subject to maximum penalties of a $1,000 fine and six months' imprisonment for first offenses, with double these amounts for repeat offenders (Fischer et al. 2003).

The early 2000s were characterized by a liberal shift in drug policy, when Canada legalized medical marijuana in 2000 (Rough 2017), and in 2002 a special committee of the Canadian Senate recommended the legalization of cannabis possession and use (Canada 2002). Under the model proposed by the Senate committee, cannabis would have been treated similarly to alcohol, with use and access to supply regulated—the committee also recommended the expungement of criminal records for the approximately six hundred thousand Canadians previously convicted of marijuana possession.

Although the Canadian government did not follow through on the Senate committee's recommendation to legalize marijuana, in 2003, legislation was proposed that marijuana be decriminalized, with maximum penalties of a $500 fine for adults and $250 for individuals under the age of eighteen for possession of fifteen grams or less (Russo 2004). The proposal to decriminalize marijuana was not passed before (Liberal) Prime Minister Jean Chrétien left office, but incoming prime minister Paul Martin indicated his intention to soften marijuana laws when he commented that it achieves "absolutely nothing to give a criminal record to young people caught with small amounts [of marijuana]" (quoted in J. Brown 2003).

Despite indications that Canada might relax its marijuana policies in the mid-2000s, the election of Stephen Harper's Conservative Party to a minority government in 2006 signaled a change in direction in the country's marijuana policies (and some of the harm-reduction practices that were in place at the time: e.g., the allowance of safe-injection drug facilities for intravenous drug users [Mosher 2011b]). Under the National Anti-drug Strategy, launched in 2007, Harper's government introduced Bill C-26, which, among other things, imposed mandatory minimum sentences for growing marijuana and proposed shutting down the Vancouver safe-drug-injection facility known as Insite. Harper was reelected in the 2011 Canadian federal election, with his party forming a majority government, and in 2012, his government initiated a new drugs policy, which mandated deep cuts in Health Canada's budget for drug treatment, while at the same time providing significant increases in the budgets for drug enforcement in the criminal justice system (Geddes 2012).

In the Canadian federal election in the fall of 2015, Liberal Party leader Justin Trudeau (whose father, Pierre Trudeau, was prime minister of Canada for nearly sixteen years and had hinted that he would consider marijuana legalization in 1976 [Mosher 1999]) included marijuana legalization as a major platform of his campaign. The Liberal Party had earlier adopted an official platform to "legalize, regulate, and restrict access to marijuana" to "keep marijuana out of the hands of children, and the profits [from the illegal trade in marijuana] out of the hands of criminals" and to "prevent Canadians from acquiring criminal records for possessing small amounts of the substance" (Liberal Party of Canada, n.d.). Trudeau (who admitted he had smoked marijuana in the past, including while as a sitting member of Parliament) came out in favor of legalizing marijuana in 2013, noting, "In many cases, it's more difficult for young people to get their hands on cigarettes than it is to get their hands on weed" (quoted in Geddes 2017). In the 2015 Canadian election, Trudeau's Liberal Party captured 184 seats in the 338-seat parliament (Austen 2015), forming a majority government, and discussions regarding the specifics of marijuana legalization commenced.

In 2016, a Government of Canada discussion paper on marijuana legalization noted that the current approach to marijuana in the country was "not working" and that the primary goals of legalization were to reduce the burdens on the criminal justice system associated with the enforcement of marijuana laws—estimated to be about $500 million per year (Picard 2014)—and to prevent Canadians from entering the criminal justice system and receiving criminal records for simple possession of marijuana. The discussion paper estimated that the illegal marijuana trade in Canada provided as much as $7 billion in annual income for organized crime groups (although what constituted an organized crime group was not defined).

In June 2016, the Canadian government appointed a task force (chaired by Anne McLellan, who had served as minister of public safety, health, and justice in the governments of previous prime ministers Jean Chrétien and Paul Martin) to make recommendations regarding the implementation of marijuana legalization (Health Canada 2016). The main objectives of this task force, consistent with Prime Minister Justin Trudeau's charge, were to (1) protect young Canadians by keeping cannabis out of the hands of children and youth, (2) keep profits out of the hands of criminals (in particular, organized crime), (3) reduce the burdens on law enforcement and the justice system associated with the processing of simple possession of cannabis offenses, and (4) prevent Canadians from entering the criminal justice system and receiving criminal records as a result of simple possession of cannabis offenses (Health Canada 2016).

To inform their recommendations, members of the task force traveled to Colorado, Washington, and Uruguay (where recreational marijuana has been legalized) and conducted extensive consultations across Canada. The task force proceeded from the assumption that "the harms associated with the use of tobacco or alcohol are greater than those associated with the use of cannabis" and that their overall recommendations would "reflect a public health approach to reduce harm and promote health" (Health Canada 2016, 16).

Although the task force was concerned about the harms associated with high-THC-content cannabis products, they did not believe that limiting THC content was the most effective way to address these harms. Instead, they recommended variable taxation rates linked to the THC level of products (Health Canada 2016), similar to the pricing models currently applied in Canada for beer, wine, and spirits, which are taxed at different levels, and the clear labeling of THC (and CBD) levels on cannabis products. The committee noted that higher prices would help in reducing use, but prices that were too high would push consumers to the illicit market—however, the task force made no specific recommendations on the price issue. The task force also recommended comprehensive restrictions on advertising and promotion of cannabis, plain packaging for products, and prohibition of any product that might be appealing to children (Health Canada 2016).

The task force recommended that the federal government regulate the production of cannabis and its derivatives, use licensing and controls on production to stimulate a "diverse, competitive market" that would allow for inclusion of small producers, and implement a seed-to-sale tracking system to prevent diversion. With respect to retail sales, some members of the task force supported a centralized, government monopoly (similar to how most Canadian provinces regulate alcohol sales), while others advocated for a private-enterprise model. In the end, the task force recommended that retail sales of cannabis should be regulated by the provinces and territories in collaboration with local governments (Health Canada 2016). Additional recommendations included limiting the density and location of marijuana storefronts (including "appropriate" distances from schools, community centers, and public parks) and providing access to cannabis products via a direct-to-consumer mail-order system. The task force also argued that there should be no colocation of alcohol or tobacco and cannabis sales, a provision that would prevent large Canadian drugstore chains (some of whom had expressed an interest in offering retail cannabis products) from participation in the market (Robertson and McArthur 2016).

The issue of personal cultivation of marijuana generated some of the strongest opinions heard by the task force, and the members ultimately decided on a limit of four plants per residence. Personal possession of marijuana would be limited to thirty grams, and while recommending limits on public smoking of cannabis similar to those governing public smoking of tobacco and the use of vaping products (which are mostly prohibited in Canadian jurisdictions), the task force also suggested that local jurisdictions should be allowed to license dedicated venues such as cannabis lounges and tasting rooms (Health Canada 2016).

There was also considerable debate in Canada regarding the age limit for purchasing and legally possessing cannabis. Given the emerging science on brain development and the effects of marijuana consumption on adolescent brains, some who testified before the task force preferred an age limit of twenty-five. The Canadian Medical Association (CMA), adopting a stance similar to its AMA counterpart in the United States, published an article in reaction to marijuana legalization in Canada that noted, "Most of us know a young person whose life was derailed [as a result of marijuana use]" and argued that "simply put, cannabis should not be used by young people." However, the CMA advocated for a lower age limit of twenty-one for cannabis purchases; and although it is by no means clear how such regulations would be implemented or enforced, the CMA also recommended restricting the quantities and potency of cannabis sold to those under the age of twenty-five (Kelsall 2017).

In emphasizing the potential problems with an age limit that was set too high, Dr. Perry Kendall, the chief medical officer of British Columbia and a member of the task force, commented, "So banning smoking by the age group 19 to 25, who are the heaviest users and smoke most of it, is basically going to criminalize them all. . . . You don't want people who are ignoring the laws, but neither do you want to drive them to the black market" (quoted in Shaw and Penner 2016). Thus, recognizing that an age limit that was too high could result in further criminalization of youth and potentially lead them to obtain marijuana from the illicit market, the task force ultimately recommended an age limit of eighteen (while at the same time allowing provinces and territories to harmonize their own age limits with the age limit for purchase of alcohol, which varies across Canada) (Health Canada 2016). And, somewhat controversially, task force chair Anne McLellan recommended continued enforcement of the criminal laws against marijuana until legalization was fully implemented.

Marijuana legalization opponents in Canada reacted strongly to the task force report and its recommendations. For example, Pamela McColl of the Canadian chapter of SAM argued that the recommendations of the task force were "a disaster." McColl rather alarmingly (and we would argue, inappropriately) compared the potential harm that legalization of marijuana would cause to people under the age of twenty-five to the damage caused by thalidomide in the early 1960s:[7] "This is going to take out an entire generation." McColl also vowed that "we are going to find a way to sue them [pre-

7. Worldwide, it is estimated that between ten thousand and twenty thousand babies were born disabled as a result of the use of thalidomide by their mothers (Thalidomide Victims Association of Canada, n.d.).

sumably, the Canadian government]" (quoted in Shaw and Penner 2016). A somewhat less strident reaction to the report was offered by an editorial in the *Globe and Mail* (2016), which referred to the recommendations as "slightly hallucinogenic" and pointed out that there was no discussion in the report of how to destigmatize individuals with previous convictions for marijuana offenses.

In March 2017, with the passage of Bill C-45, the Canadian government announced plans to fully implement marijuana legalization on July 1, 2018. Although there are still many specific issues to be clarified, the proposed regulations were consistent with the recommendations of the task force report. The legislation sets the minimum age for purchase of cannabis at eighteen, although provinces can set a higher limit if they choose to (the age limit for alcohol purchases and consumption in Canada is eighteen in Alberta, Manitoba, and Quebec; however, in the rest of the country the age limit is nineteen). There were also strict rules regarding the marketing of marijuana, with considerations of whether producers will be required to use plain packaging, whether there will be a prohibition on endorsements, and whether there will be requirements that products be packaged in child-proof containers (Kassam 2017). The legislation also included provisions that individuals under eighteen years of age found in possession of up to five grams of marijuana would not face criminal charges. And although marijuana edibles are widely available at currently illegal marijuana shops in Canada and online, when recreational sales begin in July 2018, only dried marijuana and cannabis oil will be available to consumers (Jacquie Miller 2017).

Given that there is wide variation across provinces with respect to public opinion on the acceptance of recreational marijuana and the willingness to allow for retail sales that could potentially lead some provinces to prohibit sales, the legislation also provided for mail delivery of cannabis from federally licensed producers for individuals in jurisdictions that might not have access to the substance (Kassam 2017). The legislation also created new penalties for illegally supplying marijuana to minors, which could result in up to fourteen years' imprisonment (MacCharles 2017).

There were indications that some provinces in Canada would not be ready to set up systems for distribution and retail sales of cannabis by the July 1, 2018, date, and the Canadian Association of Chiefs of Police requested that the federal government reconsider allowing home cultivation (because of the assertion that it would make it easier for young people to get access to marijuana) and delay implementation of the law (Gillies 2017). But even the relatively conservative Canadian newspaper the *Globe and Mail* (2017) conceded, "In this day and age, it is entirely appropriate for marijuana to be legal, provided it is properly regulated."

As noted previously, there is likely to be considerable variation across Canadian provinces in the implementation of marijuana legalization. In the province of Ontario, despite public opinion polls indicating the majority of residents preferred that cannabis be sold in dedicated dispensaries (Schmader 2017), the government announced that legal marijuana would eventually be sold in 150 government-operated stores (overseen by the province's Liquor Control Board), up to 40 of which were scheduled to open on July 1, 2018, and via a government-run website (Thibedeau and Crawley 2017). Under the plan, sales would be restricted to individuals nineteen years of age and over, and public consumption would be prohibited (Druzin 2017). Also under the regulations, dedicated stores would sell only cannabis (not alongside alcohol), and "trained and knowledgeable staff will sell products in a safe and socially-responsible manner to restrict access for minors and give consumers the information they need" (Ontario Ministry of Finance 2017).

Uruguay

> The traditional approach hasn't worked, someone has to be the first to do this.
> —URUGUAY PRESIDENT JOSÉ MUJICA, commenting on marijuana legalization, quoted in Dave Bewley-Taylor, Tom Blickman, and Martin Jelsma, *The Rise and Decline of Cannabis Prohibition*

In considering marijuana legalization in the larger political context, it is important to note that Uruguay has a relatively long history of progressive legislation, being the first country in South America in which women were allowed to vote (in 1927); the country also decriminalized abortion in 2012 and legalized same-sex marriage in 2013 (Walsh and Ramsey 2016).[8] Gambling and prostitution are legal and regulated by the government of Uruguay (Miroff 2017), and the country also enacted harm-reduction drug policies in the mid-1990s (including providing injecting drug users with easier access to clean needles) (Walsh and Ramsey 2016).

While consumption of marijuana has been technically legal in Uruguay since 1974, production and sale of the drug were prohibited, creating a legal conundrum (Cruz, Queirolo, and Boidi 2016), roughly similar to the situation in the Netherlands, where people can consume cannabis in coffee shops, but trafficking in the drug is illegal. President Mujica and the Uruguay legislators viewed marijuana legalization as a strategy to reduce consumption and remove profits from organized crime (an estimated 80 percent of Uru-

---

8. Although Uruguay is the only Latin American country where marijuana is legal, there have been several interesting developments with respect to marijuana legislation (and drug legislation more generally) in a number of other countries in the region in recent years. Colombia legalized medical marijuana in 2015 (Garcia 2015); Chile decriminalized marijuana possession in 2005 (Marple 2015); and in December 2016, the Mexican Senate passed legislation approving the use of marijuana for medical purposes (Orsi 2016).

guayan drug traffickers' business was believed to be related to marijuana) (Simpson 2014). Julio Calzada, the country's national drug coordinator, emphasized that legalization would be beneficial to marijuana consumers, who would be better informed about the nature of the product: "Today we have to take action with marijuana because those who buy it don't know what they're buying, just the same as what happened with people buying alcohol in 1930" (quoted in Bewley-Taylor, Blickman, and Jelsma 2014, 56). The Uruguay legislation was also motivated by concerns over the increasing use of a cracklike drug known as "pasta base," which consumers were purchasing from the same drug dealers (largely from the neighboring country of Paraguay) who sold cannabis (Walsh and Ramsey 2016). It was believed that marijuana legalization might serve to separate the markets for these two drugs and thereby reduce drug-related harms.

Uruguay is an example of a top-down marijuana legalization process (Leon and Weitzer 2014). In perhaps the most interesting case of such action thus far, despite considerable public opposition to legalization (an estimated 61 percent of Uruguayans did not support the legislation) President Mujica, along with the national legislature, took unilateral actions to legalize the drug (Cruz, Queirolo, and Boidi 2016; Haberkorn, 2016).

Under marijuana legalization in Uruguay, the regulations specify three ways by which individuals (who are citizens of the country and at least eighteen years of age) can obtain marijuana: (1) purchasing up to forty grams of the drug from licensed pharmacies; (2) growing their own marijuana (up to six female plants), with a limit of 480 grams per year; or (3) joining cannabis cooperatives with between fifteen and forty-five members, which could grow up to ninety-nine plants but could not provide more than 480 grams of marijuana to each of their members per year (Haberkorn 2014; Walsh and Ramsey 2016). Joining a cooperative requires a $400 enrollment fee and monthly payments of $92 (Haberkorn 2015). Interestingly, the regulations prohibit individuals from obtaining cannabis from more than one of these sources, although it is not clear how this regulation will be enforced (Walsh and Ramsey 2016). Additional controversial issues with the legislation were related to the cost of marijuana and its potency. In an attempt to undercut the black market, the government does not add additional taxes on the substance and the price was set at just over U.S.$1.00 per gram (pharmacies sell a five-gram packet for approximately U.S.$6.50 [Goni 2016]). Individuals may purchase a maximum of ten grams per week or forty grams per month, and THC concentrations must remain lower than 15 percent (Goni 2016). The relatively low price led to concerns that marijuana-use levels would increase, and the comparatively lower THC level might lead consumers to seek higher-strength versions on the black market (Walsh and Ramsey 2016).

As has been the case in many other jurisdictions that have legalized medical or recreational marijuana, there were delays in the implementation of the law in Uruguay; as of July 2016, only fifty of the estimated twelve hundred pharmacies in the country had registered to sell marijuana—apparently, many were concerned about security and the amount of paperwork involved in registering (Haberkorn 2016). Joe Walsh and Geoff Ramsey (2016) note that the delays in implementation are also related to the views of incoming Uruguay president Tabaré Vazquez, who was concerned that the law would lead to more problematic use of marijuana and who suggested using the registry of consumers and growers as a way to have them enter drug-treatment programs.

As Ladean Cher (2016) comments, "Rather than serving as a model for other countries contemplating cannabis legalization, Uruguay has become a cautionary tale about the difficulties of creating a marijuana market." Perhaps not surprisingly, the International Narcotics Board has criticized Uruguay's legalization of marijuana as a breach of the country's international treaty obligations, and the country has also faced criticism from the bordering countries of Argentina and Brazil, whose officials are concerned that Uruguayan marijuana may cross into their countries (Walsh and Ramsey 2016).

Despite delays, Uruguay began selling cannabis in pharmacies as of July 2017. Uruguayan citizens (or permanent residents) who wish to purchase marijuana are required to sign up for a registry—machines will scan buyers' fingerprints at each purchase (Londoño 2017). These fingerprint scans will be linked to a government database that informs the pharmacy how much the individual is eligible to purchase.

What Have We Learned Following Legalization?

The legalization of recreational marijuana in nine U.S. states (and Washington, D.C.) and two countries signals that we are entering a new era with respect to regulation of this plant. As discussed earlier, there are several differences in the specifics of the legalization schemes adopted in various states. And even within states that have legalized, reflecting that there is still not a consensus that marijuana should be legal, some jurisdictions have chosen to prohibit sales. Government officials in states where recreational marijuana has been legalized have been responsive to the problems created by legalization and have altered their regulations to address these issues.

Contrary to the predictions of legalization opponents, although findings are not unequivocal, what is clear is that the legalization of recreational marijuana has not resulted in dramatically negative consequences, in part because of the relative safety of marijuana across several indicators of harm, particularly in comparison to alcohol, tobacco, and certain prescription drugs. And legalization has also not, to this point at least, resulted in dramatic increases in motor vehicle accidents and fatalities attributed to marijuana intoxication, nor have there been increases in youth use of the substance. Even Nora Volkow, director of NIDA, has conceded that use by young people has not significantly increased following marijuana legalization. Although this may surprise (and perhaps even disappoint?) many, it really should not, as marijuana was widely available and easily accessible to virtually anyone who wanted to consume it prior to legalization—as noted elsewhere in this book, *legalization did not invent marijuana.*

Among the most significant incentives for recreational marijuana legalization is that the substance can be regulated, controlled, and taxed by government entities rather than the regulation and profit remaining in the hands of criminal enterprises. These revenues, in turn, can be (and have been) used to fund a variety of societal needs, including drug prevention and treatment programs, general health services, and public education.

For governments that have legalized recreational marijuana, the tax revenue has been substantial, far exceeding expectations. Retail sales of medical and recreational marijuana in the United States were roughly $10 billion in 2017 (Morris 2017), and between the commencement of sales of recreational marijuana on January 1, 2014, and May 31, 2017, Colorado collected $506 million in marijuana-based tax revenue (K. Newman 2017). In Washington State, where sales of recreational marijuana began on July 8, 2014, tax revenues were $65 million for fiscal year 2015, $189 million for 2016, and $319 million for 2017 (Washington State Liquor and Cannabis Board 2018). California began the sale of recreational marijuana on January 1, 2018, and sales are predicted to reach $3.7 billion in the first year of legalization, generating a potential $1 billion in tax revenue for the state (Berke 2018). While legalization opponents argue that the collection of tax revenues is not sufficient justification for marijuana legalization, in the absence of legalization, marijuana consumption still occurs, and *zero* taxes are collected.

Many additional states are considering the legalization of recreational marijuana, in part lured by the tax revenues that can be generated from legal sales of the substance. The marijuana legalization "policy experiments" in the pioneering legalized states have provided blueprints for these other states and have generally shown that legalization is not accompanied by serious negative outcomes. However, as we discuss in the concluding chapter, a number of unresolved issues remain.

7

Unfinished Business and Emerging Issues

I n our research tracking changes in the regulation of cannabis over the last several years, we have been struck how it constitutes a rapidly moving target with changes occurring on an almost monthly basis. In this chapter, we examine a number of emerging issues and unfinished business surrounding marijuana regulation—given the seemingly constant change, at least some of the issues we address are by necessity speculative.

We begin with a discussion of arguably the key issue surrounding the future of marijuana regulation—that is, the drug's classification in Schedule I of the Controlled Substances Act—followed by an examination of two issues directly related to scheduling: Section 280e of the Tax Code (which prevents cannabis businesses from deducting normal business expenses on their tax returns) and issues related to banking/financial services for marijuana businesses. We then proceed to a discussion of other continuing controversial issues, including whether states with legal marijuana should allow public consumption of the substance (and if so, how this should be regulated); how states and local jurisdictions are trying to address a lack of minority involvement in the cannabis industry; to what extent the marijuana industry might become corporatized and the related issue of how much advertising of marijuana products is appropriate; and whether the black market in cannabis has grown or been reined in under legalization.

We then undertake a detailed consideration of developments surrounding marijuana under the new administration of President Donald Trump—in particular, the views and actions of Attorney General Jeff Sessions. We provide a discussion of a number of proposals to change marijuana-related legislation at the federal level, the most radical of which is the Marijuana Justice Act, proposed by New Jersey senator Corey Booker, which would fully legalize marijuana at the federal level. We conclude by examining what we believe is next in the shifting landscape of marijuana policy as of mid-2018.

Marijuana Rescheduling

> Schedule I is the statutory nerve of drug prohibition in the United States and the bane of marijuana fans and policy reformers everywhere.
> —MIKE LUDWIG, "It's Time to Legalize Marijuana"

We begin this book by noting that in August 2016, the DEA refused to re-classify marijuana as a Schedule II drug. In many respects, the rescheduling of marijuana (or, as an increasing number of individuals and organizations are advocating for, its complete removal from the Controlled Substances Act) is the central issue regarding marijuana in the United States today. Among other things, the substance's Schedule I status creates barriers to research on marijuana, affects the ability of marijuana-related businesses to secure financial services from banks, prevents the Environmental Protection Agency from regulating pesticides and other chemicals used on cannabis crops, and ultimately gives the federal government the ability to overturn both medical and recreational legalization of marijuana in states.

In an interesting development with respect to the scheduling of mari-juana, in December 2016, the medical marijuana activist group Americans for Safe Access filed a petition under the federal Information Quality Act, asserting in its forty-five-page publication, *The Dangers and Consequences of Marijuana Use*, that the DEA was influencing public policy by making nu-merous false statements about marijuana (Staggs 2016a). Americans for Safe Access noted that many elected officials rely on information provided by the DEA in making marijuana-related policy decisions and in informing their colleagues about the benefits and risks of cannabis: "The presentation of sci-entifically unfounded information alongside scientifically accurate informa-tion obscures and diminishes the utility of the accurate information and can jeopardize public health. . . . The disingenuous presentation of inaccurate information makes it difficult for public officials and medical providers to make informed decisions regarding the viability of medical cannabis treat-ment options" (quoted in Meehan 2016).

The Information Quality Act requires federal government agencies (in-cluding the DEA) to create guidelines to ensure the "quality, objectivity, and integrity of information" they disseminate and to "establish administrative mechanisms allowing affected persons to seek and obtain correction of information maintained and disseminated by the agency that does not comply with the guidelines" (Americans for Safe Access 2016). Americans for Safe Access noted that many of the statements regarding marijuana on the DEA website have been debunked[1]—in some cases, even by the DEA itself. For example, the DEA claims that marijuana smoke is riskier than tobacco smoke and has been proven to cause cancer; however, the agency reported in August 2016 that there was little to no connection between marijuana use and cancer. Similarly, the DEA website indicates that cognitive abilities decline over time for marijuana consumers, but the agency noted in its August 2016 decision on rescheduling that cognitive deficits do not occur among those who initiate marijuana use after fifteen years of age. The DEA also claims that there is an association between cannabis use and psychosis; however, the agency recently conceded that marijuana use increases the risk of psychosis only among individuals who are already predisposed to develop such disorders (Americans for Safe Access 2016).

A particularly problematic aspect of the DEA's misinformation regarding marijuana is related to the refusal of the agency to let go of the gateway drug theory. Although not specifically acknowledging that they obtained this information from the DEA website, prominent federal legislators, including Democrat Dianne Feinstein (the ranking member of the Senate Judiciary Committee) and Attorney General Jeff Sessions, have invoked the gateway drug theory to justify their opposition to medical and recreational marijuana legalization. For example, in a 2015 Senate drug caucus hearing discussing barriers to conducting research on the medical benefits of cannabis, Senator Feinstein commented, "It concerns me greatly because young people use it. . . . It is also a gateway drug. . . . They go on to other things" (quoted in Americans for Safe Access 2016). Similarly, in a 2016 drug caucus hearing to investigate whether the DEA had been derelict in its enforcement of marijuana laws, then-senator Sessions commented, "You can see that [marijuana] is in fact a very real danger, you can see the accidents and traffic deaths related to marijuana jumped by 20%. These are the kind of things we're going to see throughout the country and you'll see heroin and cocaine increase more than it would have. . . . Children will be damaged . . . and if they go on to more serious drugs which tends to happen, and you can deny it if you want to, but it tends to happen" (quoted in Americans for Safe Access 2016).

While it is unlikely that the Americans for Safe Access petition will be successful, it has served to further underscore the hypocrisy of the DEA. And interestingly, in February 2017, the DEA removed the section "The Dangers and Consequences of Marijuana Use" from its website (Zuccaro 2017). In response to this action, Steph Sherer, executive director of Americans for

---

1. The DEA website is available at https://www.dea.gov.

Safe Access, commented, "The DEA's removal of these popular myths about cannabis from their website could mean the end of Washington gridlock. This is a victory for medical cannabis patients across the nation, who rely on cannabis to treat serious illness" (quoted in Zuccaro 2017).

Banking and Section 280e of the Tax Code

The world of cannabis banking is so full of contradiction that one business can truck money to a federal facility while the other is left to play a high-stakes game of hide-and-seek with its cash.
—JAMES RUFUS KOREN, "Why Some Pot Businesses Hide Their Cash"

In a prime example of the federal government wanting (and having) it both ways, on the one hand, the Internal Revenue Service (IRS) gladly accepts tax dollars from individuals and companies involved in the marijuana industry; on the other hand, with some exceptions, the IRS will not allow them to bank or deduct standard business expenses on their taxes. Both the lack of access to financial services and the inability to deduct business expenses are a result of marijuana's status as a Schedule I drug.

Under provisions of Section 280e of the Tax Code, marijuana businesses cannot deduct routine business expenses (including the rent of their facility, employee salaries, utilities, and marketing or advertising costs) because they are technically trafficking in a federally controlled substance. Under this legislation, "no deduction or credit shall be allowed for any amount paid or incurred during the taxable year in carrying on any trade or business if such trade or business . . . consists of trafficking in controlled substances (within the meaning of Schedule I and II of the Controlled Substances Act)."[2] This legislation was passed in 1982, after Jeffrey Edmondson, a Minnesota cocaine dealer, attempted to deduct business expenses on his taxes and was denied by the IRS. Edmondson sued in tax court and partially won his case, leading members of Congress to enact the federal regulation prohibiting such deductions (Baca 2016b). Not surprisingly, the omnipresent Kevin Sabet of SAM supports this IRS rule: "Like any special interest group they [marijuana business owners] are after one thing: money. . . . It's particularly audacious to demand that the government allow you to deduct expenses when you're breaking federal law" (quoted in Hotakainen 2015).

But Americans can be innovative in creating schemes to work around tax laws, and cannabis businesses are no different. To reduce their tax burden and restrictions imposed by section 280e, some retail marijuana outlets have engaged in "bundling"—selling marijuana at a relatively cheap price

---

2. For the text of the code, see https://www.law.cornell.edu/uscode/text/26/280E.

while increasing the price of other items, such as lighters and marijuana paraphernalia, that have a lower tax rate (Camden 2016; see also E. Bush 2015a). Other stores have split their operations into two parts—one selling paraphernalia, and the other, marijuana products (to claim rent reductions on the part of the operation selling paraphernalia); still others claim that some of their employees spend a portion of their time cleaning the store, and thus part of their salaries can qualify as legitimate tax deductions (Healy 2015).

As is true in other domains related to marijuana, there have been proposals to change IRS section 280e. Oregon senator Ron Wyden and representative Earl Blumenauer have proposed legislation to create a small-business tax-equity act that would allow owners of state-regulated marijuana businesses to deduct expenses from their federal taxes (Hotakainen 2015), and some states, including Colorado, have changed their own tax laws to permit marijuana businesses to claim deductions on their state tax returns (Healy 2015).

With respect to financial services for marijuana businesses, in essence, because marijuana remains a Schedule I drug, a financial institution is technically committing money laundering by accepting deposits derived from the sale of marijuana (Armstrong 2016). While this lack of access to legal financial services most directly affects marijuana producers, distributors, and retailers, the same restrictions technically apply to ancillary businesses involved with marijuana, including manufacturers of greenhouse lighting supplying marijuana growers, companies involved in the marketing of cannabis products, and producers of cannabis packaging products (Engen 2016).

In 2014, the Financial Crimes Enforcement Network (FinCEN), part of the U.S. Treasury Department, published guidelines for financial institutions seeking to work with marijuana businesses. These guidelines require that the institutions monitor the businesses they are dealing with for activities that might be in violation of the 2013 Cole memorandum. As of March 2017, there were an estimated 368 banks and credit unions serving the marijuana industry, which represents a small fraction of the approximately twelve thousand financial institutions in the United States (Koren 2017).

In addition to the inconveniences for both marijuana businesses and customers (who cannot use credit cards to purchase marijuana products) created by these federal restrictions on banking, there are significant threats to the safety of employees of marijuana businesses. As Michael Elliott, executive director of the Marijuana Industry Group, commented, "When you put it all together it looks like they [the federal government] want a cash-only industry that can't protect itself. That's part of their game plan—to make our businesses unsafe, to basically terrorize us and create public safety issues that they try to blame on us" (quoted in Wheeler 2014). And it is clear that these concerns regarding public safety are warranted: from the beginning of legal recreational sales in Colorado in January 2014 through March 2016, the Denver Police Department registered more than two hundred burglaries at marijuana businesses (Quinton 2016). While we are not suggesting that changes to federal banking laws with respect to the marijuana industry will eliminate the occurrence of such incidents, such changes would likely reduce the frequency of their occurrence.

Changes in financial services for marijuana businesses are also occurring at the state level. In 2016 in Oregon, for example, House Bill 4094 exempted banks from criminal liability for engaging in business with the marijuana industry (the legislation passed by a vote of 56–3) (Hansen 2016). In defending this legislation, State Representative Tobias Read noted that the best solution to the banking problem would be to ease the federal restrictions (a development he believed was unlikely to occur): "However you may feel about the underlying issue of marijuana legalization, I hope you will agree with me that having an entire segment of the economy, a growing industry, based on cash, is not a good thing. Duffel bags of cash are not good for public safety, they're not good for the collection of required tax revenue" (quoted in Hansen 2016).

In 2017, several cannabis companies formed a national organization, the New Federalism Fund, to support state-based marijuana regulatory systems and to lobby for policies to change federal tax and banking laws related to the industry. In particular, this group is focused on changing federal laws to ensure that marijuana businesses are not penalized by Section 280e of the Tax Code and allowing the businesses to openly and legally bank (Wallace 2017h).

Public Consumption of Marijuana

An additional problematic issue relates to public consumption of marijuana in jurisdictions where the drug is legal. Colorado in particular has experienced problems with public consumption of cannabis, especially with "pot tourists" visiting the city of Denver (and other Colorado tourist destinations in mountain communities), who purchase cannabis and do not have venues in which to consume the product. As Denver mayor Michael Hancock commented, "When you start looking at what the users are doing, whether they're visitors, walking up and down the mall and smoking in our parks, you recognize that if someone doesn't have a residence here that they have to have an outlet" (quoted in Meyer 2016). And as John Hudak comments, an additional problem associated with the ban on smoking cannabis in public is that it may lead tourists, who are less educated with respect to the effects of edible cannabis products, to purchase and consume these products: "Perversely, if unintentionally, current policies drive tourists to the edible market, creating risks for public health and safety" (Hudak 2014, 19).

Public consumption has also been a prominent issue with marijuana legalization in Alaska. The state attracts more than two million tourists per year, approximately half of whom arrive on cruise ships, and those who wish to purchase marijuana will have no place they can legally consume the substance. A proposal in Alaska would have allowed public consumption of marijuana at retail outlets; however, it was narrowly rejected by the Alaska Marijuana Control Board (Bohrer and Thiessen 2017). And of course public consumption of marijuana will be an issue in Nevada, especially in Las Vegas, which attracts an estimated forty-two million tourists each year, at least some of whom may wish to consume marijuana (Lockhead 2017). Current Nevada legislation classifies public consumption of marijuana as a misdemeanor, which can result in a fine of up to $600.

In 2015 in Washington State, House Bill 2126 banned all marijuana clubs and created a Class C felony offense for providing either temporary or permanent space for public marijuana consumption. At least partially as a result of this legislation, in 2015, organizers of Seattle's widely popular annual "Hempfest" event, which typically attracted about one hundred thousand people and where open consumption of marijuana was generally tolerated by law enforcement officials, chose not to host the event (Ellison 2015a).

Although the legality of such establishments are in question, some marijuana businesses in Colorado have attempted to circumvent bans on public consumption through the creation of "private clubs" where individuals can smoke or otherwise consume their own cannabis—these clubs usually charge annual membership fees as well as additional fees for each visit (Meyer 2016).

A more formal solution to the public consumption issue in the Denver occurred in the November 2016 elections when 54 percent of voters approved a four-year pilot program allowing public consumption of their own cannabis marijuana in set-off outdoor or indoor areas (although the latter would have to abide by the Colorado's indoor smoking prohibition) (Murray 2017). Under the legislation, applicants for licenses must be able to demonstrate support from a registered neighborhood association, a business improvement district's board, or some other relevant group. Businesses expressing an interest in applying for licenses have included yoga studios, coffee shops, and bars and restaurants; however, businesses holding liquor licenses will likely be excluded because of state rules banning the mixture of alcohol and marijuana (Murray 2017). In addition, existing marijuana businesses in Denver, including dispensaries, would not be able to apply for permits.

The Colorado Senate also attempted to address the public consumption issue statewide in the spring of 2017, with proposed legislation that would permit jurisdictions in the state to license "bring-your-own pot clubs" (Wyatt 2017a). However, the legislation did not specify whether members of such clubs could smoke marijuana indoors, prompting concerns from Governor

John Hickenlooper, who indicated he would oppose the bill if it allowed indoor smoking and who also expressed concerns about a possible federal government crackdown: "Given the uncertainty in Washington [D.C.], this is not the time to be . . . trying to carve out new turf and expand markets and make dramatic statements about marijuana" (quoted in Wyatt 2017a).

Racial Issues

As we discuss in Chapters 1 and 2, racial issues have been a central component of discussions related to marijuana, from the passage of the Marihuana Tax Act in 1937, to President Nixon's launching of the drug war, to the hundreds of thousands of arrests of blacks and Hispanics for marijuana offenses. However, as legalization of medicinal and recreational marijuana has occurred, a new issue has emerged: How can we ensure that members of minority groups, who bore the brunt of the drug war, can now reap the profits of legalization? Given the racial disparities in the enforcement of drug laws in general, and marijuana laws in particular, Arwa Mahdawi (2017) has gone as far as to suggest that blacks should receive reparations (similar to arguments for reparations for slavery): "Every business now exploiting the legalization of marijuana should forfeit at least 50% of their pot-based profits to a fund that gives reparations to people whose lives were destroyed by the U.S.'s discriminatory war on drugs."

Nationwide, it is estimated that only 1 percent of marijuana dispensaries in the United States have black owners (Mahdawi 2017); in Washington State, as of July 2016, blacks, who make up 3.6 percent of the state's population, constituted 2.7 percent of the 782 people who had ownership interests in the state's retail marijuana stores (Latinos and Asians were also underrepresented) (Young 2016). There are of course several barriers to minority participation in marijuana businesses. Many states prohibit convicted felons from the involvement in the industry,[3] which disproportionately affects minorities because of their higher conviction rates. Many states have also set prohibitively high application, license, and start-up fees for entry into the marijuana industry, which creates difficulties for members of minority groups who typically do not have sufficient financial capital (Jan and Nirappil 2017). For example, in Pennsylvania (which legalized medical marijuana in 2016), individuals interested in growing cannabis legally must pay a $10,000 nonrefundable application fee, as well as a $200,000 deposit, and provide proof that they could obtain $2 million in funding, with at least $500,000 in bank accounts (Hackman 2017).

---

3. Massachusetts is the first state not to prohibit former convicted felons from operating in and around the cannabis industry (Hackman 2017).

The issue of African American involvement in the cannabis industry has been a particularly prominent issue in Maryland, where the Legislative Black Caucus has continually worked to ensure that blacks are represented in the state's medical marijuana businesses. A 2014 Maryland law promoted diversity among marijuana growers, but as of the fall of 2016, not one of the fifteen cultivation licenses issued by the Maryland Medical Cannabis Commission had been granted to African Americans, who make up 30 percent of the state's population (Wiggins 2016). In early 2017, the Legislative Black Caucus proposed legislation that would change the membership of the sixteen-person Medical Cannabis Commission to reflect the diversity of the state, while also calling for a rescoring of applications for marijuana cultivation licenses to give more weight to applications submitted by African Americans (Nirappil 2017).

Oakland, California, has taken even more assertive steps to ensure that minorities are represented in marijuana businesses. In that city, whose population is approximately one-third black, one-third Hispanic, and one-third white, 77 percent of arrests for marijuana offenses in 2015 were of blacks (and 95 percent were people of color) (Hackman 2017). The city has established an "equity permit program" under which at least half of new medical cannabis business license holders (to a maximum of eight per year) must be allocated to "equity applicants" (defined as individuals who earn less than 80 percent of the median income in Oakland and are either residents of police beats that have been disproportionately targeted by police or have been incarcerated on marijuana-related charges within the last twenty years) (Hackman 2017; see also Debolt 2017).

The city of Portland, Oregon, has dedicated a portion of the tax revenue from sales of recreational marijuana to invest into "communities disproportionately impacted by cannabis prohibition" and to partially finance the expungement of records for individuals with convictions for marijuana offenses (Hackman 2017); California will similarly require that a portion of taxes collected from retail sales of marijuana be reinvested in communities that have been negatively impacted by federal and state drug policies.

Corporatization of the Marijuana Industry?

As we discuss in Chapter 5, one of the primary themes of the influential anti-marijuana legalization group SAM (as well as other organizations and some drug policy experts[4]) is that marijuana businesses will be taken over by large corporations and evolve into a corporate model similar to that of the alcohol,

---

4. For example, Jonathan Caulkins of Carnegie Mellon University predicts that the marijuana industry will evolve into a "behemoth" with substantial lobbying influence on governments (quoted in Stern 2016).

tobacco, and pharmaceutical industries. Drug policy expert Mark Kleiman (2014) of New York University comments, "It's easy to imagine the cannabis equivalent of an Anheuser-Busch InBev peddling low-cost, high octane cannabis in Super Bowl commercials." We will concede that this is possible and should be a central concern, but at the same time, we tend to agree with the comments of the Dutch drug policy scholars Cyrille Fijnaut and Brice De Ruyver: "Since cannabis is a drug which nowadays can be produced, rather easily, almost everywhere in the world and which is consumed all around the world . . . the production of cannabis will not be dominated by just a few international companies anytime soon" (2015, 175). Concerns that the marijuana industry will inevitably be dominated by large corporations neglects the fact that such a model would seem to be safer than the existing black market. As John Hudak and Jonathan Rauch comment, "For many decades the marijuana industry has been in the hands of profit-driven business enterprises—criminal ones" (2016, 2).

Some, such as marijuana cooking specialist Laurie Wolf, have argued that the marijuana industry is at a crossroads: "Down one path is a future that resembles the wine business, or the farm-to-table movement: boutique pot growers turning out harvests that reflect local climates and customs. Down the other is Big Weed: industrial farms, joints by Marlboro and pot cookies by General Mills, Monsanto patenting genetically modified strains of Purple Kush" (quoted in Widdicombe 2017).

As of mid-2018, it appears as though it is too early to determine whether the corporatization/consolidation predicted by many will manifest. While some have suggested that the involvement of companies like Scotts Miracle-Grow (a lawn-care company) in purchasing companies that supply hydroponics for cannabis growers or the involvement of Microsoft in providing inventory-tracking services for marijuana growers portend the inevitable corporatization of the industry, these large companies are (currently, at least) involved only in ancillary businesses related to the marijuana industry. And the legalization policies in Washington State and California initially prohibited vertical integration of the various sectors of the marijuana industry.[5] At the same time, there may be lessons from the craft beer industry in the United States, which has seen "dramatic" consolidation in recent years (Koch 2017). Hudak and Rauch predict that some consolidation will occur in the industry but that it is highly unlikely that it will become a copycat of Big Tobacco: "to the contrary, that seems among the *least* likely of outcomes" (2016, 9; emphasis in original), at least partially because of the lessons learned from the problems created by Big Tobacco, which led to further

---

5. However, legislation proposed by California governor Jerry Brown in the spring of 2017 would allow single businesses in the state to hold multiple licenses to grow, distribute, manufacture, and sell retail marijuana (Blood and Elias 2017).

regulation of the tobacco industry. Instead, they believe that the industry will continue to evolve along a structural continuum, with both small and larger companies. And importantly, Hudak and Rauch note that "for policymakers, the concern should be *bad* marijuana, not *big* marijuana (2016, 2; emphasis in original).

Advertising Cannabis Products

Advertising of cannabis products is related to corporatization. Businesses are trying to accomplish two goals with advertising—market their products to convince users of such products that their brand is better than others and, perhaps more important, encourage those who do not currently use their product to try it—that is, to create new consumers (Vara 2016). Marijuana businesses are no exception to this general rule, and in response some have gone as far as recommending a comprehensive ban on all forms of advertising for marijuana products (Pacula et al. 2014).

States that have legalized marijuana have responded to potential problems with advertising by enacting new regulations. For example, in Washington State, concerns regarding the relatively lax regulations related to cannabis businesses' advertising under the original I-502 legalization measure, as well as concerns that these regulations could trigger the attention of the federal government, led legislators to pass Senate Bill 5131 in July 2017. This legislation limited marijuana retail license holders to two signs (with a maximum size of sixteen hundred square inches) that were required to be permanently attached to their building and prohibited other forms of outdoor advertising: "sign spinners [people holding or spinning signs on sidewalks], sandwich boards, inflatables, persons in costumes, etc." (Washington State Liquor and Cannabis Board 2017a). The legislation also stipulated that the signs include text stating that marijuana products can be purchased only by individuals over the age of twenty-one and could not contain depictions of marijuana plants or products.

Some critics have contended that billboard advertising by marijuana businesses should be prohibited entirely, especially given that under the 1998 settlement agreement between the tobacco companies in forty-six states, the companies agreed to stop using billboard advertising (Santos 2017). The 2017 Washington State legislation required that retail outlets could use billboards "solely for the purpose of identifying the name of the business, nature of the business, and providing the public with directional information to the licensed retail outlet" (Washington State Liquor and Cannabis Board 2017a; see also Camden 2017). In addition, the legislation included a general ban on any advertising that might appeal to children and allowed for cities, towns, or counties in Washington State to enact more restrictive rules.

In Oregon, cannabis advertising is regulated by the Oregon Liquor Control Commission, whose regulations (similar to the rules for advertising alcohol and tobacco in the state) stipulate that marijuana ads cannot contain misleading statements, target minors or use cartoon images, encourage transport of the substance across state lines, make claims with respect to health effects of the drug, or display the consumption of marijuana (Silowski 2016).

Regulation of television, radio, and web-based advertising of cannabis is even more problematic. The first-ever television commercial for a marijuana product was scheduled for broadcast on a Denver-based ABC station but was pulled at the last second (Silowski 2016). And although it did not actually show marijuana, the Martha Stewart/Snoop Dog T-Mobile advertisement that aired during the 2017 Super Bowl provides an example of such an ad. There have also been television advertisements for businesses/services related to the cannabis industry, such as an ad for the Hoban Law Group (which specializes in hemp and medical marijuana issues) that appeared on CNN, Fox News, and MSNBC (Barcott 2017).

A controversial aspect of California's Proposition 64 was a provision that could potentially allow marijuana companies to advertise their products in print ads, online, and on radio and television. The legislation states that "any advertising or marketing placed in broadcast, cable, radio, print, and digital communication shall only be displayed where at least 71.6% of the audience is reasonably expected to be 21 years of age or older, as determined by reliable, up-to-date audience composition data" (quoted McGreevy 2016b). In fact, this provision was one of the primary reasons that California senator Dianne Feinstein opposed marijuana legalization: "[It] allows marijuana smoking ads in prime time, on programs with millions of children and teenage viewers" (quoted in Nichols 2016). Oregon has a provision similar to California's, stipulating that marijuana businesses "may not utilize television, radio, billboards, print media or internet advertising unless the licensee has reliable evidence that no more than 30 percent of the audience . . . is reasonably expected to be under the age of 21" (quoted in Silowski 2016). Of course, a key question with respect to both the California and Oregon provisions on such advertising is how it will be determined that no more than 30 percent (or 28.4 percent) of the audience is under the age of twenty-one, and as a spokesman for the "No on Proposition 64" campaign noted, this threshold is so low that only a handful of shows, such as Saturday-morning cartoons, would be prohibited from running marijuana advertisements (Nichols 2016). Washington State's stipulations on television advertising essentially defer to the federal government and emphasize that "television and radio carry across state lines as well as places where children can see or hear. TV and radio are also regulated by the Federal Communications Commission. Licensees should consult their attorney and media-buyer or other advertising sales representative to ensure cannabis-related advertisements are permissible" (Washington State Liquor and Cannabis Board 2016).

Up until now, television advertisements for marijuana products have certainly not been pervasive. And although the Federal Communications Commission does not have a rule that specifically bans television ads for marijuana in states that have legalized the drug (Nichols 2016), a primary reason that we have not seen many marijuana ads on television is that, as in other areas of marijuana regulation, marijuana is a Schedule I substance. Television broadcasters are licensed by the federal government, and it seems unlikely that stations will air advertisements for marijuana, as they risk having their licenses revoked (Ingraham 2016g; see also McGreevy 2016b). At the same time, although official data are not available, several radio stations in states where marijuana is legalized have been airing advertisements fairly frequently, such as in the Portland, Oregon, metropolitan area. There has also been a proliferation of marijuana ads in "alternative" newspapers in the Portland area (such as the *Willamette Week* and the *Portland Mercury*).

Diversion: Reining in the Black Market

One of the key provisions of the 2013 Cole memorandum (since rescinded by Attorney General Jeff Sessions) was that states with marijuana legalization policies need to ensure that marijuana was not diverted to the black market. In considering the issue of diversion, it is important to stress that most legalization proponents did not claim that legalization would completely eliminate the black market in marijuana, which will undoubtedly continue to exist and arguably even thrive until consumers in every state can legally purchase the substance.

Diversion of marijuana was the basis of a lawsuit filed by the attorneys general of Nebraska and Oklahoma against Colorado in 2015 in which they claimed that Colorado's marijuana legalization conflicts with federal law and had created problems in their states by increasing the amount of marijuana coming into their states. The lawsuit claimed that "if this entity [the state of Colorado] were based south of the border, the federal government would prosecute it as a drug cartel" (Ingold and Baca 2016). U.S. solicitor general Donald Verrilli Jr. recommended that the Supreme Court reject the suit, noting that the alleged diversion of marijuana into Nebraska and Oklahoma was being caused by individuals breaking the law, not the state of Colorado itself: "This is not an appropriate case for the exercise of the court's original jurisdiction. Entertaining the type of dispute at issue here—essentially that one state's laws make it more likely that third parties will violate federal and state laws in another state—would represent a substantial and unwarranted expansion of the court's original jurisdiction" (quoted in Baca 2015f). The

Supreme Court ultimately voted 6–2 (with Justices Clarence Thomas and Samuel Alito dissenting) to decline to hear the case (Ingold and Baca 2016).

But there is no doubt that diversion of cannabis from states with legal marijuana is occurring. In Colorado, for example, one problem with the legislation that was alleged to be causing diversion inside and outside the state (albeit not to the extent claimed in the 2015 Rocky Mountain HIDTA report we discuss in detail in Chapter 5) was that medical caregivers in the state were initially allowed to grow up to 495 plants. Changes in the Colorado law that went into effect on January 21, 2017, limited the number of plants caregivers could grow to 99 (Rodgers 2016), but this reduction apparently did not significantly reduce diversion. In supporting a further reduction in the number of plants that could be grown, the police chief of Greenwood Village, Colorado, commented, "The current limit of 99 plants is a massive loophole in our state law that attracts criminal elements from across our nation in search of a quick buck" (quoted in Eason 2017). In March 2017, the Colorado House approved Bill 1220, which limited the number of cannabis plants that could be grown by caregivers to sixteen and permitted local jurisdictions to impose further restrictions (the city of Denver had previously imposed a twelve-plant limit) (Eason 2017). Later, a Colorado Senate committee approved a measure to limit the number of plants to twelve per residential property, but medical marijuana patients and their caregivers would be allowed up to twenty-four plants. The plant limit for medical patients and caregivers is higher because a large number of plants are needed to produce cannabis oils and other medical treatments these patients need (Wyatt 2017b).

Significant diversion of cannabis from the state of Oregon is also occurring, according to a report by the Oregon State Police (2017) (although, as we discuss later, the Oregon State Police superintendent has expressed concerns about the veracity of this report). This report referred to Oregon as an "epicenter of cannabis production" and estimated that the state produces between 132 tons and 900 tons more marijuana than what state residents could consume. The report commented that marijuana legalization in Oregon "has provided an effective means to launder cannabis products and proceeds, where, in essence actors can exploit legal mechanisms to obscure products' origins and conceal true profits, thereby blurring the boundaries of the illegal market and complicating enforcement efforts." And in California, a study commissioned by the California Department of Food and Agriculture estimated that California farms produce approximately 13.5 million pounds of marijuana yearly, while consumption by state residents is estimated to be about 2.5 million pounds (Rosenhall 2017). In contrast to the situation in Colorado and Oregon, it appears that Washington State's comparatively strict monitoring of cannabis producers, in particular its prohibition on personal cultivation for nonmedical marijuana registrants, has led to considerably less "leakage" of cannabis across state lines (Coughlin-Bogue 2017).

State officials are not unaware of these concerns surrounding diversion and the black market in cannabis. In Oregon, legislation requiring that regulators track all marijuana grown in the state's legal market (including both medical and recreational—prior to this law, only recreational marijuana was tracked) was passed in the summer of 2017, and Washington State planned on implementing an improved tracking system that would be "highly secure, reliable, scalable and flexible" as of November 1, 2017 (Selsky 2017). Despite claims to the contrary, it is not entirely clear that marijuana smuggling has become a greater problem under legalization than it was in the past; as Oregon Democratic representative Earl Blumenauer commented, "Marijuana has left Oregon for decades. What's different is that now we have better mechanisms to try and control it" (quoted in Selsky 2017).

Harvard University economist Jeffrey Miron (2017) has suggested that the solution to the continued black market problem is "trivial: full legalization" but adds that such legalization must not be accompanied by excessive regulation or taxation. With respect to the issue of diversion, it is also worth considering the comments of Alison Holcomb, primary architect of Washington State's Initiative 502: "If people are smoking Washington marijuana, isn't that better than smoking Mexican marijuana?" (quoted in Keefe 2013).

The Trump Administration

I'm very capable of changing anything I want to.
—DONALD TRUMP, quoted in Steve Coll, "Trump's Intervention"

Anyone who thinks that in the United States the prohibition
of cannabis is abolished is wrong. It really is not over yet.
—CYRILLE FIJNAUT AND BRICE DE RUYVER, *The Third Way*

As is the case in many other policy domains and issues, President Donald Trump's position on marijuana (he claims to have never smoked it) is not entirely clear. In April 1990, Trump apparently supported the legalization of all drugs, commenting to a reporter, "We're losing badly the war on drugs. You have to legalize drugs to win that war. You have to take the profits away from these drug czars" (quoted in J. Johnson 2015).[6] Trump (rhetorically, at least) has also been a champion of states' rights; campaigning in 2015, he commented, "In terms of marijuana legalization, I think it should be a state issue, state-by-state" and, with respect to medical marijuana, suggested that

---

6. We are presuming this comment was not intended to apply to drug czars appointed by presidents.

he was "100 percent" in favor of medical marijuana (quoted in Kaplan 2017): "Marijuana is such a big thing. I think medical should happen—right? Don't we agree? I think so. And then I really believe we should leave it up to the states" (quoted in J. Johnson 2015).

However, perhaps portending what may occur with respect to marijuana under his administration, when asked about legalization in Colorado (by Fox News talk show host Sean Hannity) at a Conservative Political Action Conference in 2015, Trump suggested, "If they vote for it, they vote for it. But you know, they have got a lot of problems going on right now in Colorado, some big problems. . . . And I love Colorado and the people are great, but there's a question as to how it's all working out there, you know? That's not going exactly trouble-free" (quoted in J. Johnson 2015). Trump also presented himself as a "law-and-order" candidate and has indicated that he approves of reinstating "stop-and-frisk" policies (Lichtblau 2017), which were used, especially in New York City, to target minorities who possessed marijuana. As marijuana activist Steve D'Angelo notes, the foci of marijuana regulation during the eight years of the Obama administration were social justice and civil liberties issues, including marijuana prohibition's contribution to mass incarceration and racial disparities in the enforcement of drug laws: "Those issues resonated under Obama. We don't anticipate those issues to resonate well with the Trump administration" (quoted in Wallace 2017j).

Attorney General Jeffrey Sessions

> I reject the idea that America will be a better place if marijuana is sold in every corner store. And I am astonished to hear people suggest that we can solve our heroin crisis by legalizing marijuana—so people can trade one life-wrecking dependency for another that's only slightly less awful. Our nation needs to say clearly once again that using drugs will destroy your life.
> —JEFF SESSIONS, "Attorney General Jeff Sessions Delivers Remarks on Efforts to Combat Violent Crime"

While the current president's position on marijuana is not entirely clear, there is considerably less ambiguity in the stance of his Attorney General Jeff Sessions. As noted previously, Sessions subscribes to the marijuana as a gateway drug theory and has referred to the substance as "a very real danger. We need grown-ups in Washington to say marijuana is not the kind of thing that ought to be legalized" (quoted in Fuller 2016a). He also said that "good people don't smoke marijuana" (quoted in Wallace 2016a), and at a Senate drug caucus hearing in April 2016, Sessions commented, "To give that [marijuana] away and make it socially acceptable, creates the demand, increased demand that results in people being addicted or impacted adversely" (quoted in Wallace 2016a).

Sessions also claimed that there was "more violence around marijuana than one would think" (quoted in Wallace 2017g) and expressed skepticism regarding the utility of medical marijuana, especially its serving as a substitute for opioid drugs. At a talk before the National Association of Attorneys General in February 2017, Sessions commented, "I see a line in the Washington Post today that I remember from the '80s. Marijuana is a cure for opiate abuse. How stupid is that. Give me a break. This is the kind of argument that has been made out there to just—almost a desperate attempt to defend the harmlessness of marijuana or even its benefits. I doubt that's true. Maybe science will prove me wrong" (quoted in Ingraham 2017b). As the review of research in Chapter 3 indicates, there is considerable evidence to suggest that science has already proven that Sessions is wrong on this issue.

Sessions has indicated that he intends to increase the use of asset-forfeiture provisions, which could result in federal agents seizing cash, property, and supplies from marijuana businesses in states with legalized marijuana (Berenson 2017). Sessions requested that the Senate Appropriations Committee rescind the Rohrabacher-Farr amendment, which prevents the Department of Justice from using funds to prevent "any state or jurisdiction from implementing a law that authorizes the use, distribution, possession, or cultivation of medical marijuana" (Washburn 2017b), but the committee refused to do so. And although it is too early to tell what impact this will have, some three days after legal sales of recreational marijuana commenced in California on January 1, 2018, Sessions rescinded the Cole memorandum, directing "all U.S. Attorneys to use previously established prosecutorial principles that provide them all the necessary tools to disrupt criminal organizations, tackle the growing drug crisis, and thwart violent crime across our country" (quoted in Zapotosky, Horwitz, and Achenbach 2018).

Sessions's more general views on drugs and crime are also relevant here. In his role as a federal prosecutor in Mobile, Alabama, in the 1980s and 1990s (he also served as Alabama attorney general from 1994 to 1996 and as an Alabama senator from 1996 to 2016), Sessions vigorously pursued drug cases, and his policies "helped southern Alabama establish a federal drug conviction rate that was almost four times the national average" (P. Levy 2017). Later, as chair of the Senate Judiciary Committee, Sessions blocked proposals to reduce sentences for drug offenses and criticized the Obama administration's efforts to reduce the federal prison population by scaling back the use of mandatory minimum sentences (Ludwig 2016). Sessions has also spoken favorably about stop-and-frisk practices by law enforcement, and it has been speculated that the attorney general could tie federal funding for police departments to the use of these aggressive practices (Ludwig 2016).

Other Trump administration officials who have hinted that the federal government may take a more aggressive approach to marijuana include Homeland Security secretary (and, as of August 2017, White House chief of staff) John Kelly. Retired marine general Kelly does not support the use of medical marijuana, has been vocal in his criticism of marijuana legalization, and is also a member of the marijuana as a gateway drug team (Ingraham 2016o). Speaking at George Washington University in April 2017, Kelly commented, "Let me be clear about marijuana. It's a potentially dangerous drug that frequently leads to the use of harder drugs" (quoted in *Columbian* 2017). "Its use and possession is against federal law and until the law is changed by the U.S. Congress, we in DHS [Department of Homeland Security] are sworn to uphold all the laws on the books" (quoted in K. Williams 2017). Kelly also signaled that the Transportation and Security Administration would take "appropriate action" if marijuana was discovered at security checkpoints and/or baggage screenings and, importantly, that "Immigration and Customs Enforcement will continue to use marijuana possession, distribution, and convictions as essential elements as they build their deportation/removal apprehension packages for targeted operations against illegal aliens" (quoted in K. Williams 2017).

Jeff Sessions's Letters to Governors and the Governors' Responses

> Mr. Sessions is committed to cherry-picking information that fits into his worldview. When it comes to Mr. Sessions and marijuana, ignorance seems to be a pre-existing condition, and he has no interest in seeking treatment for that ailment.
> —JOHN HUDAK, quoted in Alicia Wallace, "Sessions Raises 'Serious Questions' about Colorado's Marijuana Management in Letter to Gov"

Perhaps the most interesting development with respect to marijuana up to this point in the Trump administration involves letters sent by Attorney General Sessions to the governors of four states and the responses of those governors. In April 2017, Governors Bill Walker (Alaska), John Hickenlooper (Colorado), Kate Brown (Oregon), and Jay Inslee (Washington) wrote a letter to the attorney general and Secretary of the Treasury Steve Mnuchin, urging the Trump administration to consult with them before making changes in federal marijuana regulations. The letter emphasized that the 2013 Cole memorandum had provided "the necessary framework for state regulatory programs centered on public safety and health protections" and expressed concern that overturning the Cole memorandum could lead to diversion of marijuana to the black market and possibly compromise public safety. Importantly, while noting that they themselves had "expressed apprehensions before our states adopted current [marijuana] laws," the governors indicated that they were "committed to implementing the will of our citizens and have worked cooperatively with our legislatures to establish robust regulatory structures that prioritize public health and public safety, reduce inequitable incarceration and expand our economies" (Brown et al. 2017).

In response to this letter, in July 2017, Sessions sent (separate, although with similar themes) letters to each governor detailing his concerns regarding the situation of legalized recreational marijuana in each state, framing these concerns in the context of the provisions of the 2013 Cole memorandum and relying heavily on (largely outdated and widely discredited) law enforcement reports. Each of the four letters noted that "Congress has determined that marijuana is a dangerous drug" and that "the Department [of Justice] remains committed to enforcing the Controlled Substances Act." Sessions's letters further emphasized that the Cole memorandum included the statement, "Nothing herein precludes investigation or prosecution, even in the absence of any one of the factors listed above" (Sessions 2017d).

Rather curiously, and apparently assuming that the governors of the four states (or at least, their respective staffs) were not aware of these reports, Sessions's letters also attached the law enforcement reports on marijuana whose data he refers to in his letter (in the letter to the Alaska governor, a 2015 report by the Alaska State Troopers; in Colorado, the 2016 Rocky Mountain HIDTA report; in Oregon, a 2017 report by the Oregon State Troopers; and in Washington State, a 2016 report by the Northwest HIDTA). We outline the specifics of the letters to each state, as well as the response from the respective governors.

> We encourage you to keep in mind why we are having this conversation. State and federal prohibition of marijuana failed to prevent its widespread use, which was generating huge profits for violent criminal organizations. The people of Washington State chose by popular vote to try a different path. Under Washington's system, responsible adults are allowed access to a highly regulated product that returns substantial tax revenues to the government even as it displaces illegal activity. (Inslee and Ferguson 2017)

In his letter to Washington State's governor Jay Inslee and attorney general Bob Ferguson, drawing on the report from the Northwest HIDTA, Sessions (2017c) noted that Washington marijuana had been shipped to forty-three other states (although it is by no means clear that this involved marijuana diverted from the legal recreational market) and that seventeen THC-extraction labs exploded in the state in 2014. Sessions (or, more likely, his staff) did not carefully read the Northwest HIDTA report, as there was no indication there that these were labs regulated by the state of Washington.

In their response to Sessions, in a letter that did not mince words, Governor Inslee and Attorney General Ferguson (2017) commented. "Your letter, citing the March 2016 Northwest High Intensity Drug Trafficking Area report on marijuana in Washington, makes a number of allegations that are outdated, incorrect, or based on incomplete information. . . . No licensed extraction business has exploded—the incidents referred to were black-or gray-market facilities. . . . In the history of our licensing system, no legal extraction lab has ever had an explosion." With respect to Sessions's claim that Washington marijuana had been diverted to forty-three other states, Inslee and Ferguson noted that the assertion was based on data from a period "several years before our recreational sales began and reveals nothing about whether the source of the marijuana was legal or illegal."

One of the more curious references in Sessions's (2017c) letter was that 61.9 percent of drivers "do not believe marijuana makes a difference in their driving ability." But the study Sessions referred to made no such claim. In fact, the study reported that 97 of 893 drivers who were surveyed reported having previously used marijuana within two hours of driving. Of this group, 61.9 percent (sixty) indicated that marijuana did not affect their driving ability, which translates to 6.7 percent of the drivers involved in the survey.

Perhaps most tellingly, Inslee and Ferguson (2017) suggested that Sessions had not properly distinguished "between marijuana activity that is legal and illegal" and that "some of the statistics cited in your letter are simply incorrect, or based on misreading of their context." Inslee and Ferguson added that the report relied on "incomplete and unreliable data that does not provide the most accurate snapshot of our efforts since the marketplace opened in 2014" (quoted in Anderson 2017), or, as the *Seattle Times* (2017) noted, "Sessions' data, in fact, comes from the prohibition era he apparently favors." Ferguson added, "Honestly, it's hard to take him [Sessions] seriously if he relies on such outdated information" (quoted in Young 2017a). In an additional interesting twist, and likely in response to Sessions's attachment of the Northwest HIDTA report to his letter, Inslee and Ferguson included an attachment of their own—a 2017 report by the Washington State Liquor and Cannabis Board, which describes how Washington State's regulatory system is designed to comply with the priorities of the Cole memorandum. Inslee and Ferguson (2017) concluded their letter with a request to discuss with Sessions a number of issues, including "whether DOJ intends to follow its recommendations from its Task Force on Crime Reduction and Public Safety—in particular, its reported recommendation to continue previous federal policy on state legalization of marijuana" and "whether President Trump's previous statements of support for medical marijuana, and leaving recreational marijuana legalization to the states, represent the policy of the federal government."

Editorial boards of major papers in the state of Washington also responded critically to Sessions's stance on marijuana. The Vancouver *Columbian* (2017) reiterated its previous position that "it is incumbent upon

Congress to end an unnecessary fight and legalize recreational [marijuana] use nationally" and referred to Sessions's "illogical thinking on the issue," characterizing his views as a "maddening collection of falsehoods, innuendo, and outdated thinking." Importantly, the *Columbian* noted that Sessions's threats of interference in states that had legalized marijuana was hypocritical with respect to his position on states' rights in other domains: "He has championed states' rights regarding bathrooms for transgender citizens and the Voting Rights Act. In other words, the Attorney General of the United States supports states' rights—except when he doesn't."

The editorial board of the *Seattle Times* (2017) was similarly critical of Sessions's threat of intervention in Washington State, suggesting the data Sessions referred to in his letter to Inslee and Ferguson were "misleading and cherry-picked" and "wrongly portrayed Washington's marijuana experiment as a circus, with exploding marijuana-extraction labs and stoned teens weaving across the roadway." The editorial also noted that Sessions was seemingly unaware that marijuana legalization was at least partially the product of the failed policy of prohibition that had resulted in the arrests and incarceration of drug users, with disproportional impacts on members of minority groups. Alison Holcomb, the primary architect of Washington State's recreational marijuana law, added, "Sessions is on thin political ice, and public opinion on cannabis—and states' rights to determine how their law enforcement resources should be used with respect to cannabis—makes this a losing issue for him. I'm surprised he decided this was the best way to rally his supporters" (quoted in Young 2017a).

The first two paragraphs of Sessions's (2017d) letter to Colorado governor Hickenlooper were virtually identical to those of the other three letters and referred exclusively to data (again, including attaching the full report itself as an appendix) from the Rocky Mountain HIDTA report. Indicating that the HIDTA report "raises serious questions about the efficacy of marijuana 'regulatory structures' in your state," Sessions (2017d) provided eight bullet points focusing on alleged evidence that Colorado marijuana was being transported across state lines, alleged increases in youth marijuana use in the state, increases in marijuana-related emergency room visits, and alleged increases in marijuana-related traffic deaths in the state.

In reaction to Sessions's letter to Hickenlooper, Ricardo Baca (2017), former editor of the *Denver Post*'s *Cannabist*, wrote an op-ed urging Governor Hickenlooper and Attorney General Cynthia Coffman to call out the "unreliable, misleading, and inaccurate misinformation" from the Rocky Mountain HIDTA report referenced in Sessions's letter. More specifically, Baca suggested that Hickenlooper and Coffman should compare the HIDTA data on youth use of cannabis to the findings from the Healthy Kids Colorado Survey and the HIDTA data on motor vehicle collisions and fatalities to those provided by the Colorado State Patrol and state departments of Transportation and Public Safety "and ask yourself why these agencies' data differ so wildly from those of HIDTA." (As Baca mentions, Sessions's letters to the governors relied exclusively on the law enforcement reports and completely excluded more credible scientific studies on the impacts of marijuana legalization, both those published in academic journals and other reports from various regulatory agencies in each state.)

In an August 2017 reply to Sessions's letter, Governor Hickenlooper and Attorney General Coffman rebutted Sessions's claims, albeit in a more conciliatory tone than that adopted by Governor Inslee and Attorney General Ferguson. Among many points made in their response, Hickenlooper and Coffman noted that "multiple data sources indicate that youth marijuana use in Colorado has remained stable following legalization," that out-of-state diversion was largely the result of "abusive residential marijuana cultivation activities that take place under the guise of lawful medical marijuana production," and that data on marijuana-related motor vehicle crash fatalities and emergency department visits indicated a decrease for both measures for the most recent time period for which data were available (Hickenlooper and Coffman 2017, 1–2) .

Sessions's (2017b) letter to Alaska governor Bill Walker emphasized similar themes and also referred to a 2015 report from the Alaska State Troopers Association (which included a three-paragraph section on marijuana) that mentioned that "marijuana is available throughout the state and is often viewed as a gateway drug for young adults and teenagers," that 19.0 percent of high school students in the state had used marijuana in the past 30 days, and that "demand for Alaskan-grown marijuana continues to be high as a result of its exceptional tetrahydrocannabinol (THC) content" (Alaska State Troopers 2015, 10). Interestingly, although certainly not surprisingly, Sessions was seemingly not concerned about much stronger statements regarding the problems associated with alcohol use and abuse in the state made in the same report: "Alaska's criminal justice professionals recognize that alcohol is the primarily abused substance in Alaska. Alcohol is involved in many violent, suicidal, and accidental deaths" (5), as well as violent crimes such as sexual assault and domestic violence. Governor Bill Walker and Attorney General Jahna Lindemuth apparently found it rather curious that Sessions's letter referenced data from 2015, since legal sales of recreational marijuana did not commence in the state until 2016 (Pasquariello and Washburn 2017).

Sessions's letter to Oregon governor Kate Brown specifically focused on the issue of diversion of cannabis from the state and referred to a 2017 report by the Oregon State Police (OSP), which was partially drafted by Ravi Channell, who works for the Oregon-Idaho HIDTA (Crombie 2017b). However, Brown (and, in fact, OSP superintendent Travis Hampton himself) discredited the report; Hampton sent a letter to Sessions indicating that the report (which was leaked to the Portland-based *Oregonian* newspaper) "is not a published report and is regrettably utilized to represent Oregon's efforts and compliance surrounding marijuana enforcement" and that it included many "subjective or invalidated sources" (Hampton 2017). In her letter to Sessions, Governor Kate Brown (2017) noted that, beginning in January 2017, all recreational and medicinal marijuana sold legally in the state was being tracked from seed to sale (to prevent diversion) and commented, "Despite the concerns surrounding legalization of marijuana, there can be no denying that Oregon has benefited from this industry. Oregon has already realized $60.2 million in revenue and created over 16,000 jobs for Oregonians. . . . This does not even take into account cost savings to the criminal justice system."

Sessions's letters to the governors did not outline what specific (if any) actions the federal government would take with respect to marijuana, "leaving government and industry officials to read the letters as tea leaves and interpret them differently" (Anderson 2017). Sessions's rather threatening letters also seem curious in light of the fact that the Task Force on Crime Reduction and Public Safety, commissioned by Sessions in 2017, did not suggest any new policy recommendations with respect to marijuana (Gurman 2017).

Can the Genie Be Put Back in the Bottle?

While some cannabis legalization proponents claim their movement has grown too big to fail, it has also proved too significant for the federal government to ignore.
—ALICIA WALLACE, "Something's Going to Have to Give"

While most drug policy experts believe the Trump administration will not fully reinitiate the war on marijuana, the letters sent to governors by Sessions, as well as the rescindment of the Cole memorandum, suggest that it is unlikely there will be no response. In February 2017, then White House press secretary Sean Spicer commented, "I do believe you'll see greater enforcement of it [federal marijuana laws]. . . . It's something that the Department of Justice I think will be further looking into" (quoted in Young 2017b). Revealing that he (and, ostensibly, the president) did not understand that under federal law there is no difference between medicinal and recreational marijuana (because it is a Schedule I drug), Spicer indicated that Trump saw a "big difference" between the use of marijuana for medicinal purposes and for recreation (Wagner and Zapotosky 2017). Perhaps not surprisingly, Spicer also revealed that he was unaware that some research indicates marijuana can serve as a substitute for opioids: "I think that when you see something like the opioid addiction crisis blossoming in so many states around this country, the last thing we should be doing is encouraging people. There is still a federal law we need to abide by" (quoted in Wagner and Zapotosky

2017). Somewhat ironically, Spicer's comments with respect to the primacy of federal marijuana law came one day after the Trump administration revoked protections for transgendered students initiated by President Obama, arguing that decisions on such protections should be left to the states (Young 2017b). Spicer's comments also seem inconsistent with the views of the Environmental Protection Agency's administrator Scott Pruitt, who has criticized the Obama administration's policies of "intruding on the autonomy given to states on environmental laws" (quoted in Revesz 2017).

Speculating on the specific actions the Trump administration will take on marijuana, John Hudak, an expert on marijuana policy at the Brookings Institution, suggests that there are several possible courses of action. He notes that while the administration could decide to enforce existing federal marijuana laws, this could create problems because federal agents could not force state or local officials to assist them in these efforts (Wallace 2017m). And should the federal government decide to engage in such a crackdown, there is also the complicated issue of how law enforcement agents would distinguish between businesses involved in recreational rather than medical marijuana, since in most states that have legalized recreational marijuana, at the level of production and sales, there is essentially no distinction between the two. Another potential strategy would be for the federal government to withhold certain federal funds from states that do not comply with federal marijuana laws, similar to what it has done with "sanctuary cities" that have vowed to protect undocumented immigrants (Coughlin-Bogue 2017). It has also been speculated that the federal government could seize tax revenues being collected by states from marijuana businesses, since technically, these funds are criminal proceeds (Wallace 2017e).

An additional crucial factor in how the response to marijuana may change under the new administration involves appointments to key government positions that directly or indirectly address drug issues, as well as the appointment of U.S. attorneys and judges. As of March 2018 Trump had not yet appointed a permanent director for the Substance Abuse and Mental Health Services Administration and the leadership of the CDC has been in turmoil. Anne Schuchat was appointed head of the CDC in January 2018 after former Trump appointee, Brenda Fitzgerald, resigned when it became known that she had invested in tobacco stock shortly after being named CDC's director (one of the CDCs goals is to reduce tobacco use [Quinn 2018]). It appears as though Nora Volkow (who is largely opposed to marijuana legalization) will remain as director of the NIDA, and in August 2017, Trump appointed David Muhlhausen, a research fellow at the right-wing Heritage Foundation, to be director of the National Institute of Justice (AllGov 2017). Although we were unable to find evidence on Muhlhausen's specific views on marijuana, he has written articles criticizing community-oriented police services and prisoner reentry programs and is pro–death penalty (AllGov 2017).

When Trump took office, the ONDCP website was "wiped clean" (Jiminez 2017),[7] and a draft memorandum obtained by CNN in May 2017 indicated that the ONDCP budget would be cut by 94 percent (from $380 million to $24 million) (Merica 2017). After concerns expressed by numerous individuals and organizations regarding how these massive cuts would hinder attempts to address the country's opioid epidemic, the White House backed off and announced that the reductions to the ONDCP budget would amount to only approximately 3 percent (Shesgreen 2017). In September 2017, the president nominated Tom Marino, a former district attorney and federal prosecutor, for the position of ONDCP director. Marino, the person Trump had tasked with leading the fight against the nation's opioid epidemic, was forced to withdraw his name from consideration. It was revealed that Marino had earned nearly $100,000 from pharmaceutical lobbyists while simultaneously backing legislation making it easier for drug companies to distribute opioids and avoid DEA oversight (Higham and Bernstein 2017). In February 2018 Trump nominated Jim Carroll, his deputy chief of staff, who had formerly worked at Ford Motor Company as well as at the Justice and Treasury Departments, to be drug czar. Carroll is not known to have any prior experience or expertise in drug policy (Barcott 2018).

In early March 2017, the Trump administration ordered the resignation of forty-six U.S. attorneys who had been appointed under the Obama administration (Savage and Haberman 2017). Although at the time of writing it is not known who will be appointed to these vacant positions, it is at least possible that, in line with the pronouncements of Sean Spicer and Jeff Sessions discussed previously, some may take a more aggressive stance toward marijuana. Drug policy expert Alex Kreit noted that with these appointments, enforcement of federal marijuana laws may end up "looking like a patchwork quilt. Instead of seeing raids and prosecutions in every state, enforcement will likely vary based on the approach taken by individual federal prosecutors" (quoted in Coughlin-Bogue 2017), who are likely to respond to local concerns in any actions they may take. Trump will also have the opportunity to fill more than one hundred judicial vacancies in federal courts, and his vow to choose conservative judges who hold views similar to those of late Supreme Court Justice Antonin Scalia could have implications for marijuana-related cases that might be heard before these judges (Rucker and Barnes 2016).

As revealed in the responses of governors to Attorney General Sessions's letters, and in other actions and statements, government officials in states with legal recreational marijuana appear ready to resist any federal intervention. Even before the exchange of letters between Sessions and Washington

---

7. WhiteHouse.gov pages about climate change, health care, and lesbian, gay, bisexual, and transgender rights also disappeared at the same time (Rocheleau 2017).

State officials, Attorney General Bob Ferguson (who was also the first state attorney general to sue the federal government over the controversial January 2017 Trump executive order banning immigration and travel from seven Muslim countries) commented, "I will resist any efforts by the Trump administration to undermine the will of the voters in Washington State" (quoted in Young 2017b). In emphasizing that the problems associated with opioid drugs were far more important to address, Ferguson added, "To the extent that DOJ [Department of Justice] chooses to reallocate anti-drug resources, we encourage it to work even more closely with states to combat the opioid scourge; research suggests that decriminalized marijuana is associated with lower rates of opioid abuse and fewer opioid-related fatalities" (quoted in Hawkins 2017).

Governor John Hickenlooper indicated that he would not approve of the federal government intervening in Colorado. In an interview with *Cannabist* reporter Alicia Wallace, Hickenlooper commented, "We haven't seen a spike in teenage use. We haven't seen a giant increase in people's consumption of marijuana. Seems like people who were using marijuana before it was legal, still are. Seems like the people who weren't using marijuana before it was legal, still aren't." Hickenlooper emphasized that the "old system," which fostered a black market in marijuana was "a disaster," and noted that under legalization, a portion of the tax revenues collected were being allocated for drug education and prevention programs (quoted in Wallace 2017d).

Attorney General Xavier Becerra also announced his intention to oppose federal intervention in California: "I took an oath to enforce the laws that California has passed. If there is action from the federal government on this subject [marijuana] I will respond in an appropriate way to protect the interests of California" (quoted in Halper and McGreevy 2017). And although at the time of writing the status of this legislation is not known, in anticipation of federal intervention, a "sanctuary marijuana state" bill (Bill 1578) was introduced in the California Assembly that would prevent state and local law enforcement agencies from assisting federal agencies and officials in pursuing marijuana consumers or businesses who were in compliance with the state's law (Staggs 2017). The proposed legislation in California is similar to a proposed law that would prevent law enforcement agencies in the state from assisting federal immigration officials in targeting illegal immigrants (McGreevy 2017).

Finally, in Nevada (which legalized recreational marijuana in 2016), Democratic Senate majority leader Aaron Ford released a statement indicating that his state's attorney general, Adam Laxalt, "must make it immediately clear that he will vigorously defend Nevada's recreational laws from federal overreach. Not only did voters overwhelmingly vote to approve the legalization of recreational marijuana, the Governor's proposed education budget depends on tax revenue from recreational marijuana sales. Any action by the Trump administration would be an insult to Nevada voters and would pick the pockets of Nevada's students" (quoted in Wallace 2017l).

Marijuana Law Reform at the Federal Level?

As of 2018, there were several federal marijuana bills under consideration, many of which have been proposed by the Cannabis Caucus in Congress. This caucus, which has the goal of protecting legalized marijuana, is headed by Representatives Earl Blumenauer (Democrat, Oregon), Jared Polis (Democrat, Colorado), Dana Rohrabacher (Republican, California, who is a supporter of President Donald Trump), and Don Young (Republican, Alaska) (Wallace 2017f), all of whom have previously been active in marijuana law reform.

In 2017, Blumenauer teamed with fellow Oregon Democratic senator Ron Wyden to announce the "Path to Marijuana Reform," which involved three proposed bills that address a number of issues related to marijuana (Wallace 2017b). The first of these bills, the Small Business Tax Equity Act, would create an exception to Section 280e of the Tax Code and would allow marijuana businesses that are compliant with the laws of their state to claim tax deductions. The Responsibly Addressing the Marijuana Policy Gap Act removes federal penalties and the possibility of civil asset forfeiture for cannabis businesses complying with state laws and also recommends the expungement of criminal records for those convicted of low-level marijuana offenses. Finally, the Marijuana Revenue and Regulation Act proposes to completely remove the substance from the Controlled Substances Act and would regulate marijuana at the federal level in a manner similar to that of alcohol (Ludwig 2017b; see also Wallace 2017b). As we discuss in Chapter 3, Blumenauer also introduced the Veterans Equal Access Act, which would remove restrictions on VA doctors recommending medical marijuana to their patients (Reilly 2016).

Perhaps even more surprisingly, in September 2017, Republican senator Orrin Hatch of Utah, who is strongly opposed to the use of recreational marijuana, and Democratic senator Brian Schatz of Hawaii introduced the Marijuana Effective Drug Study Act (MEDS Act). Among other things, the proposed legislation would facilitate research on marijuana's medicinal uses by "streamlining the research registration process" and making marijuana more available for researchers (Labak 2017). In announcing the proposal, Senator Hatch produced a statement that was rather comically filled with marijuana puns:

> It's high time to address research into medical marijuana. Our country has experimented with a variety of state solutions without properly delving into the weeds of the effectiveness, safety, dosing, ad-

ministration, and quality of medical marijuana. All the while the federal government strains to enforce regulations that do more harm than good. To be blunt, we need to remove the administrative barriers that sometimes do more harm than good. (Quoted in Labak 2017)

Other recent developments include a policy resolution by the National Conference of State Legislatures (NCSL), a bipartisan, nongovernmental organization that serves members and staff of state legislatures, recommending that cannabis be removed from the Controlled Substances Act (McClure 2017). The NCSL emphasized that marijuana's classification as a Schedule I drug, which restricts the ability of marijuana companies to do business with financial institutions and forces most of them to operate on a cash-only basis, "attracts criminal activity and creates substantial public safety risks" (quoted in McClure 2017).

And at the same time that Sessions was issuing his letters to the governors of states with legalized recreational marijuana, New Jersey senator Cory Booker proposed the Marijuana Justice Act (Senate of the United States 2017). Certainly the most radical proposal regarding marijuana at the federal level to date, the Marijuana Justice Act calls for legalizing the substance at the federal level. The proposal also includes provisions that would withhold federal funds for prison construction from states that have disproportionate (both with respect to minorities and low-income populations) marijuana arrest or incarceration rates and recommends expungement of federal convictions for cannabis possession. In addition, any individual "who is aggrieved by a disproportionate incarceration rate of a state may bring a civil action in an appropriate district court of the U.S." (Senate of the United States 2017, 9). Finally, the Booker proposal would establish a community reinvestment fund (for job training and prisoner reentry services, among others) for communities that have been most affected by the war on drugs. Given the rather radical nature of this proposal, and given that Republicans control the House and Senate, it is highly unlikely that this legislation will pass. However, Booker may be a candidate for president in the 2020 election, and marijuana legalization will likely be a prominent issue in that year.

While it thus seems unlikely that marijuana will be legalized at the federal level in the United States in the near future, it is also probable that several states will consider (both medical and recreational) legalization in the 2018 and 2020 elections. The Marijuana Policy Project (n.d.) is working to change marijuana laws through legislatures or ballot initiatives. These efforts include but may not be limited to recreational marijuana legalization in Connecticut, Delaware, Hawaii, Illinois, Maryland, Michigan, New Hampshire, and Rhode Island. MPP is also lobbying for medical marijuana legislation in Louisiana, Nebraska, South Carolina, Texas, and West Virginia. Similar to the recent legalization of recreational marijuana in Vermont, and in contrast to the legalization of recreational marijuana in the other eight recreationally legalized states and Washington, D.C., in some of these states the substance could be legalized as a result of legislative action instead of ballot measures. For example, in New Jersey, new governor Philip Murphy, emphasizing social and racial justice issues, has proposed to legalize marijuana (Rouse 2018).

What's Next?

> The tipping point for cannabis has arrived, and there is no question about where we are headed. Full legalization will come to the world sooner or later.
> —STEVE D'ANGELO, *The Cannabis Manifesto*

While we are not as convinced as Steve D'Angelo that worldwide legalization of marijuana is going to occur in the near future, we do agree that we are at a tipping point, and it will be fascinating to observe developments in marijuana legislation both in the United States and in other countries in the coming years. Outcomes from the legalization of recreational cannabis in several states and Washington, D.C., indicate that, with some exceptions, these policy experiments have largely been successful—dramatically negative consequences have not occurred, and many would argue that substantial benefits have accrued.

As we note elsewhere in this book, predictions of increases in youth use of marijuana following legalization—one of the primary concerns of marijuana prohibitionists—have not manifested, and government regulation of marijuana may be serving to limit access to the substance by children and adolescents. Findings from studies on increases in automobile collisions and associated fatalities in states where marijuana has been legalized are mixed but generally do not indicate substantial increases in such outcomes. While marijuana is a psychoactive substance and therefore can affect the ability to operate a motor vehicle, research indicates it is less incapacitating than alcohol in this regard. Whereas alcohol can cause people to underestimate their impairment and drive erratically, marijuana may cause some to be "overcautious"—overestimating their level of impairment and driving more carefully (Neavyn et al. 2014; Sewell, Poling, and Sofuoglu 2009). Some drivers (especially those at a high risk of being involved in collisions, such as heavy drinkers and young males) may also be substituting marijuana for alcohol to some degree.

Contrary to the predictions of certain marijuana prohibitionists, violent crime and crime more generally have not increased under marijuana legalization.[8] This should not be surprising, as it has been well established that

---

8. At the same time, we need to be cognizant of the fact that the war on marijuana in the United States is far from over. Arrest statistics released by the FBI in 2017 revealed that

marijuana is typically not aggression inducing and may even lead to a decrease in the likelihood of aggression and violence (Hoaken and Stewart, 2003; Smith et al. 2014). We would argue that the central reason that serious negative outcomes related to marijuana legalization have not occurred is that *legalization did not invent marijuana.*

We have also seen several positive outcomes of marijuana legalization. As we discuss in Chapter 6, retail sales of medical and recreational marijuana reached approximately $10 billion in 2017 and generated hundreds of millions of dollars in tax revenue (Morris 2017); legalization of recreational marijuana in California is expected to generate more than $1 billion in tax revenue annually (Berke 2018). Obviously, these revenues would be left uncollected in the absence of legalization. Although the specifics vary by state, most states direct the tax revenues obtained from legalization to public needs and services, including drug prevention and treatment programs and funding of K–12 education. States with legalized recreational marijuana have also realized significant criminal justice system cost savings from not having to enforce laws against marijuana possession and processing marijuana offenders. And although social and racial/ethnic justice issues remain even in states that have legalized, far fewer people of all races/ethnicities are being subject to criminal justice sanctions (and the attendant additional negative collateral consequences) for marijuana possession.

As of mid-2018, many other issues remain unresolved. Perhaps most important, marijuana remains a Schedule I substance under the Controlled Substances Act, inhibiting scientific research on the substance (including research on its medicinal uses but also research on the potential harms of high-potency marijuana that has become increasingly common under legalization). The Schedule I status of marijuana also prevents legal cannabis businesses from accessing financial services (which, ironically, prevents appropriate taxation, entices robbery, and threatens public safety). The Schedule I status also provides the federal government with the means to overturn both medical and recreational legalization of marijuana in states that have legalized. Although we suspect that the genie cannot be put back in the bottle—that is, the federal government will not use its powers to intervene in marijuana-legal states—the actions of the Trump administration are difficult to predict, and Attorney General Jeff Sessions is staunchly anti-marijuana. At the same time, there are a number of reasons why large-scale federal intervention is unlikely. One of these is the reticence of the federal government (especially conservative administrations, at least in rhetoric) to

---

there were 587,700 arrests for marijuana possession in 2016, representing a 2.2 percent increase from the previous year (Federal Bureau of Investigation 2017a). Arrests for marijuana possession are still one of the single largest offense categories in the United States, constituting more than 5 percent of all arrests in 2016 and greater than the total number of arrests for all violent crimes combined.

intercede in states' rights, particularly in a political context in which an apparently ever-increasing majority of Americans favor marijuana legalization (64 percent as of October 2017 [J. McCarthy 2017]). Another is the challenge of enforcing restrictions against recreational marijuana and not medical marijuana (unless the choice is to go after both, which would be even more problematic given that the majority of states have legalized medical marijuana).

The black market for marijuana is also a concern, as is the diversion of legally produced marijuana to the black market; these issues will remain a concern unless and until the drug is legalized nationwide. Attention will also focus on the regulation of marijuana advertising, which may be important in attempts to prevent the legalization of recreational marijuana from creating new users of the substance over and above that which occurs under criminalization (MacCoun 2010) and the related potential for the corporatization of the marijuana industry. Although we agree that the corporatization of marijuana is a concern, we believe that the characteristics of the marijuana industry make it less likely to follow the paths taken by Big Tobacco, Big Pharma, and Big Alcohol. Marijuana can be produced easily almost anywhere, and with the exception of Washington State, all states that have legalized recreational marijuana allow home growing, making it less likely that the industry will be dominated by a few big players. And even if this scenario proves to be the case, we see legalized, regulated, and taxed "Big Weed" as preferable to the marijuana market being in the hands of profit-driven criminal enterprises.

We return to a key point we make earlier in this book: Viewed in a larger historical perspective, the prohibition of cannabis in the United States (and other nations) is a historical anomaly. "It's not the wave of legalization that is radical, prohibition was radical" (Hari 2015, 273). While the damage to countless individuals who have been denied access to a plant that has demonstrated medicinal benefits (and is far less harmful than a host of currently legal drugs) and to the millions of people who have experienced criminal justice system sanctions (with particularly deleterious effects on members of racial/ethnic minority groups) cannot be undone, there are signs that we are entering a new era of rationality in regulating this plant. Yes, marijuana has been legalized, and the sky has not fallen.

References

Abcarian, Robin. 2016. "Now What? A Dispensary Owner, a Scientist, a Defense Expert and a City Manager Reflect on the New Pot Law." *Los Angeles Times*, November 13. Available at http://www.latimes.com/local/abcarian/la-me-abcarian-cannabis -voices-20161112-story.html.

Abel, Ernest. 1980. *Marijuana: The First Twelve Thousand Years*. New York: Premium Press.

Abrams, Donald I., Hector P. Vizoso, Starley B. Shade, Cheryl Jay, M. E. Kelly, and N. L. Benowitz. 2007. "Vaporization as a Smokeless Cannabis Delivery System: A Pilot Study." *Clinical Pharmacology and Therapeutics* 82 (5): 572–578.

Adams, Mike. 2016. "Federal Drug Agency Releases Apocalyptic Report on Marijuana Legalization in Colorado." *Merry Jane*, September 2. Available at https://merryjane .com/news/fda-report-marijuana-legalization-colorado.

Advisory Committee on Drug Dependence. 1968. "Cannabis: Report by the Advisory Committee on Drug Dependence." Available at https://peopleofstort.files.wordpress .com/2014/09/woottonreport1969.pdf.

Aguilar, John. 2016. "Marijuana Gap Divides Colorado Towns That Sell Pot, Those That Don't." *Denver Post*, January 1. Available at https://www.denverpost.com/2016/01/ 01/marijuana-gap-divides-colorado-towns-that-sell-pot-those-that-don't.

Alaska State Troopers. 2015. "2015 Annual Drug Report." Available at https://dps.alaska .gov/getmedia/06618bea-e1b5-42ea-8c09-c1705ebd947c/2015-annual-drug-report; .aspx.

Aldrich, Michael. 2006. "The Remarkable W. B. O'Shaughnessy." *O'Shaughnessy's*, Spring, pp. 26–27.

Alexander, Bruce. 1990. *Peaceful Measures: Canada's Way out of the War on Drugs*. Toronto: University of Toronto Press.

Allentuck, Samuel, and Karl Bowman. 1942. "The Psychiatric Aspects of Marijuana Intoxication." *American Journal of Psychiatry* 99:248–250.

AllGov. 2017. "Director of the National Institute of Justice: Who Is David Muhlhausen?" August 6. Available at http://www.allgov.com/news/top-stories/director-of-the -national-institute-of-justice-who-is-david-muhlhausen-170806?news=860268.

Altieri, Erik. 2013. "First Medical Marijuana Sale Reported in Washington, DC." National Organization for the Reform of Marijuana Laws, July 30. Available at http://blog .norml.org/2013/07/30/first-medical-marijuana-sale-reported-in-washington-dc.

American Academy of Neurology. 2017. "Cannabis-Based Medicine May Cut Seizures in Half for Those with Tough-to-Treat Epilepsy." April 18. Available at https://www .aan.com/PressRoom/Home/PressRelease/1544.

American Academy of Pediatrics. 2015. "American Academy of Pediatrics Reaffirms Opposition to Legalizing Marijuana for Recreational or Medical Use." January 26. Available at https://www.aap.org/en-us/about-the-aap/aap-press-room/pages/ American-Academy-of-Pediatrics-Reaffirms-Opposition-to-Legalizing-Marijuana -for-Recreational-or-Medical-Use.aspx.

American Cancer Society. 2017. "Cancer Treatment and Survivorship: Facts and Figures, 2016–2017." Available at https://www.cancer.org/content/dam/cancer-org/research/ cancer-facts-and-statistics/cancer-treatment-and-survivorship-facts-and-figures/ cancer-treatment-and-survivorship-facts-and-figures-2016-2017.pdf.

American Civil Liberties Union. 2013. "The War on Marijuana in Black and White." Available at https://www.aclu.org/files/assets/aclu-thewaronmarijuana-rel2.pdf.

American Civil Liberties Union of Washington. 2014. "Court Filings for Adult Marijuana Possession Plummet." Available at https://www.aclu-wa.org/news/court -filings-adult-marijuana-possession-plummet.

American College of Cardiology. 2017. "Marijuana Use Associated with Increased Risk of Stroke, Heart Failure." Available at http://www.acc.org/about-acc/press-releases/ 2017/03/09/14/05/marijuana-use-associated-with-increased-risk-of-stroke-heart -failure.

American Mercury. 1935. "The Menace of Marijuana." December, pp. 487–490.

American Psychiatric Association. 2013. "Position Statement on Marijuana as Medicine." Available at https://www.psychiatry.org/home/policy-finder?g=2c2d5a6a -7605-48f9-80ef-9206adf4a9c5&Page=9.

Americans for Safe Access. 2016. "Petition before the United States Department of Justice Information Quality Guidelines Staff." December 5. Available at http://ameri can-safe-access.s3.amazonaws.com/documents/DOJ%20IQA%20Petition.pdf.

Anderson, D. Mark, Benjamin Hansen, and Daniel I. Rees. 2012. "Medical Marijuana Laws and Teen Marijuana Use." Institute for the Study of Labor Discussion Paper 6592. Available at http://ftp.iza.org/dp6592.pdf.

Anderson, Rick. 2017. "Sessions Says He Has 'Serious Concerns' about Legal Marijuana: Now States Wonder What's Next." Los Angeles Times, August 9. Available at http:// www.latimes.com/nation/la-na-sessions-marijuana-20170809-story.html.

Angell, Tom. 2017. "Feds Scale Back Marijuana 'Addiction' and 'Overdose' Talk." Mass-Roots, August 28. Available at https://www.massroots.com/news/feds-scale-back -marijuana-addiction-and-overdose-talk.

Anslinger, Harry. 1943. "The Psychiatric Aspects of Marihuana Intoxication." Journal of the American Medical Association 121:212–213.

———. 1945. "More on Marihuana and Mayor LaGuardia's Committee Report." Journal of the American Medical Association 128:1187.

Are We Sure? n.d.a. "The Issue—RI." Available at https://arewesure.net/the-issue-ri (accessed June 18, 2018).

———. n.d.b. "The Issue—VT." Available at https://arewesure.net/the-issue-vt (accessed June 18, 2018).

Arit, John. 2015. "Marijuana Activists Cheer Michele Leonhart's Exit from the DEA." *Bloomberg*, April 21. Available at https://www.bloomberg.com/news/articles/2015 -04-22/marijuana-activists-cheer-michele-leonhart-s-exit-from-the-dea.

Armstrong, Marc. 2016. "Public Banks Could Break the Impasse over Marijuana Money." *Truthout*, August 24. Available at https://truthout.org/articles/public -banks-could-break-the-impasse-over-marijuana-money.

Associated Press. 2014. "Marijuana in California: Jerry Brown Opposes Legalization, Says 'We Need to Stay Alert.'" *Mercury News*, March 2. Available at https://www .mercurynews.com/2014/03/02/marijuana-in-california-jerry-brown-opposes -legalization-says-we-need-to-stay-alert.

Atakan, Zerrin. 2012. "Cannabis, a Complex Plant: Different Compounds and Different Effects on Individuals." *Therapeutic Advances in Psychopharmacology* 2:241– 254.

Atkins, Drew. 2017. "DEA's Marijuana-Eradication Program Still Targets Washington, Where (Some) Pot Is Legal." *Seattle Times*, January 7. Available at https://www .seattletimes.com/seattle-news/marijuana/deas-marijuana-eradication-program -still-targets-washington.

Auer, Reto, Eric Vittinghoff, Kristine Yaffe, Arnaud Künzi, Stefan G. Kertesz, Deborah A. Levine, Emiliano Albanese, et al. 2016. "Association between Lifetime Marijuana Use and Cognitive Function in Middle Age: The Coronary Artery Risk Development in Young Adults (CARDIA) Study." *JAMA Internal Medicine* 176:352–361.

Austen, Ian. 2015. "Justin Trudeau and the Liberal Party Prevail with Stunning Rout in Canada." *New York Times*, October 19. Available at https://www.nytimes.com/2015/ 10/20/world/americas/canada-election-stephen-harper-justin-trudeau.html.

Aydelotte, Jayson D., Lawrence H. Brown, Kevin M. Luftman, Alexandra L. Mardock, Pedro G. R. Teixeira, Ben Coopwood, and Carlos V. R. Brown. 2017. "Crash Fatality Rates after Recreational Marijuana Legalization in Washington and Colorado." *American Journal of Public Health* 107 (8): 1329–1331.

Baca, Ricardo. 2014. "See the Christmas Card the Marijuana Policy Project Sent to Maureen Dowd." *Denver Post*, December 24. Available at https://www.denverpost .com/2014/12/24/see-the-christmas-card-the-marijuana-policy-project-sent-to -maureen-dowd.

———. 2015a. "Cannabis Journalism: It's a Class You Can Now Take at University of Denver." *The Cannabist*, May 14. Available at https://www.thecannabist.co/2015/05/ 14/cannabis-journalism-marijuana-class-university-denver/34936.

———. 2015b. "Halloween 2015: Is Marijuana Candy Really a Concern for Trick-or-Treaters?" *The Cannabist*, October 19. Available at https://www.thecannabist.co/ 2015/10/19/halloween-marijuana-halloweed/42455.

———. 2015c. "House Passes Bill to Prevent DOJ from Interfering in States' Medical Pot Laws." *The Cannabist*, June 3. Available at https://www.thecannabist.co/2015/06/03/ house-medical-pot-marijuana/35704.

———. 2015d. "Roseanne Barr Is Going Blind, Using Pot to Relieve the 'Pressure in My Eyes.'" *The Cannabist*, April 23. Available at https://www.thecannabist.co/2015/04/ 23/roseanne-barr-blind-marijuana/34074.

———. 2015e. "Teen Pot Use: Colorado Leads U.S., but State's Youth Use Remains Unchanged." *The Cannabist*, December 21. Available at https://www.thecannabist.co/ 2015/12/21/teen-pot-use-colorado-marijuana/45367.

———. 2015f. "Top Federal Lawyer to SCOTUS: Reject Colorado Marijuana Suit." *The Cannabist*, December 16. Available at https://www.thecannabist.co/2015/12/16/us-government-colorado-marijuana-lawsuit-oklahoma-nebraska/45190.

———. 2016a. "Poll Shows Little Regret in Colorado over Legalizing Marijuana." *Denver Post*, September 20. Available at https://www.denverpost.com/2016/09/20/legalize-marijuana-poll.

———. 2016b. "Rescheduling Marijuana: The Good, the Bad, and the Ugly Unknowns of Schedule II." *The Cannabist*, June 27. Available at https://www.thecannabist.co/2016/06/27/rescheduling-marijuana-schedule-ii-cannabis/56769.

———. 2016c. "This Major Publisher of Travel Guides Now Includes Sections on Marijuana Tourism." *The Cannabist*, July 1. Available at https://www.thecannabist.co/2016/07/01/travel-guidebook-marijuana-denver-colorado/57450.

———. 2016d. "Willie Nelson Is Now Hiring Employees for His New Weed Company in Colorado." *The Cannabist*, June 20. Available at https://www.thecannabist.co/2016/06/20/willie-nelson-weed-hiring/56231.

———. 2017. "Op-Ed: Colorado Officials Should Speak Out on Fake Marijuana Data Used by Feds." *The Cannabist*, August 21. Available at https://www.thecannabist.co/2017/08/21/marijuana-data-jeff-sessions-federal-hidta-reports/86449.

Bachhuber, Marcus, Brendan Saloner, Chinazo Cunningham, and Colleen Barry. 2014. "Medical Cannabis Laws and Opioid Analgesic Overdose Mortality in the United States, 1990–2010." *JAMA Internal Medicine* 174:1668–1673.

Bailey, Everton. 2015. "Marijuana-Sniffing Dogs on the Way Out for Some Oregon Police Agencies as Pot Legalization Kicks In." *The Oregonian*, January 31. Available at https://www.oregonlive.com/pacific-northwest-news/index.ssf/2015/01/marijuana-sniffing_dogs_on_way.html.

Baker, Charlie, Maura Healey, and Martin Walsh. 2016. "Mass. Should Not Legalize Marijuana." *Boston Globe*, March 4. Available at https://www.bostonglobe.com/opinion/editorials/2016/03/04/mass-should-not-legalize-marijuana/njYep84wtERutHNIHByu4J/story.html.

Baker, Mike. 2011. "States Reassess Marijuana Laws after Fed Warnings." *Associated Press*, May 3. Available at http://archive.boston.com/news/local/rhode_island/articles/2011/05/03/states_reassess_marijuana_laws_after_fed_warnings.

Baker, Russ. 2002. "George Soros's Long Strange Trip." In *Busted*, edited by Mike Gray, 51–61. New York: Thunder's Mouth Press.

Balko, Radley. 2014a. "Colorado's Poster Boy for 'Stoned Driving' Was Drunk off His Gourd." *Washington Post*, June 6. Available at https://www.washingtonpost.com/news/the-watch/wp/2014/06/06/colorados-poster-boy-for-stoned-driving-was-drunk-off-his-gourd.

———. 2014b. "The Drug War's Profit Motive." *Washington Post*, February 17. Available at https://www.washingtonpost.com/news/the-watch/wp/2014/02/17/the-drug-wars-profit-motive.

Barcott, Bruce. 2015. *Weed the People: The Future of Legal Marijuana in America*. New York: Time Books.

———. 2017. "First Cannabis Ad Runs on CNN, Fox News, and MSNBC." *Leafly*, September 9. Available at https://www.leafly.com/news/politics/first-cannabis-ad-runs-on-cnn-fox-news-and-msnbc.

———. 2018. "Jim Carroll Tapped as Trump's Drug Czar." *Leafly*, February 9. Available at https://www.leafly.com/news/politics/jim-carroll-tapped-as-trumps-drug-czar.

Barcott, Bruce, and Michael Scherer. 2015. "The Great Pot Experiment." *Time*, May 14. Available at http://time.com/3858353/the-great-pot-experiment.

Barrus, Daniel G., Kristen L. Capogrossi, Sheryl C. Cates, Camille K. Gourdet, Nicholas C. Peiper, Scott P. Novak, Timothy W. Lefever, and Jenny L. Wiley. 2016. "Tasty THC: Promises and Challenges of Cannabis Edibles." *Methods Report (RIT Press)*, November. Available at https://www.ncbi.nlm.nih.gov/pmc/articles/PMC5260817.

Baum, Dan. 2016. "Legalize It All: How to Win the War on Drugs." *Harper's Magazine*, April. Available at https://harpers.org/archive/2016/04/legalize-it-all.

Bava, Sunita, Joanna Jacobus, Rachel E. Thayer, and Susan F. Tapert. 2013. "Longitudinal Changes in White Matter Integrity among Adolescent Substance Users." *Alcoholism: Clinical and Experimental Research* 37:E181–189.

Bealum, Ngaio. 2015. "Stoned Rabbits Are the Anti-marijuana Movement's Weakest Ploy Yet." *The Guardian*, March 3. Available at https://www.theguardian.com/commentisfree/2015/mar/03/marijuana-stoned-rabbits-utah-weakest-ploy-yet-legal-weed.

Becker, Howard. 1963. *Outsiders: Studies in the Sociology of Deviance*. New York: Free Press.

Beckett, Lois. 2017. "How Jeff Sessions and Donald Trump Have Restarted the War on Drugs." *The Guardian*, August 21. Available at https://www.theguardian.com/us-news/2017/aug/21/donald-trump-jeff-sessions-war-on-drugs.

Bell, Karissa. 2015. "High There Is a Dating App for Pot Smokers." *Mashable*, February 5. Available at https://mashable.com/2015/02/05/high-there-app/#rCB.89sOdmqo.

Belville, Russ. 2013. "Project SAM's Kevin Sabet Claims 39% Washington Teens Use Dispensary Pot, Reality Is 9.4%." *Huffington Post*, May 24. Available at https://www.huffingtonpost.com/russ-belville/project-sams-kevin-sabet-_b_3328352.html.

———. 2014. "11 U.S. Presidents Who Smoked Marijuana." *High Times*, February 17. Available at https://hightimes.com/culture/11-us-presidents-who-smoked-marijuana.

———. 2015. "Kevin Sabet Is Misleading You Again about Marijuana Legalization." *Huffington Post*, September 24. Available at https://www.huffingtonpost.com/russ-belville/kevin-sabet-is-misleading_b_8192098.html.

Bennett, Jessica. 2014. "'Vape' Joins Pot Lingo as Oxford's Word of the Year." *New York Times*, November 21. Available at https://www.nytimes.com/2014/11/23/fashion/vape-joins-pot-lingo-as-oxfords-word-of-the-year.html.

Bennett, Sukee, and Aylin Y. Woodward. 2017. "Study Says Marijuana Users at Increased Risk of Stroke, Heart Failure." *The Cannabist*, March 16. Available at https://www.thecannabist.co/2017/03/16/marijuana-health-effects-stroke-heart-failure-risk/75663.

Bennett, William, and John Walters. 1996. "Medical Reefer Madness." *Weekly Standard*, December 8. Available at https://www.weeklystandard.com/william-j-bennett-and-john-p-walters/medical-reefer-madness.

Bennett, William, and Robert White. 2015. *Going to Pot: Why the Rush to Legalize Marijuana Is Harming America*. New York: Center Street.

Benson, Kate. 2008. "Dope Smokers Not So Mellow." *Sydney Morning Herald*, July 30. Available at https://www.smh.com.au/news/health/dope-smokers-not-so-mellow-any-more/2008/07/29/1217097241179.html.

Berenson, Tessa. 2017. "How Jeff Sessions Could Crack Down on Legal Marijuana (and Why He Might Not)." *Time*, July 27. Available at http://time.com/4876286/jeff-sessions-legal-marijuana.

Berg, Sven. 2017. "Legal Weed, Idaho Consumers Breathe Life into Tiny Oregon Town, Irk Otter." *Idaho Statesman*, March 4. Available at http://www.idahostatesman.com/news/local/article136552113.html.

Berke, Jeremy. 2018. "California's Cannabis Market Is Expected to Soar to $5.1 Billion—and It's Going to Be Bigger Than Beer." *Business Insider*, February 28. Available at http://www.businessinsider.com/california-legalizing-weed-on-january-1-market-size-revenue-2017-12.

Bertram, Eva, Morris Blachman, Kenneth Sharpe, and Peter Andreas. 1996. *Drug War Politics: The Price of Denial.* Berkeley: University of California Press.

Bess, Gabby. 2015. "Why Is This Pipe Also a Dildo?" *Broadly*, October 20. Available at https://broadly.vice.com/en_us/article/d3ggq7/hey-why-is-this-pipe-also-a-dildo.

Bewley-Taylor, Dave, Tom Blickman, and Martin Jelsma. 2014. *The Rise and Decline of Cannabis Prohibition.* Swansea, UK: Global Drug Policy Observatory.

Biello, David. 2006. "Large Study Finds No Link between Marijuana and Lung Cancer." *Scientific American*, May 24. Available at https://www.scientificamerican.com/article/large-study-finds-no-link.

Bienenstock, David. 2014. "Maureen Dowd Freaked Out on Weed Chocolate Because She's Stupid." *Vice*, June 5. Available at https://www.vice.com/en_us/article/yvqbav/maureen-dowd-freaked-out-on-weed-chocolate-because-shes-stupid.

Blickman, Tom, and Martin Jelsma. 2009. *Drug Policy Reform in Practice.* Amsterdam: Transnational Institute.

Blood, Michael R., and Paul Elias. 2017. "California Police Not Down with Gov. Brown's Marijuana Plan." *The Cannabist*, April 6. Available at https://www.thecannabist.co/2017/04/06/california-marijuana-regulations-recreational-police/76761.

Bohrer, Becky. 2015. "Alaska First State to OK Option for Social Pot Use." *The Cannabist*, November 19. Available at https://www.thecannabist.co/2015/11/19/alaska-marijuana-regulations-edibles-social-pot-use/44104.

Bohrer, Becky, and Mark Thiessen. 2016. "Alaska on Track to Be First State to Allow Toking in Pot Shops." *The Cannabist*, April 28. Available at https://www.thecannabist.co/2016/04/28/alaska-pot-shops-onsite-consumption/52973.

———. 2017. "Alaska Marijuana Board Rejects Onsite Use at Retail Shops." *The Cannabist*, February 2. Available at https://www.thecannabist.co/2017/02/02/alaska-marijuana-onsite-consumption/72905.

Bond, Bradley, and Benjamin Compton. 2015. "Gay On-Screen: The Relationship between Exposure to Gay Characters on Television and Heterosexual Audiences' Endorsement of Gay Equality." *Journal of Broadcasting and Electronic Media* 59:717–732.

Bonn-Miller, Marcel O., and Glenna S. Rousseau. 2017. "Marijuana Use and PTSD among Veterans." National Center for PTSD, May 10. Available at https://www.ptsd.va.gov/professional/co-occurring/marijuana_use_ptsd_veterans.asp.

Borchardt, Debra. 2017. "Marijuana Industry Projected to Create More Jobs Than Manufacturing by 2020." *Forbes*, February 22. Available at https://www.forbes.com/sites/debraborchardt/2017/02/22/marijuana-industry-projected-to-create-more-jobs-than-manufacturing-by-2020.

Bostwick, J. Michael. 2012. "Medicinal Use of Marijuana." *New England Journal of Medicine* 368:866–867.

Boudreau, Craig. 2016. "Colorado City Bans Marijuana Sales, Then Votes to Allow Pot Shops." *Daily Caller*, August 24. Available at http://dailycaller.com/2016/08/24/colorado-city-bans-marijuana-sales-then-votes-to-allow-pot-shops.

Bouquet, J. 1944. "Marihuana Intoxication." *Journal of the American Medical Association* 124:1010–1011.

Bowman, Karl. 1944. "Psychiatric Aspects of Marijuana Intoxication." *Journal of the American Medical Association* 125:376.

Bradford, Ashley, and W. David Bradford. 2016. "Medical Marijuana Laws Reduce Prescription Medication Use in Medicare Part D." *Health Affairs* 35 (7): 1230–1236.

Brandeis, Jason. 2012. "The Continuing Vitality of *Ravin v. The State*: Alaskans Still Have a Constitutional Right to Possess Marijuana in Their Homes." *Alaska Law Review* 29:175–236.

Brecher, Edward. 1972. *Licit and Illicit Drugs*. Boston: Little, Brown.

Bringetto, Christina. 2016. "Weed Recipes: Top 10 Best Cannabis Cookbooks." *Heavy*, June 30. Available at https://heavy.com/marijuana/2016/06/weed-recipes-top-10 -best-cannabis-cookbooks.

Britton, John. 2017. "Death, Disease and Tobacco." *The Lancet* 389:1861–1862.

Bromberg, Walter. 1939. "Marihuana: A Psychiatric Study." *Journal of the American Medical Association* 113:4–12.

Brown, Jim. 2003. "Martin to Roll Out His Own Pot Bill." International Hempology 101 Society, December 18. Available at http://www.hempology.ca/2003/12/18/martin-to -roll-his-own-pot-bill.

Brown, Kate. 2017. Letter to Attorney General Jeff Sessions. August 22. Available at https://s3.amazonaws.com/big.assets.huffingtonpost.com/OregonResponseTo Sessions.pdf.

Brown, Kate, John Hickenlooper, Jay Inslee, and Bill Walker. 2017. Letter to Attorney General Jeff Sessions and Secretary Steve Mnuchin. April 3. Available at https:// www.thecannabist.co/2017/08/17/jeff-sessions-letters-marijuana-policy-alaska -colorado-oregon-washington/86246.

Brulliard, Karin. 2016. "What Happens When Animals Get into Your Weed Stash?" *The Cannabist*, October 31. Available at https://www.thecannabist.co/2016/10/31/pets -marijuana-accidental-ingestion/66439.

Buckley, William. 1996. "The War on Drugs Is Lost." *National Review*, February 12. Available at https://www.nationalreview.com/2014/07/war-drugs-lost-nro-staff.

Bureau of Justice Statistics. 2010. "Alcohol and Crime: Data from 2002 to 2008." Available at https://www.bjs.gov/content/acf/ac_conclusion.cfm.

Burke, Caitlin. 2017. "New Study Links Marijuana Usage to Decreased Academic Success." *CBN News*, July 28. Available at http://www1.cbn.com/cbnnews/us/2017/july/ new-study-links-marijuana-usage-to-decreased-academic-success.

Burke, Jill. 2010. "Irwin Ravin, Alaska Marijuana Activist, Dies." *Anchorage Daily News*, April 12. Available at https://www.adn.com/alaska-news/article/irwin-ravin-alaska -marijuana-rights-activist-dies/2010/04/13.

Bush, Evan. 2015a. "Bill Aims to Simplify Taxes on Pot Businesses." *Seattle Times*, January 21. Available at http://old.seattletimes.com/html/localnews/2025515369 _pottax1xml.html.

———. 2015b. "Day-Tripping Pot-Tour Startups See Wine-Industry Future." *Seattle Times*, February 28. Available at https://www.seattletimes.com/seattle-news/day -tripping-pot-tour-startups-see-wine-industry-future.

———. 2015c. "Pot of Gold: The New Legal Marijuana Business Has Created a Once-in-a-Lifetime Opportunities." *Seattle Times*, July 16. Available at https://www .seattletimes.com/pacific-nw-magazine/pot-of-gold-the-new-legal-marijuana -business-has-created-once-in-a-lifetime-opportunities.

Bush, George H. W. 1989. "Address to the Nation on the National Drug Control Strategy." September 5. Available at http://www.presidency.ucsb.edu/ws/?pid=17472.

Bush, George W. 2002. "Remarks on the 2002 National Drug Control Strategy." February 12. Available at https://www.gpo.gov/fdsys/pkg/WCPD-2002-02-18/pdf/WCPD-2002-02-18-Pg220.pdf.

Calabria, Bianca, Louisa Degenhardt, Wayne Hall, and Michael Lynskey. 2010. "Does Cannabis Use Increase the Risk of Death? Systematic Review of Epidemiological Evidence on the Adverse Effects of Cannabis Use." *Drug and Alcohol Review* 29:318–330.

Calabria, Stephen. 2016. "Law of the Land: Recreational Cannabis in Washington, D.C." *Herb*, November 1. Available at https://herb.co/marijuana/news/law-land-washington-dc.

California Medical Association. 2011. "Cannabis and the Regulatory Void." Available at https://www.cmanet.org/files/pdf/news/cma-cannabis-tac-white-paper-101411.pdf.

———. 2016. "CA Medical Association Announces Support for Responsible Marijuana Ballot Initiative." Available at http://www.cmanet.org/news/press-detail/?article=ca-medical-association-announces-support-for.

Camden, Jim. 2015. "State Could Get 222 More Pot Stores." *Spokesman-Review*, December 16. Available at http://www.spokesman.com/stories/2015/dec/16/state-could-get-222-more-pot-stores.

———. 2016. "Pot Store Employees Can Receive Tips, Board Says." *Spokesman-Review*, March 15. Available at http://www.spokesman.com/stories/2016/mar/15/pot-store-employees-in-washington-can-receive-tips.

———. 2017. "Washington Could Crack Down on Pot Shop Advertising." *Spokesman-Review*, April 21. Available at http://www.spokesman.com/stories/2017/apr/21/washington-could-crack-down-on-pot-shop-advertisin.

Cami, Jordi, and Magi Farre. 2003. "Drug Addiction." *New England Journal of Medicine* 349:975–986.

Cannabis Training University. n.d. "About Us." Available at https://www.cannabistraininguniversity.com/about-ctu.

Cano, Regina Garcia, and Scott Sonner. 2017. "Here's What's Legal—and What's Not—in Nevada as Recreational Weed Sales Begin." *The Cannabist*, June 30. Available at https://www.thecannabist.co/2017/06/30/nevada-marijuana-laws-las-vegas/82792.

Carson, Rob. 2012. "Washington's Marijuana Legalization Measure Creates Strange Bedfellows." *Governing*, October 15. Available at http://www.governing.com/news/state/Washingtons-Marijuana-Legalization-Measure-Creates-Strange-Bedfellows.html.

Carter, Jimmy. 1977. "Drug Abuse Message to Congress." August 2. Available at http://www.presidency.ucsb.edu/ws/?pid=7908.

Carvajal, Nikki, and Sidney Sullivan. 2018. "Map: See Where Legal Marijuana Is Sold around Alaska." *KTUU*, April 5. Available at http://www.ktuu.com/content/news/MAP-Where-legal-marijuana-sales-are-coming-and-how-soon-they-could-be-here-395195701.html.

Casarett, David. 2015. *Stoned: A Doctor's Case for Medical Marijuana*. New York: Current.

Castelli, M. Paola, Camilla Madeddu, Alberto Casti, Angelo Casu, Paola Casti, Maria Scherma, Liana Fattore, Paola Fadda, and M. Grazia Ennas. 2014. "Delta-9 Tetrahydrocannabinol Prevents Methamphetamine-Induced Neurotoxicity." *PLOS One*,

May 20. Available at http://journals.plos.org/plosone/article?id=10.1371/journal .pone.0098079.

Caulkins, Jonathan. 2016. "The Real Dangers of Marijuana." *National Affairs*, Winter. Available at https://www.nationalaffairs.com/publications/detail/the-real-dangers -of-marijuana.

Centers for Disease Control and Prevention. 2009. "Health-Risk Behaviors and Academic Achievement." Available at https://www.cdc.gov/healthyyouth/health_and _academics/pdf/health_risk_behaviors.pdf.

———. 2015. "Alcohol Poisoning Deaths." Available at https://www.cdc.gov/vitalsigns/ alcohol-poisoning-deaths/index.html.

———. 2016. "Alcohol Use and Your Health." Available at https://www.cdc.gov/alcohol/ pdfs/alcoholyourhealth.pdf.

———. 2017a. "Drug Overdose Death Data." Available at https://www.cdc.gov/ drugoverdose/data/statedeaths.html.

———. 2017b. "Impaired Driving: Get the Facts." Available at https://www.cdc.gov/ motorvehiclesafety/impaired_driving/impaired-drv_factsheet.html.

Cerda, Magdalena, Melanie Wall, and Tianshu Feng. 2017. "Association of State Recreational Marijuana Laws with Adolescent Marijuana Use." *JAMA Pediatrics* 171 (2): 142–149. Available at http://jamanetwork.com/journals/jamapediatrics/article -abstract/2593707.

Chatwin, Caroline. 2003. "Drug Policy Developments within the European Union." *British Journal of Criminology* 43:567–582.

Cher, Ladan. 2016. "Uruguay's Half-Baked Marijuana Experiment." *Foreign Policy*, March 21. Available at http://foreignpolicy.com/2016/03/21/uruguay-marijuana -legalization.

Chokshi, Niraj. 2015. "Alaska Legalizes Marijuana Today: Here's How Its Law Compares to All the Others." *Washington Post*, February 24. Available at https://www .washingtonpost.com/blogs/govbeat/wp/2015/02/24/alaska-legalizes-marijuana -today-heres-how-its-law-compares-to-all-the-others.

Choo, Esther, Madeline Benz, Nikolas Zaller, Otis Warren, Kristin L. Rising, and K. John McConnell. 2014. "The Impact of State Medical Marijuana Legislation on Adolescent Marijuana Use." *Journal of Adolescent Health* 55:160–166.

Clarke, Thomas H. 2013. "Vermont Marijuana Decriminalization Law Takes Effect Monday." *Daily Chronic*, June 29. Available at http://www.thedailychronic.net/2013/ 24232/vermont-marijuana-decriminalization-law-takes-effect-monday.

Clemency Report. 2015. "Fifty-Four Marijuana Offenders Given Federal Life Sentences since 1996." Previously available at http://www.clemencyreport.org/fifty-four -marijuana-offenders-given-federal-life-sentences-since-1996.

Cohen, Peter. 1994. "The Case of the Two Dutch Drug Policy Commissions: An Exercise in Harm Reduction, 1968–1976." Paper presented at the 5th International Conference on the Reduction of Drug Related Harm, March 7–11. Available at http://www .cedro-uva.org/lib/cohen.case.html.

Cole, James. 2013. "Memorandum for All United States Attorneys." Available at https:// www.justice.gov/iso/opa/resources/3052013829132756857467.pdf.

Coll, Steve. 2017. "Trump's Intervention." *New Yorker*, April 17, p. 19.

Colorado Department of Public Safety. 2016. *Marijuana Legalization in Colorado: Early Findings*. Denver: Colorado Department of Public Safety.

Colorado Department of Revenue. 2018. "Marijuana Tax Data." Available at https://www .colorado.gov/pacific/revenue/colorado-marijuana-tax-data.

Columbian. 2014. "Marijuana for Sale." July 17, p A6.

———. 2017. "In Our View: Sessions Off Base on Pot." August 18. Available at http://www.columbian.com/news/2017/aug/18/in-our-view-sessions-off-base-on-pot.

Commonwealth of Australia. 1977. *Drug Problems in Australia: An Intoxicated Society? Report from the Senate Standing Committee on Social Welfare.* Canberra: Australian Government Printing Service.

Compton, Richard. 2017. "Marijuana-Impaired Driving: A Report to Congress." Available at https://www.nhtsa.gov/sites/nhtsa.dot.gov/files/documents/812440-marijuana-impaired-driving-report-to-congress.pdf.

Compton, Richard, and Amy Berning. 2015. *Drugs and Alcohol Crash Risk.* Washington, DC: U.S. Department of Transportation.

Cooper, Michael. 2011. "2 Governors Asking U.S. to Ease Rules on Marijuana to Allow for Its Medical Use." *New York Times,* November 30. Available at https://www.nytimes.com/2011/12/01/us/federal-marijuana-classification-should-change-gregoire-and-chafee-say.html.

Corbyn, Zoe. 2015. "Dreaming of the Billion-Dollar High in California's Marijuana Green Rush." *The Guardian,* November 6. Available at https://www.theguardian.com/society/2015/nov/06/california-marijuana-green-rush-billion-dollar-high.

Coughlin-Bogue, Tobias. 2017. "Washington's Legal Pot Experiment: Can It Survive Trump?" *Crosscut,* March 17. Available at http://features.crosscut.com/legal-marijuana-trump-sessions-enforcement.

Crombie, Noelle. 2015. "Eastern Oregon Residents Didn't Vote for Legal Marijuana, Urge OLCC to Keep a Tight Rein." *The Oregonian,* January 23.Available at https://www.oregonlive.com/marijuana/index.ssf/2015/01/eastern_oregon_residents_didnt.html.

———. 2016a. "In a First, Oregon State Fair to Feature Marijuana Plants." *The Oregonian,* July 27. Available at https://www.oregonlive.com/marijuana/index.ssf/2016/07/in_a_first_oregon_state_fair_t.html.

———. 2016b. "No More 'Girl Scout Cookies,' Other Popular Names on Pot Packaging, State Says." *The Oregonian,* September 30. Available at https://www.oregonlive.com/marijuana/index.ssf/2016/09/worried_about_pots_appeal_to_k.html.

———. 2016c. "Oregon Collects $3.48 Million in Revenue from First Month of Taxed Recreational Marijuana Sales." *The Oregonian,* March 17. Available at https://www.oregonlive.com/marijuana/index.ssf/2016/03/first_month_of_taxed_recreatio.html.

———. 2017a. "Big Change: Medical Marijuana Dispensaries No Longer Selling Rec Pot." *The Oregonian,* January 9. Available at https://www.oregonlive.com/marijuana/index.ssf/2017/01/oregon_reaches_another_pot_mil.html.

———. 2017b. "Gov. Brown Mounts Vigorous Defense of Legal Pot in Oregon." *The Oregonian,* August 22. Available at https://www.oregonlive.com/marijuana/index.ssf/2017/08/gov_kate_brown_blasts_oregon_s.html.

———. 2017c. "Oregon Pays Out $85 Million in Pot Taxes to School Fund, Cops, Other Services." *The Oregonian,* October 6. Available at https://www.oregonlive.com/marijuana/index.ssf/2017/10/oregon_pays_out_85_million_in_1.html.

Cruz, Jose, Rosario Queirolo, and Maria Boidi. 2016. "Determinants of Public Support for Marijuana Legalization in Uruguay, the United States, and El Salvador." *Journal of Drug Issues* 46 (4): 1–18.

Daily Kos. 2007. "Pot Smoking Presidents Sons and the Not So Radical Politics of Legalized Marijuana." November 27. Available at https://www.dailykos.com/stories/2007/11/27/414565/-.

Daley, Haven. 2016. "Bench Press Your Bong: World's First Cannabis Gym Opening." *The Cannabist*, July 7. Available at https://www.thecannabist.co/2016/07/07/marijuana-exercise-gym/57725.

D'Angelo, Steve. 2015. *The Cannabis Manifesto*. Berkeley, CA: North Atlantic Books.

Darnell, A. J., and K. Bitney. 2017. "I-502 Evaluation and Benefit-Cost Analysis: Second Required Report." Washington State Institute for Public Policy, September. Available at http://www.wsipp.wa.gov/ReportFile/1670/Wsipp_I-502-Evaluation-and-Benefit-Cost-Analysis-Second-Required-Report_Report.pdf.

Davenport-Hines, Richard. 2001. *The Pursuit of Oblivion: A Global History of Narcotics*. London: Weidenfeld and Nicholson.

Davies, Jag. 2015. "U.S. Surgeon General Says 'Marijuana Can Be Helpful.'" Drug Policy Alliance, February 3. Available at http://www.drugpolicy.org/blog/us-surgeon-general-says-marijuana-can-be-helpful.

Davis, Aaron C. 2016. "Stark Racial Divide Remains in Pot Arrests in D.C." *Washington Post*, April 5. Available at https://www.washingtonpost.com/local/dc-politics/stark-racial-divide-remains-in-pot-arrests-in-dc/2016/04/05/775594b0-fa7f-11e5-80e4-c381214de1a3_story.html.

Davis, Julie Hirschfeld. 2015. "Michelle Leonhart, Head of D.E.A., to Retire over Handling of Sex Scandal." *New York Times*, April 21. Available at https://www.nytimes.com/2015/04/22/us/michele-leonhart-top-dea-official-is-expected-to-resign.html.

Deam, Jenny. 2014. "Student's Death in Colorado Raises Questions on Pot and Health." *Los Angeles Times*, April 7. Available at http://www.latimes.com/nation/la-na-colorado-pot-woes-20140407-story.html.

Debolt, David. 2017. "Oakland Reserves Marijuana Biz Permits for People Who Served Time for Weed." *The Cannabist*, March 9. Available at https://www.thecannabist.co/2017/03/09/oakland-marijuana-business-permits-convictions/75252.

Degenhardt, Louisa, Harvey A. Whiteford, Alize J. Ferrari, Amanda J. Baxter, Fionna J. Charlson, Wayne D. Hall, Greg Freedman, et al. 2013. "Global Burden of Disease Attributable to Illicit Drug Use and Dependence: Findings from the Global Burden of Disease Study 2010." *The Lancet* 382:1564–1574.

Denver Post. 2012. "Amendment 64—Legalize Marijuana Election Results." Available at http://data.denverpost.com/election/results/amendment/2012/64-legalize-marijuana.

Devaney, Tim. 2015. "Most Young Republicans Support Legalizing Pot." *The Hill*, March 2. Available at http://thehill.com/regulation/234321-most-young-republicans-support-marijuana-legalization.

Devinsky, Orrin, J. Helen Cross, Linda Laux, Eric Marsh, Ian Miller, Rima Nabbout, Ingrid E. Scheffer, Elizabeth A. Thiele, and Stephen Wright. 2017. "Trial of Cannabidiol for Drug-Resistant Seizures in the Dravet Syndrome." *New England Journal of Medicine* 376:2011–2020.

Dickinson, Tim. 2012. "The Next Seven States to Legalize Pot." *Rolling Stone*, December 18. Available at https://www.rollingstone.com/politics/politics-news/the-next-seven-states-to-legalize-pot-113828.

———. 2013. "Ethan Nadelmann: The Real Drug Czar." *Rolling Stone*, June 6. Available at https://www.rollingstone.com/culture/culture-news/ethan-nadelmann-the-real-drug-czar-92837.

———. 2016. "Why America Can't Quit the Drug War." *Rolling Stone*, May 5. Available at https://www.rollingstone.com/culture/culture-news/why-america-cant-quit-the-drug-war-47203.

Dilley, J., L. Hitchcock, N. McGroder, L. A. Greto, and S. M. Richardson. 2017. "Community-Level Responses to State Marijuana Legalization in Washington State." *International Journal of Drug Policy* 42:102–108.

Dills, Angela, Sieste Goffard, and Jeffrey Miron. 2016. "Dose of Reality: The Effect of State Marijuana Legalizations." Cato Institute Policy Analysis no. 799. Available at https://www.cato.org/publications/policy-analysis/dose-reality-effect-state-marijuana-legalizations.

Dischner, Molly. 2015. "Alaskans Join Ranks of Americans with Legal Recreational Marijuana." *SeattlePI*, February 23. Available at https://blog.seattlepi.com/marijuana/2015/02/23/alaskans-join-ranks-of-americans-with-legal-recreational-marijuana.

Dorris, Jennie. 2016. "Marijuana: Past, Present, Future." *Carnegie Mellon Today*, February 22. Available at https://www.cmu.edu/cmtoday/artsculture_publicpolicy/effects-marijuana-legalization-policy.

Dowd, Maureen. 2014. "Don't Harsh Our Mellow, Dude." *New York Times*, June 3. Available at https://www.nytimes.com/2014/06/04/opinion/dowd-dont-harsh-our-mellow-dude.html.

Downs, David. 2015. "Morgan Freeman: Only Pot Cures My Pain." *Seattle Post-Intelligencer*, May 10. Available at https://blog.seattlepi.com/marijuana/2015/05/10/morgan-freeman-only-pot-cures-my-pain.

———. 2016a. "DEA's Pot Ruling Slammed by Lawmakers, Doctors, Advocates." *San Francisco Chronicle*, August 15. Available at https://blog.sfgate.com/smellthetruth/2016/08/15/deas-pot-ruling-slammed-by-lawmakers-doctors-advocates.

———. 2016b. "Major Victory: Feds Drop Case against Harborside Health Center." *East Bay Express*, May 3. Available at https://www.eastbayexpress.com/LegalizationNation/archives/2016/05/03/major-victory-feds-drop-case-against-harborside-health-center.

Dravet Syndrome Foundation. n.d. "What Is Dravet Syndrome?" Available at https://www.dravetfoundation.org/what-is-dravet-syndrome.

Drug Enforcement Administration. n.d. "DEA History." Available at https://www.dea.gov/about/history.shtml.

———. 2005. "Drugs of Abuse." Available at https://www.naabt.org/documents/Drugs%20of%20abuse%20DEA.pdf.

———. 2014. "The Dangers and Consequences of Marijuana Abuse." Available at https://www.getsmartaboutdrugs.gov/sites/getsmartaboutdrugs.com/files/publications/The_Dangers_and_Consequences_of_Marijuana_Abuse%20May2014_Accessible%20version.pdf.

———. 2016. "Residential Marijuana Grows in Colorado: The New Meth Houses?" Available at https://www.dea.gov/divisions/den/2016/den062216.pdf.

———. 2017. "Drugs of Abuse." Available at https://www.dea.gov/pr/multimedia-library/publications/drug_of_abuse.pdf.

Drug Policy Alliance. n.d. "A Brief History of the Drug War." Available at http://www.drugpolicy.org/issues/brief-history-drug-war.

———. 2013. "Removing Marijuana from the Controlled Substances Act." Available at https://www.drugpolicy.org/sites/default/files/DPA_Fact%20sheet_Marijuana%20Reclassification_May%202013.pdf.

———. 2014a. "Annual Report." Available at http://www.drugpolicy.org/sites/default/files/DPA_Annual_Report_2014_0.PDF.

———. 2014b. "The DEA: Four Decades of Impeding and Rejecting Science." June 9. Available at http://www.drugpolicy.org/sites/default/files/DPA-MAPS_DEA_Science _Final.pdf.

———. 2014c. "Race, Class and Marijuana Arrests in Mayor DeBlasio's Two New Yorks." Available at http://www.drugpolicy.org/resource/race-class-and-marijuana-arrests -mayor-de-blasios-two-new-yorks-nypds-marijuana-arrest.

———. 2016a. "Marijuana Facts." Available at https://www.drugpolicy.org/sites/default/ files/DPA_Marijuana_Facts_Booklet.pdf.

———. 2016b. "So Far, So Good: What We Know about Marijuana Legalization in Colorado, Washington, Alaska, Oregon, and Washington, D.C." Available at http:// www.drugpolicy.org/news/2016/10/so-far-so-good-what-we-know-about -marijuana-legalization-colorado-washington-alaska-ore.

Drug Policy Alliance and Marijuana Arrest Research Project. 2017. "Unjust and Unconstitutional: 60,000 Jim Crow Marijuana Arrests in Mayor de Blasio's New York." Available at http://www.drugpolicy.org/sites/default/files/Marijuana-Arrests-NYC --Unjust-Unconstitutional--July2017_2.pdf.

Druzin, Randi. 2017. "The Ontario Proposition: Details and Feedback from the Scene." *Leafly*, September 8. Available at https://www.leafly.com/news/politics/the-ontario -proposition-details-and-feedback-from-the-scene.

D'Souza, Deepak Cyril, Jose A. Cortes-Briones, Mohini Ranganathan, Halle Thurnauer, Gina Creatura, Toral Surti, Beta Planeta, et al. 2016. "Rapid Changes in CB1 Receptor Availability in Cannabis Dependent Males after Abstinence from Cannabis." *Biological Psychiatry* 1:6–67.

Dumcius, Gintautas. 2018a. "Massachusetts Marijuana Retail Shops in These Three Towns Up for State Approval This Week." *MassLive*, August 7. Available at https://www .masslive.com/news/index.ssf/2018/08/massachusetts_marijuana_retail_2.html.

———. 2018b. "When Can You Legally Buy Marijuana in Massachusetts? Here's the Timeline." *MassLive*, January 17. Available at https://www.masslive.com/news/ index.ssf/2018/01/when_can_people_in_massachuset.html.

DuPont, Robert L. 2016. "Marijuana Has Proven to Be a Gateway Drug." *New York Times*, April 26. Available at https://www.nytimes.com/roomfordebate/2016/04/26/ is-marijuana-a-gateway-drug/marijuana-has-proven-to-be-a-gateway-drug.

Dyer, Trey. 2018. "The Democratic Party Policies on Substance Abuse." *DrugRehab.com*, May 30. Available at https://www.drugrehab.com/featured/democrats-substance -abuse-policies.

Earleywine, Mitch. 2002. *Understanding Marijuana: A New Look at the Scientific Evidence*. New York: Oxford University Press.

———. 2004. "Gateway Beliefs Wreck Drug Abuse Prevention." In *Addiction: Opposing Viewpoints*, edited by Louise I. Gerdes, 74–77. London: Thomson Gale.

Eason, Brian. 2017. "Colorado House OKs Efforts to Crack Down on Illegal Marijuana." *The Cannabist*, March 13. Available at https://www.thecannabist.co/2017/03/13/ colorado-illegal-marijuana-crackdown/75462.

Eddy, Mark. 2010. "Medical Marijuana: Review and Analysis of Federal and State Policies." *Congressional Research Service*, April 2. Available at https://fas.org/sgp/crs/ misc/RL33211.pdf.

Edge, Megan, and Laurel Andrews. 2014. "Timeline: Notable Moments in 40 Years of Alaska's History with Marijuana." *Anchorage Daily News*, April 13. Available at https://www.adn.com/cannabis-north/article/alaska-weed-history/2014/04/14.

Egan, Timothy. 2010. "Reefer Gladness." *New York Times*, September 29. Available at https://opinionator.blogs.nytimes.com/2010/09/29/reefer-gladness.

Egelko, Bob. 2011. "Is Obama Changing His Tune on Marijuana?" *Cannabis Culture*, July 6. Available at https://www.cannabisculture.com/content/2011/07/06/obama-changing-his-tune-marijuana.

———. 2015. "Justice Dept. Memo Lets Feds Shut Down Pot Dispensaries." *San Francisco Chronicle*, August 5. Available at https://www.sfgate.com/nation/article/Justice-Dept-memo-lets-feds-shut-down-pot-6427452.php.

Elkins, Chris. 2018. "The Republican Party Policies on Substance Abuse." *DrugRehab.com*, May 30. Available at https://www.drugrehab.com/featured/republicans-substance-abuse-policies.

Ellis, Ronald J., Will Toperoff, Florin Vaida, Geoffrey van den Brande, James D. Gonzales, Ben D. Gouaux, Heather Bentley, and Joseph Hampton Atkinson. 2009. "Smoked Medical Cannabis for Neuropathic Pain in HIV: A Randomized, Crossover Clinical Trial." *Neuropsychopharmacology* 34:672–680.

Ellison, Jake. 2013. "Is This How the Feds Might Fight State's Marijuana Market?" *Seattle Post-Intelligencer*, June 2. Available at https://blog.seattlepi.com/marijuana/2013/06/02/dea-letters-is-this-how-the-feds-might-fight-states-marijuana-market.

———. 2014a. "Marijuana: What's Law Enforcement Actually Grousing about in Washington?" *Seattle Post-Intelligencer*, June 19. Available at https://blog.seattlepi.com/marijuana/2014/06/19/marijuana-whats-law-enforcement-actually-grousing-about-in-washington.

———. 2014b. "Study: Genes Linked to Schizophrenia May Drive Marijuana Use (Not Vice Versa)." *Seattle Post-Intelligencer*, June 24. Available at https://blog.seattlepi.com/marijuana/2014/06/24/study-genes-linked-to-schizophrenia-may-drive-marijuana-use-not-vise-versa.

———. 2015a. "Hempfest 2015: Seattle Festival Forced to Abandon Adult-Only 'Marijuana Gardens.'" *Seattle Post-Intelligencer*, August 11. Available at https://blog.seattlepi.com/marijuana/2015/08/11/hempfest-2015-seattle-festival-forced-to-abandon-adult-only-marijuana-gardens.

———. 2015b. "Today in No Sh*t: DEA Admits the Blindingly Obvious about Marijuana." *Seattle Post-Intelligencer*, August 5. Available at https://blog.seattlepi.com/marijuana/2015/08/05/today-in-no-sht-dea-admits-the-blindingly-obvious-about-marijuana.

———. 2015c. "Why Anti-pot Crusaders Need Marijuana to Change the Brain." *Seattle Post-Intelligencer*, February 11. Available at https://blog.seattlepi.com/marijuana/2015/02/11/why-anti-pot-crusaders-need-marijuana-to-change-the-brain.

Engen, John. 2016. "Dangerous Haze: Banking Is Not Yet Going to Pot." *American Banker*, July 31. Available at https://www.americanbanker.com/news/dangerous-haze-banking-is-not-yet-going-to-pot.

Englund, Michelle M., Jessica Siebenbruner, Elizabeth M. Oliva, Byron Egeland, Chu-Ting Chung, and Jeffrey D. Long. 2013. "The Developmental Significance of Late Adolescent Substance Use for Early Adult Functioning." *Developmental Psychology* 49 (8): 1554–1564. Available at https://www.ncbi.nlm.nih.gov/pmc/articles/PMC3568218.

Evans, Erica. 2016. "Pot Opponents Question Validity of Colorado Study." *Los Angeles Times*, June 22. Available at http://www.latimes.com/nation/la-na-colorado-pot-20160621-snap-story.html.

Fabian, Jordan. 2017. "VA Chief: Medical Marijuana Could Help Vets." *The Hill*, May 31. Available at http://thehill.com/homenews/administration/335782-va-chief-medical-marijuana-could-help-vets.

Falkstedt, D., V. Wolff, P. Allebeck, T. Hemmingsson, and A. K. Danielsson. 2017. "Cannabis, Tobacco, Alcohol Use, and the Risk of Early Stroke." *Stroke* 48 (2): 265–270. Available at https://www.ahajournals.org/doi/pdf/10.1161/STROKEAHA.116.015565.

Fang, Lee. 2016. "Police and Prison Guard Groups Fight Marijuana Legalization in California." *The Intercept*, May 18. Available at https://theintercept.com/2016/05/18/ca-marijuana-measure.

Federal Bureau of Investigation. 2017a. "Estimated Number of Arrests: United States, 2016." Available at https://ucr.fbi.gov/crime-in-the-u.s/2016/crime-in-the-u.s.-2016/topic-pages/tables/table-18.

———. 2017b. "FBI Releases 2016 Crime Stats." September 25. Available at https://www.fbi.gov/news/pressrel/press-releases/fbi-releases-2016-crime-statistics.

Ferguson, Bob. 2014. "Whether Statewide Initiative Establishing System for Marijuana Producers, Processors, and Retailers Preempts Local Ordinances." January 16. Available at https://www.atg.wa.gov/ago-opinions/whether-statewide-initiative-establishing-system-licensing-marijuana-producers.

———. 2015. "Cities and Counties Have a Right to Ban the Sale of Marijuana." *Seattle Times*, February 8. Available at http://old.seattletimes.com/html/opinion/2025642344_fergusonopedmarijuana09xml.html.

Ferner, Matt. 2016. "New DEA Chief: 'Heroin Is Clearly More Dangerous Than Marijuana.'" *Huffington Post*, December 19. Available at https://www.huffingtonpost.com/entry/dea-chief-marijuana-heroin-danger_us_55c25079e4b0f7f0bebb4ef5.

Ferraiolo, Kathleen. 2007. "From Killer Weed to Popular Medicine: The Evolution of American Drug Control Policy, 1937–2000." *Journal of Policy History* 19:147–179.

Fijnaut, Cyrille. 2014. "Legalisation of Cannabis in Some American States." *European Journal of Crime, Criminal Law, and Criminal Justice* 22:207–217.

Fijnaut, Cyrille, and Brice De Ruyver. 2015. *The Third Way: A Plea for a Balanced Cannabis Policy*. Leiden, Netherlands: Brill Nijhoff.

Fine, Doug. 2012. *Too High to Fail*. New York: Gotham Books.

Fischer, Benedikt, Kari Ala-Leppilampi, Eric Single, and Amanda Robins. 2003. "Cannabis Law Reform in Canada: Is the 'Saga of Promise and Retreat' Coming to an End?" *Canadian Journal of Criminology and Criminal Justice* 45:265–298.

Fisher, Marc. 2014. "Marijuana's Rising Acceptance Comes after Many Failures: Is It Now Legalization's Time?" *Washington Post*, February 22. Available at http://www.washingtonpost.com.

Fisher, Marc, Aaron Davis, and Perry Stein. 2015. "With Marijuana Legalization, Green Rush Is on in D.C." *Washington Post*, February 25. Available at https://www.washingtonpost.com/politics/marijuanas-rising-acceptance-comes-after-many-failures-is-it-now-legalizations-time/2014/02/22/9adc8502-98dd-11e3-80ac-63a8ba7f7942_story.html.

Flatow, Nicole. 2013. "Caltech Physicist: If All Science Were Run like Marijuana Research, Creationists Would Control Paleontology." *ThinkProgress*, February 25. Available at https://thinkprogress.org/caltech-physicist-if-all-science-were-run-like-marijuana-research-creationists-would-control-a6518ebde671.

Forman, James. 2017. *Locking Up Our Own: Crime and Punishment in Black America*. New York: Macmillan.

Forman, Jolene. 2016. "It's Not Legal Yet: Nearly 500,000 Marijuana Arrests in California in the Last Decade." Drug Policy Alliance, August 17. Available at http://www.drugpolicy.org/blog/its-not-legal-yet-nearly-500000-marijuana-arrests-california-last-decade.

Fox, Steve, Paul Armentano, and Mason Tvert. 2009. *Marijuana Is Safer, So Why Are We Driving People to Drink?* White River Junction, VT: Chelsea Green.

Fried, Peter, Barbara Watkinson, Deborah James, and Robert Gray. 2002. "Current and Former Marijuana Use: Preliminary Findings of a Longitudinal Study of Effects on IQ in Young Adults." *Canadian Medical Association Journal* 167:887–891.

Friedersdorf, Conor. 2011. "The War on Drugs Turns 40." *The Atlantic*, June 15. Available at https://www.theatlantic.com/politics/archive/2011/06/the-war-on-drugs-turns-40/240472.

Frisher, Martin, Ilana Crome, Orsolina Martino, and Peter Croft. 2009. "Assessing the Impact of Cannabis Use on Trends in Diagnosed Schizophrenia in the United Kingdom from 1996 to 2005." *Schizophrenia Research* 113:123–138.

Fuller, Thomas. 2016a. "Californians Legalize Marijuana in Vote That Could Echo Nationally." *New York Times*, November 9. Available at https://www.nytimes.com/2016/11/09/us/politics/marijuana-legalization.html.

———. 2016b. "Medical Marijuana Is Legal in California, Except When It's Not." *New York Times*, November 21. Available at https://www.nytimes.com/2016/11/22/us/medical-marijuana-is-legal-in-california-except-when-its-not.html.

———. 2017a. "Marijuana Goes Industrial in California." *New York Times*, April 15. Available at https://www.nytimes.com/2017/04/15/us/california-marijuana-industry-agriculture.html.

———. 2017b. "Marijuana Industry Presses Ahead in California's Wine Country." *New York Times*, March 18. Available at https://www.nytimes.com/2017/03/18/us/california-marijuana-wine-country.html.

———. 2017c. "Nevada Rushes to Address Shortage of Newly Legalized Marijuana." *New York Times*, July 13. Available at https://www.nytimes.com/2017/07/13/us/nevada-legal-marijuana-shortage.html.

Fulton, Greg. 2015. "Legal Pot in Colorado: How It's Affected Trucking." *Truckinginfo*, November 17. Available at https://www.truckinginfo.com/156435/legal-pot-in-colorado-how-its-affected-trucking.

Gahlinger, Paul. 2001. *Illegal Drugs: A Complete Guide to Their History, Chemistry, Use and Abuse.* Salt Lake City, UT: Sagebrush Press.

Gaither, Julie R., John M. Leventhal, Sheryl A. Ryan, and Deepa R. Camenga. 2016. "National Trends in Hospitalizations for Opioid Poisonings among Children and Adolescents, 1997 to 2012." *JAMA Pediatrics* 170:1195–1201.

Galal, Ahmed M., Desmond Slade, Waseem Gul, Abir T. El-Alfy, Daneel Ferreira, and Mahmoud A. Elsohly. 2009. "Naturally Occurring and Related Synthetic Cannabinoids and Their Potential Therapeutic Applications." *Recent Patents on CNS Drug Discovery* 4:112–136.

Galliher, John, and Allynn Walker. 1977. "The Puzzle of the Social Origins of the Marijuana Tax Act of 1937." *Social Problems* 34:367–376.

Galston, William A., and E. J. Dionne. 2013. "The New Politics of Marijuana Legalization." Brookings Institution, May 29. Available at https://www.brookings.edu/research/the-new-politics-of-marijuana-legalization-why-opinion-is-changing.

Garber, Andrew, and Steve Miletich. 2011. "Former U.S. Attorney McKay Backs Effort to Legalize Pot in Washington." *Seattle Times*, June 21. Available at https://www

.seattletimes.com/seattle-news/former-us-attorney-mckay-backs-effort-to-legalize
-pot-in-washington.

Garcia, Jacobo. 2015. "Colombia Legalizes Medical Marijuana with President's Decree."
The Cannabist, December 22. Available at https://www.thecannabist.co/2015/12/22/
colombia-marijuana-president-decree-medical-marijuana/45527.

Gardner, Fred. 2015. "Legalization in 2016?" *Counterpunch*, January 26. Available at
https://www.counterpunch.org/2015/01/26/legalization-in-2016.

Geddes, John. 2012. "Harper's Anti-drug Strategy Gets a Little Less Compassionate."
Macleans, July 25. Available at https://www.macleans.ca/news/canada/drug-money.

———. 2017. "Justin Trudeau and the Dangers of Legalizing Weed." *Macleans*, April
12. Available at https://www.macleans.ca/news/canada/justin-trudeau-and-the
-dangers-of-legalizing-weed.

Geiger, Abigail. 2016. "Support for Marijuana Legalization Continues to Rise." Pew
Research Center, October 12. Available at http://www.pewresearch.org/fact-tank/
2016/10/12/support-for-marijuana-legalization-continues-to-rise.

Gelacak, Michael. 1997. *Cocaine and Federal Sentencing Policy*. Washington, DC: United
States Sentencing Commission.

Gettman, Jon. 2009. "Marijuana Arrests in the United States (2007): Arrests, Usage, and
Related Data." *Bulletin of Cannabis Reform*, November 5. Available at https://www
.drugscience.org/Archive/bcr7/Gettman_Marijuana_Arrests_in_the_United
_States.pdf.

———. 2015. "Racial Disparities in Marijuana Arrests in Virginia (2003–2013)." Drug
Policy Alliance. Available at http://www.drugpolicy.org/sites/default/files/Racial
_Disparities_in_Marijuana_Arrests_in_Virginia_2003-2013.pdf.

Gillies, Rob. 2017. "Canadian Police Ask Government to Postpone Marijuana Legalization." *The Cannabist*, September 12. Available at https://www.thecannabist.co/2017/
09/12/canada-marijuana-legalization-police-postpone/87933.

Gilman, Alfred, and Louis Goodman. 1956. *The Pharmacological Basis of Therapeutics*.
New York: Macmillan.

Gilman, Jodi M., John K. Kuster, Sang Lee, Myung Joo Lee, Byoung Woo Kim, Nikos
Makris, Andre van der Kouwe, Anne J. Blood, and Hans C. Breiter. 2014. "Cannabis
Use Is Quantitatively Associated with Nucleus Accumbens and Amygdala Abnor-
malities in Young Adult Recreational Users." *Journal of Neuroscience* 34:5529–5538.

Glaser, Steph. 2014. "How People in Colorado Feel about the 'Bud Bowl.'" *Matador
Network*, February 2. Available at https://matadornetwork.com/sports/how-people
-in-colorado-feel-about-the-bud-bowl.

Globe and Mail. 2016. "Marijuana Legalization Report Wants People to Have Their Pot
and Not Smoke It, Too." December 13. Available at https://www.theglobeandmail
.com/opinion/editorials/marijuana-legalization-report-wants-people-to-have-their
-pot-and-not-smoke-it-too/article33316378.

Goni, Uki. 2016. "Uruguay's Legal Marijuana Policy En Route to Next Phase of Regulation." *The Guardian*, March 24. Available at https://www.theguardian.com/world/
2016/mar/24/uruguay-legal-marijuana-next-phase-regulation.

Governing the States and Localities. 2018. "State Same-Sex Marriage State Laws Map."
Available at http://www.governing.com/gov-data/same-sex-marriage-civil-unions
-doma-laws-by-state.html.

Government of Canada. 2016. "Toward the Legalization, Regulation and Restriction of
Access to Marijuana: Discussion Paper." Available at https://www.canada.ca/
content/dam/hc-sc/healthy-canadians/migration/health-system-systeme-sante/

consultations/legalization-marijuana-legalisation/alt/legalization-marijuana
-legalisation-eng.pdf.

Grabus, Sheri. 2016. "Study Questions Role for Marijuana in Teen Users' IQ Decline."
National Institute on Drug Abuse, August 1. Available at https://www.drugabuse
.gov/news-events/nida-notes/2016/08/study-questions-role-marijuana-in-teen
-users-iq-decline.

Graf, Tyler. 2014. "Commissioners Ban Recreational Marijuana Facilities outside City
Limits." *The Columbian*, May 26. Available at https://www.columbian.com/news/
2014/may/26/commissioners-ban-recreational-marijuana-facilitie.

Graham, Gillian. 2017. "Recreational Marijuana Is Now Legal in Maine: Here's What
You Need to Know." *Portland Press Herald*, January 30. Available at https://www
.pressherald.com/2017/01/30/recreational-marijuana-is-now-legal-in-maine-heres
-what-you-need-to-know.

Graves, Lucia. 2014. "The Last Drug Czar?" *The Atlantic*, March 13. Available at https://
www.theatlantic.com/politics/archive/2014/03/the-last-drug-czar/439419.

Gray, Eliza. 2015. "Dope Dreams." *Time*, April 20. Available at http://columbian.tiffin
.k12.oh.us/subsites/Ann-Reddy/documents/Legalization%20of%20Marijuana/
Dope%20Dreams.pdf.

Gray, James. 2001. *Why Our Drug Laws Have Failed and What We Can Do about It.*
Philadelphia: Temple University Press.

Greer, George, Charles Grob, and Adam Halberstadt. 2014. "PTSD Symptoms of Patients
Evaluated for the New Mexico Medical Cannabis Program." *Journal of Psychoactive
Drugs* 46:73–77.

Griffin, Bill. 2016. "The Slow Death of the Cannabis Coffeeshop." *Marijuana Times*,
April 26. Available at http://www.marijuanatimes.org/the-slow-death-of-the-can
nabis-coffeeshop.

Grimley, Brynn. 2016. "Pierce County Ban on Pot Businesses Vetoed by County Executive." *News Tribune*, June 30. Available at https://www.thenewstribune.com/news/
local/marijuana/article86980287.html.

Grinspoon, Lester. 1998. "Prescribing the Forbidden Medicine." *Playboy*, August 1, p. 42.

Grinspoon, Lester, and James Bakalar. 1995. "Marihuana as Medicine: A Plea for Reconsideration." *Journal of the American Medical Association* 273:1875–1876.

Grotenhermen, Franjo. 2007. "The Toxicology of Cannabis and Cannabis Prohibition."
Chemistry and Biodiversity 4:1744–1768.

Grotenhermen, Franjo, Gero Leson, Gunter Berghaus, Olaf H. Drummer, Hans-Peter
Kruger, Marie C. Longo, Herbert Moskowitz, et. al. 2007. "Developing Limits for
Driving under Cannabis." *Addiction* 102:1910–1917.

Grund, Jean-Paul, and Joost Breeksema. 2013. *Coffeeshops and Compromise.* New York:
Open Society Foundations. Available at https://www.opensocietyfoundations.org/
sites/default/files/coffee-shops-and-compromise-20130713.pdf.

Grush, Loren. 2014. "Casual Marijuana Use Linked with Brain Abnormalities, Study
Finds." *Fox News*, April 15. Available at http://www.foxnews.com/health/2014/04/
15/casual-marijuana-use-linked-with-brain-abnormalities-study-finds.html.

GSS Data Explorer. n.d. "Should Marijuana Be Made Legal." Available at https://
gssdataexplorer.norc.org/trends/Civil%20Liberties?measure=grass.

Guerino, Paul, Paige Harrison, and William Sabol. 2011. *Prisoners in 2010.* Washington,
DC: Bureau of Justice Statistics.

Gupta, Sanjay. 2009. "Why I Would Vote No on Pot." *Time*, January 8. Available at http://
content.time.com/time/subscriber/article/0,33009,1552034,00.html.

———. 2013. "Why I Changed My Mind on Weed." *CNN*, August 8. Available at https://www.cnn.com/2013/08/08/health/gupta-changed-mind-marijuana/index.html.

Gurciullo, Briana, and Karen Mawdley. 2015. "Marijuana Law Creates Confusion but Finds Growing Acceptance in the District." *Washington Post*, August 9. Available at https://www.washingtonpost.com/local/marijuana-law-creates-confusion-but -finds-growing-acceptance-in-district/2015/08/09/1ea3b040-3d47-11e5-9c2d -ed991d848c48_story.html.

Gurman, Sadie. 2017. "Sessions' Marijuana Task Force Report Gives Him No Ammo to Go after Legal States." *The Cannabist*, August 4. Available at https://www.the cannabist.co/2017/08/04/sessions-marijuana-task-force-report/85436.

Gusovsky, Dina. 2016. "Americans Consume the Vast Majority of the World's Opioids." *CNBC*, April 27. Available at https://www.cnbc.com/2016/04/27/americans-consume -almost-all-of-the-global-opioid-supply.html.

Haberkorn, Leonardo. 2014. "Uruguay Leader Calls Colorado Pot Law 'a Fiction.'" *Yahoo!*, May 3. Available at https://www.yahoo.com/news/uruguay-leader-calls -colorado-pot-law-fiction-001421961.html.

———. 2015. "Marijuana Clubs Sprouting Up in Uruguay." *Associated Press*, June 12. Available at https://apimagesblog.com/blog/2015/06/12/uruguay-marijuana-clubs.

———. 2016. "A Majority of Pharmacists in Uruguay Don't Want to Sell Pot: Here's Why." *The Cannabist*, July 6. Available at https://www.thecannabist.co/2016/07/06/ uruguay-marijuana-pharmacies/57627.

Hackman, Rose. 2017. "A Billion-Dollar Industry, a Racist Legacy." *The Guardian*, June 15. Available at https://www.theguardian.com/us-news/2017/jun/15/legal-marijuana -industry-racism-portland-jesce-horton.

Hadland, Scott E., Maxwell S. Krieger, and Brandon D. L. Marshall. 2017. "Industry Payments to Physicians for Opioid Products, 2013–2015." *American Journal of Public Health* 107:1493–1495.

Haglage, Abby. 2013. "Meet Mark Kleiman, the Man Who Will Be Washington State's Pot Czar." *Daily Beast*, March 21. Available at https://www.thedailybeast.com/meet -mark-kleiman-the-man-who-will-be-washington-states-pot-czar.

———. 2016. "The DEA Just Blew It on Pot." *Daily Beast*, August 11. Available at https://www.thedailybeast.com/the-dea-just-blew-it-on-pot.

Haines, Gavin. 2016. "Why Are Amsterdam's Cannabis 'Coffeeshops' Closing?" *The Telegraph*, December 5. Available at https://www.telegraph.co.uk/travel/desti nations/europe/netherlands/amsterdam/articles/future-of-coffeeshops-in-doubt-as -amsterdams-oldest-cannabis-cafe-faces-closure.

———. 2017. "Everything You Need to Know about Marijuana Smoking in the Netherlands." *The Telegraph*, February 21. Available at https://www.telegraph.co.uk/travel/ destinations/europe/netherlands/amsterdam/articles/everything-you-need-to -know-about-smoking-marijuana-in-the-netherlands.

Hall, Wayne. 2015. "What Has Research over the Past Two Decades Revealed about the Adverse Health Effects of Recreational Cannabis Use?" *Addiction* 110:19–35.

Halper, Evan. 2014. "Marijuana Legalization Backers Anxious as Costs Mount, Donors Waiver." *Los Angeles Times*, November 27, p. 31.

———. 2015. "Marijuana Legalization Gets a Boost on Capitol Hill." *Los Angeles Times*, March 10. Available at http://www.latimes.com/nation/politics/politicsnow/la-pn -marijuana-senate-20150310-story.html.

Halper, Evan, and Patrick McGreevy. 2017. "Trump Administration Signals a Possible Crackdown on States over Marijuana." *Los Angeles Times*, February 23. Available

at http://www.latimes.com/politics/la-na-pol-trump-marijuana-20170223-story
.html.

Halperin, Alex. 2016. "Canada's Legal Weed: What You Need to Know." *Rolling Stone*,
April 17. Available at https://www.rollingstone.com/culture/culture-news/canadas
-legal-weed-what-you-need-to-know-116460.

Hampton, Travis. 2017. Letter to Jefferson B. Sessions III. August 16. Available at http://
media.heartlandtv.com/documents/Hampton+Sessions+Letter.pdf.

Hancock-Allen, Jessica, Lisa Barker, Michael Van Dyke, and Dawn Holmes. 2015. "Notes
from the Field: Death Following Ingestion of an Edible Marijuana Product—Colorado, March, 2014." *Centers for Disease Control Morbidity and Mortality Weekly* 64
(28): 771–772.

Hansen, Kristena. 2016. "Working in Unison, Oregon Pot Bills Find Easy Passage
through Legislature." *The Cannabist*, February 17. Available at https://www
.thecannabist.co/2016/02/17/oregon-marijuana-pot-proposals-bills-regulation-gain
-support-legalization/48638.

Harbarger, Molly. 2015. "Now You Can Order Marijuana to Be Delivered by Drone—Just
Not in Oregon." *The Oregonian*, August 6. Available at https://www.oregonlive.com/
business/index.ssf/2015/08/now_you_can_order_marijuana_to.html.

Hari, Johann. 2015. *Chasing the Scream: The First and Last Days of the War on Drugs.*
New York: Bloomsbury.

Harkinson, Josh. 2015. "Adventures of a Pot Pioneer." *Mother Jones*, August 17. Available at https://www.motherjones.com/politics/2015/08/steve-deangelo-harborside
-marijuana-interview.

Haroutounian, Simon, Yael Ratz, Yehuda Ginosar, Kayina Furmanov, Fayez Saifi, Ronit
Meidan, and Elyad Davidson. 2016. "The Effect of Medical Cannabis on Pain and
Quality-of-Life Outcomes in Chronic Pain: A Prospective Open-Label Study."
Clinical Journal of Pain 32:1036–1043.

Harper, Sam, Erin Strumpf, and Jay Kaufman. 2012. "Do Medical Marijuana Laws Increase Marijuana Use? Replication Study and Extension." *Annals of Epidemiology*
22:207–212.

Harper's New Monthly Magazine. 1858. "Hasheesh and Hasheesh Eaters." April, pp.
653–658.

Harshman, Marissa. 2017. "Merging of Marijuana Markets Gets Mixed Reviews." *The
Columbian*, August 1. Available at https://www.columbian.com/news/2017/aug/01/
merging-of-marijuana-markets-gets-mixed-reviews.

Hart, Carl. 2016. "The DEA's Decision to Keep Pot Restrictions Perpetuates Hypocrisy."
Scientific American, October 1. Available at https://www.scientificamerican.com/
article/the-dea-s-decision-to-keep-pot-restrictions-perpetuates-hypocrisy.

Hart, Carl, and Charles Ksir. 2015. *Drugs, Society and Human Behavior.* 15th ed. New
York: McGraw-Hill.

Hasin, Deborah S., Melanie Wall, Katherine M. Keyes, Magdalena Cerda, John Schulenberg, Patrick M. O'Malley, Sandro Galea, Rosalie Pacula, and Tianshu Feng. 2015.
"Medical Marijuana Laws and Adolescent Marijuana Use in the USA from 1991 to
2014: Results from Annual, Repeated Cross-sectional Surveys." *Lancet Psychiatry*
2:601–608.

Haskell, Meg. 2009. "Medical Marijuana Access Law OK'd." *Bangor Daily News*, November 3. Available at https://bangordailynews.com/2009/11/03/politics/medical
-marijuana-access-law-okrsquod.

Hawkins, Derek. 2017. "Sean Spicer Correlated Marijuana Use to Opioid Addiction: Medical Research Is Not on His Side." *The Cannabist*, February 24. Available from https://www.thecannabist.co/2017/02/24/opioid-addiction-marijuana-research -sean-spicer/74348.

Hayes, Marie, and Mark Brown. 2014. "Legalization of Medical Marijuana and Incidence of Opioid Mortality." *JAMA Internal Medicine* 174:1673–1674.

Health Canada. 2016. *A Framework for the Legalization and Regulation of Cannabis in Canada*. Ottawa: Health Canada.

Health Commission of New South Wales. 1973. *The Use and Abuse of Drugs*. Canberra: Health Commission of New South Wales.

Healy, Jack. 2014a. "After 5 Months of Sales, Colorado Sees the Downside of a Legal High." *New York Times*, May 31. Available at https://www.nytimes.com/2014/06/01/ us/after-5-months-of-sales-colorado-sees-the-downside-of-a-legal-high.html.

———. 2014b. "Denver Symphony's Pot-Party Fundraiser a Mellow Affair." *Seattle Times*, May 24. Available at https://www.seattletimes.com/nation-world/denver -symphonyrsquos-pot-party-fundraiser-a-mellow-affair.

———. 2015. "Legal Marijuana Faces Another Federal Hurdle: Taxes." *New York Times*, May 9. Available at https://www.nytimes.com/2015/05/10/us/politics/legal-mari juana-faces-another-federal-hurdle-taxes.html.

Healy, Jack, and Kirk Johnson. 2014. "Next Gold Rush: Legal Marijuana Feeds Entre-preneurs' Dreams." *New York Times*, July 18. Available at https://www.nytimes.com/ 2014/07/19/us/new-gold-rush-legal-marijuana-feeds-entrepreneurs-dreams.html.

Hellerman, Caleb. 2017. "Scientists Say Government's Only Pot Farm Has Moldy Sam-ples—and No Federal Testing Standards." *PBS News Hour*, March 8. Available at https://www.pbs.org/newshour/nation/scientists-say-governments-pot-farm-moldy -samples-no-guidelines.

Hendrix, Steve. 2017. "You Can Get Weed Delivered to Your Door in D.C. Just like Pizza, but Is It Legal?" *Washington Post*, May 22. Available at https://www.washingtonpost .com/local/you-can-get-weed-delivered-to-your-door-in-dc-just-like-pizza-but-is-it -legal/2017/05/22/186da532-3cb9-11e7-8854-21f359183e8c_story.html.

Herb. 2015. "Dope Puns: 10 Awesome Weed Puns." July 14. Available at https://herb.co/ marijuana/news/dope-puns-10-awesome-weed-puns.

Hero Grown. n.d. "Our Mission." Available at https://herogrown.org.

Hesse, Josiah. 2016a. "The Bud+Breakfast: The Marijuana Inn Where Wake and Bake Is Serious Business." *The Guardian*, March 10. Available at https://www.theguardian .com/society/2016/mar/10/bud-breakfast-colorado-marijuana-wake-and-bake-inn.

———. 2016b. "Scientists Frustrated with Low Quality Weed from Government, Want Dispensary Pot." *MassRoots*, May 27. Available at https://www.massroots.com/ news/scientists-frustrated-with-low-quality-weed-from-government-want-dis pensary-pot.

———. 2016c. "Why Are People Going to the Emergency Room for Weed?" *The Can-nabist*, January 14. Available at https://www.thecannabist.co/2016/01/14/pot -emergency-room-marijuana-er/42939.

Hickenlooper, John, and Cynthia Coffman. 2017. Letter to Attorney General Jeff Ses-sions. August 24. Available at http://www.cpr.org/news/story/hickenlooper-ag -coffman-to-sessions-the-colorado-way-on-pot-is-a-model-for-other-states.

Hickman, Matt, Peter Vickerman, John Macleod, Glyn Lewis, Stan Zammit, James Kirkbride, and Peter Jones. 2009. "If Cannabis Caused Schizophrenia—How Many

Cannabis Users Need to Be Prevented in Order to Prevent One Case of Schizophrenia? England and Wales Calculations." *Addiction* 104 (11): 1856–1861.

Higham, Scott, and Lenny Bernstein. 2017. "The Drug Industry's Triumph over the DEA." *Washington Post*, October 15. Available at https://www.washingtonpost.com/graphics/2017/investigations/dea-drug-industry-congress.

High There. n.d. "Who We Are." Available at https://www.highthere.com/about (accessed July 15, 2017).

Hill, Kevin. 2015. "Medical Marijuana Does Not Increase Adolescent Marijuana Use." *Lancet Psychiatry* 2:572–573.

Himmelstein, Jerome. 1983. *The Strange Career of Marijuana*. Westport, CT: Greenwood Press.

Hinton, Elizabeth. 2016. *From the War on Poverty to the War on Crime*. Cambridge, MA: Harvard University Press.

Hoaken, Peter, and Sherry Stewart. 2003. "Drugs of Abuse and the Elicitation of Human Aggressive Behavior." *Addictive Behaviors* 28:1533–1554.

Hobbs, Andy. 2015. "Washington State Veterans Form Support Group to Promote Medical Pot." *The Cannabist*, July 21. Available at https://www.thecannabist.co/2015/07/21/washington-state-veterans-medical-marijuana/38295.

Hoeffel, John. 2010. "Prop. 19: Marijuana Initiative Drew Strongest Support in Bay Area, but Failed in 'Emerald Triangle.'" *Los Angeles Times*, November 3. Available at http://latimesblogs.latimes.com/lanow/2010/11/measure-to-legalize-marijuana-drew-strongest-support-from-bay-area-but-failed-in-emerald-triangle.html.

Holden, Dominic. 2012. "The Sheriff and His Opponent Fight over Who Wants to Legalize Pot More." *The Stranger*, October 1. Available at https://www.thestranger.com/slog/archives/2012/10/01/the-sheriff-and-his-opponent-fight-over-who-wants-to-legalize-pot-more.

———. 2013. "The Starbucks of Pot." *Slate*, May 31. Available at http://www.slate.com/articles/news_and_politics/jurisprudence/2013/05/jamen_shively_and_the_starbucks_of_pot_obama_should_let_big_business_marijuana.html.

Horwitz, Sari. 2012. "Marijuana Legalization on Ballot in 3 States, but Justice Department Remains Silent." *Washington Post*, October 11. Available at https://www.washingtonpost.com/world/national-security/marijuana-legalization-on-ballot-in-3-states/2012/10/11/db15f5f6-13a8-11e2-ba83-a7a396e6b2a7_story.html.

Hotakainen, Rob. 2013a. "Drug Czar Gil Kerlikowske Talks Tough on Marijuana as Pressure Grows." *Miami Herald*, April 24. Available at https://www.miamiherald.com/latest-news/article1950666.html.

———. 2013b. "Recovering Drug Addict Patrick Kennedy Now Leads Fight against Legalizing Marijuana." *McClatchy*, June 20. Available at https://www.mcclatchydc.com/news/politics-government/article24750262.html.

———. 2015. "Tax Day Is Source of Unhappiness for Marijuana Industry." *McClatchy*, April 14. Available at https://www.mcclatchydc.com/news/nation-world/national/economy/article24783028.html.

Hsu, Jeremy. 2016. "Could Medical Cannabis Break the Painkiller Epidemic?" *Scientific American*, September 1. Available at https://www.scientificamerican.com/article/could-medical-cannabis-break-the-painkiller-epidemic.

Hu, Winnie. 2017. "When Retirement Comes with a Daily Dose of Cannabis." *New York Times*, February 19. Available at https://www.nytimes.com/2017/02/19/nyregion/retirement-medicinal-marijuana.html.

Hudak, John. 2014. "Colorado's Rollout of Legal Marijuana Is Succeeding." Brookings Institution, July. Available at https://www.brookings.edu/wp-content/uploads/2016/06/CEPMMJCOv2.pdf.

Hudak, John, and Jonathan Rauch. 2016. "Worry about Bad Marijuana—Not Big Marijuana." Brookings Institution, June. Available at https://www.brookings.edu/wp-content/uploads/2016/07/big-marijuana-1.pdf.

Hudak, Marissa, Daniel Severn, and Kimberly Nordstrom. 2015. "Edible Cannabis-Induced Psychosis: Intoxication and Beyond." *American Journal of Psychiatry* 172:911–912.

Hudson Institute. n.d. "About." Available at https://www.hudson.org/about (accessed August 10, 2017).

Huffington Post. 2013. "Operation Pipe Dream: 10 Years Later." February 26. Available at https://www.huffingtonpost.com/the-/operation-pipe-dream-10-y_b_2745740.html.

Hughes, Trevor. 2016. "New Pot Laws May Affect 84M Americans." *USA Today*, October 28. Available at http://ee.usatoday.com/subscribers/shared/ShowArticle.aspx?doc=USA%2F2016%2F10%2F28&entity=Ar00102&sk=86BC0BCA.

Human Rights Watch. 2016. "Every 25 Seconds: The Human Toll of Criminalizing Drug Use in the United States." October 12. Available at https://www.hrw.org/report/2016/10/12/every-25-seconds/human-toll-criminalizing-drug-use-united-states.

Humphreys, Keith. 2017. "These College Students Lost Access to Legal Pot—and Started Getting Better Grades." *Washington Post*, July 25. Available at https://www.washingtonpost.com/news/wonk/wp/2017/07/25/these-college-students-lost-access-to-legal-pot-and-started-getting-better-grades.

Imtiaz, Sameer, Kevin D. Shield, Michael Roerecke, Joyce Cheng, Svetlana Popova, Paul Kurdyak, Benedikt Fischer, and Jurgen Rehm. 2016. "The Burden of Disease Attributable to Cannabis Use in Canada." *Addiction* 111:653–662.

Indian Hemp Drugs Commission. 1894. *Report of the Indian Hemp Drugs Commission, 1893–94.* Simlaj, India: Government Central Printing Office.

Ingold, John. 2010. "New Medical-Marijuana Regs Now Law in Colorado." *Denver Post*, June 7. Available at https://www.denverpost.com/2010/06/07/new-medical-marijuana-regs-now-law-in-colorado.

———. 2012. "The Inside Story of How Marijuana Became Legal in Colorado." *Denver Post*, December 28. Available at http://blogs.denverpost.com/thespot/2012/12/28/story-marijuana-legal-colorado/87640.

———. 2016. "No Change in Colorado Teens' Marijuana Use before and after Legalization, Study Finds." *Denver Post*, December 28. Available at https://www.denverpost.com/2016/12/28/colorado-teens-marijuana-use-legalization-study.

Ingold, John, and Ricardo Baca. 2016. "Supreme Court Denies Oklahoma and Nebraska Challenge to Colorado Pot." *Denver Post*, March 21. Available at https://www.denverpost.com/2016/03/21/supreme-court-denies-oklahoma-and-nebraska-challenge-to-colorado-pot.

Ingraham, Christopher. 2015a. "DEA Warns of Stoned Rabbits If Utah Passes Medical Marijuana." *Washington Post*, March 2. Available at https://www.washingtonpost.com/news/wonk/wp/2015/03/02/dea-warns-of-stoned-rabbits-if-utah-passes-medical-marijuana.

———. 2015b. "Federal Court Tells the DEA to Stop Harassing Medical Marijuana Providers." *Washington Post*, October 20. Available at https://www.washingtonpost

.com/news/wonk/wp/2015/10/20/federal-court-tells-the-dea-to-stop-harassing
-medical-marijuana-providers.

———. 2015c. "Why Congress Wants to Cut DEA's Cannabis Eradication Budget." *Denver Post*, November 27. Available at https://www.denverpost.com/2015/11/27/why
-congress-wants-to-cut-deas-cannabis-eradication-budget.

———. 2016a. "A Casino Magnate Is Spending Millions to Fight Legal Marijuana in Three States." *Washington Post*, October 26. Available at https://www.washingtonpost
.com/news/wonk/wp/2016/10/26/a-casino-magnate-is-spending-millions-to-fight
-legal-marijuana-in-three-states.

———. 2016b. "DEA Laments That 'Media Attention' Is Making It Tough to Put People in Jail for Pot." *Washington Post*, December 8. Available at https://www.wash
ingtonpost.com/news/wonk/wp/2016/12/08/dea-laments-that-media-attention
-is-making-it-tough-to-put-people-in-jail-for-pot.

———. 2016c. "The DEA Spent $73,000 to Eradicate Marijuana Plants in Utah: It Didn't Find Any." *Washington Post*, October 7. Available at https://www.washingtonpost
.com/news/wonk/wp/2016/10/07/the-dea-spent-73000-to-eradicate-marijuana
-plants-in-utah-it-didn't-find-any.

———. 2016d. "Drug Cops Raid an 81-Year Old Woman's Garden to Take Out a Single Marijuana Plant." *Washington Post*, October 7. Available at https://www
.washingtonpost.com/news/wonk/wp/2016/10/07/drug-cops-raid-an-81-year-old
-grandmothers-garden-to-take-out-a-single-marijuana-plant.

———. 2016e. "Gallup: Support for Marijuana Legalization Surges to New Highs." *Washington Post*, October 19. Available at https://www.washingtonpost.com/news/
wonk/wp/2016/10/19/gallup-support-for-marijuana-legalization-surges-to-new
-highs.

———. 2016f. "Marijuana Reform Went 8 for 9 on the Ballot This Week: It Could Be the Tipping Point." *Washington Post*, November 10. Available at https://www
.washingtonpost.com/news/wonk/wp/2016/11/10/marijuana-reform-went-8-for-9
-on-the-ballot-this-week-it-could-be-the-tipping-point.

———. 2016g. "The 'Mostly False' Argument That Could Derail Legal Weed in California." *Washington Post*, August 24. Available at https://www.washingtonpost.com/
news/wonk/wp/2016/08/24/the-mostly-false-argument-that-could-derail-legal
-weed-in-california.

———. 2016h. "Now We Know What Happens to Teens When You Make Pot Legal." *Washington Post*, June 21. Available at https://www.washingtonpost.com/news/
wonk/wp/2016/06/21/colorado-survey-shows-what-marijuana-legalization-will-do
-to-your-kids.

———. 2016i. "One Striking Chart Shows Why Pharma Companies Are Fighting Legal Marijuana." *Washington Post*, July 13. Available at https://www.washingtonpost
.com/news/wonk/wp/2016/07/13/one-striking-chart-shows-why-pharma
-companies-are-fighting-legal-marijuana.

———. 2016j. "Scientists: Adolescent Marijuana Use Is Absolutely Not Linked with Lower IQs." *Washington Post*, January 18. Available at https://www.denverdonate
.com/denver/denver-news/scientists-adolescent-marijuana-use-is-absolutely-not
-linked-with-lower-iqs.

———. 2016k. "Senators Held a Hearing to Remind You That 'Good People Don't Smoke Marijuana.'" *Washington Post*, April 5. Available at https://www.washingtonpost
.com/news/wonk/wp/2016/04/05/senators-one-sided-marijuana-hearing-is-heavy
-on-anecdote-light-on-data.

———. 2016l. "Stark Gap in How Doctors and the Government View Marijuana." *Washington Post*, August 29. Available at https://www.washingtonpost.com/news/wonk/ wp/2016/08/29/the-stark-difference-in-how-doctors-and-the-government-view -marijuana.

———. 2016m. "Study: States Are Losing Out on Billions of Dollars by Keeping Pot Illegal." *Washington Post*, May 16. Available at https://www.washingtonpost.com/ news/wonk/wp/2016/05/16/study-states-are-losing-out-on-billions-by-keeping-pot -illegal.

———. 2016n. "What Happens When You Get Stoned Every Day for Five Years?" *Washington Post*, February 1. Available at https://www.washingtonpost.com/news/wonk/ wp/2016/02/01/what-happens-when-you-get-stoned-every-single-day-for-five -years.

———. 2016o. "What Trump's Pick for Department of Homeland Security Could Mean for Legal Weed." *The Cannabist*, December 8. Available at https://www.thecannabist .co/2016/12/08/john-kelly-trump-dhs-pick/68963.

———. 2016p. "Where Opiates Killed the Most People in 2015." *Washington Post*, December 13. Available at https://www.washingtonpost.com/news/wonk/wp/2016/12/ 13/where-opiates-killed-the-most-people-in-2015.

———. 2016q. "Why Elizabeth Warren Thinks Legalizing Marijuana Could Help End America's Opioid Addiction Crisis." *Washington Post*, February 13. Available at https://www.washingtonpost.com/news/wonk/wp/2016/02/13/why-elizabeth -warren-thinks-legalizing-marijuana-could-help-end-americas-opioid-addiction -crisis.

———. 2017a. "A Big Thing Marijuana Opponents Warned You about Is Definitely Not Happening." *Washington Post*, March 21. Available at https://www.washingtonpost .com/news/wonk/wp/2017/03/21/a-big-thing-marijuana-opponents-warned-you -about-is-definitely-not-happening.

———. 2017b. "Dear Jeff Sessions: Here's That Science on Marijuana and Opioids You Were Asking For." *The Cannabist*, March 1. Available at https://www.thecannabist .co/2017/03/01/sessions-marijuana-opioid-research/74584.

———. 2017c. "11 Charts That Show Marijuana Has Gone Mainstream." Washington Post, April 19. Available at https://www.washingtonpost.com/news/wonk/wp/2017/ 04/19/11-charts-that-show-marijuana-has-truly-gone-mainstream.

———. 2017d. "Study: Nationwide Medical Marijuana Laws Would Save Lives—and a Billion Taxpayer Dollars." *Washington Post*, April 20. Available at https://www .washingtonpost.com/news/wonk/wp/2017/04/20/study-nationwide-medical -marijuana-laws-would-save-lives-and-a-billion-taxpayer-dollars.

———. 2017e. "What Marijuana Legalization Did to Car Accident Rates." *Washington Post*, June 26. Available at https://www.washingtonpost.com/news/wonk/wp/2017/ 06/26/what-marijuana-legalization-did-to-car-accident-rates.

Inslee, Jay, and Bob Ferguson. 2017. Letter to Jefferson B. Sessions III. August 15. Available at https://s3.amazonaws.com/big.assets.huffingtonpost.com/Inslee-Ferguson -Sessions.pdf.

Insurance Institute for Highway Safety. 2017. "High Claims: Legalizing Recreational Marijuana Is Linked to Increased Crashes." *Status Report*, June 22. Available at http://www.iihs.org/iihs/sr/statusreport/article/52/4/1.

Isikoff, Michael. 1989. "Drug Buy Set Up for Bush Speech." *Washington Post*, September 22. Available at https://www.washingtonpost.com/wp-srv/local/longterm/tours/ scandal/bushdrug.htm.

Jackson, Nicholas J., Joshua D. Isen, Rubin Khoddam, Daniel Irons, Catherine Tuvblad, William G. Iocono, Matt McGue, Adrian Raine, and Laura A. Baker. 2016. "Impact of Adolescent Marijuana Use on Intelligence: Results from Two Longitudinal Twin Studies." *Proceedings of the National Academy of Sciences* 113:E500–508.

Jaffe, Matthew. 2016. "Patrick Kennedy Opens Up about Addiction, Pushes for Mental Health Reform." *CNN*, May 2. Available at https://www.cnn.com/2016/05/02/politics/patrick-kennedy-the-axe-files/index.html.

James, Tom. 2016. "The Failed Promise of Legal Pot." *The Atlantic*, May 9. Available at https://www.theatlantic.com/politics/archive/2016/05/legal-pot-and-the-black-market/481506.

Jan, Tracy, and Fenit Nirappil. 2017. "Battling the Racial Roadblocks to Joining the Legalized Marijuana Trade." *Washington Post*, June 2. Available at https://www.washingtonpost.com/business/economy/battling-the-racial-roadblocks-to-joining-the-legalized-marijuana-trade/2017/06/02/7321de02-416f-11e7-9869-bac8b446820a_story.html.

Janssen, Wallace F. 1981. "The Story of the Laws behind the Labels." *FDA Consumer*, June. Available at https://www.fda.gov/downloads/AboutFDA/History/FOrgsHistory/EvolvingPowers/UCM593437.pdf.

Jetly, Rakesh, Alexander Heber, George Fraser, and Denis Boisvert. 2015. "The Efficacy of Nabilone, a Synthetic Cannabinoid, in the Treatment of PTSD-Associated Nightmares: A Preliminary, Randomized, Double-Blind, Placebo-Controlled Cross-over Design Study." *Psychoneuroendocrinology* 51:585–588.

Jiminez, Daniel M. 2017. "Is Federal Drug Control Policy Office on the Chopping Block in Fed Budget?" *The Cannabist*, February 22. Available at https://www.thecannabist.co/2017/02/22/office-national-drug-control-policy-budget/74149.

Johnson, Gene. 2014a. "ACLU: Steep Drop in Pot Cases has Freed Resources." *Seattle Times*, March 20. Available at https://www.seattletimes.com/seattle-news/aclu-steep-drop-in-pot-cases-has-freed-up-resources.

———. 2014b. "Reports of Problems Vex Washington Pot Lottery." *Seattle Times*, April 25. Available at https://www.seattletimes.com/seattle-news/reports-of-problems-vex-washington-pot-lottery.

Johnson, Jenna. 2015. "Trump Softens Position on Marijuana Legalization." *Washington Post*, October 29. Available at https://www.washingtonpost.com/news/post-politics/wp/2015/10/29/trump-wants-marijuana-legalization-decided-at-the-state-level.

Johnson, Tamra. 2017. "Young Millennials Top List of Worst Behaved Drivers." *AAA Newsroom*, February 15. Available at https://newsroom.aaa.com/2017/02/young-millennials-top-list-worst-behaved-drivers.

Johnston, James. 1855. "The Narcotics We Indulge In: Indian Hemp." In *The Hasheesh Eater's Companion*, edited by David Gross, 65–76. N.p.: Createspace Independent Publishing Platform, 2007.

Journal of Mental Science. 1894. Review of *Return, East India*. 40:107–108.

Journal of the American Medical Association. 1942. "Recent Investigations of Marihuana." 120:1128–1129.

———. 1945. "Marihuana Problems." 127:1129.

Joy, Janet, Stanley Watson, and John Benson, eds. 1999. *Marijuana and Medicine: Assessing the Science Base*. Washington, DC: National Academy Press.

Jurgensen, John. 2015. "TV Experiments with Pot." *Wall Street Journal*, February 12. Available at https://www.wsj.com/articles/tv-experiments-with-pot-1423780600.

Kaczynski, Andrew. 2014. "Almost Everything Barack Obama's Ever Said about Marijuana over the Years." *BuzzFeed*, January 21. Available at https://www.buzzfeednews.com/article/andrewkaczynski/barack-obama-weed.

Kampia, Rob. 2011. "Obama: From First to Worst on Medical Marijuana." *Huffington Post*, October 9. Available at https://www.huffingtonpost.com/rob-kampia/obama-from-first-to-worst_b_1001781.html.

Kandel, Denise. 2003. "Does Marijuana Use Cause the Use of Other Drugs?" *Journal of the American Medical Association* 289:482–483.

Karlin, Mark. 2015. "NYPD Commissioner Stricken with Giuliani Syndrome, Blames Marijuana for Increase in Murder Rate." *Buzzflash*, March 5. Available at http://buzzflash.com/commentary/nypd-commissioner-stricken-with-giuliani-syndrome-blames-marijuana-for-increased-murder-rate.

Kaskie, Brian, Padmaja Ayyagari, Gary Milavetz, Dan Shane, and Kanika Arora. 2017. "The Increasing Use of Cannabis among Older Americans: A Public Health Crisis or Viable Policy Alternative?" *The Gerontologist* 57 (6): 1166–1172.

Kassam, Ashifa. 2017. "Canadian Government Aims to Legalise Marijuana by 1 July 2018." *The Guardian*, March 27. Available at https://www.theguardian.com/world/2017/mar/27/canada-legal-marijuana-july-2018.

Kassirer, Jerome. 1997. "Federal Foolishness and Marijuana." *New England Journal of Medicine* 336:366–367.

Kastor, Elizabeth. 1986. "The Great Drug Debate." *Washington Post*, October 22. Available at https://www.washingtonpost.com/archive/lifestyle/1986/10/22/the-great-drug-debate/df37470c-2763-444c-be93-3a1ae842b022.

Kaufman, Marc. 2006. "Study Finds No Marijuana-Cancer Connection." *Washington Post*, May 26. Available at http://www.washingtonpost.com/wp-dyn/content/article/2006/05/25/AR2006052501729.html.

Keefe, Patrick Radden. 2013. "Buzzkill: Washington State Discovers That It's Not So Easy to Create a Legal Marijuana Economy." *New Yorker*, November 18. Available at https://www.newyorker.com/magazine/2013/11/18/buzzkill.

Kelsall, Diane. 2017. "Cannabis Legislation Fails to Protect Canada's Youth." *Canadian Medical Association Journal* 189 (21): E737–E738. Available at http://www.cmaj.ca/content/189/21/E737.

Kerlikowske, R. Gil. 2012. "Principles of Modern Drug Policy." May 21. Available at https://obamawhitehouse.archives.gov/ondcp/news-releases-remarks/principles-of-modern-drug-policy-directors-remarks-at-the-world-federation-against-drugs.

Keyes, Scott. 2015. "Marijuana Industry Rides High Thanks to Celebrity Investors." *The Guardian*, October 12. Available at https://www.theguardian.com/society/2015/oct/12/celebrity-marijuana-investors-snoop-dogg-willie-nelson.

Kirkbride, James B., Antonia Errazuriz, Tim J. Croudace, Craig Morgan, Daniel Jackson, Jane Boydell, Robin M. Murray, and Peter B. Jones. 2012. "Incidence of Schizophrenia and Other Psychoses in England, 1950–2009: A Systematic Review and Meta-analyses." *PLOS ONE* 7 (3). Available at http://journals.plos.org/plosone/article?id=10.1371/journal.pone.0031660.

Kleiman, Mark. 2014. "How Not to Make a Hash out of Cannabis Legalization." *Washington Monthly*, March–May. Available at https://washingtonmonthly.com/magazine/marchaprilmay-2014/how-not-to-make-a-hash-out-of-cannabis-legalization.

Koch, Jim. 2017. "Is It Last Call for Craft Beer?" *New York Times*, April 7. Available at https://www.nytimes.com/2017/04/07/opinion/is-it-last-call-for-craft-beer.html.

Kohn, Howard. 1989. "Cowboy in the Capital: Drug Czar Bill Bennett." *Rolling Stone*, November 2. Available at https://www.rollingstone.com/politics/politics-news/ cowboy-in-the-capital-drug-czar-bill-bennett-45472.

Kolansky, Harold, and William Moore. 1971. "Effects of Marihuana on Adolescents and Young Adults." *Journal of the American Medical Association* 216:486–492.

Komp, Ellen. 2011. "Mark Twain's 'Hasheesh' Experience in San Francisco." *San Francisco Chronicle*, October 2. Available at https://www.sfgate.com/opinion/article/ Mark-Twain-s-hasheesh-experience-in-S-F-2328992.php.

Koren, James Rufus. 2017. "Why Some Pot Businesses Hide Their Cash—and Others Truck It Straight to a Federal Vault." *Los Angeles Times*, July 7. Available at http:// www.latimes.com/business/la-fi-cannabis-banking-20170707-story.html.

Korf, Dirk, Marije Wouters, and Annemieke Benschop. 2011. "The Return of the Underground Cannabis Retail Market?" *Bonger International Bulletin* 1 (1). Available at https://pure.uva.nl/ws/files/1259644/99646_Bonger_International_Bulletin_Vol_1 _nr_1.pdf.

Kruesi, Kimberlee. 2015. "Taking the High Road: Another State Changes Mile 420 to 419.9." *The Cannabist*, August 18. Available at https://www.thecannabist.co/2015/ 08/18/idaho-420-signs/39569.

Kunkle, Fredrick. 2014. "Like, Wow: Police Chief Hoaxed on Pot Perils." *Washington Post*, February 26. Available at https://www.washingtonpost.com/local/md-politics/ like-wow-police-chief-is-hoaxed-on-pot-perils/2014/02/25/42bd0592-9e94-11e3 -9ba6-800d1192d08b_story.html.

———. 2016. "Eyes on the Road: Study Finds Fewer Traffic Fatalities in Medical Marijuana States." *The Cannabist*, December 20. Available at https://www.thecannabist .co/2016/12/20/marijuana-driving-stats-traffic-fatalities-medical-marijuana-laws/ 69770.

Kuruvilla, Matthai. 2014. "Feds Raid Oaksterdam University, Founders Home." *San Francisco Chronicle*, July 8. Available at https://www.sfgate.com/crime/article/Feds -raid-Oaksterdam-University-founder-s-home-3452743.php.

Kush Tours. n.d. "Welcome to Kush Tourism." Available at https://kushtourism.com (accessed July 17, 2017).

Labak, Aleta. 2015. "Attorney General Nominee Loretta Lynch against Legalizing Marijuana." *The Cannabist*, January 28. Available at https://www.thecannabist.co/ 2015/01/28/loretta-lynch-marijuana-attorney-general-senate-confirmation -hearing/28774.

———. 2017. "Sen. Orrin Hatch Pushes to Ease Marijuana Research Barriers with MEDS Act." *The Cannabist*, September 13. Available at https://www.thecannabist.co/2017/ 09/13/meds-act-marijuana-research-bill-senate-orrin-hatch/88013.

Labigalini, Eliseu, Lucio Rodrigues, and Dartiu Da Silveira. 1999. "Therapeutic Use of Cannabis by Crack Addicts in Brazil." *Journal of Psychoactive Drugs* 31:451–455.

Lacher, Irene. 1992. "The Way Patti Sees It." *Los Angeles Times*, April 30. Available at http://articles.latimes.com/1992-04-30/news/vw-1989_1_nancy-reagan.

La Ganga, Maria L. 2016. "California Recreational Marijuana Initiative Will Be on the November Ballot." *The Guardian*, May 4. Available at https://www.theguardian .com/society/2016/may/04/california-marijuana-election-2016.

Lagos, Marisa. 2010. "State Downgrades Pot Possession to Infraction." *San Francisco Chronicle*, October 2. Available at https://www.sfgate.com/news/article/State -downgrades-pot-possession-to-infraction-3251355.php.

Lake, Stefani, Thomas Kerr, and Julio Montaner. 2015. "Prescribing Medical Cannabis in Canada: Are We Being Too Cautious?" *Canadian Journal of Public Health* 106: 328–330.

The Lancet. 1963. "Pot." 2:989–990.

Lapidos, Juliet. 2014. "The Public Lightens Up about Weed." *New York Times*, July 26. Available at https://www.nytimes.com/2014/07/27/opinion/sunday/high-time-the -public-lightens-up-about-weed.html.

Law Enforcement against Prohibition (LEAP). 2016a. "Law Enforcement against Pro- hibition (LEAP) Endorses FL Medical Marijuana Initiative." November 7. Avail- able at http://copssaylegalize.blogspot.com/2016/11/press-release-law-enforce ment-against.html.

———. 2016b. "LEAP Declares Support for California Marijuana Legalization, Prop. 64." July 13. Available at http://copssaylegalize.blogspot.com/2016/07/press-release-leap -declares-support-for.html.

League of Oregon Cities. 2016. "Local Government Regulation of Marijuana in Oregon (Fourth Edition)." Available at https://www.orcities.org/Portals/17/Library/ 2016LocalRegulationofMarijuanAinOregon12-09-16.pdf.

Le Dain, Gerald. 1972. *Cannabis: The Report of the Commission of Inquiry into the Non- medical Use of Drugs*. Ottawa: Information Canada. Available at http://www .druglibrary.org/schaffer/library/studies/ledain/ldctoc.html.

Lee, Martin. 2012. *Smoke Signals*. New York: Scribner.

Legislative Research Bureau. 1974. *Effects of the Oregon Laws Decriminalizing Posses- sion and Use of Small Quantities of Marijuana*. Salem, OR: Legislative Research Bureau.

Legum, Gary. 2014. "Reagan Drug Czar Says Weed Won't Make You Gay Anymore but Will Still Kill You." *Wonkette*, October 30. Available at https://www.wonkette.com/ reagan-drug-czar-says-weed-wont-make-you-gay-anymore-but-will-still-kill-you.

Leon, Kenneth, and Ronald Weitzer. 2014. "Legalizing Recreational Marijuana: Com- paring Ballot Outcomes in Four States." *Journal of Qualitative Criminal Justice and Criminology* 2:193–218.

Leonhardt, David, and Alicia Parlapiano. 2015. "Why Gun Control and Abortion Are Different from Gay Marriage." *New York Times*, June 30. Available at https://www .nytimes.com/2015/06/30/upshot/why-gun-control-and-abortion-are-different -from-gay-marriage.html.

Lester, Barry, Lynne Andreozzi, and Lindsey Appiah. 2004. "Substance Use during Pregnancy: Time for Policy to Catch Up with Research." *Harm Reduction Journal* 1:1–44.

Levin, Sam. 2016. "Expots: Medical Marijuana Draws Parents to US for Their Children's Treatments." *The Guardian*, May 9. Available at https://www.theguardian.com/ society/2016/may/09/medical-marijuana-families-move-to-colorado-epilepsy.

Levine, Harry. 2013. "The Scandal of Racist Marijuana Arrests—and What to Do about It." *The Nation*, October 30. Available at https://www.thenation.com/article/scandal -racist-marijuana-arrests-and-what-do-about-it.

Levy, Pema. 2017. "The Harsh, Petty, and Highly Political Law of Jeff Sessions." *Mother Jones*, May–June. Available at https://www.motherjones.com/politics/2017/04/jeff -sessions-alabama-trump-voting.

Levy, Sharon. 2013. "Effects of Marijuana Policy on Children and Adolescents." *JAMA Pediatrics* 167:600–602.

Lewis, Amanda Chicago. 2016. "Marijuana Arrests Down in Colorado for White Teens, Up for Black and Latino Teens." *BuzzFeed*, May 10. Available at https://www .buzzfeednews.com/article/amandachicagolewis/marijuana-arrests-down-in-colo rado-for-white-teens-up-for-bl.

Liberal Party of Canada. n.d. "Marijuana." Available at http://www.liberal.ca./real change/marijuana (accessed June 12, 2016).

Lichtblau, Eric. 2017. "Obama Legacy of Freeing Prisoners May Come under Trump Siege." *New York Times*, January 15. Available at https://www.nytimes.com/2017/ 01/15/us/politics/obama-prisoners.html.

Lindblom, Mike. 2017. "As Deaths Mount, Lawmakers Seek to Ban All Handheld Device Use in Cars." *News Tribune*, January 3. Available at https://www.thenewstribune .com/news/politics-government/article124185194.html.

Lippman, Matthew. 2014. *Essential Criminal Law*. Thousand Oaks, CA: Sage.

Livingston, Melvin, Tracey E. Barnett, Chris Delcher, and Alexander C. Wagenaar. 2017. "Recreational Cannabis Legalization and Opioid-Related Deaths in Colorado, 2000–2015." *American Journal of Public Health* 107:1827–1829.

Lizza, Ryan. 2013. "The Middleman." *New Yorker*, May 13. Available at https://www .newyorker.com/magazine/2013/05/13/the-middleman-2.

Lockhead, Colton. 2017. "20 Things to Know about Legal Marijuana in Nevada." *Las Vegas Review Journal*, January 2. Available at https://www.reviewjournal.com/ news/pot-news/20-things-to-know-about-legal-marijuana-in-nevada.

Logan, Barry, Sherri Kacinko, and Douglas Beirness. 2016. *An Evaluation of Data from Drivers Arrested for Driving under the Influence in Relation to per Se Limits for Cannabis*. Washington, DC: American Automobile Association.

Londoño, Ernesto. 2017. "Uruguay's Marijuana Law Turns Pharmacists into Dealer." *New York Times*, July 19. Available at https://www.nytimes.com/2017/07/19/world/ americas/uruguay-legalizes-pot-marijuana.html.

Los Angeles Times Editorial Board. 2016. "It's Time to Legalize and Regulate Marijuana in California: Yes on Proposition 64." *Los Angeles Times*, September 16. Available at http://www.latimes.com/opinion/editorials/la-ed-proposition-64-20160918-snap -story.html.

Lucas, Phillipe Gabriel, Amanda Reiman, Mitch Earleywine, Stephanie K. McGowan, Megan Oleson, Michael P. Coward, and Brian Thomas. 2013. "Cannabis as a Substitute for Alcohol and Other Drugs: A Dispensary-Based Survey of Substitution Effect in Canadian Medical Cannabis Patients." *Addiction Research and Theory* 21:425–442.

Lucas, Phillipe, Zach Walsh, Kim Crosby, Robert Callaway, Lynne Belle-Isle, Robert Kay, Rielle Capler, and Susan Holtzman. 2016. "Substituting Cannabis for Prescription Drugs, Alcohol and Other Substances among Medical Cannabis Patients: The Impact of Contextual Factors." *Drug and Alcohol Review* 35:326–333.

Ludwig, Mike. 2016. "Will Donald Trump and Jeff Sessions Revamp the War on Drugs to Preserve White Power?" *Truthout*, December 1. Available at https://truthout.org/ articles/will-donald-trump-and-jeff-sessions-revamp-the-war-on-drugs-to -preserve-white-power.

———. 2017a. "It's Time to Legalize Marijuana and Abolish the Drug Czar." *Truthout*, April 20. Available at https://truthout.org/articles/it-s-time-to-legalize-marijuana -and-abolish-the-drug-czar.

———. 2017b. "Marijuana Reforms Gain Momentum as Trump Administration Mulls a Crackdown." *Truthout*, April 7. Available at https://truthout.org/articles/marijuana -reforms-gain-momentum-as-trump-administration-mulls-a-crackdown.

Lynskey, Michael T., Andrew C. Heath, Kathleen K. Bucholz, Wendy S. Slutske, Pamela A. F. Madden, Elliot C. Nelson, Dixie J. Statham, and Nicholas G. Martin. 2003. "Escalation of Drug Use in Early Onset Cannabis Users vs. Co-twin Controls." *Journal of the American Medical Association* 289:427–433.

MacCoun, Robert. 2010. "What Can We Learn from the Dutch Cannabis Coffeeshop Experience?" Rand Working Paper WR-768-RC. Available at https://www.rand.org/content/dam/rand/pubs/working_papers/2010/RAND_WR768.pdf.

MacCoun, Robert, and Michelle Mello. 2015. "Half-Baked: The Retail Promotion of Marijuana Edibles." *New England Journal of Medicine* 372:989–991.

MacCoun, Robert, and Peter Reuter. 2001. *Drug War Heresies*. Cambridge: Cambridge University Press.

MacLeod, Ian. 2015. "Pot Shots: The Long War over Marijuana Legalization." *Vancouver Sun*, December 27. Available at https://vancouversun.com/news/national/pot-shots-the-long-war-over-marijuana-legalization.

Mahdawi, Arwa. 2017. "America's Lucrative New Weed Industry Should Compensate the Black Victims of the Country's War on Drugs." *The Guardian*, August 27. Available at https://www.theguardian.com/commentisfree/2017/aug/27/americas-lucrative-new-weed-industry-should-compensate-the-black-victims-of-the-countrys-war-on-drugs.

Main St. Marijuana. 2018. "Main Street Marijuana Longview." Available at http://www.mainstmj.com/longview-menu.

Maine State Legislature. 2018. "Recreational Marijuana in Maine." Available at https://legislature.maine.gov/lawlibrary/recreational_marijuana_in_maine/9419.

Manderson, Desmond. 1999. "Formalism and Narrative in Law and Medicine: The Debate over Medical Marijuana Use." *Journal of Drug Issues* 29:121–134.

Mapes, Jeff. 2014a. "Marijuana Legalization: How Your Neighbors Voted." *The Oregonian*, November 26. Available at https://www.oregonlive.com/mapes/index.ssf/2014/11/marijuana_legalization_how_you.html.

———. 2014b. "Marijuana Legalization: The Rise of a Drug from Outlaw Status to Retail Shelves." *The Oregonian*, November 9. Available at https://www.oregonlive.com/mapes/index.ssf/2014/11/marijuana_legalization_the_ris.html.

Marcus, Ruth. 2014. "The Myths of Smoking Pot." *Washington Post*, June 24. Available at https://www.washingtonpost.com/opinions/ruth-marcus-national-institute-on-drug-abuse-chief-attacks-myths-of-pot-smoking/2014/06/24/12010d84-fbd9-11e3-8176-f2c941cf35f1_story.html.

Marie, Olivier, and Ulf Zolitz. 2015. "'High' Achievers? Cannabis Access and Academic Performance." Institute for the Study of Labor Discussion Paper 8900. Available at http://ftp.iza.org/dp8900.pdf.

———. 2017. "'High' Achievers? Cannabis Access and Academic Performance." *Review of Economic Studies* 84:210–237.

Marijuana Policy Project. n.d. "About Us." Available at https://www.mpp.org/about (accessed June 15, 2016).

———. 2017. "Summary of Oregon's Measure 91." Available at https://www.mpp.org/states/oregon/summary-of-oregons-measure-91.

———. 2018. "Maine." Available at https://www.mpp.org/states/maine.

Marist Poll. 2017. "Weed and the American Family." Available at http://maristpoll.marist.edu/yahoo-newsmarist-poll.

Marks, Gene. 2017. "Business Is Booming: North American Marijuana Sales Up 30 Percent in 2016." *The Cannabist*, January 6. Available at https://www.thecannabist.co/2017/01/06/marijuana-sales-figures-2016/70821.

Marple, Olivia. 2015. "Chile Considers Cannabis Decriminalization, Highlighting Growing Movement in Latin America." *Council on Hemispheric Affairs*, August 18. Available at http://www.coha.org/chile-considers-cannabis-decriminalization-highlights-a-growing-movement-in-latin-america.

Martin, Alyson, and Nushin Rashidian. 2014. *A New Leaf: The End of Cannabis Prohibition*. New York: New Press.

Martin, Jonathan. 2012. "Children's Alliance Backs Pot Measure on Ballot." *Seattle Times*, September 10. Available at https://www.seattletimes.com/seattle-news/childrens-alliance-backs-pot-measure-on-ballot.

———. 2015. "Should Marijuana Home Grows Be Legal in Washington?" *Seattle Times*, January 28. Available at http://blogs.seattletimes.com/opinionnw/2015/01/28/should-marijuana-home-grows-be-legal-in-washington.

Marum, Anna. 2017. "In Trump Era, Oregon Post Industry Leaders Surprisingly Chill about Crackdown." *The Oregonian*, March 3. Available at https://www.oregonlive.com/marijuana/index.ssf/2017/03/recreational_marijuana_oregon_trump_era.html.

Mayor's Committee on Marihuana. 1944. *The La Guardia Committee Report: The Marihuana Problem in the City of New York*. New York: New York Academy of Medicine. Available at http://www.druglibrary.org/schaffer/library/studies/lag/lagmenu.htm.

McCarthy, Justin. 2017. "Record-High Support for Legalizing Marijuana Use in U.S." Gallup, October 25. Available at https://news.gallup.com/poll/221018/record-high-support-legalizing-marijuana.aspx.

McCarthy, Pat. 2016. Letter to Doug Richardson. June 30. Available at http://www.co.pierce.wa.us/DocumentCenter/View/42379.

McClure, James. 2017. "Cannabis Prohibition 'Creates Substantial Public Safety Risks,' State Lawmakers Say." *Civilized*, August 8. Available at https://www.civilized.life/articles/cannabis-prohibition-endangers-public-safetyis-a-risk-to-public-safety.

McCullum, April. 2017. "Gov. Scott Vetoes Legal Marijuana, but Summer Could Bring Compromise." *Burlington Free Press*, May 24. Available at https://www.burlingtonfreepress.com/story/news/politics/2017/05/24/gov-scott-vetoes-marijuana-legalization-bill/336048001.

McGhee, Tom. 2014. "More Pot Arrests at Denver Schools, but No Sign of Increasing Usage." *Denver Post*, December 19. Available at https://www.denverpost.com/2014/12/19/more-pot-arrests-at-denver-schools-but-no-sign-of-increasing-usage.

McGreal, Chris. 2016. "'Commercialization Won Out': Will Legal Marijuana Be the Next Big Tobacco?" *The Guardian*, October 31. Available at https://www.theguardian.com/society/2016/oct/14/legal-marijuana-tobacco-industry-california-colorado-vote.

McGreevy, Patrick. 2016a. "Billionaire Activists like Sean Parker and George Soros Are Fueling the Campaign to Legalize Pot." *Los Angeles Times*, November 2. Available at http://www.latimes.com/politics/la-pol-ca-proposition64-cash-snap-20161102-story.html.

———. 2016b. "California Initiative Draws Fire for Opening the Door to TV Ads That Promote Pot Smoking." *Los Angeles Times*, July 31. Available at http://www.latimes.com/politics/la-pol-ca-california-pot-ads-20160731-snap-story.html.

———. 2016c. "10 Things You Need to Know about Legalized Pot in California." *Los Angeles Times*, November 7. Available at http://www.latimes.com/politics/la-pol-ca-proposition-64-marijuana-legalization-explained-20161107-story.html.

———. 2016d. "Weed's Legal in California, but Activists Fear a Battle Ahead with Jeff Sessions, Trump's Pick for Attorney General." *Los Angeles Times*, December 1. Available at http://www.latimes.com/politics/la-pol-ca-marijuana-legalization-jeff-sessions-snap-20161201-story.html.

———. 2017. "California Lawmakers Want to Block Police from Helping Federal Drug Agents Take Action against Marijuana License Holders." *Los Angeles Times*, March 23. Available at http://www.latimes.com/politics/la-pol-sac-pot-enforcement-legislation-20170323-story.html.

McLoughlin, B.C., J. A. Pushpa-Rajah, D. Gillies, J. Rathbone, H. Variend, E. Kalakouti, and K. Kyprianou. 2014. "Cannabis and Schizophrenia." *Cochrane Database of Systematic Reviews* 14 (10). Available at https://www.ncbi.nlm.nih.gov/pubmed/25314586.

McMaken, Ryan. 2016. "63 Million Americans Now Live in States with Legal Recreational Marijuana." Mises Institute, November 9. Available at https://mises.org/wire/63-million-americans-now-live-states-legal-recreational-marijuana.

Medline Plus. 2009. "PTSD: A Growing Epidemic." Winter. Available at https://medlineplus.gov/magazine/issues/winter09/articles/winter09pg10-14.html.

Meehan, Maureen. 2016. "Americans for Safe Access Legally Challenge DEA Misinformation about Pot." *High Times*, December 7. Available at https://hightimes.com/news/americans-for-safe-access-legally-challenge-dea-misinformation-about-pot.

Meier, Madeline H., Avshalom Caspi, Antony Ambler, HonaLee Harrington, Renate Houts, Richard S. E. Keefe, Kay McDonald, Aimee Ward, Richie Poulton, and Terrie E. Moffitt. 2012. "Persistent Cannabis Users Show Neuropsychological Decline from Childhood to Midlife." *Proceedings of the National Academy of Sciences* 109:E2657–E2664. Available at http://www.pnas.org/content/109/40/E2657.

Memmott, Mark. 2012. "'We've Got Bigger Fish to Fry' Than Going after Pot Smokers, Obama Says." *NPR*, December 14. Available at https://www.npr.org/sections/thetwo-way/2012/12/14/167244381/weve-got-bigger-fish-to-fry-than-going-after-pot-smokers-obama-says.

Meola, Stacy D., Caitlin Tearney, Sharlee A. Haas, Timothy B. Hackett, and Elisa Mazzaferro. 2012. "Evolution of Trends in Marijuana Toxicosis in Dogs Living in a State with Legalized Medical Marijuana." *Journal of Veterinary Emergency and Critical Care* 22:690–696.

Mercury. 2017. "Toke Talks." April 19, p. 48.

Merica, Dan. 2017. "White House Drug Policy Office Facing Massive Cuts, Draft Memo Says." *CNN*, May 5. Available at https://www.cnn.com/2017/05/05/politics/white-house-office-drug-policy-cut/index.html.

Merritt, Jeralyn. 2004. "Reagan's Drug War Legacy." *AlterNet*, June 18. Available at https://www.alternet.org/story/18990/reagan%27s_drug_war_legacy.

Meyer, Jeremy. 2016. "Three Years after Banning Pot Clubs, Denver's Mayor Rethinks His Position." *The Cannabist*, January 18. Available at https://www.thecannabist.co/2016/01/18/pot-clubs-mayor-michael-hancock/46804.

Meza, Summer. 2015. "Teen Boredom May Be More of a 'Gateway' Than Marijuana." *Seattle Post-Intelligencer*, July 7. Available at https://blog.seattlepi.com/marijuana/2015/07/07/teen-boredom-may-be-more-of-a-gateway-than-marijuana.

Michaelson, Jay. 2017. "Legal Weed's No. 1 Warrior Puts Down His Pipe." *Daily Beast*, April 28. Available at https://www.thedailybeast.com/legal-weeds-no-1-warrior-puts-down-his-pipe.

Migoya, David. 2015. "University of Denver Adds Pot Business to Law School Curriculum." *Denver Post*, January 16. Available at https://www.denverpost.com/2015/01/16/university-of-denver-adds-pot-business-to-law-school-curriculum.

Military Surgeon. 1933. "Mariajuana [*sic*] Smoking in Panama." 73. Available at http://www.druglibrary.org/schaffer/library/studies/panama/panama1.htm.

Miller, Jacquie. 2017. "Cannabis Gummy Bears and Cookies: Edible Products Pose a Challenge as Canada Moves to Legalize Pot." *Ottawa Citizen*, June 18. Available at https://ottawacitizen.com/news/local-news/feature-on-edibles.

Miller, Joshua. 2016. "It's Official: Marijuana Is Legal in Massachusetts." *Boston Globe*, December 14. Available at https://www.bostonglobe.com/metro/2016/12/14/official-marijuana-legal-midnight-massachusetts/10Rl2inZQMjSPrNAMSBkCJ/story.html.

Mills, Evan. 2012. "The Carbon Footprint of Indoor Cannabis Production." *Energy Policy* 46:58–67.

Miroff, Nick. 2017. "In Uruguay's Marijuana Experiment, the Government Is Your Pot Dealer." *Washington Post*, July 7. Available at https://www.washingtonpost.com/world/the_americas/in-uruguays-marijuana-experiment-the-government-is-your-pot-dealer/2017/07/07/6212360c-5a88-11e7-aa69-3964a7d55207_story.html.

Miron, Jeffrey. 2015. "The Case to Reclassify Grass." *Newsweek*, March 10. Available at https://www.newsweek.com/case-reclassify-grass-312845.

———. 2017. "This Economist Has a Strategy to Kill the Marijuana Black Market." *The Cannabist*, August 14. Available at https://www.thecannabist.co/2017/08/14/marijuana-black-market-economy/85968.

Mogensen, Jackie Flynn. 2017. "A Quick Guide to Legal Pot in California." *Mother Jones*, December 26. Available at https://www.motherjones.com/politics/2017/12/a-quick-guide-to-legal-pot-in-california.

Mohanraj, Rajiv, and Martin J. Brodie. 2006. "Diagnosing Refractory Epilepsy: Response to Sequential Treatment Schedules." *European Journal of Neurology* 13:277–282.

Mokrysz, C., R. Landy, S. H. Gage, M. R. Munafo, J. P. Roiser, and H. V. Curran. 2016. "Are IQ and Educational Outcomes in Teenagers Related to Their Cannabis Use? A Prospective Cohort Study." *Journal of Psychopharmacology* 30:159–168.

Monitoring the Future. 2016. "Teen Use of Any Illicit Drug Other Than Marijuana at New Low, Same True for Alcohol." Available at http://www.monitoringthefuture.org/pressreleases/16drugpr_complete.pdf.

Montgomery, Lori, and Craig Whitlock. 2003. "Medical Marijuana Bill Passes." *Washington Post*, March 27. Available at https://www.washingtonpost.com/archive/local/2003/03/27/medical-marijuana-bill-passes/86c1bfbf-c9a9-4665-8cdc-dc1b4c9b803c.

Mooney, Chris. 2005. *The Republican War on Science*. New York: Basic Books.

Morral, Andrew, Daniel McCaffrey, and Susan Paddock. 2002. "Reassessing the Marijuana Gateway Effect." *Addiction* 38:1493–1504.

Morris, Chris. 2017. "Legal Marijuana Sales Are Expected to Hit $10 Billion This Year." *Fortune*, December 6. Available at http://fortune.com/2017/12/06/legal-marijuana-sales-10-billion.

Morrissey, Mitchell. 2016. Letter to No on 64 Campaign and SAM Action. October 12. Available at https://www.westword.com/news/legal-pot-harms-colorado-and-other-states-need-to-know-denver-da-says-8466009.

Mosendz, Polly. 2016. "Weed Dog Treats Booming Business across America." *The Cannabist*, December 27. Available at https://www.thecannabist.co/2016/12/27/marijuana-dog-treats-growing-business/70077.

Mosher, Clayton. 1999. "Imperialism, Irrationality and Illegality. The First 90 Years of Canadian Drug Policy." *New Scholars—New Visions* 3:1–40.

———. 2011a. "Anslinger, Harry." In *Encyclopedia of Drug Policy*, edited by Mark Kleiman and James Hawdon, 27–28. Thousand Oaks, CA: Sage.

———. 2011b. "Convergence or Divergence? Recent Developments in Drug Policies in Canada and the United States." *American Review of Canadian Studies* 41:370–386.

Mosher, Clayton, and Scott Akins. 2014. *Drugs and Drug Policy: The Control of Consciousness Alteration*. Thousand Oaks, CA: Sage.

Mosher, Clayton, Terance Miethe, and Timothy Hart. 2011. *The Mismeasure of Crime*. Thousand Oaks, CA: Sage.

Murkin, George. 2016. "Will Drug Use Rise? Exploring a Key Concern about Decriminalising or Regulating Drugs." Transform, June. Available at https://www.tdpf.org.uk/sites/default/files/Use-report-2016.pdf.

Murray, David W., Brian Blake, and John P. Walters. 2017. "Countering the Threat of Legalized Marijuana: A Blueprint for Federal, Community, and Private Action." Hudson Institute, February 27. Available at https://www.hudson.org/research/13392-countering-the-threat-of-legalized-marijuana-a-blueprint-for-federal-community-and-private-action.

Murray, Jon. 2017. "Denver Issues Final Social Marijuana Rules, Dropping Waiver and Ventilation Plan Requirements." *Denver Post*, June 30. Available at https://www.denverpost.com/2017/06/30/denver-final-social-marijuana-use-rules.

Murrieta, Ed. 2015. "Mark Twain's 1865 Hashish Escapade Inspires Revisit." *The Cannabist*, September 18. Available at https://www.thecannabist.co/2015/09/18/mark-twain-san-francisco-hashish-mania/41175.

Musto, David. 1999. *The American Disease*. New Haven, CT: Yale University Press.

Nadelmann, Ethan. 2016. "Fears of Marijuana's Gateway Effect Vastly Exceed the Evidence." *New York Times*, April 26. Available at https://www.nytimes.com/roomfordebate/2016/04/26/is-marijuana-a-gateway-drug/fears-of-marijuanas-gateway-effect-vastly-exceed-the-evidence.

Nathan, David, H. Westley Clark, and Jocelyn Elders. 2017. "The Physicians' Case for Marijuana Legalization." *American Journal of Public Health* 107:1746–1747.

Nathman, Avital Norman. 2016. "The Complete Rundown of Celebrity Cannabis Businesses." *Merry Jane*, September 23. Available at https://merryjane.com/culture/celebrity-cannabis-businesses.

National Academies of Sciences, Engineering, and Medicine (NASEM). 2017. *The Health Effects of Cannabis and Cannabinoids: The Current State of Evidence and Recommendations for Research*. Washington, DC: National Academies Press.

National Center for Post-traumatic Stress Disorder (NCPTSD). 2018. "Understanding PTSD and PTSD Treatment." Available at https://www.ptsd.va.gov/public/understanding_ptsd/booklet.pdf.

National Commission on Marihuana and Drug Abuse. 1972. *Marihuana: A Signal of Misunderstanding*. Available at http://www.druglibrary.org/schaffer/library/studies/nc/ncmenu.htm.

National Conference of State Legislatures. 2018. "State Medical Marijuana Laws." June 27. Available at http://www.ncsl.org/research/health/state-medical-marijuana-laws.aspx.

National Criminal Justice Association Center for Justice Planning. n.d. "Byrne JAG Program." Available at http://www.ncjp.org/byrne_jag (accessed June 16, 2017).

National Highway Traffic Safety Administration. 2014. "Drug and Human Performance Fact Sheets." Available at https://www.nhtsa.gov/sites/nhtsa.dot.gov/files/809725 -drugshumanperformfs.pdf.

National Institute on Drug Abuse. n.d. "About NIDA." Available at http://www .drugabuse.gov/about-nida (accessed December 12, 2016).

———. 2018. "Marijuana: Facts Parents Need to Know." Available at https://d14 rmgtrwzf5a.cloudfront.net/sites/default/files/mj_parents_facts_brochure.pdf.

National Institutes of Health (NIH). 1997. "Workshop on the Medical Utility of Marijuana." Available at https://maps.org/research/mmj/mmj-news/1402-nih-workshop -on-the-medical-utility-of-marijuana.

National Organization for the Reform of Marijuana Laws. 2013. "About NORML." Available at http://norml.org/about.

———. 2018. "State Laws." Available at http://norml.org/laws.

Neavyn, Mark J., Eike Blohm, Kavita M. Babu, and Steven B. Bird. 2014. "Medical Marijuana and Driving: A Review." *Journal of Medical Toxicology* 10:269–279.

Nelson, Steven. 2016. "Marijuana Is Harder Than Ever for Younger Teens to Find." *U.S. News and World Report*, December 13. Available at https://www.usnews.com/news/ data-mine/articles/2016-12-13/marijuana-is-harder-than-ever-for-younger-teens-to -find.

Netherland, Julie. 2016. "Making Drug Policy More Evidence-Based: The Role of Scientists and Scholars." Drug Policy Alliance, May 5. Available at http://www.drugpolicy .org/blog/making-drug-policy-more-evidence-based-role-scientists-and-other -scholars.

Newman, Katelyn. 2017. "Milestoned: Colorado Pot Tax Revenue Surpasses $500M." *U.S. News and World Report*, July 20. Available at https://www.usnews.com/news/ best-states/colorado/articles/2017-07-20/colorado-pot-tax-revenue-surpasses-500 -million.

Newman, Tony. 2005. "After Drug War Zealots Pressure AARP the Magazine to Kill Medical Marijuana Story, the L.A. Times Runs Version on Front Page of Today." Drug Policy Alliance, April 27. Available at https://www.drugpolicy.org/index.php/ news/2005/04/after-drug-war-zealots-pressure-aarp-magazine-kill-medical -marijuana-story-la-times-run.

Newport, Frank. 2017. "Wyoming, North Dakota and Mississippi Most Conservative." Gallup, January 31. Available at https://news.gallup.com/poll/203204/wyoming -north-dakota-mississippi-conservative.aspx.

News Medical. 2013. "Psychiatrist Claims Medical Marijuana Dangerous for Treatment of Psychiatric Problems." January 22. Available at https://www.news-medical.net/ news/20130122/Psychiatrist-claims-medical-marijuana-dangerous-for-treatment -of-psychiatric-problems.aspx.

Newsweek. 1954. "Reefers on KPFA." May 10, p. 17.

New Yorker. 1951. "Saw-Toothed." August 11, pp. 18–19.

New York Times. 1974. "Mrs. Ford May Favor Softer Marijuana Laws." September 8. Available at https://www.nytimes.com/1974/09/08/archives/mrs-ford-may-favor -softer-marijuana-laws.html.

———. 1976. "A Carter Son Confirms He Smoked Marijuana." September 7. Available at https://www.nytimes.com/1976/09/07/archives/a-carter-son-confirms-he -smoked-marijuana.html.

———. 2014. "Repeal Prohibition, Again." July 27. Available at https://www.nytimes.com/interactive/2014/07/27/opinion/sunday/high-time-marijuana-legalization.html.

———. 2016a. "Outrageous Sentences for Marijuana." April 14. Available at https://www.nytimes.com/2016/04/14/opinion/outrageous-sentences-for-marijuana.html.

———. 2016b. "Stop Treating Marijuana like Heroin." August 12. Available at https://www.nytimes.com/2016/08/13/opinion/a-small-victory-for-more-sensible-marijuana-policies.html.

Nichols, Chris. 2016. "Feinstein's Claim about Marijuana Ads on 'Prime Time' TV Goes Up in Smoke." *Politifact*, August 5. Available at https://www.politifact.com/california/statements/2016/aug/05/dianne-feinstein/feinsteins-claim-about-prime-time-marijuana-tv-ads.

Nicholson, Kieran. 2015. "Fed Study Says Pot Use by Youth on Rise in Colorado, Leads Nation." *Denver Post*, December 17. Available at https://www.denverpost.com/2015/12/17/fed-study-says-pot-use-by-youth-on-rise-in-colorado-leads-nation.

Nirappil, Fenit. 2017. "Black Md. Lawmakers Push Bills to Diversify Medical Marijuana Industry." *Washington Post*, January 27. Available at https://www.washingtonpost.com/local/md-politics/black-md-lawmakers-push-bills-to-diversify-medical-marijuana-industry/2017/01/27/c63d4f1e-e4a3-11e6-ba11-63c4b4fb5a63_story.html.

Nixon, Richard. 1971. "Remarks about an Intensified Program for Drug Abuse Prevention and Control." June 17. Available at http://www.presidency.ucsb.edu/ws/?pid=3047.

Noon, Alison. 2017. "You Could Find Weed for Sale in a New State as Soon as July 1." *The Cannabist*, February 9. Available at https://www.thecannabist.co/2017/02/09/nevada-recreational-marijuana-start/73373.

Northwest High Intensity Drug Trafficking Area. 2016. *Washington State Marijuana Impact Report*. Seattle: Northwest High Intensity Drug Trafficking Area. Available at https://drive.google.com/file/d/0Bxs3xMLjUamANHhRRkluWkRobXM/view?pref=2&pli=1.

Nutt, David. 2009. "Government vs Science over Drug and Alcohol Policy." *The Lancet*, 374:1731–1733.

———. 2012. *Drugs without the Hot Air*. Cambridge, UK: UIT Cambridge.

Nutt, David, Leslie King, William Saulsbury, and Colin Blakemore. 2007. "Development of a Rational Scale to Assess the Harms of Drugs." *The Lancet* 369:1047–1053.

Office of National Drug Control Policy. 2003. "Who's Really in Prison for Marijuana?" Available at https://www.ncjrs.gov/ondcppubs/publications/pdf/whos_in_prison_for_marij.pdf.

———. 2010. "President Obama Releases National Strategy to Reduce Drug Use and Its Consequences." May 11. Available at https://obamawhitehouse.archives.gov/realitycheck/the-press-office/president-obama-releases-national-strategy-reduce-drug-use-and-its-consequences.

———. 2011. "Advancing a New Approach to Drug Policy: Key Accomplishments." June. Available at https://www.ncjrs.gov/pdffiles1/ondcp/newapproach.pdf.

———. 2014. *National Drug Control Strategy, 2014*. Washington, DC: Office of National Drug Control Policy. Available at https://obamawhitehouse.archives.gov/sites/default/files/ondcp/policy-and-research/ndcs_2014.pdf.

Ogden, David. 2009. "Memorandum for Selected United States Attorneys: Investigations and Prosecutions in States Authorizing the Medical Use of Marijuana." U.S.

Department of Justice, October 19. Available at https://www.aclu.org/files/assets/DOJ_Memorandum_to_US_Attorneys_re_medical_marijuana_enforcement.pdf.

Oliere, Stephanie, Antoine Jolette-Riopel, Stephane Potvin, and Didier Jutras-Aswad. 2013. "Modulation of the Endocannabinoid System: Vulnerability Factor and New Treatment Target for Stimulant Addiction." *Front Psychiatry* 4:109.

Onders, Bridget, Marcel J. Casavant, Henry A. Spiller, Thiphalak Chounthirath, and Gary A. Smith. 2016. "Marijuana Exposure among Children Younger Than Six Years in the United States." *Clinical Pediatrics* 55:428–436.

O'Neill, Brian. 2012. "I-502 Discussion Important—and Entertaining." *Tacoma News Tribune*, October 14.

Ontario Ministry of Finance. 2017. "Ontario's Cannabis Retail and Distribution Model." September 8. Available at https://news.ontario.ca/mof/en/2017/09/ontarios-cannabis-retail-and-distribution-model.html.

On the Issues. 2016. "Joe Biden on Drugs." June 15. Available at http://www.ontheissues.org/2016/Joe_Biden_Drugs.htm.

Oregon Department of Revenue. 2018. "Statistics from Oregon Marijuana Tax Returns: Calendar Year 2016." Available at https://www.oregon.gov/DOR/programs/gov-research/Documents/marijuana-tax-report_2016.pdf.

Oregon Liquor Control Commission. 2017. "Active Marijuana Retail Licenses Approved as of May 12, 2017." Available at https://digital.osl.state.or.us/islandora/object/osl%3A84992.

Oregon Secretary of State. 2012. "Voters' Pamphlet." Available at https://sos.oregon.gov/elections/Documents/pamphlet/2012/general-book18.pdf.

———. 2014. "November 4, 2014, General Election, Official Abstract of Votes." Available at https://sos.oregon.gov/elections/Documents/results/results-2014-general-election.pdf.

Oregon State Police. 2017. *A Baseline Evaluation of Cannabis Enforcement Priorities in Oregon*. Salem: Oregon State Police.

Orsi, Peter. 2016. "Mexico Moves Closer to Medical Marijuana with Overwhelming Senate Approval." *The Cannabist*, December 14. Available at https://www.thecannabist.co/2016/12/14/mexico-moves-closer-to-legal-medical-marijuana-with-overwhelming-senate-approval/69470.

O'Shaughnessy, William. 1843. "On the Preparations of the Indian Hemp, or Gunjah (*Cannabis Indica*)." *Provincial Medical Journal*, no. 123 (1843): 343–347, 363–369.

Overton, Penelope. 2017. "Lawmakers Propose 20% Tax on Recreational Marijuana." *Portland Press Herald*, July 25. Available at https://www.pressherald.com/2017/07/25/maine-recreational-pot-sales-would-be-taxed-at-20-percent-under-proposal.

Pacula, Rosalie Liccardo, Beau Kilmer, Alexander C. Wagenaar, Frank J. Chaloupka, and Jonathan P. Caulkins. 2014. "Developing Public Health Regulations for Marijuana: Lessons from Alcohol and Tobacco." *American Journal of Public Health* 104:1021–1028.

Pasquariello, Alex. 2017. "Legalization Opponent Kevin Sabet Takes On Colorado at Anti-marijuana Event." *The Cannabist*, October 6. Available at https://www.thecannabist.co/2017/10/06/colorado-marijuana-legalization-symposium-kevin-sabet-sam/89545.

Pasquariello, Alex, and Polly Washburn. 2017. "Alaska and Washington Govs Push Back on Sessions' Marijuana Enforcement Letters." *The Cannabist*, August 16. Available at https://www.thecannabist.co/2017/08/16/jeff-sessions-marijuana-alaska-washington-letters/86224.

Payne, John. 2013. "The Hidden History of the Pot Lobby." *Reason*, May 25. Available at http://reason.com/archives/2013/05/25/the-hidden-history-of-the-pot-lobby.

Peele, Stanton. n.d. "The General McCaffrey Scientific Fool Award." Available at http://www.peele.net/mccaffrey/mccaffrey.html (accessed January 21, 2017).

Pew Research Center. 2017. "Support for Same-Sex Marriage Grows, Even among Groups That Had Been Skeptical." June 26. Available at http://www.people-press.org/2017/06/26/support-for-same-sex-marriage-grows-even-among-groups-that-had-been-skeptical.

Pfaff, John. 2017. *Locked In*. New York: Basic Books.

Phillips, Noelle. 2016. "Some Colorado Pols Paint Dark Picture for Legal Weed." *The Cannabist*, November 1. Available at https://www.thecannabist.co/2016/11/01/marijuana-legalization-colorado-pols-paint-dark-picture/66527.

Picard, Andre. 2014. "Canada's Pot Policy Needs to Sober Up." *Globe and Mail*, August 21. Available at https://www.theglobeandmail.com/news/national/canadas-pot-policy-needs-to-sober-up/article20166378.

———. 2017. "Ontario's Pot-Store Plan Is Legitimate—and Pathetic." *Globe and Mail*, September 11. Available at https://www.theglobeandmail.com/opinion/ontarios-pot-store-plan-is-legitimate-and-pathetic/article36227649.

Piper, Brian J., Rebecca M. DeKeuster, Monica L. Beals, Catherine M. Cobb, Corey A. Burchman, Leah Perkinson, Shayne T. Lynn, Stephanie D. Nichols, and Alexander T. Abess. 2017. "Substitution of Medical Cannabis for Pharmaceutical Agents for Pain, Anxiety, and Sleep." *Journal of Psychopharmacology* 31 (5): 569–575.

Poison Control. 2015. "Poison Statistics: National Data, 2014." Available at https://www.poison.org/poison-statistics-national-data-from-2014.

Pollan, Michael. 2001. *The Botany of Desire*. New York: Random House.

Powell, Betsy. 2016. "Pot Tax Revenue Pays for Denver Sidewalks and Schools: Would It Work Here?" *Toronto Star*, January 15. Available at https://www.thestar.com/news/city_hall/2016/01/15/pot-tax-revenue-pays-for-denver-sidewalks-and-schools-would-it-work-here.html.

Power, Robert A., Karin H. J. Verweij, Mohd Zuhair, G. W. Montgomery, Anjali K. Henders, A. Christopher Heath, Pamela A. F. Madden, S. E. Medland, Naomi R. Wray, and Nicholas G. Martin. 2014. "Genetic Predisposition to Schizophrenia Associated with Increased Use of Cannabis." *Molecular Psychiatry* 19:1201–1204.

Proceedings: White House Conference on Narcotic and Drug Abuse. 1962. Washington, DC: Government Printing Office.

Pulkkinen, Levi. 2013. "Charge: High Driver Killed Teen Pedestrian." *Seattle Post-Intelligencer*, March 3. Available at https://www.seattlepi.com/local/article/Charge-High-driver-killed-teen-pedestrian-4348939.php.

Quinn, Melissa. 2018. "Trump CDC Director Resigns after Stock Purchases in Global Tobacco Company Revealed." *Washington Examiner*, January 31. Available at https://www.washingtonexaminer.com/trump-cdc-director-resigns-after-stock-purchases-in-global-tobacco-company-revealed.

Quinton, Sophie. 2016. "Why Marijuana Businesses Still Can't Get Bank Accounts." Pew, March 22. Available at http://www.pewtrusts.org/en/research-and-analysis/blogs/stateline/2016/03/22/why-marijuana-businesses-still-cant-get-bank-accounts.

Raby, John. 2017. "West Virginia Governor Signs Medical Marijuana Bill." *WHSV*, April 19. Available at http://www.whsv.com/content/news/West-Virginia-governor-signs-medical-marijuana-bill-419889323.html.

Ray, Oakley, and Charles Ksir. 2004. *Drugs, Society, and Human Behavior*. New York: McGraw-Hill.

Reilly, Mollie. 2016. "Congress Clears Way for Veterans to Get Medical Marijuana." *Huffington Post*, May 19. Available at https://www.huffingtonpost.com/entry/medical-marijuana-veterans-congress_us_573de75de4b0646cbeec57ed.

Reiman, Amanda. 2009. "Cannabis as a Substitute for Alcohol and Other Drugs." *Harm Reduction Journal* 6. Available at https://harmreductionjournal.biomedcentral.com/articles/10.1186/1477-7517-6-35.

———. 2015a. "Two New Antidotes for Reefer Madness." Drug Policy Alliance, August 10. Available at http://www.drugpolicy.org/blog/two-new-antidotes-reefer-madness.

———. 2015b. "Why People in the Health Field Are Changing Their Minds about Marijuana Policy." Drug Policy Alliance, February 3. Available at http://www.drugpolicy.org/blog/why-people-health-field-are-changing-their-minds-about-marijuana-policy.

Reinarman, Craig. 2002. "Why Dutch Drug Law Threatens the U.S." In *Busted*, edited by Mike Gray, 127–133. New York: Thunder's Mouth Press/Nation Books.

Reis, Jared, Reto Auer, Michael P. Bancks, David C. Goff Jr., Cora E. Lewis, Mark J. Pletcher, Jamal S. Rana, James M. Shikany, and Stephen Sidney. 2017. "Cumulative Lifetime Marijuana Use and Incident Cardiovascular Disease in Middle Age: The Coronary Artery Risk Development in Youth Adults (CARDIA) Study." *American Journal of Public Health* 107:601–606.

Remnick, David. 2014. "Going the Distance: On and Off the Road with Barack Obama." *New Yorker*, January 27. Available at https://www.newyorker.com/magazine/2014/01/27/going-the-distance-david-remnick.

Revesz, Richard. 2017. "According to Scott Pruitt, States Only Have the Right to Pollute, Not Protect Their Environments." *Los Angeles Times*, March 20. Available at http://www.latimes.com/opinion/op-ed/la-oe-revesz-pruitt-epa-federalism-20170320-story.html.

Riggs, Mike. 2013. "Obama's War on Pot." *The Nation*, October 30. Available at https://www.thenation.com/article/obamas-war-pot.

Rindels, Michelle. 2016. "Things to Know about Nevada's Marijuana Ballot Measure." *The Cannabist*, September 26. Available at https://www.thecannabist.co/2016/09/26/nevada-marijuana-ballot-measure/63939.

Rittiman, Brandon. 2016. "Where Does All That Colorado Pot Tax Go?" *9News*, August 15. Available at https://www.9news.com/article/news/where-does-all-that-colorado-pot-tax-go/73-298554132.

Robertson, Grant, and Greg McArthur. 2016. "Shoppers Drug Mart Eyes Sales of Medical Marijuana." *Globe and Mail*, February 23. Available at https://www.theglobeandmail.com/report-on-business/shoppers-drug-mart-shows-budding-interest-in-selling-medical-pot/article28863445.

Rocha, Francisco Carlos Machado, Jair Guilherme dos Santos Junior, Sergio Carlos Stefano, and Dartiu Xavier da Silveira. 2014. "Systematic Review of the Literature on Clinical and Experimental Trials on the Antitumor Effects of Cannabinoids in Gliomas." *Journal of Neuro-Oncology* 116:11–24.

Rocheleau, Matt. 2017. "Why Are Whitehouse.gov Web Pages Disappearing?" *Boston Globe*, January 20. Available at https://www.bostonglobe.com/metro/2017/01/20/why-are-whitehouse-gov-web-pages-disappearing/gd0HEAAU49hrLZMCiOQwuN/story.html.

Rocky Mountain High Intensity Drug Trafficking Area. 2015. *The Legalization of Marijuana in Colorado: The Impact.* Denver: Rocky Mountain High Intensity Drug Trafficking Area. Available at https://studylib.net/doc/8711951/the-legalization-of -marijuana-in-colorado--the-impact.

Rodgers, Jakob. 2016. "Number of Colorado Marijuana Plants Caregivers Can Grow Will Drastically Drop in 2017." *The Cannabist,* December 28. Available at https://www .thecannabist.co/2016/12/28/colorado-marijuana-plants-caregivers-2017/70131.

Roffman, Roger. 2014. *Marijuana Nation.* New York: Pegasus Books.

Rogeberg, Ole. 2013. "Correlations between Cannabis Use and IQ Change in the Dunedin Cohort Are Consistent with Confounding from Socioeconomic Status." *Proceedings of the National Academy of Sciences* 110 (11): 4251–4254.

Rogeberg, Ole, and Rune Elvik. 2016. "The Effects of Cannabis Intoxication on Motor Vehicle Collision Revisited and Revised." *Addiction* 111:1348–1359.

Rohrabacher, Dana. 2016. "Rohrabacher Urges Continuation of Medical Marijuana Amendment." October 26. Available at https://rohrabacher.house.gov/media-center/ press-releases/rohrabacher-urges-continuation-of-medical-marijuana-amendment.

Romero, Dennis. 2016. "Why This Time Will Be Different for Marijuana Legalization." *Los Angeles Times,* August 20. Available at http://www.latimes.com/opinion/op-ed/ la-oe-romero-prop64-marijuana-legalization-20160819-snap-story.html.

Rose, Joseph. 2016. "Oregon's First Marijuana Drive-Thru Coming to Gold Beach." *The Oregonian,* January 31. Available at https://www.oregonlive.com/pacific-northwest -news/index.ssf/2016/01/oregons_first_marijuana_drive-.html.

Rosenberg, Chuck. 2016. Letter to Gina M. Raimondo, Jay R. Inslee, and Bryan A. Krumm. August 11. Available at https://www.deadiversion.usdoj.gov/schedules/ marijuana/Acting_Adminstrator_Rosenberg_Response_to_Request_Marijuana _Rescheduling.pdf.

Rosenhall, Laura. 2017. "Why Black Market Marijuana Could Remain Huge in California." *Los Angeles Daily News,* August 5. Available at https://www.dailynews.com/ 2017/08/05/why-black-market-marijuana-could-remain-huge-in-california.

Rottenberg, Josh. 2015. "Talk Show Host's Stoner Dream Comes True, and It's High Time." *Los Angeles Times,* February 9. Available at http://www.latimes.com/local/ great-reads/la-et-c1-stoner-talk-show-20150209-story.html.

Rouse, Karen. 2018. "Racial Justice Drives Fight for, and against, Legal Pot in New Jersey." *New York Times,* March 11. Available at https://www.nytimes.com/2018/03/11/ nyregion/nj-legal-marijuana-racial-justice.html.

Rucker, Philip, and Robert Barnes. 2016. "Trump to Inherit More Than 100 Court Vacancies, Plans to Reshape Judiciary." *Washington Post,* December 25. Available at https://www.washingtonpost.com/politics/trump-to-inherit-more-than-100-court -vacancies-plans-to-reshape-judiciary/2016/12/25/d190dd18-c928-11e6-85b5 -76616a33048d_story.html.

Russo, R. 2004. "Tougher Pot Penalties Might Prevent Increased Border Scrutiny." *Vancouver Sun,* January 21.

Sabet, Kevin. n.d. "About." Available at http://kevinsabet.com/about (accessed June 21, 2016).

———. 2013a. "Civil Liberties Erode When Drug Use Widens." James A. Baker III Institute for Public Policy, May 21. Available at https://blog.chron.com/bakerblog/ 2013/05/civil-liberties-erode-when-drug-use-widens.

———. 2013b. "Marijuana: What the Evidence Shows as It Relates to the Impact of Use and What Can Be Learned from Washington State and Colorado." Available at https://olis.leg.state.or.us/liz/2013I1/Downloads/CommitteeMeetingDocument/31779.

Saint Louis, Catherine. 2015. "New Challenge for Police: Finding Pot in Lollipops and Marshmallows." *New York Times*, May 16. Available at https://www.nytimes.com/2015/05/17/us/new-challenge-for-police-finding-pot-in-lollipops-and-marshmallows.html.

Salsberg, Bob. 2017. "Massachusetts Opens Hearings on Recreational Marijuana Regulation." *The Cannabist*, March 20. Available at https://www.thecannabist.co/2017/03/20/massachusetts-recreational-marijuana-regulation-panel-hearings/75811.

Santaella-Tenorio, Julian, Christine M. Mauro, Melanie M. Wall, June H. Kim, Magdalena Cerda, Katherine M. Keyes, Deborah S. Hasin, Sandro Galea, and Silvia Saboia Martins. 2016. "US Traffic Fatalities, 1985–2014, and Their Relationship to Medical Marijuana Laws." *American Journal of Public Health* 107 (2): 336–342.

Santos, Melissa. 2017. "'I'm So High Right Meow?' State Lawmakers Don't Think Pot Billboards Should Be Appealing to Kids." *News Tribune*, April 21. Available at https://www.thenewstribune.com/news/local/marijuana/article146061419.html.

Savage, Charlie, and Maggie Haberman. 2017. "Trump Abruptly Orders 46 Obama-Era Prosecutors to Resign." March 10. Available at https://www.nytimes.com/2017/03/10/us/politics/us-attorney-justice-department-trump.html.

Savage, David G. 1990. "Bennett, First U.S. Drug Czar, Quits." *Los Angeles Times*, November 9. Available at http://articles.latimes.com/1990-11-09/news/mn-4120_1_drug-policy.

Scarboro, Morgan. 2017. "How High Are Marijuana Taxes in Your State?" Tax Foundation, June 1. Available at https://taxfoundation.org/marijuana-taxes-state.

Schatz, Bryan. 2015. "Obama Just Granted Clemency to a Pot Lifer, but Dozens More Remain behind Bars." *Mother Jones*, July 15. Available at https://www.motherjones.com/politics/2015/07/obama-commuted-drug-senteces-marijuana-lifer.

Schmader, Dave. 2017. "Ontario Shocker: Province to Restrict Legal Cannabis Sales to 150 Government-Run Stores and One Website." *Leafly*, September 8. Available at https://www.leafly.com/news/canada/ontario-shocker-province-to-restrict-legal-cannabis-sales-to-150-government-run-stores.

Schulenberg, John E., Lloyd D. Johnston, Patrick M. O'Malley, Jerald G. Bachman, Richard A. Miech, and Megan E. Patrick. 2017. *Monitoring the Future National Survey Results on Drug Use, 1975–2016.* Vol. 2, *College Students and Adults Ages 19–55.* Ann Arbor: University of Michigan. Available at http://www.monitoringthefuture.org/pubs/monographs/mtf-vol2_2016.pdf.

ScienceDaily. 2014. "Brain Changes Associated with Casual Marijuana Use in Young Adults, Study Finds." April 15. Available at https://www.sciencedaily.com/releases/2014/04/140415181156.htm.

Scientific American. 1936. "Marijuana Menaces Youth." March, pp. 150–151.

Scott, Eugene. 2017. "A New High: Poll Finds Record Support for Pot Legalization." *CNN*, April 20. Available at https://www.cnn.com/2017/04/20/politics/marijuana-poll-legalization/index.html.

Seattle Times. 2012. "Editorial: Approve Initiative 502—It's Time to Legalize, Regulate, and Tax Marijuana." September 22. Available at http://old.seattletimes.com/html/editorials/2019226555_editmarijuanainitiative502xml.html.

———. 2016. "Reefer Madness at the DEA—When Will the Feds Catch Up?" August 12. Available at https://www.seattletimes.com/opinion/editorials/reefer-madness-at-the-dea-when-will-the-feds-catch-up.

———. 2017. "Jeff Sessions, Pot Prohibition Is So 2011." August 17. Available at https:// www.seattletimes.com/opinion/editorials/jeff-sessions-pot-prohibition-is-so-2011.

Selsky, Andrew. 2016. "The Tides Are Shifting in Oregon over Legal Marijuana." *All Bud*, May 16. Available at https://www.allbud.com/learn/aggarticle/2296?page=7.

———. 2017. "Legal Marijuana States Try to Curb Interstate Smuggling to Fend Off Feds." *The Cannabist*, August 14. Available at https://www.thecannabist.co/2017/08/ 14/legal-marijuana-states-smuggling/85939.

Senate of the United States. 2017. "Marijuana Justice Act of 2017." Available at https:// www.congress.gov/bill/115th-congress/senate-bill/1689.

Sensible Colorado. n.d. "History of Colorado's Medical Marijuana Laws." Available at http://sensiblecolorado.org/history-of-co-medical-marijuana-laws (accessed October 12, 2016).

Sessions, Jeff. 2017a. "Attorney General Jeff Sessions Delivers Remarks on Efforts to Combat Violent Crime and Restore Public Safety before Federal, State, and Local Law Enforcement." March 15. Available at https://www.justice.gov/opa/speech/attorney -general-jeff-sessions-delivers-remarks-efforts-combat-violent-crime-and-restore.

———. 2017b. Letter to Bill Walker. July 24. Available at https://assets.documentcloud .org/documents/3933501/Jeff-Sessions-Marijuana-Policy-Letter-to-Alaska.pdf.

———. 2017c. Letter to Jay Inslee and Robert Ferguson. July 24. Available at https:// agportal-s3bucket.s3.amazonaws.com/uploadedfiles/Another/News/Press _Releases/8%202%2017%20Ltr%20from%20J%20Sessions%20%28002%29.pdf.

———. 2017d. Letter to John Hickenlooper. July 24. Available at https://images.westword .com/media/pdf/sessions_letter.pdf.

Sewell, Andrew, James Poling, and Mehmet Sofuoglu. 2009. "The Effect of Cannabis Compared with Alcohol on Driving." *American Journal on Addictions* 18:185–193.

Shapiro, Fred. 2006. *The Yale Book of Quotations*. New Haven, CT: Yale University Press.

Shapiro, Katie. 2016a. "NYC Police Commissioner Bill Bratton Dispenses Some Confusing Cannabis Logic." *The Cannabist*, May 28. Available at https://www.thecannabist .co/2016/05/26/nyc-police-chief-bill-bratton-confusing-cannabis-logic/54902.

———. 2016b. "Why Police and Prison Groups Worry about California Legalization." *The Cannabist*, May 19. Available at https://www.thecannabist.co/2016/05/19/police -prison-groups-worried-california-legalization/54441.

Shapiro, Nina. 2012. "Alison Holcomb: Pot Mama." *Seattle Weekly*, September 25. Available at http://archive.seattleweekly.com/news/872582-129/story.html.

Shaw, Bob, and Derrick Penner. 2016. "Setting Age Limit for Pot a Balancing Act, Says B.C. MD on Federal Panel." *Vancouver Sun*, December 13. Available at https:// vancouversun.com/news/local-news/setting-age-limit-for-pot-a-balancing-act-says -b-c-md-on-federal-panel.

Shepherd, Michael. 2016. "What Stands between Maine and Legitimate Marijuana Use?" *Bangor Daily News*, May 4. Available at https://bangordailynews.com/2016/05/04/ the-point/what-stands-between-maine-and-legal-marijuana-use.

Shesgreen, Deirdre. 2017. "White House Backs Off Proposed Cuts to Anti-drug Programs." *USA Today*, May 23. Available at https://www.usatoday.com/story/news/ politics/2017/05/23/white-house-backs-off-proposed-cuts-anti-drug-programs/ 102057676.

Shi, Yuyan. 2017. "Medical Marijuana Policies and Hospitalizations Related to Marijuana and Opioid Pain Reliever." *Drug and Alcohol Dependence* 173:144–150.

Shorto, Russell. 2013. *Amsterdam: A History of the World's Most Liberal City*. New York: Vintage Books.

Silowski, Vince. 2016. "Marijuana Advertising: Room to Maneuver (in Oregon, at Least)." July 26. Available at https://www.cannalawblog.com/marijuana-advertising-room-to-maneuver-in-oregon-at-least.

Simpson, Jeffrey. 2014. "Should Canada Do a Uruguay on Pot?" *Globe and Mail*, December 3. Available at https://www.theglobeandmail.com/opinion/should-canada-do-a-uruguay-on-pot/article21886003.

Smart Approaches to Marijuana. n.d.a. "Marijuana and Who's in Prison." Available at https://learnaboutsam.org/the-issues/marijuana-and-whos-in-prison (accessed July 15, 2017).

———. n.d.b. "Mission and Vision." Available at https://learnaboutsam.org/who-we-are/mission-vision (accessed January 12, 2013).

———. 2014. "Casual Pot Use Linked to Big Brain Changes." April 24. Available at https://learnaboutsam.org/casual-pot-use-linked-big-brain-changes.

———. 2017. "The Cole Memo: 4 Years Later; Status Report on State Compliance of Federal Enforcement Policy." August. Available at https://learnaboutsam.org/wp-content/uploads/2017/08/SAM-The-Cole-Memo-4-Years-Later-Status-Report.pdf.

Smith, Graeme. 2002. "Many Other Countries Try Decriminalization." *Globe and Mail*, December 11. Available at https://www.theglobeandmail.com/news/national/many-other-countries-try-decriminalization/article1028851.

Smith, Nancy. 2014. "Why Is Sheldon Adelson Opposing Medical Marijuana?" *Sunshine State News*, June 15. Available at http://sunshinestatenews.com/story/why-sheldon-adelson-opposing-medical-marijuana.

Smith, Philip H., Gregory G. Homish, Rebecca L. Collins, Gary A. Giovino, Helene Raskin White, and Kenneth E. Leonard. 2014. "Couples' Marijuana Use Is Inversely Related to Their Intimate Partner Violence over the First 9 Years of Marriage." *Psychology of Addictive Behaviors* 28:734–742.

S. N. 2017. "Why Amsterdam's Coffeeshops Are Closing." *The Economist*, January 10. Available at https://www.economist.com/the-economist-explains/2017/01/10/why-amsterdams-coffeeshops-are-closing.

Socias, Maria Eugenia, Thomas Kerr, Evan Wood, Huiru Dong, Stephanie Lake, Kanna Hayashi, Kora DeBeck, Didier Jutras-Aswad, Julio Montaner, and M.-J. Milloy. 2017. "Intentional Cannabis Use to Reduce Crack Cocaine Use in a Canadian Setting: A Longitudinal Analysis." *Addictive Behaviors* 72:138–143.

Sonner, Scott. 2017. "Nevada Sells a Lot More Weed in Its Adult-Use Rollout Than Other States." *The Cannabist*, September 29. Available at https://www.thecannabist.co/2017/09/29/nevada-recreational-marijuana-rollout-outpaces-other-states/89108.

Sonner, Scott, and Michelle Rindels. 2015. "Historic Day in Nevada: First Medical Marijuana Sales after 15-Year Wait." *The Cannabist*, July 31. Available at https://www.thecannabist.co/2015/07/31/nevada-medical-marijuana/38822.

Sottile, Leah. 2016. "Denvontre Thomas Is 19: He Could Face a Year in Prison for a Gram of Marijuana." *Willamette Week*, July 26. Available at https://www.wweek.com/news/2016/07/26/devontre-thomas-is-19-he-could-face-a-year-in-prison-for-a-gram-of-marijuana.

Southey, Tabatha. 2017. "Stirring the Pot Legislation." *Globe and Mail*, April 21. Available at https://www.theglobeandmail.com/opinion/stirring-the-pot-legislation/article34774871.

Staggs, Brooke. 2016a. "DEA Website Called Out over Debunked Statements about Marijuana Health Risks." *The Cannabist*, December 15. Available at https://www.thecannabist.co/2016/12/15/dea-health-risks-website/69504.

———. 2016b. "Marijuana: Is It Safe? Is It Addictive? Sorting Fact from Fiction." *The Cannabist*, June 27. Available at https://www.thecannabist.co/2016/06/27/marijuana-research-fact-fiction/57027.

———. 2016c. "Parents Facing Custody Issues See Hope with California Legalization." *The Cannabist*, December 15. Available at https://www.thecannabist.co/2016/12/15/california-legalization-gives-parents-hope/69516.

———. 2017. "California vs. Trump Administration: Bill Would Create Sanctuary State for Marijuana." *The Cannifornian*, February 20. Available at http://www.thecannifornian.com/cannabis-news/california-news/california-vs-trump-bill-create-sanctuary-state-marijuana.

Stamper, Norm. 2005a. *Breaking Rank*. New York: Nation Books.

———. 2005b. "Let Those Dopers Be." *Los Angeles Times*, October 16. Available at http://articles.latimes.com/2005/oct/16/opinion/op-legalize16.

Starling, Boris. 2016. "The Tide Effect: How the World Is Changing Its Mind on Cannabis Legalisation." Available at https://static1.squarespace.com/static/56eddde762cd9413e151ac92/t/582eecc6e3df2844237ca6dc/1479470281332/The+Tide+Effect+WEB+VERSION.pdf.

State of Nevada Department of Taxation. 2018. "FAQs for Marijuana Establishments." Available at https://tax.nv.gov/FAQs/Retail_Marijuana.

Statista. 2017. "Percentage of the Population in the U.S. Who Were Medical Marijuana Patients as of 2017, by State." August 15. Available at https://www.statista.com/statistics/743485/medical-marijuana-patient-population-united-states-by-state.

Steffen, Jordan. 2014. "Pot Edibles Were Big Surprise in First Year of Recreational Sales." *Denver Post*, December 26. Available at https://www.denverpost.com/2014/12/19/pot-edibles-were-big-surprise-in-first-year-of-recreational-sales.

———. 2015. "A Preview of Pot's Possible Role in Insanity Defense in Denver Murder." *Denver Post*, September 26. Available at https://www.denverpost.com/2015/09/26/a-preview-of-pots-possible-role-in-insanity-defense-in-denver-murder.

———. 2016. "Lawsuit against Marijuana Company over Deadly Denver Shooting Could Be First of Its Kind." *Denver Post*, May 10. Available at https://www.denverpost.com/2016/05/10/lawsuit-against-marijuana-company-over-deadly-denver-shooting-could-be-first-of-its-kind.

Stern, Ray. 2016. "Why Did Arizona Just Say No to Marijuana Legalization in 2016?" *Phoenix New Times*, November 10. Available at https://www.phoenixnewtimes.com/news/why-did-arizona-just-say-no-to-marijuana-legalization-in-2016-8814965.

StoptheDrugWar.org. 2014. "The 2014 National Drug Control Strategy: Baby Steps in the Right Direction." July 10. Available at https://stopthedrugwar.org/chronicle/2014/jul/09/the_2014_national_drug_control_strategy.

Strekal, Justin. 2017. "House Committee Blocks Veterans Equal Access Amendments." July 26. Available at http://blog.norml.org/2017/07/26/house-committee-blocks-veterans-equal-access-amendments.

Stringer, Richard, and Scott Maggard. 2016. "Reefer Madness to Marijuana Legalization: Media Exposure and American Attitudes toward Marijuana (1975–2012)." *Journal of Drug Issues* 46:428–445.

Stroup, Keith. 1996. "NORML's Testimony on Medical Marijuana before Congress." March 6. Available at http://norml.org/library/item/norml-s-testimony-on-medical-marijuana-before-congress-1996-keith-stroup-esq.

Stroup, Keith, and Paul Armentano. 2002. "The Problem Is Not Prohibition." In *Busted*, edited by Mike Gray, 223–224. New York: Thunder's Mouth Press/Nation Books.

Subritzky, Todd, Simone Pettigrew, and Simon Lenton. 2016. "Issues in the Implementation and Evolution of the Commercial Recreational Cannabis Market in Colorado." *International Journal of Drug Policy* 27:1–12.

Substance Abuse and Mental Health Services Administration. 1999. *Treatment of Adolescents with Substance Use Disorders*. Rockville, MD: SAMHSA. Available at https://www.ncbi.nlm.nih.gov/books/NBK64350.

———. 2015. "Behavioral Health Trends in the United States: Results from the 2014 National Survey on Drug Use and Health." Available at https://www.samhsa.gov/data/sites/default/files/NSDUH-FRR1-2014/NSDUH-FRR1-2014.pdf.

———. 2016. "Key Substance Use and Mental Health Indicators in the United States: Results from the 2015 National Survey on Drug Use and Health." Available at https://www.samhsa.gov/data/sites/default/files/NSDUH-FFR1-2015/NSDUH-FFR1-2015/NSDUH-FFR1-2015.pdf.

———. 2017. "Results from the 2016 National Survey on Drug Use and Health: Detailed Tables." Available at https://www.samhsa.gov/data/sites/default/files/NSDUH-DetTabs-2016/NSDUH-DetTabs-2016.pdf.

Sullum, Jacob. 2014. "Anti-pot Republicans Forsake Federalism in Medical Marijuana Vote." *Forbes*, May 30. Available at https://www.forbes.com/sites/jacobsullum/2014/05/30/anti-pot-republicans-forsake-federalism-in-medical-marijuana-vote/#6f4176bcbc35.

———. 2015. "Bill Bennett's Gateway Theory (and Harry Anslinger's)." *Forbes*, February 10. Available at https://www.forbes.com/sites/jacobsullum/2015/02/10/bill-bennetts-marijuana-gateway-theory-and-harry-anslingers/#7013a4d4a5ea.

———. 2016. "Marijuana Arrests Hit a Two-Decade Low but Are Still an Outrage." *Forbes*, September 29. Available at https://www.forbes.com/sites/jacobsullum/2016/09/29/marijuana-arrests-hit-a-two-decade-low-but-are-still-an-outrage/#170718121bb4.

Suri, Sameer. 2017. "'Can o'Bisque?' Snoop Dogg and Martha Stewart Rib the Rapper's Famous Penchant for Marijuana in T-Mobile Super Bowl Ad." *Daily Mail*, February 5. Available at http://www.dailymail.co.uk/tvshowbiz/article-4194596/Snoop-Dogg-Martha-Stewart-cut-T-Mobile-Super-Bowl-ad.html.

Survey Graphic. 1938. "Danger." April, p. 221.

Swift, Art. 2016. "Support for Legal Marijuana Use Up to 60% in U.S." Gallup, October 19. Available at https://news.gallup.com/poll/196550/support-legal-marijuana.aspx.

Szalavitz, Maia. 2010. "The Link between Marijuana and Schizophrenia." *Time*, July 21. Available at http://content.time.com/time/health/article/0,8599,2005559,00.html.

———. 2014. "No, Weed Won't Rot Your Brain." *Daily Beast*, April 17. Available at https://www.thedailybeast.com/no-weed-wont-rot-your-brain.

Tablang, Kristin. 2016. "The Pot List: 12 Celebrities in the Marijuana Business." *Forbes*, April 19. Available at https://www.forbes.com/sites/kristintablang/2016/04/19/12-celebrities-marijuana-business-bob-marley-woody-harrelson-willie-nelson-whoopi-goldberg-snoop-dogg-wiz-khalifa/#6d0fe99275b4.

Tashkin, Donald. 2013. "Effects of Marijuana Smoking on the Lung." *Annals of the American Thoracic Society* 10:239–247.

Task Force on Narcotics and Drug Abuse. 1967. *Task Force Report: Narcotics and Drug Abuse*. Washington, DC: U.S. Government Printing Office.

Tefft, Brian. 2016a. *Acute Sleep Deprivation and the Risk of Motor Vehicle Crash Involvement*. Washington, DC: American Automobile Association.

———. 2016b. *Prevalence of Marijuana Involvement in Fatal Crashes, 2010–2014*. Washington, DC: American Automobile Association.

———. 2016c. *The Prevalence of Motor Vehicle Crashes Involving Road Debris, United States 2011–2014*. Washington, DC: American Automobile Association.

Thalidomide Victims Association of Canada. n.d. "The Canadian Tragedy." Available at https://thalidomide.ca/en/the-canadian-tragedy (accessed January 2, 2017).

Thibedeau, Hannah, and Mike Crawley. 2017. "Ontario to Create Cannabis Control Board, Open Up Storefronts." *CBC*, September 8. Available at https://www.cbc.ca/news/politics/ontario-to-create-cannabis-control-board-1.4280073.

Thomas, Madeleine. 2013a. "After the Raid: First Oaksterdam, Then Legal Battles for Harborside Health Center." *Oakland North*, April 18. Available at https://oaklandnorth.net/2013/04/18/after-the-raid-first-oaksterdam-then-legal-battles-for-harborside-health-center.

———. 2013b. "After the Raid: One Year after Federal Agents Raided Oaksterdam, What's Changed?" *Oakland North*, April 2. Available at https://oaklandnorth.net/2013/04/02/after-the-raid-one-year-after-federal-agents-raided-oaksterdam-whats-changed.

Throckmorton, Douglas C. 2016. "FDA Regulation of Marijuana: Past Actions, Future Plans." Available at https://www.fda.gov/downloads/AboutFDA/CentersOffices/OfficeofMedicalProductsandTobacco/CDER/UCM498077.pdf.

Time. 1945. "The Weed." July 19, p. 45.

———. 2017. "For the Record." August 10. Available at http://time.com/4894991/for-the-record.

Tracy, Brianne. 2017. "Woody Harrelson Reveals He Quit Smoking Pot." *People*, March 20. Available at https://people.com/celebrity/woody-harrelson-quit-smoking-pot.

United States Congressional Record. 1974. *The Marihuana-Hashish Epidemic and Its Impact on U.S. Security*. Washington, DC: United States Congressional Record.

United States Sentencing Commission. 2014. "Primary Drug Type of Offenders Sentenced under Drug Guidelines." Available at https://www.ussc.gov/sites/default/files/pdf/research-and-publications/annual-reports-and-sourcebooks/2014/Table33.pdf.

Urbina, Ian. 2012. "Addiction Diagnoses May Rise under Guideline Changes." *New York Times*, May 11. Available at https://www.nytimes.com/2012/05/12/us/dsm-revisions-may-sharply-increase-addiction-diagnoses.html.

U.S. Department of Justice. 1988. "In the Matter of Marijuana Rescheduling Petition." Available at http://www.druglibrary.org/schaffer/library/studies/young/index.html.

U.S. Department of Veterans Affairs. 2018. "VA and Marijuana—What Veterans Need to Know." Available at https://www.publichealth.va.gov/marijuana.asp.

Vancouver Sun. 1969. "Pot Law Very Stupid, Indefensible." November 3, p. 1.

Vara, Vauhini. 2016. "The Art of Marketing Marijuana." *The Atlantic*, April. Available at https://www.theatlantic.com/magazine/archive/2016/04/the-art-of-marketing-marijuana/471507.

Vekshin, Alison. 2016. "Stoked and Toked for Super Bowl 50: Bay Area Weed Shops Taking Advantage." *The Cannabist*, February 4. Available at https://www.thecannabist.co/2016/02/04/super-bowl-50-bay-area-pot-shops-san-francisco/47626.

Ventura, Jesse, with Jen Hobbs. 2016. *Marijuana Manifesto*. New York: Skyhorse.

Vestal, Christine. 2017. "Medical Marijuana Could Help Combat Opioid Epidemic." *The Cannabist*, February 28. Available at https://www.thecannabist.co/2017/02/28/medical-marijuana-opioid-epidemic-research/74558.

Villeneuve, Marina. 2016. "Superhero Powers: Does the Gov Have the Right to Stop Maine Marijuana Legalization?" *The Cannabist*, December 22. Available at https://www.thecannabist.co/2016/12/22/maine-marijuana-paul-lepage-fact-check/69889.

Villeneuve, Marina, and Patrick Whittle. 2016. "'These Towns Have Their Head in the Sand': Moratoriums Coming after Maine Voters Legalize Marijuana." *The Cannabist*, December 28. Available at https://www.thecannabist.co/2016/12/28/maine-marijuana-towns-consider-moratoriums/70091.

Virtue, Graeme. 2017. "Baked Off: Your 4/20 Guide to the Best Weed on TV." *The Guardian*, April 20. Available at https://www.theguardian.com/tv-and-radio/2017/apr/20/420-guide-best-weed-tv-shows.

Volkow, Nora D., Ruben D. Baler, Wilson M. Compton, and Susan R. B. Weiss. 2014. "Adverse Health Effects of Marijuana Use." *New England Journal of Medicine* 370:2219–2227.

VS Strategies. 2017. "Colorado Exceeds $500 Million in Cannabis Revenue since Legalization." Available at http://vsstrategies.com/wp-content/uploads/VSS-CO-MJ-Revenue-Report-July-2017.pdf.

Wagner, John, and Matt Zapotosky. 2017. "Spicer: Feds Could Step Up Enforcement against Marijuana Use in States." *Washington Post*, February 23. Available at https://www.washingtonpost.com/news/post-politics/wp/2017/02/23/spicer-feds-could-step-up-anti-pot-enforcement-in-states-where-recreational-marijuana-is-legal.

Wallace, Alicia. 2016a. "Trump's Pick for Attorney General Not a Fan of Legal Weed." *The Cannabist*, November 18. Available https://www.thecannabist.co/2016/11/18/trump-attorney-general-marijuana-legalization-enforcement/67892.

———. 2016b. "U.S. Drug Czar: The Feds Have Dragged Their Feet on Pot Research." *Denver Post*, October 5. Available at https://www.denverpost.com/2016/10/05/us-drug-czar-feds-dragged-their-feet-pot-research.

———. 2016c. "Why Beer Distributors, Alcohol Trade Groups Are Fighting Legal Marijuana with Lots of Cash." *The Cannabist*, September 15. Available at https://www.thecannabist.co/2016/09/15/anti-legalization-beer-distributors/63259.

———. 2017a. "After Years of Lobbying by Veterans, Colorado Adds PTSD as Medical Marijuana Condition." *The Cannabist*, June 6. Available at https://www.thecannabist.co/2017/06/06/colorado-ptsd-medical-marijuana-veterans/80819.

———. 2017b. "Bipartisan 'Path to Marijuana Reform' Bills Introduced to Decriminalize, Protect, Regulate Cannabis Industry." *The Cannabist*, March 30. Available at https://www.thecannabist.co/2017/03/30/marijuana-federal-decriminalization-legislation-cannabis-industry/76346.

———. 2017c. "Colorado Marijuana Sales Top $131M, Set Record in March 2017." *The Cannabist*, May 10. Available at https://www.thecannabist.co/2017/05/10/colorado-marijuana-sales-statistics-march-2017/79215.

———. 2017d. "Exclusive: Here's How Colorado Gov. John Hickenlooper Really Feels about Marijuana." *The Cannabist*, March 31. Available at https://www.thecannabist.co/2017/03/31/colorado-governor-john-hickenlooper-marijuana-2017/76411.

———. 2017e. "Federal Marijuana Law Enforcement: What You Need to Know." *The Cannabist*, March 7. Available at https://www.thecannabist.co/2017/03/07/federal-marijuana-enforcement-trump-administration-experts-questions/74933.

———. 2017f. "How Congress Is Getting Serious about Cannabis amid White House Uncertainty." *The Cannabist*, February 6. Available at https://www.thecannabist.co/2017/02/06/congress-marijuana-legislation-cannabis-caucus/72897.

———. 2017g. "Jeff Sessions to AGs: 'We Don't Need to Be Legalizing Marijuana.'" *The Cannabist*, February 28. Available at https://www.thecannabist.co/2017/02/28/jeff-sessions-marijuana-legalization-to-nations-ags/74535.

———. 2017h. "Powerhouse Cannabis Firms Form Lobby Group to Protect State-Based Weed Laws." *The Cannabist*, March 23. Available at https://www.thecannabist.co/2017/03/23/new-federalism-fund-marijuana-lobbying-congress/75988.

———. 2017i. "Sessions Raises 'Serious Questions' about Colorado's Marijuana Management in Letter to Gov." *The Cannabist*, August 4. Available at https://www.thecannabist.co/2017/08/04/jeff-sessions-colorado-marijuana-letter-hickenlooper/85404.

———. 2017j. "'Something's Going to Have to Give': An Untenable Conflict between Feds, Legalized States." *The Cannabist*, March 6. Available at https://www.thecannabist.co/2017/03/06/trump-marijuana-legalization-industry-lobbyists/74960.

———. 2017k. "Studies Offer Conflicting Conclusions on Marijuana Legalization's Role in Car Crashes, Fatalities." *The Cannabist*, June 23. Available at https://www.thecannabist.co/2017/06/23/conflicting-studies-marijuana-legalization-car-crashes-fatalities/82309.

———. 2017l. "Trump Administration Puts Recreational Marijuana in Crosshairs." *The Cannabist*, February 23. Available at https://www.thecannabist.co/2017/02/23/sean-spicer-marijuana-medical-recreational-trump-administration/74255.

———. 2017m. "What Will Be AG Jeff Sessions' First Move on Marijuana?" *The Cannabist*, February 8. Available at https://www.thecannabist.co/2017/02/08/attorney-general-jeff-sessions-marijuana-scenarios/73321.

———. 2018. "Molson Coors Calls Legal Marijuana a 'Risk Factor' for Its Beer Business." *The Cannabist*, February 14. Available at https://www.thecannabist.co/2018/02/14/molson-coors-legal-marijuana-beer/99014.

Walsh, John, and Geoff Ramsey. 2016. "Uruguay's Drug Policy: Major Innovations, Major Challenges." Brookings Institution. Available at https://www.brookings.edu/wp-content/uploads/2016/07/Walsh-Uruguay-final.pdf.

Walsh, J. T. 1894. "Hemp Drugs and Insanity." *Journal of Mental Science* 40:21–36.

Walsh, Zach, Raul Gonzalez, Kim Crosby, Michelle S. Thiessen, Chris Carroll, and Marcel O. Bonn-Miller. 2017. "Medical Cannabis and Mental Health: A Guided Systematic Review." *Clinical Psychology Review* 51:15–29.

Walters, John P. 2002. "The Myth of 'Harmless' Marijuana." *Washington Post*, May 1. Available at https://www.washingtonpost.com/archive/opinions/2002/05/01/the-myth-of-harmless-marijuana/1cb7937f-6f6d-4a53-984b-0885456c9183.

———. 2014. "The Presidency Goes to Pot." *Weekly Standard*, February 3. Available at https://www.weeklystandard.com/john-p-walters/the-presidency-goes-to-pot.

Wang, George Sam, Marie-Claire Le Lait, Sara J. Deakyne, Alvin C. Bronstein, Lalit Bajaj, and Genie Roosevelt. 2016. "Unintentional Pediatric Exposures to Marijuana in Colorado, 2009–2015." *Jama Pediatrics*. Available at https://jamanetwork.com/journals/jamapediatrics/fullarticle/2534480.

Wang, George, Sandeep Narang, Kathryn Wells, and Ryan Chuang. 2011. "A Case Series of Marijuana Exposures in Pediatric Patients Less Than 5 Years of Age." *Child Abuse and Neglect* 35:5563–5565.

Wang, George, Genie Roosevelt, and Kennon Heard. 2013. "Pediatric Marijuana Exposures in a Medical Marijuana State." *JAMA Pediatrics* 167 (7): 630–633.

Washburn, Polly. 2017a. "Public Support for Medical and Recreational Marijuana Legalization Hits All-Time High." *The Cannabist*, August 8. Available at https://www.thecannabist.co/2017/08/08/marijuana-legalization-opinion-poll-americans/85562.

———. 2017b. "Senate Committee, Rejecting Request from Sessions, Keeps Protection for Medical Marijuana States." *The Cannabist*, July 27. Available at https://www.thecannabist.co/2017/07/27/senate-appropriations-medical-marijuana/84714.

Washington Post. 2014. "D.C. Voters Should Reject the Rush to Legalize Marijuana." September 14. Available at https://www.washingtonpost.com/opinions/dc-voters-should-reject-the-rush-to-legalize-marijuana/2014/09/14/aca37112-3ab6-11e4-bdfb-de4104544a37_story.html.

Washington Secretary of State. 2012. "Initiative Measure No. 502 Concerns Marijuana— County Results." Available at https://results.vote.wa.gov/results/20121106/Initiative-Measure-No-502-Concerns-marijuana_ByCounty.html.

Washington State Department of Health. n.d. "Medical Marijuana." Available at http://www.doh.wa.gov/YouandYourFamily/Marijuana/MedicalMarijuana (accessed August 15, 2017).

Washington State Liquor and Cannabis Board. n.d. "Marijuana Compliance Checks: 18 of 157 Recreational Marijuana Stores Sell to Minors." Available at https://lcb.wa.gov/pressreleases/marijuana-compliance-checks-18-157-recreational-marijuana-stores-sell-minors (accessed January 23, 2017).

———. 2016. "Frequently Asked Questions about Marijuana Advertising." Available at https://lcb.wa.gov/mj2015/faq_i502_advertising.

———. 2017a. "Changes to Marijuana Advertising Laws." July 3. Available at https://lcb.wa.gov/sites/default/files/publications/Marijuana/5131-Advertising-Notice.pdf.

———. 2017b. "Marijuana Dashboard." September. Available at https://data.lcb.wa.gov/stories/s/WSLCB-Marijuana-Dashboard/hbnp-ia6v.

———. 2018. "Annual Report, Fiscal Year 2017." Available at https://lcb.wa.gov/sites/default/files/publications/annual_report/2017-annual-report-final2-web.pdf.

Washington State Senate. n.d. "History of Washington State Marijuana Laws." Available at http://www.ncsl.org/documents/summit/summit2015/onlineresources/wa_mj_law_history.pdf (accessed January 12, 2017).

Wax-Thibodeaux, Emily. 2014. "More Veterans Press VA to Recognize Medical Marijuana as Treatment Option." *Washington Post*, November 15. Available at https://www.washingtonpost.com/politics/more-veterans-press-va-to-recognize-medical-marijuana-as-treatment-option/2014/11/15/51666986-6a7b-11e4-b053-65cea7903f2e_story.html.

Way, Art. 2017. "Colorado and Washington Laid the Groundwork for California to Set New Gold Standard of Marijuana Legalization." Drug Policy Alliance, January 3. Available at http://www.drugpolicy.org/blog/colorado-and-washington-laid-groundwork-california-set-new-gold-standard-marijuana-legalization.

WCBV News. 2017. "Governor Baker to Sign Massachusetts Marijuana Bill; Here's What Will Change." July 27. Available at https://www.wcvb.com/article/governor-baker-to-sign-massachusetts-marijuana-bill-heres-what-will-change/10374397.

Weil, Andrew, and Winnifred Rosen. 1998. *From Chocolate to Morphine.* Boston: Houghton Mifflin.

Weiner, Rachel. 2012. "Obama: I've Got 'Bigger Fish to Fry' Than Pot Smokers." *Washington Post*, December 14. Available at https://www.washingtonpost.com/news/post-politics/wp/2012/12/14/obama-ive-got-bigger-fish-to-fry-than-pot-smokers.

Weiss, Jeff. 2015. "The Making of the Modern Stoner." *Vulture*, June 29. Available at http://www.vulture.com/2015/06/making-of-the-modern-stoner.html.

Wente, Margaret. 2015. "Deep in the Weeds: How Colorado Is Dealing with Legalized Marijuana." *Globe and Mail*, May 15. Available at https://www.theglobeandmail.com/news/world/how-colorado-is-dealing-with-legalized-marijuana/article24457303.

Wentling, Nikki. 2017. "American Legion Adopts Resolution Supporting Medical Marijuana." *Stars and Stripes*, August 24. Available at https://www.stripes.com/news/us/american-legion-adopts-resolution-supporting-medical-marijuana-1.484362.

Wenzel, John. 2015. "Weed Goes Wide: The Subtle Mainstreaming of Cannabis in Colorado." *Denver Post*, December 28. Available at https://www.denverpost.com/2015/12/28/weed-goes-wide-the-subtle-mainstreaming-of-cannabis-in-colorado.

Westervelt, Amy. 2017. "Marijuana Sales Give Nevada a Taste of the Green Rush, but High Demand Outstrips Supply." *Washington Post*, July 15. Available at https://www.washingtonpost.com/national/marijuana-sales-give-nevada-a-taste-of-the-green-rush-but-high-demand-outstrips-supply/2017/07/15/46899bc2-68da-11e7-8eb5-cbccc2e7bfbf_story.html.

Westneat, Danny. 2012. "King County Sheriff Makes Case for Pot." *Seattle Times*, October 3. Available at http://old.seattletimes.com/text/2019324549.html.

Wheeler, William. 2014. "Chronic Insecurity." *Playboy*, July–August. Available at http://williamscannabisinternational.com/playboy-magazine-chronic-insecurity.

White House. 1998. Reauthorization Act of 1998. Available at https://obamawhitehouse.archives.gov/ondcp/reauthorization-act.

———. 2016. "High Intensity Drug Trafficking Areas (HIDTA) Program." Available at https://obamawhitehouse.archives.gov/ondcp/high-intensity-drug-trafficking-areas-program.

Widdicombe, Lizzie. 2017. "The Martha Stewart of Marijuana Edibles." *New Yorker*, April 24. Available at https://www.newyorker.com/magazine/2017/04/24/the-martha-stewart-of-marijuana-edibles.

Wiedeman, Reeves. 2015. "The Bong Next Door: Ambling through America's Most Stoned Suburbs." *New York Magazine*, November 4. Available at http://nymag.com/daily/intelligencer/2015/11/americas-most-stoned-suburbs.html.

Wiggins, Ovetta. 2016. "Could Maryland Pause the Medical Marijuana Program until Racial Issues Are Resolved?" *The Cannabist*, October 7. Available at https://www.thecannabist.co/2016/10/07/maryland-marijuana-reform/64825.

Wile, Rob. 2015. "Americans Are High on Weed Approximately 288 Million Hours a Week." *Splinter*, June 13. Available at https://splinternews.com/americans-are-high-on-weed-approximately-288-million-ho-1793848378.

Williams, Janice. 2017. "Anne Coulter Blames Marijuana for Making 'People Retarded' and 'Destroying the Country.'" *Newsweek*, August 1. Available at https://www.newsweek.com/ann-coulter-marijuana-legal-america-645040.

Williams, Katie Bo. 2017. "DHS Chief Reverses Marijuana Comments." *The Hill*, April 18. Available at http://thehill.com/policy/national-security/department-of-homeland-security/329307-dhs-chief-reverses-marijuana.

Wilson, Reid. 2014. "Legal Pot Faces Myriad Obstacles." *The Columbian*, April 8. Available at https://www.columbian.com/news/2014/apr/08/legal-pot-faces-myriad -obstacles.

Wing, Nick. 2015. "Police Arrested Someone for Weed Possession Every 51 Seconds in 2014." *Huffington Post*, September 28. Available at https://www.huffingtonpost.com/ entry/marijuana-arrests-2014_us_560978a7e4b0768126fe6506.

Wyatt, Kristen. 2015. "A New Symbol to ID Colorado Pot Edibles: THC 'Stop Sign.'" *The Cannabist*, August 11. Available at https://www.thecannabist.co/2015/08/11/ colorado-pot-edibles-symbol-thc-stop-sign/39288.

———. 2016. "Enter 'Mad Men'—Marijuana Industry Turns to Branding." *The Cannabist*, January 6. Available at https://www.thecannabist.co/2016/01/06/marijuana -marketing-brands-willie-nelson-snoop-dogg/45906.

———. 2017a. "Colorado Ends Plans for Pot Clubs over Trump Uncertainty." *Associated Press*, April 14. Available at https://www.apnews.com/0cdd3900384e45738df3887b 2943c239/Colorado-ends-plans-for-pot-clubs-over-Trump-uncertainty

———. 2017b. "Colorado Senate Committee Lowers Marijuana Plant Limit to 12, or 24 with Registration." *The Cannabist*, March 23. Available at https://www.thecannabist .co/2017/03/23/colorado-marijuana-plant-limit-bill/76003.

Young, Bob. 2014. "Pot Grower's 'Beast Mode' Strain Packs Punch." *Seattle Times*, January 27. Available at https://www.seattletimes.com/seattle-news/pot-grow errsquos-lsquobeast-modersquo-strain-packs-punch.

———. 2016. "Minorities, Punished Most by War on Drugs, Underrepresented in Legal Pot." *Seattle Times*, July 1. Available at https://www.seattletimes.com/seattle-news/ marijuana/blacks-latinos-underrepresented-in-pot-shop-ownership.

———. 2017a. "U.S. Attorney General Sessions Criticizes Washington State's Legal Marijuana System." *Seattle Times*, August 4. Available at https://www.seattletimes .com/seattle-news/sessions-raises-concerns-over-washingtons-marijuana -legalization.

———. 2017b. "Washington State Will Resist Federal Crackdown on Legal Weed, AG Ferguson Says." *Seattle Times*, February 23. Available at https://www.seattletimes .com/seattle-news/marijuana/washington-state-will-resist-federal-crackdown-on -legal-weed-ag-ferguson-says.

Young, William Mackworth, and John Kaplan. 1969. *Marijuana: Report of the Indian Hemp Drugs Commission, 1893–1894*. Silver Spring, MD: Thomas Jefferson.

YouTube. 2016. "Bill Maher Smokes Giant Joint on Live TV." February 13. Available at https://www.youtube.com/watch?v=MVr5tJ1VvSw.

Zapotosky, Matt, Sari Horwitz, and Joel Achenbach. 2018. "Justice Department Ending Policy That Let Legal Pot Flourish." *Washington Post*, January 5. Available at https:// www.heraldnet.com/nation-world/justice-department-to-end-policy-that-let-legal -pot-flourish.

Zeese, Kevin. 2002. "Once-Secret 'Nixon Tapes' Show Why the U.S. Outlawed Pot." *AlterNet*, March 20. Available at https://www.alternet.org/story/12666/once-secret _%22nixon_tapes%22_show_why_the_u.s._outlawed_pot.

Zezima, Katie. 2018. "Vermont Is the First State to Legalize Marijuana through the Legislature." *Washington Post*, January 24. Available at https://www.washingtonpost .com/news/post-nation/wp/2018/01/23/vermont-is-the-first-state-to-legalize -marijuana-through-legislature.

Zhang, Li Rita, Hal Morgenstern, Sander Greenland, Shen-Chih Chang, Philip Lazarus, M. Dawn Teare, Penella J. Woll, et al. 2015. "Cannabis Smoking and Lung Cancer

Risk: Pooled Analysis in the International Lung Cancer Consortium." *International Journal of Cancer* 136:894–903.

Zimmer, Lynn, and John Morgan. 1997. *Marijuana Myths, Marijuana Facts*. New York: Lindesmith Center.

Zuccaro, Anna. 2017. "DEA Removes Marijuana Misinformation from Website after Months of Public, Legal Pressure." Americans for Safe Access, February 13. Available at https://www.safeaccessnow.org/iqa_victory.

Zukerberg, Paul. 2013. "It's Time for D.C. to Stop Wrecking Lives over a Bag of Weed." *Washington Post*, May 24. Available at https://www.washingtonpost.com/opinions/its-time-for-dc-to-stop-wrecking-lives-over-a-bag-of-weed/2013/05/24/e3bbc8cc-c314-11e2-914f-a7aba60512a7_story.html.

Index

Clayton J. Mosher is a Professor of Sociology at Washington State University. He is the coauthor of *Drugs and Drug Policy: The Control of Consciousness Alteration*, coauthor of *The Mismeasure of Crime*, and author of *Discrimination and Denial: Systemic Racism in Ontario's Legal and Criminal Justice System, 1892–1961*.

Scott Akins is an Associate Professor of Sociology in the School of Public Policy at Oregon State University. He is the coauthor of *Drugs and Drug Policy: The Control of Consciousness Alteration*.

www.ingramcontent.com/pod-product-compliance
Lightning Source LLC
Chambersburg PA
CBHW040146270326
41929CB00025B/3402